PRO-SLAVERY THOUGHT IN THE OLD SOUTH

PRO-SLAVERY THOUGHT IN THE OLD SOUTH

By

WILLIAM SUMNER JENKINS, Ph.D.

Assistant Professor of Political Science in the University of North Carolina
Sometime Research Assistant in the Institute for Research in
Social Science in the University of North Carolina

Gloucester, Mass.

PETER SMITH

1960

To

WILLIAM WHATLEY PIERSON

PREFACE

A NUMBER of specialized fields must be investigated before a definitive history of American political thought can be accomplished. It is hoped that this study of pro-slavery thought will serve to forward the larger task. In it the author has attempted to analyze the whole body of thought that developed in the Old South in justification of the peculiar system of society which existed there. The field is inclusive, the sources practically unlimited; one despairs of producing a work that is actually exhaustive. In the manifold ramifications of the study, therefore, it has not been possible always to trace an idea back to its origin, or to follow a theory through to its ultimate culmination.

The purpose has been to indicate the various thought trends, to evaluate their significance, and to estimate their weight in the entire body of pro-slavery thought. The primary conclusion resulting from the study is that the Southern mind was absorbed in making a defense of slavery. The whole Southern civilization, which had many distinctive features as a way of life, was so completely identified with slavery as to make its very existence seem to depend upon the defense of that institution. The misfortune to the South was that its mental power was taken out of other fields of endeavor at a time when it could have been most fruitful in the development of a higher civilization. The South produced profound intellects; but mental energy was so much used up in the perfection of an irrefutable justification of slavery that the finer features of Southern life were neglected, and consequently imperilled. And, as a consequence, it was also tragedy that the North in attacking slavery, attacked everything Southern. The abolitionist, believing that slavery vitiated the entire way of Southern life, could have no appreciation of the social values inherent in the South.

Sophistical as some of the argument was, special pleading as much of it was—it was also realistic in its sympathy and its knowledge—there were constructive elements in it, as to institutional organization and constitutional law, as to ideas of republican government and of liberty, and as to an equable society. The ensuing pages will declare the truth of this statement. This is the thesis of the work. Significant as this contribution was, it might have been greater but for the exigency of making the defense.

The theories of the slaveholder gave offense to those who thought chattel slavery morally wrong, and these theories caused a certain regimentation of Southern life. Conclusive among these ideas, as the Southerner thought, was the "Positive Good" theory, which claimed for the laborer, and in application provided, social security. Chattel slavery today may provoke the interest only of the antiquarian; but, with the compensating element of security for the workman, slave society may well challenge the interest and study of those seeking such security, through a fairer distribution of the social product, in a free society, from which a system of wage slavery has not yet been eradicated.

Dr. J. G. de Roulhac Hamilton, in the spring of 1925, suggested that the author make a study of theories of the Southern slaveholder. The work was begun the following year under the direction of Dr. W. W. Pierson, funds being generously provided by the Institute for Research in Social Science. During the decade through which the work has been pursued, assistance has been rendered by many individuals, and this opportunity is taken to express sincere appreciation to all of them. A special debt of gratitude is due to Dr. Fletcher M. Green, of Emory University, for many helpful suggestions as to procedure in the early period of research; to the late Professor Ulrich B. Phillips, of Yale University, for valuable advice as to approach, and for the use of his rich collection of notes; to Dr. Hamilton for suggestions as to procedure and the location of materials, and for many constructive criticisms of the manuscript; and to Dr. Pierson, for an intimate and stimulating guidance throughout the work, and for the inspiration that has led to the completion of the book.

The librarians of the following institutions rendered kind assistance in gathering materials: the University of North Carolina, the University of South Carolina, Harvard University, Duke University, the Charleston Library Society, Lawson McGhee Library, the North Carolina State Library, the Virginia State Library, and the Library of Congress; the late Professor Yates Snowden, of the University of South Carolina, the late August Kohn, of Columbia, South Carolina, and Mr. J. Rion McKissick of Greenville, South Carolina, made their rich private collections available; and Mr. and Mrs. Geo. P. Coleman of Williamsburg, Virginia, graciously permitted the use of the valuable Tucker manuscripts. Miss Georgia Faison of the University of North Carolina Library staff has been most helpful in locating and checking rare titles; Dr. Charles B. Robson and Dr. Carl H. Pegg have read the entire manuscript and given important advice as to form and content; Dr. Joseph C. Russell has read the proof; Mrs. N. B. Adams has rendered a valuable service in reading the entire proof and checking the bibliography; and Dr. Katharine Jocher has supervised the preparation and editing of the manuscript.

W. S. J.

May 17, 1935.
Chapel Hill

CONTENTS

[xi]

PRO-SLAVERY THOUGHT IN THE OLD SOUTH

INTRODUCTION

L ONG before the first settlements were made in the western hemisphere the arguments in justification of the social institution of domestic slavery had become hackneyed. Slavery, as ancient in the history of the world as society itself, early became the subject of philosophic inquiry. The greatest of the Greek thinkers justified slavery in logic as conforming to nature. The legalistic thought of the Romans constructed a basis for it both in the *jus civile* and in the *jus gentium*. The patristic writers of the early Christian era surrounded the institution with the sanction of religion and the church; and, throughout the long span of the Middle Ages, it remained securely embedded in the customs and practice of the nations of the world. Justified in the mind of mankind at the outset of the modern era, the royal ordinances of Spain prepared the way for its introduction into the New World; and installation began when Las Casas, with benevolent motives, ordered that Negroes be imported to work in the mines of the Indies. Before the advent of American history, Aristotle, Ulpian, St. Augustine, St. Thomas Aquinas, Pufendorf and many other great names among the philosophers had contributed ideas which formed a large body of pro-slavery thought.

It is true, then, that pro-slavery thought did not have its inception in America; it is doubtful, indeed, that any distinct aspect of it was indigenous to the peculiar system of human bondage that was planted in America. With so full a heritage from the Old World, the American controversialists of slavery freely drew upon ancient and medieval sources in constructing their opposite cases. As all the basic types of argument were inherited, it was necessary only to restate, re-

[1]

arrange, and elaborate these arguments in different form. Many of the details of this restatement, of course, were dictated or modified by peculiar social, economic, and political factors present in American history from time to time.

Viewing the history of American slavery in perspective, one is likewise impressed with the similarity in the character of the basic types of arguments, at whatever period presented, either in attack or in defense of slavery. This fact is apparent whether the argument was offered in a casual defense against a lone crusader for emancipation in 1690, or in a more deliberate response to the extreme application of the Revolutionary philosophy; whether it was made in apathetic apology during the period of quiescence, in righteous indignation aroused by the abolition intermeddler of the Garrisonian period, or finally with the studied rebuttal when the defense had reached its consummation. The development of pro-slavery thought was rather in the general nature of the defense as it grew from an apathetic condition to assume a position of belligerency. This fact, it is hoped, will become clear as we proceed with the historical resumé. The purpose of the first two chapters is to follow the growth of the slavery defense, from its earliest utterances in America, through the many ramifications of its expression, to its complete statement. In certain periods the only evidences of a pro-slavery theory were negative expressions; at other times, controversies more pertinent to the day submerged and crowded out interest in slavery; yet as the political controversy over the institution assumed various new aspects, positive expressions of pro-slavery thought constantly recurred, changing from time to time in emphasis and content, never entirely dying out.

CHAPTER I

THE ORIGINS OF SLAVERY THOUGHT IN AMERICA, 1660-1790

PURITANISM AND SLAVERY

THE institution of domestic slavery had an early origin in both the Northern and Southern Colonies. The earliest records of slavery in New England coincide with the Pequot War, 1637, when the captured Indians were enslaved.[1] Negro slaves were shortly thereafter imported, the practice of trading the Indian for the blackamoor arising because the latter was better suited by nature for enslavement.[2] It would seem that this custom was given positive legal recognition first in the Body of Liberties enacted in 1641, a legal sanction which remained unrepealed throughout the Colonial period.[3] When the New England Confederation was formed in 1643 to promote matters of common concern for the New England Colonies one provision of the compact was for the rendition of bond servants.[4]

Throughout the seventeenth century it is impossible to discern a public attitude for emancipation in New England. The voices of Roger Williams and John Eliot were raised in behalf of the enslaved, but their efforts were directed at mitigation of the severity of the practices rather than at the over-

[1] George H. Moore, *Notes on the History of Slavery in Massachusetts* (New York, 1866), p. 1.

[2] John Josselyn mentions seeing Negroes in Massachusetts about this time. "An Account of Two Voyages to New England" (1670), *Massachusetts Historical Society Collections*, XXIII, 231.

[3] Moore, *op. cit.*, p. 11; J. C. Hurd, *The Law of Freedom and Bondage in the United States* (Boston, 1857), I, 198. Reprint with remarks by F. C. Gray in *Massachusetts Historical Society Collections*, XXVIII, 231.

[4] *New Haven Colonial Records*, 1653-1665, pp. 562-566.

throw of the institution itself.[5]   The single exception of an
anti-slavery tenor to the accepted theory and practice of enslavement of the time was the statute passed in Rhode Island
by the General Court of Warwick, May 19, 1652, the first
legislative enactment for the emancipation of the slave in
America.[6]   Provision was made for granting freedom after
a service of ten years; however, the statute was probably
never enforced.[7]

In the opening year of the new century the first positive
statement of the anti-slavery theory was published in Boston.
Samuel Sewell, then Judge of the Superior Court, "essayed
to prevent Negroes and Indians being rated as cattle, but
could not succeed."[8]   His pamphlet, *The Selling of Joseph,
A Memorial,* was widely distributed and influenced the progress of the early anti-slavery movement in other parts of the
colonies.[9]   The following year John Saffin printed a reply
to Sewell, answering one by one his arguments and making
probably the first written defense of slavery in American history.[10]   In these two pamphlets appears for the first time in
published form the clash of opinion over the slavery question;

[5] For Williams' suggestion to set captives free after a period of years, probably dated 1637, see Moore, *op. cit.,* p. 3, quoting from Williams' letters in
Massachusetts Historical Society Collections, XXXVII, 214. For Eliot's "Remonstrance to the Governor and Council," see Moore, *op. cit.,* pp. 36-37, quoting
from *Plymouth Colony Records,* X, 451-452.

[6] *Rhode Island Colonial Records,* I, 243.

[7] U. B. Phillips, *American Negro Slavery* (New York, 1918), p. 106; Moore,
op. cit., p. 73.

[8] Quoted from the diary of Sewell in Joshua Coffin, *A Sketch of the History of
Newbury, Newburyport, and West Newbury, from 1635 to 1845* (Boston, 1845),
p. 338.

[9] Reprinted from an original in Moore, *op. cit.,* pp. 83-87, also in *Massachusetts
Historical Society Proceedings,* 1863-1864, VII, 161-165.

[10] A / Brief and Candid Answer to a late / Printed Sheet, entitled / The
Selling of Joseph / whereunto is annexed, / a True and Particular Narrative by
Way of Vindication of the / Authors Dealing with and Prosecution of his Negro
Man Servant / for his vile and exhorbitant Behavior towards his Master and
his / Tenant, Thomas Shepard; which hath been wrongfully represented / to
their Prejudice and Defamation (Boston, 1701). Reprinted in Moore, *op. cit.,*
pp. 251-256.

the issue was clearly drawn, and the details of the early attack and defense are preserved for us. Sewell's appeal was
largely religious, "all men, as they are the Sons of Adam,
are Co-heirs, and have equal Right unto Liberty"; *caveat
emptor,* title to property cannot result from man stealing:
"evil must not be done," bring Negroes from a pagan country, "that good may come of it," that is, that they may be
Christianized; do unto others as you would have them do
unto you, "for this is the Law and the Prophets."

Saffin, in his reply to Sewell, brought the defense of
slavery under the Puritan theory of election:

. . . True, but what is all this to the purpose, to prove that all
men have equal right to Liberty, and all outward comforts of this
life; which Position seems to invert the order that God hath set in
the World, who hath ordained different degrees and orders of
men, some to be High and Honourable, some to be Low and
Despicable; some to be Monarchs, . . . Masters, . . . others to
be subjects, and to be Commanded; Servants of sundry sorts and
degrees, bound to obey, yea some to be born Slaves, and so to remain during their lives, as hath been proved. Otherwise there
would be a mere parity among men, contrary to that of the
Apostle, I *Cor.* 12 *from the* 13 *to the* 26 *verse,* where he sets forth
(by way of comparison) the different sorts and offices of the
Members of the Body, indigitating that they are all of use, but
not equal, and of like dignity. So God hath set different Orders
and Degrees of men in the World, both in Church and Common
Weal. Now, if this Position of parity should be true, it would then
follow that the ordinary course of Divine Providence of God in
the World should be wrong and unjust, (which we must not dare
to think, much less to affirm) and all the sacred Rules, Precepts
and Commands of the Almighty which he hath given the Son of
Men to observe and keep in their respective Places, Orders and
Degrees, would be to no purpose; which unaccountability derogates
from the Divine Wisdom of the most High, who hath made

nothing in vain, but hath Holy Ends in all his Dispensations to the Children of men.[11]

Here in its initial state Saffin rested the pro-slavery theory on the two pillars of the Bible argument, Leviticus 24: 44-46, the divine dispensation to Israel to possess slaves, and I Corinthians XII: 13-26, where St. Paul set forth his philosophy of grades and orders. He also made use of the argument from Old Testament prophecy, the curse on Canaan, by which he distinguished the enslavement of the depraved Negro from the selling of Joseph, one of God's chosen people. These specific sanctions for slavery used during the formative stage, reappear with each later stage of the slavery controversy and were cited as long as the institution remained to be defended.

Attacks on slavery in Colonial New England were few and isolated and not in harmony with the prevailing sentiment of the times. There seemed to be no inconsistency between the Calvinistic theory of election and domestic slavery, nor any incongruity between a system of bondage and the Puritan practice in religious and governmental institutions. Puritan political views were strongly influenced by religion, but by the Old Testament religion; they patterned their institutions as prototypes of the Old Hebrew society, and the Law of Moses, with ultimate divine sanction, was their standard. The doctrine of election in the realm of religion, moreover, was fundamentally out of harmony with a theory of social equality. There were orders and grades in God's kingdom; so there should be distinctions in the worldly. The Negro, according to Puritan theory, was a heritage of God's elect. Cotton Mather typically expressed their idea when he wrote in his diary in 1706 that he considered the gift of a slave to him a singular blessing and "a mighty smile of heaven

[11] *Ibid.*, pp. 251-252.

upon his family."[12]   Whatever views the Puritan advocate of the slave had were humanitarian, for the care of his soul and for the amelioration of his physical hardships, rather than equalitarian, for the absolving of his status. The seeds of the anti-slavery crusade were not indigenous to Puritanism, nor did the climate of New England nourish their growth, until shortly before the Revolution when the fertile thought of the American patriot was implanted with them to stimulate a rapid and luxuriant growth.

SLAVERY AND QUAKERISM

The earliest concerted movement for the abolition of slavery on the American continent had its origin with the Quakers and kindred pietistic sects.   As early as 1671 George Fox, the father of Quakerism, in a public discourse advised the inhabitants of the Barbadoes to use their slaves kindly and to reward them with freedom after they had served a number of years in bondage,[13] which speech, in pamphlet form, was circulated and read by many Friends in the Colonies on the continent.[14]   Following this suggestion, William Penn in 1682, in the "Articles of the Free Society of Traders," provided that Negro slaves should be set free after serving a period of fourteen years.[15]

The earliest written record preserved for us penned in America protesting against the existence of domestic slavery

[12] W. B. O. Peabody, *Life of Cotton Mather*, in Jared Sparks, *The Library of American Biography* (New York, 1849), VI, 305.   In his *Essays To Do Good*, 1710, Mather made a strong plea for religious instruction of the slave but made no suggestion for emancipation (Massachusetts Sabbath Society edition, Boston, 1845), pp. 108-110.

[13] R. M. Jones, *The Quakers in the American Colonies* (London, 1911), p. 510.

[14] For references to the influence of Fox's discourse see John Hepburn, *The American Defense of the Christian Golden Rule* (London, 1713); Ralph Sandiford, *A Brief Examination of the Practice of the Times*, quoted in S. M. Janney, *A History of the Religious Society of Friends, from its rise to the year 1828* (Philadelphia, 1867), p. 241.

[15] A. C. and R. H. Thomas, "History of the Society of Friends," *American Church History*, XII, 243.   The provision was never carried into effect.

emanated from a group of Mennonites and German Quakers living at Germantown, Pennsylvania. In the handwriting of Francis Daniell Pastorius this protest against "the traffic of mens-body" and "the handling of men as cattle" was submitted to the Monthly Meeting and later to the Yearly Meeting, 1688, without receiving a positive judgment by the society.[16] The reasoning of the protest was primarily religious, an application of the Golden Rule, with a political note stressing the inconsistency between liberty of conscience, for which the Quakers came to America, and the denial of freedom of person to the Negro. "Here is liberty of conscience, here. ought to be likewise liberty of ye body, except of evil doers, wch is an other case. . . . In Europe there are many oppressed for Conscience sake; and here there are those oppressed wch are of a black color."[17] In 1693 George Keith, a significant figure as an early religious controversialist, issued a more lengthy tract, *An Exhortation and Caution to Friends Concerning Buying or Keeping of Negroes,* which was merely an elaboration of the religious reasons offered in the earlier protest.[18]

After 1700, an increasing spirit of opposition to slavery grew among the Quakers and was expressed in the publication of many essays and pamphlets. In 1713 John Hepburn published an essay attacking slavery, *The American Defense of the Christian Golden Rule,* in which a dialogue takes place between a slaveholder who states arguments in defense of slavery and a Christian who refutes them one by one.[19] William Burling followed with another pamphlet in 1718[20]

---

[16] Samuel W. Pennypacker, "The Settlement of Germantown and the Causes Which Led to It," *The Pennsylvania Magazine of History and Biography,* IV, 28, 30 note.

[17] Reprint of original, *ibid.,* pp. 28-30.   [18] Reprint of original, *ibid.,* XIII, 265.

[19] *Op. cit.* The only copy of this pamphlet which I have been able to locate is in the Boston Public Library.

[20] Samuel Allison, "Notes on Early Quaker Books on Slavery," *The Non Slaveholder,* II (1847), 149 refers to such a book.

and Ralph Sandiford's tract, *A Brief Examination of the Practice of the Times,* was published by Benjamin Franklin, 1729.[21]   Elihu Coleman's *Testimony against Making Slaves of Men*[22] followed in 1733, and in 1738 Benjamin Lay's *All Slave-Keepers that Keep the Innocent in Bondage, Apostates.*[23]   In these writings the seeds of the anti-slavery movement in America were sown.   They were spread to all parts of the Colonies by the preaching of a number of itinerant Quaker ministers advocating emancipation.   Of first importance in organizing and unifying Friends in the movement ranks the work of John Woolman, the great Quaker apostle of freedom.   He has recorded in his diary the difficulties that he had to surmount and the success that he attained.[24]   Supplementing the crusading endeavors of Woolman, Anthony Benezet, a prolific pamphleteer, by his writings, which extended from the middle of the century down to the eighties, was a principal medium in spreading the anti-slavery doctrines beyond the narrow circle of Friends and causing the religious motives of the pietists to coalesce with the secular motives of the patriots to form the broader anti-slavery movement of the Revolutionary period.   His writings were read by Washington and definitely influenced the thinking of Patrick Henry on the subject of slavery.[25]   Friends in their Yearly Meeting at Philadelphia in 1758 prohibited members of the society from importing, selling, or purchasing slaves, but not until 1776 did they go to the logical ex-

---

[21] *The Works of Benjamin Franklin* (Sparks, ed.), X, 403.

[22] Moore, *op. cit.,* p. 108.   [23] *Ibid.,* p. 82, note 1.

[24] *A Journal of the Life, Gospel Labours, and Christian Experiences of the Faithful Minister of Christ, John Woolman* (Dublin, 1776).   There have been many later editions.   *Cf. Some Considerations on the Keeping of Negroes.* (First printed in 1754; published with the *Journal* in 1776).

[25] See letter of Patrick Henry, Jan. 18, 1773, on receiving one of Benezet's tracts published in *Views of American Slavery Taken a Century Ago* (Philadelphia, 1858), p. 133.

treme on the issue and disowned members who refused to manumit their slaves.[26]

An analysis of the Quaker writings on slavery reveals the fact that their ideas were based fundamentally on religious and moral motives. The dislike for slavery inhered in the pietistic faith; it was a practice inconsistent with their conception of the Christian life, which was a life of simplicity of thought and humility of action. Their conviction that there was a divine spark in every man was incompatible with any system of social gradation and prohibited luxury for one man at the expense and labor of another. As Woolman expressed it, "man is born to labor, and experience abundantly sheweth that it is for our good."[27] He believed, moreover, that freedom was God's gift to man. "I have ever believed that Liberty was the natural right of all men equally."[28] The idea of property in man entailed the control of the slave as a moral being, and this was the basis of the evil to the Quaker who believed in the doctrine of the inner light whereby the individual and the deity came into direct moral contact.

Consequently, in formulating their theory against slavery, the Quakers based their arguments tangibly on the Golden Rule of Christianity, "do unto others as you would have them do unto you." From the time of Keith and Hepburn, through the entire slavery controversy, Quaker thought revolved around this Biblical injunction. Woolman declared that it was "the best criterion, by which mankind ought to judge of their own conduct, and others judge for them of theirs," explaining that "one man ought not to look upon another man, or society of men as so far beneath him; but that he should put himself in their place in all his actions toward them, and bring himself to this test; *viz.:* How should

[26] Thomas, *op. cit.*, p. 245.
[27] *Considerations*, p. 246.   [28] *Ibid.*, p. 264.

I approve of this conduct were I in their circumstances and they in mine."[29]   Likewise, Anthony Benezet interpreted the Golden Rule to be inconsistent with slaveholding.   "If we continually bear in mind the royal law of doing to others as we would be done by, we shall never think of bereaving our fellow creatures of that valuable blessing, liberty, nor endure to grow rich by their bondage."[30]

An estimate of the influence of Quaker thought on the early emancipation movement is now in order. First to become pronounced, the Quaker antagonisms for slavery converged with the natural rights philosophy in the 1760s and 1770s as the two main streams to form the current of anti-slavery opinion that flowed down through the American Revolution. The continued interest of Quakers as a group in the anti-slavery movement, after the Revolutionary period, was manifest through the organization of manumission and emancipation societies, and, during the early years of the Republic, Warner Mifflin and others of their leaders tied up the religious crusade with practical politics by petitioning Congress to exercise its powers to abolish slavery and the slave trade and to prohibit its extension into the territories.[31] The writings and preaching of individual Quakers, no longer isolated as in the Colonial period, acted as a tonic to sustain the anti-slavery movement during the early decades of the

[29] *Ibid.*, p. 261.

[30] Janney, *op. cit.*, p. 315, quoting Benezet's address at Philadelphia in 1754.

[31] A petition was presented to the Congress Wednesday, January 26, 1785, by a group of Quakers pleading for abolition. *Journals of the Continental Congress* (Fitzpatrick, ed.), XXVIII, 19. For the petition of the annual meeting of Quakers in 1790 presented to the House of Representatives, February 11, 1790, see *Annals of Congress*, 1st Cong. 1st Sess., p. 224; for the petition of the Pennsylvania Society for Promoting Abolition of Slavery, see *ibid.*, 1st Cong. 2nd Sess., p. 1239; for the petition from six societies, December 8, 1791, *ibid.*, 2nd Cong. 1st Sess., p. 241; and for the petition of Warner Mifflin, a Quaker, presented November 26, 1792, see *ibid.*, 2nd Cong. 2nd Sess., p. 728. It was over these petitions that the first debates in the Congress on the slavery question arose. Both the religious and the natural rights sanctions are appealed to in these petitions.

Republic until the abolition crusade broke into full force.[32] Allied in sentiment and conviction with the Quakers in antagonism to slavery were many of the evangelical churches. Of especial force among this group was the preaching of the itinerant Methodist divines.[33] As time passed, however, their ardor cooled, and these churches in the Southern States, unlike the Quakers wherever located, became staunch defenders of slavery.[34]

[32] For representative statements of the Quaker attitude on slavery during the early period of the American Union, see James O'Kelly, *Essay on Negro Slavery* (Baltimore, 1789); Warner Mifflin, *A Serious Expostulation with the Members of the House of Representatives* (Philadelphia, 1793), and *The Defense of Warner Mifflin against Aspersions Cast on Him on Account of His Endeavor to Promote Righteousness* (Philadelphia, 1796). For the later period, see the writings of Benjamin Lundy under whom a recrudescence of the Quaker movement took place. *The Life, Travels and Opinions of Benjamin Lundy, including his journey to Texas and Mexico; with a sketch of contemporary events and a Notice of the revolution in Hayti* (Philadelphia, 1847). For an historical summary of the part played by Friends in the anti-slavery movement, see *A Brief Statement of the Rise and Progress of the Testimony of the Religious Society of Friends, against Slavery and the Slave Trade* (Philadelphia, 1843). This was presented at the Yearly Meeting at Philadelphia, April, 1843. For the attitude of North Carolina Quakers, see *An Address to the People of North Carolina on the Evils of Slavery* (Greensboro, 1830), printed by William Swain.

[33] John Wesley, the father of Methodism, after his return from America to England began to condemn slavery and in 1774 published *Thoughts upon Slavery*, which was republished by Anthony Benezet in Philadelphia and widely circulated. L. Tyerman, *The Life and Times of John Wesley, M.A., Founder of the Methodists* (New York, 1872), III, 183. For the influence of Benezet on Wesley, see *ibid.*, p. 114. Wesley's *Thoughts* and Benezet's *Short Account* were republished together in 1858 in *Views of American Slavery Taken a Century Ago—Anthony Benezet and John Wesley* (Philadelphia, 1858). Freeborn Garretson, an early Methodist preacher, publicly condemned slavery in North Carolina and Virginia in 1773. C. B. Swaney, *Episcopal Methodism and Slavery with Sidelights on Ecclesiastical Politics* (Boston, 1926), p. 1. For the attitude of two other leaders, Thomas Coke and Francis Asbury, see *ibid.*, p. 1, and for Asbury, see *The Heart of Asbury's Journal* (E. S. Tipple, ed.; New York, 1904).

[34] For the change in attitude of Southern Methodists, see L. C. Matlock, *The Anti-Slavery Struggle and Triumph in the Methodist Episcopal Church* (New York and Cincinnati, 1881); John Nelson Norwood, *The Schism in the Methodist Episcopal Church, 1844: a study of slavery and ecclesiastical politics* (New York, 1923); and Swaney, *op. cit.* For one of the best contemporary defenses of the position of Southern Methodists, see H. B. Bascom, *Methodism and Slavery: With other matters controversial between the North and the South* (Frankfort, 1845).

THEORIES OF RELIGIOUS INSTRUCTION

At this point, while searching for the origins of slavery theories, the influence of another movement of the Colonial period upon the development of slavery thought should be considered. The philosophy behind the movement for religious instruction of the slaves contained some of the germs of the pro-slavery argument. This movement, which began at a very early date within the Established Church, accepted the validity of the relationship between master and slave and concentrated efforts toward the betterment of conditions incident to that relationship. Two main purposes were aimed at: first, to impress upon masters the Christian duty of affording their slaves the opportunity for salvation, of caring for the slave's soul as well as his body; and secondly, to offer the slave the means of salvation, while exhorting him to his proper obligations to the master under the slave relation. Instruction in these mutual obligations would result in the amelioration of the severity of the slave system but would not eventuate in the abolition of the master slave relation.

The foundation for practical religious instruction was laid by Richard Baxter in the *Christian Directory* published in 1673.[35] This work, which contained a chapter of directions to masters on the proper usage of their slaves, had an extensive circulation among the plantation owners and must have influenced many of them for the proper treatment to their slaves.[36] In the year 1685, Morgan Godwyn, a clergy-

---

[35] *The Practical Works of the Rev. Richard Baxter: With a life of the author, and a critical examination of his writings* (Wm. Orme, ed.), vols. II-VI.

[36] *Ibid.*, IV, 209-220. For Baxter's influence on slaveholders, see Charles Colcock Jones, *The Religious Instruction of the Negroes in the United States* (Savannah, 1842), p. 7. "The works of this eminent servant of God had an extensive circulation, and these Directions may have been productive of much good on the Plantations of those owners into whose hands they fell." Moore, *op. cit.*, p. 78, says that Baxter expressly recognized the lawfulness of slavery and was concerned only with the religious obligations growing out of the relation. [L. Bacon] "The Southern Apostasy," *The New Englander*, XII, (1854), 627,

man of the Church of England, appeared before James II and preached a sermon deploring the condition of the slaves and pleading that His Majesty use some endeavor toward having the Gospel ideas propagated in the Colonies.[37] The actual work of religious instruction was undertaken by the "Society for the Propagation of the Gospel in Foreign Parts" which was incorporated by William III in 1701. Many missionaries were sent out by this organization to spread the philosophy of religious instruction throughout the plantations.[38] Typical of the endeavors of clergymen of the Established Church to expound the proper relationship of master and slave were the sermons preached by the Rev. Thomas Bacon in Maryland. He taught that the slave was ingrafted into the master's family and that being equally capable of sal-

---

while admitting that Baxter did not deny absolutely and without qualification the lawfulness of slavery, contends that to have obeyed his directions meant gradual abolition. See Baxter's basis for slavery, *Works*, IV, 216. "A certain degree of servitude or slavery is lawful by necessitated consent of the innocent. That is so much (1) As wrongeth no interest of God, (2) Nor of Mankind by breaking the laws of nations, (3) Nor the person himself, by hindering his salvation, or the needful means thereof; nor those comforts of life which nature giveth to man as man, (4) Nor the commonwealth or society where we live."

[37] *Trade Preferred before Religion, and Christ Made to Give Place to Mammon: Represented in a sermon relating to the plantations* (London, 1685). Godwyn had published in 1680 *The Negroes' and Indians' Advocate, sueing for their admission into the Church* (London, 1680). He accepted the lawfulness of slavery and pleaded the right to religion of the Negro and Indian. Evelyn in his diary attests to the determination of James II to Christianize the slaves. On the 16th of September, 1685, he wrote: "I may not forget a resolution which his Majesty made, and had a little before entered upon it at the Council Board at Windsor or Whitehall, that the negroes in the Plantations should all be baptised, exceedingly disclaiming against that impiety of their masters prohibiting it, out of a mistaken opinion that they would be *ipso facto* free; but his Majesty persists in his resolution to have them Christened, which piety the Bishop blessed him for." *Works* (Bohn, ed.), II, 245. Thus on the 29th of May, 1686, the following Instruction was sent to Governor Dongan of New York. "You are with ye assistance of our Council to find out the best means to facilitate & encourage the conversion of Negroes and Indians to the Christian Religion." *New York Colonial Documents*, III, 374.

[38] Jones, *op. cit.*, p. 8 ff. David Humphrey, *An Historical Account of the Incorporated Society for the Propagation of the Gospel in Foreign Parts* (London, 1730), pp. 200-231.

vation with other members of the family he should be brought up in the knowledge and fear of God.[39]   Activity for religious instruction was not confined to the ministry of the Established Church.   Exponents of this humanitarian philosophy were found also among the Methodist missionaries[40] and among the early Puritan divines.   Of especial significance among the Puritans was the work of Cotton Mather who founded a school for the teaching of slaves.   Probably nowhere was the theory of religious instruction more clearly expounded than in the following passage from Mather's *Essays To Do Good,* published in 1710, setting forth the various methods of doing good in this world of iniquity.

Masters, yea, and mistresses too, must have their devices how to do good unto their servants; how to make them the servants of Christ, and the children of God.   God, whom you must remember to be "your Master in heaven," has brought them, and put them into your hands.   Who can tell what good he has brought

[39] *Two Sermons Preached to a Congregation of Black Slaves, at the Parish Church of St. Peter's in the Province of Maryland* (London, 1749).   *Four Sermons upon the Great Indispensable Duty of all Christian Masters and Mistresses to Bring up Their Negro Slaves in the Knowledge and Fear of God* (London, 1750).   Years later Bishop Meade of the Episcopal diocese of Virginia incorporated several of these sermons in a volume, *Sermons for Servants* (n. p. 1836).   Frederick Dalcho, *Churches of South Carolina* (Charleston, 1820), p. 148, tells of the fruits of the movement in South Carolina.   "At length through the influence and exertions of the Rev. Mr. Commissary Gasden, a School-house was built in Charles-Town by private subscription and opened on 12 Sept. 1742."

[40] For such views expressed by George Whitefield, one of the early Methodist missionaries to Georgia, see *infra,* p. 41.   Bishop Asbury was profoundly impressed with the expediency of preaching amelioration rather than abolition to the masters.   February 1, 1809, he wrote in his *Journal,* "We are defrauded of great numbers by the pains that are taken to keep the blacks from us.   Their masters are afraid of the influence of our principles.   Would not an *amelioration* in the condition and treatment of slaves have produced more practical good to the poor Africans than any attempt at their *emancipation?*   The state of society, unhappily, does not admit of this; besides the blacks are deprived of the means of instruction.   Who will take the pains to lead them into the way of salvation and watch over them that they may not stray, but the Methodists?   Well now their masters will not let them come to hear us.   What is the personal liberty of the African which he may abuse to the salvation of his soul; how may it be compared?" Tipple, *op. cit.,* p. 608.

them for? How if they should be the elect of God, fetched from Africa, or the Indies, and brought into your families, on purpose, that by the means of their being there, they may be brought home unto the Shepherd of souls!

Oh! that the souls of our slaves were of more account with us! that we gave a better demonstration that we despise not our own souls, by doing what we can for the souls of our slaves, and not using them as if they had no souls! That the poor slaves and blacks which live with us, may by our means be made the candidates of the heavenly life! How can we pretend unto Christianity, when we do no more to Christianize our slaves! Verily, you must give an account unto God concerning them. If they be lost through your negligence, what answer can you make unto "God, the Judge of all"? Methinks, common principles of gratitude should incline you to study the happiness of those, by whose obsequious labors your lives are so much accommodated. Certainly, they would be the better servants to you, the more faithful, the more honest, the more industrious, and submissive servants to you, for your bringing them into the service of your common Lord.

But if any servant of God, may be so honored by him, as to be made the successful instrument of obtaining from a British Parliament, 'an Act for the Christianizing of the slaves in the plantations,' then it may be hoped something more may be done than has yet been done, that the blood of souls may not be found in the skirts of our nation: a controversy of heaven with our colonies may be removed, and prosperity may be restored; or, however, the honorable instrument, will have unspeakable peace and joy in the remembrance of his endeavors. In the meantime, the slave trade is a spectacle that shocks humanity.[41]

[41] Quoted from the Massachusetts Sabbath School Society edition (Boston, 1845), pp. 101-104. A new edition improved by George Burdes from the latest London edition, 1807 (Boston, 1817), p. 58, note 1 following the above passage: "In the original work some observations are made in this place with respect to the usages of slaves; but as the subject has happily no connection with our country, the passage is here omitted." These observations or rules for the proper treatment of slaves are printed in full in the Massachusetts Sabbath School Society edition, pp. 104-110.

The movement to improve the conditions of slavery by means of religious instruction met with serious objections from slaveowners. Two principal ideas militated in opposition to the work of the humanitarians; first, the belief that the Negro was a different species from man, that he was without a soul, and that Christianity offered no salvation for him; and secondly, the fear that administration of the sacraments to the slave would elevate him to the plane of the master and would absolve his status as a slave. In the literature of the Colonial period may be found many evidences of the belief in the inferior capacity of the Negro, which idea made such an indelible impression on the collective mind of the slaveowners that it was not entirely removed even a century later when assaulted by the combined teachings of the churches in the South during the crest of the development of the religious theory of the unity of the races. Instead, this common belief of Negro incapacity was the Colonial heritage of the ethnological branch of the later pro-slavery thought which developed the theory of the diversity of races and plurality of their origins. Bishop Berkeley, who visited in the Colonies around 1730, testified before the "Society for the Propagation of the Gospel" that "an irrational contempt of the blacks, as creatures of another species, who had no right to be instructed or admitted to the sacraments, has proved a main obstacle to the conversion of these poor people."[42] Another writer of the same period commented on what hindered baptism among the slaves: "Talk to a *Planter* of the *Soul* of a *Negro*, and he'll be apt to tell ye (or at least his actions speak it loudly) that the Body of one of them may be worth twenty Pounds; but the Souls of an hundred of them would not yield him a Farthing; and therefore he's not at all solicitous about them. . . ."[43]

[42] Quoted from a sermon preached before the Society, February 18, 1731, *Works* (London, 1820 ed.) III, 247. ("Has" changed from "have"—author's change).

[43] *The Athenian Oracle* (London, 1728), II, 464.

Probably the main obstacle to the conversion of the Negroes was the fear of the slaveowners that baptism would alter the status of the slave. Bishop Berkeley said the notion prevailed throughout the Colonies that "being baptized is inconsistent with a state of slavery."[44] This idea probably grew out of the old patristic theory that slavery was based upon man's original sin rather than upon nature.[45] So long as the slave was a heathen or infidel, slavery was lawful,[46]

[44] *Loc. cit.* In answering the arguments against baptizing the slaves the writer in *The Athenian Oracle*, II, 462-464, contended that Christian masters were under a duty to baptize their slaves which grew out of the covenant with God, that Christ had substituted baptism for circumcision as a part of the covenant entered into between God and Abraham, Genesis 17: 12.

[45] For the theory of the early Church Fathers that slavery was a consequence of sin, see R. W. and A. J. Carlyle, *A History of Mediaeval Political Theory in the West* (Edinburgh and London, 1927), I, 116-124. The same idea was carried down into the theory of the canonists, *ibid.*, II, 119-120. In 1851 a Georgia jurist commenting upon the currency of this Colonial idea concluded "that it seems to have been derived from the authority which God gave the Jews, to take and subdue, and enslave, if they could not convert, the heathen, in the land which was their inheritance. . . ." Neal v. Farmer, 9 *Ga. Rep.*, p. 577.

[46] The idea that enslavement lawfully depended upon infidelity goes far back in the history of the common law and it is difficult to ascertain its original source. The author of the *Mirrour*, late thirteenth century, recognized heathenism as the basis for slavery. See Andrew Horn, *The Mirrour of Justices* (Robinson, ed., 1903), Ch. II, Sec. 28, p. 123. "From *Shem* and *Japheth* came the gentle Christians, and from *Cham*, the villains which the Christians may give away, or sell as they do other Chattels. . . ." Definite legal sanction was given the theory of infidelity in two early English cases. In Butts v. Penny (1677), 2 *Lev.* 20; 83 *Eng. Rep.* 518 the court held "that *negroes* being usually bought and sold among merchants, as merchandise, and also being infidels, there might be a property in them sufficient to maintain trover. . . ." Again in Gelly v. Cleve (1694), (Hill. term 5 Will. and Mar. C. B.) cited in Chamberlain v. Harvey. 1 *Ld. Raym.* 146, 91 *Eng.* Rep. 994, infidelity appears to have been the sole basis for the decision that "trover will lie for a negro boy, for they are heathens, and therefore a man may have property in them, and that the court without averment made, will take notice that they are heathens." Holdsworth traces the theory of these cases back to Coke's opinion in Calvin's Case (1608). See Wm. Holdsworth, *A History of English Law* (London), VII, 484. Coke drew upon the medieval laws of war which recognized a modified property of the captor in the captive enemy until ransom was paid. He then laid down the rule that infidels were perpetual enemies which might be killed, or, in lieu thereof, be made perpetual prisoners or slaves. *Cf.* 7 *Co. Rep.*, 1, 17 a, 17 b, 77 *Eng. Rep.* 377, 397, "All Infidels are in law *perpetui inimici*, perpetual enemies (for the law presumes not

but the administration of the sacraments washed away original sin and the basis of slavery fell. So strong was this apprehension and so effectively was it used to hinder the activities of the missionaries working for the betterment of slave conditions that the Bishop of London, who was in charge of missionary work among the plantations, sent a pastoral letter to masters in the year 1727 with the hope of dispelling all fear that baptism would destroy the property of the master in his slave:

To which it may be very truly reply'd, That Christianity, and the embracing of the Gospel, does not make the least Alteration in Civil Property, or in any of the Duties which belong to Civil Relations; but in all these Respects, it continues Persons just in the same State as it found them. The Freedom which Christianity gives, is a Freedom from the Bondage of Sin and Satan, and from the Dominion of Men's Lusts and Passions and inordinate Desires; but as to their outward Condition, whatever that was before, whether bond or free, their being baptised, and becoming Christians, makes no manner of Change in it. . . .[47]

---

that they will be converted, that being *remota potentia* (a remote possibility), for between them, as with the devils, whose subjects they be, and the Christians, there is perpetual hostility, and can be no peace. . . ." Early evidence of the belief 'in the Colonies that paganism was a justification for enslavement is found in Saffin, *loc. cit.*, p. 252: "Again, if it should be unlawful to deprive them that are lawful Captives, or Bondmen of their Liberty for life being Heatherns, it seems to be more unlawful to deprive our Brethren, of our own or other Christian nations of their Liberty, (though but for a time)." And *ibid.*, p. 255: "And therefore these florid expressions, the Sons and Daughters of the first *Adam*, the Brethren and Sisters of the Second Adam, and the Offspring of God, seem to be misapplied to impart and insinuate, that we ought to tender Pagan Negroes with all love, kindness, and equal respect as to the best of men." Biblical authority for holding the heathen in perpetual bondage was taken from Leviticus 25: 44-46.

[47] Quoted in Humphrey, *op. cit.*, pp. 257-271, 265; also Jones, *op. cit.*, pp. 16-25, 21. The Bishop cites St. Paul as authority, I Cor., 7: 20, "Let every man abide in the same calling wherein he was called." Apparently the Pauline teachings did not suggest that conversion or baptism emancipated the slave. For St. Paul's theory of slavery, see Carlyle, *op. cit.*, I, 84-89. The same seems to be true of writings of the Fathers, *ibid.*, *passim*, and of the canonists, *ibid.*, II, 116-129. For the inconsistency between ordination and a state of slavery under the canon law, see *ibid.*, pp. 122-127.

The pronouncement from the church, nevertheless, did not suffice to alleviate the fears of the slaveowners concerning the efficacy of baptism in absolving the status of the slave as a rule of the unwritten law of England.[48]   In order to

---

[48.]In the English cases there appears to be a division of authority as to the legal efficacy of baptizing the slave. Premised upon the theory that infidelity supported property in man, some of the decisions suggest the logical conclusion that conversion would destroy that property. It is difficult to trace out the origin of this legal theory. Apparently it did not come into English law through the canon law, *cf. supra*, note 47, but was present in the common law from a very early date. *Cf. The Mirrour*, Ch. II, Sec. 28, p. 124, "Villains become free many ways; some by baptism, as those *Saracans* who are taken by Christians or bought, and brought to Christianity by grace."   In the English cases supporting slavery conversion was one of the arguments presented to the courts in plea for freedom. In Butts *v.* Penny (1677), 3 *Keble* 785, 84 *Eng. Rep.*, 1011 the court seemed to accept the argument. It was an action for trover for 100 Negroes. ". . . but *per curiam*, they are by usage *tanquam bona*, and go to the administrator until they become Christians; and thereby they are enfranchised." This dictum is the closest approach to an acceptance by the English court of the conversion theory to be found in the reported cases. The question was again discussed in Sir Thomas Grantham's Case (1686), 3 *Mod.* 121, 87 *Eng. Rep.* 77. In 1696 an elaborate discussion of the question whether baptism emancipated the slave was made before the King's Bench, but because of a misconception of the form of action brought by the plaintiff, Chamberlaine *v.* Harvey, 5 *Mod.* 186, 187, 87 *Eng. Rep.* 596, the court did not make a decision. The counsel for the Negro argued: "Being baptized according to the use of the Church, he (the slave) is thereby made a Christian, and Christianity is inconsistent with slavery. And this was allowed even in the time when the Popish religion was established, as appears by Littleton; for in those days, if a villain had entered into religion, and was professed, as they called it, the Lord could not seize him; and the reason there given is, because he was dead in law, and if the Lord might take him out of his cloister, then he could not live according to his religion. The like reason may now be given for baptism being incorporated into the laws of the land; if the duties which arise thereby cannot be performed in a state of servitude, the baptism must be a manumission. That such duties cannot be performed is plain; for persons baptized are to be confirmed by the diocean, when they can give an account of their faith, and are enjoined by several acts of Parliament, to come to Church. But if the Lord hath an absolute property over him, then he might send him far enough from the performance of these duties" into an infidel land where he would not be suffered to exercise the Christian religion. But Lord Hardwicke flatly denied the validity of the contention in Pearne .*v.* Lisle (1749), I *Amb.* 75, 27 *Eng. Rep.* 47. *Cf. infra*, note 49. In the cases supporting freedom, while the conversion theory was mooted, apparently the decisions were based on another ground; namely, that there was nothing in the common law to support property in man. In Shanley *v.* Harvey (1762), 2 *Eden.* 126, 28 *Eng. Rep.* 844, Chancellor Northington gave it as his opinion that "as soon as a man sets foot

undeceive them in this regard, an opinion of His Majesty's Attorney and Solicitor Generals was procured and dispensed throughout the Colonies, in which they pledged themselves to the planters for the legal consequences of baptizing the slaves.[49]   Even then it was deemed necessary to enact statutes in some of the Colonies to override this supposed rule of the common law and set at rest the apprehension of the slaveowners in order that the work of religious instruction might proceed.[50]

---

on English ground he is free." In Smith v. Brown and Cooper, 2 Salk 666, 91 Eng. Rep. 566 Lord Holt held that "as soon as a negro comes into England, he becomes free." To the same effect was Mansfield's decision in Somerset v. Stewart (1772), Loft 1, 20 Howell's St. Trials 1, 98 Eng. Rep. 510.

It does not appear from the reported cases that the question of the ipso facto effect of conversion was ever discussed in the Colonial courts. No cases of this character are digested in the American Digest System. Nathan Dane, A General Abridgment and Digest of American Law (Boston, 1823), II, 427, states that one of the arguments presented in the suits for freedom in Massachusetts in 1773 was that Negroes "were Christians, and if held in slavery, could not perform their Christian duties."

[49] Hurd, op. cit., I, 186, note, quotes the opinion from an essay published by Granville Sharp in London, 1772: "We are of the opinion that a slave by coming from the West Indies to Great Britain or Ireland, either with or without his master, doth not become free; and that his master's property or right in him is not thereby determined or varied; and that baptism doth not bestow freedom on him, nor make any alteration in his temporal condition in these kingdoms. We are also of opinion that the master may legally compel him to return again to the Plantations. June 14, 1729. P. Yorke; C. Talbot." Bishop Berkeley commenting upon the circulation of the opinion in the Colonies hoped that it would produce the intended effect there, loc. cit. Lord Hardwicke later gave judicial sanction to the opinion in Pearne v. Lisle (1749), I Amb. 75, 27 Eng. Rep. 47, when he held that trover would lie for a slave, saying: "There was once a doubt, whether, if they were baptized they would not become free by that act, and there were precautions taken in the Colonies to prevent their being baptized, till the opinion of Lord Talbot and myself, was taken on that point. We were both of the opinion that it did not alter their state." Mansfield also refers to the opinion in the Somerset Case (1772), Lofft. 1, 98 Eng. Rep. 510.

[50] The statute law in the Colonies on this matter is quite extensive. See Va. Act 1667, C. 3: "That the conferring of baptism does not alter the condition of the person as to his bondage or freedom, that divers masters, freed from doubt, may more carefully endeavor the propagation of Christianity by permitting Children, though slaves . . . to be admitted to that sacrament." The Statutes at Large, being a collection of the laws of Virginia (W. W. Hening, ed.; New York, 1833),

The body of pro-slavery thought that developed along with the practice of religious instruction lingered on in the South; and, when a recrudescence of enthusiasm for the moral betterment of the slaves occurred at a later period, the Colonial attitudes afforded the source out of which grew the theory of the new movement.

THE NATURAL RIGHTS PHILOSOPHY AND SLAVERY

It is difficult to determine with certainty how soon the natural rights factor began to influence the development of American slavery thought. From the genesis of the anti-slavery movement there was an appeal to fundamental law, many asserting that slavery was contrary to the law of nature. But the concept of a pre-social state of nature ruled over by an immutable law of nature which guaranteed to the individual the inalienable rights of liberty and equality was not well formed in the early writings on slavery. Rather the early

---

II, 260. See also act of 1682, c. 3, *ibid.*, p. 490, Act of 1705, c. 49, Sec. 36. "That baptism of slaves shall not exempt them from bondage," *ibid.*, III, 460. For South Carolina, see Act of 1690, Sec. 2. *Statutes at Large of South Carolina* (D. J. McCord and Thomas Cooper, eds.; Columbia, 1836-1841), VII, 342; Act of 1712, Sec. 34, *ibid.*, pp. 352-364. There seems to have been no such statute enacted in Georgia or North Carolina. A significant provision, however, on the same matter appears in John Locke's "The Fundamental Constitutions of Carolina" (1669), Art. 107: "Since charity obliges us to wish well to the souls of all men, and religion ought to alter nothing in man's civil estate or right, it shall be lawful for slaves as well as others, to enter themselves, and be of what Church or profession any of them shall think best, and be as fully member as any free-man. But yet no slave shall hereby be exempted from that civil dominion his master hath over him, but be in all things in the same state and condition he was in before." F. N. Thorpe, *Constitutions*, V, 2785. Hurd, *op. cit.*, I, 250, quotes from *Plantation Laws* (London, 1705), a Maryland statute to the same effect dated 1699. In New York a similar statute was enacted in 1706, Hurd, *op. cit.*, I, 281, carried forward in Act of 1788, C. 40, Sec. 3, *ibid.*, II, 52, where baptism was not deemed to be manumission, and as late as 1801, C. 188, Sec. 1, *ibid.*, p. 53. Moore, *op. cit.*, p. 58, says that there is no evidence in the statutes of Massachusetts to show that the question of the legal effect of baptism on the slave was ever mooted in that Colony. The French *Code Noir* of 1685, prepared by Colbert, required every French planter to have his slaves baptized and instructed in Christianity. For summary of Act see Henri Martin, *Histoire de France depuis les Temps les Plus Reculés Jusqu'en 1789* (Paris, 1878), XII, 555-556.

attacks on slavery, being motivated by religion, identified nature with divine authority appealing to the law of nature and nature's God.

It may be surmised that the natural rights factor began to play a part in the slavery controversy soon after it began to affect American thinking on political matters generally. No specific evidence seems to exist, however, of its application to the slave until the decade prior to the outbreak of the American Revolution. During the preliminaries of the Revolution, while the patriots were formulating their theory of resistance to Great Britain, natural rights became a chief source for the Colonial arguments, and incidentally the right of the slave to freedom was asserted. One of the first recorded instances occurred when James Otis included the slave in his assertion of the natural and inherent rights of man as he pleaded the cause of the Colonists. Otis' thinking was not purely secular, as he seems to have identified the law of nature with divine authority and doubted the existence of a pre-social state of nature. His emphasis, nevertheless, was on the original rights of the individual in nature, an element much more pronounced in the theory of Otis than in that of earlier thinkers.

The colonists are by the law of nature free born, as indeed all men are, white or black. . . . Does it follow that 'tis right to enslave a man because he is black? Will short curl'd hair, like wool, instead of Christian hair, as 'tis called by those, whose hearts are as hard as the nether millstone, help the argument? Can any logical inference in favour of slavery, be drawn from a flat nose, a long or short face. . . .

There is nothing more evident, says Mr. Locke, than 'that creatures of the same species and rank, promiscuously born to all the same advantages of nature, and the use of the same faculties, should also be equal one among another, without subordination and subjection, unless the master of them all should by any manifest declaration of his will set one above another, and confer on him by an evident and clear appointment, an undoubted right to dominion and sovereignty.' 'The natural liberty of man is to be free from any superior power on earth, and not to be under the will or legislative authority of man, but only to have the law of nature for his rule.' This is the liberty of individual states; this is the liberty of every man out of society, and who has a mind to live so; which liberty is only abridged in certain instances, not lost to those who are born in or voluntarily enter into society; this gift of God cannot be annihilated.[51]

During the decade following the pronouncement of Otis, as the natural rights theory became an increasingly prominent factor in molding American political opinion, it also had a pronounced effect upon slavery thought. This influence was felt even by thinkers whose predominant motive was religious in character. For example, Benjamin Coleman, who believed "the oppression, bondage and slavery exercised upon our poor brethren the Africans to be a God-provoking and wrath pro-curing sin," asserted that "they are as free by nature as we, or any other people, have a natural right to liberty and freedom as much as we and it is only by power and tyranny that they are brought and kept under this cruel yoke of bondage."[52]

Soon the natural rights theory was translated into the

[51] *The Rights of the British Colonies Asserted and Proved* (Boston, 1764), pp. 29-30. Reprinted in *University of Missouri Studies*, IV, No. 3 (C. F. Mullett, ed.), Moore, *op. cit.*, pp. 109-110, thinks that Otis first protested against slavery as opposed to natural rights in his speech on the Writs of Assistance, 1661. Unfortunately the only record of this speech is found in the insufficient notes taken by John Adams. *Works*, II, 523. Another attack by Otis on slavery may be found in *A Vindication of the House of Representatives of the Province of Massachusetts Bay* (Boston, 1762), pp. 18-20. *University of Missouri Studies*, IV, 18-20. "No government has a right to make hobby horses, asses and slaves of the subject, nature having made sufficient of the two former, for all the lawful purposes of man, from the harmless peasant in the field, to the most refined politician in the Cabinet; but none of the last, which infallibly proves they are unnecessary."

[52] Joshua Coffin, *op. cit.*, p. 339, quoting from the *Essex Journal*, July 20, 1774.

activities of the group who urged liberation of the slaves by legislative action. In 1767 a bill was introduced into the Massachusetts House of Representatives "to prevent the unwarrantable and unnatural custom of enslaving mankind."[53] A few years later representatives from Salem were instructed to prevent importation of Negroes into Massachusetts "as repugnant to the natural rights of mankind,"[54] and in 1776 a resolution was introduced into the House: "That the selling and enslaving the human species is a direct violation of natural rights alike vested in all men by their Creator."[55] A clear expression of the natural rights theory was contained in the preamble of an emancipation bill drafted the following year:

Whereas ye unnatural practice in this State of holding certain persons in slavery, more particularly those transported from Africa and the children born of such persons, is contrary to the laws of nature . . . and a disgrace to all good governments, more especially to such who are struggling against oppression and in favor of the natural and unalienable rights of human nature. . . .[56]

[53] *Ibid.*, p. 338; Moore, *op. cit.*, p. 126.

[54] Joseph B. Felt, *Annals of Salem* (1845-49 ed.), II, 416.

[55] Moore, *op. cit.*, p. 149, quoting from *Journal*, p. 105; Felt, *op. cit.*, p. 417.

[56] Moore, *op. cit.*, p. 184, quoting from *Massachusetts Archives*, CXLII, 58. It is difficult to ascertain whether or not the natural rights argument was presented to the courts in the Massachusetts freedom suits of the Revolutionary period. A statement of John Adams supports the possibility. "I was concerned in several causes in which Negroes sued for their freedom, before the Revolution. The arguments in favor of their liberty were much the same as have been urged since in pamphlets and newspapers, in debates in Parliament, etc., arising from the rights of mankind, which was the fashionable word at that time. Since that time they have dropped the 'kind'." Letter to Dr. Belknap, Mch. 21, 1795, *Massachusetts Historical Society Collections*, XLIII, 401. Nathan Dane in a summary of the arguments in these suits makes no mention of natural rights apart from rights under the common law. *Loc. cit.* See also Dr. Belknap in *Massachusetts Historical Society Collections*, IV, 203, where he says that the Negroes based their right to freedom on the Royal Charter and the common law of England. See also Holyoke's Observations, *ibid.*, XLIII, 400. Unfortunately the reports of these cases are inadequate to settle the question. In the liberty cases arising after the adoption of the Constitution of 1780, however, there is strong evidence of an appeal to natural rights. See Emory Washburn, "The Extinction of Slavery in

Many similar expressions in the sermons and speeches delivered during this period show that slavery thought in New England was profoundly influenced by the natural rights philosophy. The query remains whether or not this body of anti-slavery opinion was strong enough to effect the incorporation of a liberation provision in the fundamental law of the State? Anti-slavery leaders at a later time insisted that it was the intention of the natural rights framers of the Declaration of Rights of 1780 to give legal effect to the liberation principle in the general equality clause which states that "all men are born free and equal, and have certain natural, essential and unalienable rights."[57]

Massachusetts," *Massachusetts Historical Society Collections*, XXXIV, 333-346, where the author quotes from the manuscript brief of the lawyer for the Negroes. One of the arguments pressed upon the court was that any law upholding slavery was contrary to the law of nature, that all men are equal and free by nature.

[57] Opinion of scholars on the subject has been divided as to whether the Declaration of Rights by its own force and efficacy emancipated the slaves. The historian Jeremy Belknap was of the affirmative opinion in writing to Ebenezer Hazard, Jan. 25, 1788, when he stated that "this has been pleaded in law and admitted." *Massachusetts Historical Society Collections*, XLIII, 11. But in answering the query of St. George Tucker in 1795 as to the mode by which slavery had been abolished in Massachusetts, Belknap was of the opinion "that slavery hath been abolished here by publick opinion, which began to be established about thirty years ago." *Ibid.*, IV, 201. Chief Justice Parsons in 1808 in the case of Winchendon *v.* Hatfield, 4 *Mass.* 123, 128, without citing the case referred to, stated that "in the first action involving the right of the master, which came before the Supreme Judicial Court, after the establishment of the Constitution, the judges declared that by virtue of the first Article of the Declaration of Rights, slavery in this State was no more." John G. Palfrey, the historian of New England, stated in 1845 that the declaration of the court came in 1783. *Papers on the Slave Power* (Boston, 1846), p. 4. There is no contemporaneous report of the case extant and authorities differ as to what case it was that determined the question of illegality of slavery in Massachusetts. Washburn, *loc. cit.*, says that it was the case of the Negro Quork Walker, and he assumes from a study of the manuscript brief of counsel that the court did not base the illegality of slavery mainly on the operation of the Constitution, the appeal to the fundamental law of nature appearing in the brief. Chief Justice Shaw in Commonwealth *v.* Aves (1833), 18 *Pickering* 193, 209, left it an open question when slavery was abolished in Massachusetts. Felt, *op. cit.*, II, 418, states that "the Constitution was generally understood to nullify bondage within its jurisdiction. Still some doubted." Moore, *op. cit.*, p. 203, after thoroughly weighing the available con-

In the South the application of the natural rights philosophy to the slavery problem seems to have been delayed a few years. Even then the influence was neither as widespread nor as profound as in New England. In Virginia Arthur Lee took up the cause of the slaves in the early 1760s. In an essay published in 1764 he based his attack on the institution on grounds of civil policy:

To sum up all, it is evident, that the bondage we have imposed on the Africans, is absolutely repugnant to justice. That it is highly inconsistent with civil policy; first as it tends to suppress all improvements in arts and sciences. . . . Secondly, as it may deprave the minds of the freemen. . . . And, lastly, as it endangers the community by the destructive effects of civil commotions. Need I add to these . . . that it is shocking to humanity, violative of every generous sentiment, abhorrent utterly from the Christian religion.[58]

He weakened the force of the natural rights argument against

temporary evidence, concluded that the opinion that the Declaration of Rights was a direct and intentional abolition of slavery could not be supported, and that the family tradition, which assigned to John Lowell its author, as the express motive for its origin, the intention of abolishing slavery, would not bear the test of historical criticism. Moore concluded that the whole judicial construction by which the Court made the equality clause the instrument of abolition was far in advance of the intention of the Convention and the understanding of the people when it was adopted, and that it was only gradually reached and sustained by public opinion. See also the Boston Critics on Moore, *The Historical Magazine* X, (1866), 138-143, and Moore's rejoinder, *ibid.*, pp. 186-198.

The general equality clause in the New Hampshire Constitution was construed to apply to all persons born after 1784 when the Constitution was adopted. A similar clause in the Virginia Constitution of 1776 proved to have no legal effect on the slave, although it was argued that such was intended by the framers in the debates on emancipation in the Legislature, 1831-1832. The Vermont bill of rights alone expressly abolished slavery and the Delaware bill alone has a provision against the slave trade. Some of the Southern constitutions framed after 1800 expressly confine equality to freemen: the Constitution of Mississippi, 1817, and Alabama, 1819.

[58] *An Essay in Vindication of the Continental Colonies of America, from a Censure of Mr. Adam Smith, in His Theory of Moral Sentiments. With some reflections on slavery in general. By an American* (London, 1764), p. 42.

the justice of slavery when he admitted that the individual's right to liberty was alienable under certain conditions.

Life and liberty were both the gifts of God. In a state of nature they were both equally sacred. When the increase, and other necessities of men, made the establishment of societies requisite, it followed necessarily, that a portion of natural liberty should be sacrificed to the more effectual preservation of the rest. This first subjected men to laws. The power of enacting these was lodged, by a majority of suffrages in each society, in a select number, denominated from thence the *legislative* body. Penal laws became soon necessary to the well-being of society; and were proportioned to the nature of offenses. For atrocious crimes, a deprivation of life was the most general punishment. Now, as liberty was subjected to the same power which made life the atonement for certain crimes, that certainly might have been sacrificed for similar or different offenses. In this view therefore the origin of slavery seems just and legal.[59]

A closer approach to the natural rights argument was made in his article published in the *Virginia Gazette*, March 19, 1767. There he declared that "as freedom is unquestionably the birthright of all mankind, Africans as well as Europeans, to keep the former in a state of slavery is a constant violation of that right and therefore of justice."[60] He then went on to refute the legal bases on which writers had justified slavery, that is consent, force, and birth.

For surely a man's own will and consent can not be allowed to introduce so important an innovation into society as slavery, or to make himself an outlaw, which is really the state of a slave, since, neither consenting to nor aiding the laws of society in which he lives, he is neither bound to obey them nor entitled to their protection.

To found any right in force is to frustrate all right and involve everything in confusion, violence, and rapine. With these two

[59] *Ibid.*, p. 32.
[60] Republished in *Views of American Slavery Taken a Century Ago*, p. 109.

the last must fall, since, if the parent cannot justly be made a slave neither can the child be born in slavery. . . .[61]

A certain degree of opposition to slavery appeared in the enactments of several of the Colonial assemblies regarding the foreign slave trade. South Carolina passed a law entirely prohibiting the importation of slaves.[62] Maryland, Virginia, and South Carolina, at various times, laid import taxes with the idea of reducing the number of Negroes being imported.[63] These acts were disallowed by the Crown and the Governors instructed to veto them if passed again.[64] The records show, however, that the efforts to abolish or limit the importations of slaves were not prompted by a regard for the rights of man. They were motivated primarily by the fear and the grave danger that the Negroes would become so numerous as to upset the safe ratio of the races and create a social peril and a military menace. The imported barbarian had an undermining effect on established institutions and a harmful influence upon the acclimated Negro

[61] *Ibid.* Jonathan Boucher writing about this time referring to the articles printed by Lee thought that they had done more harm than good. *Causes and Consequences of the American Revolution* (London, 1797), p. 39

[62] A total prohibition act passed the Provincial Assembly in 1760, but was disallowed by the Crown and the Governor was rebuked for assenting to it. *Cf.* William Burge, *Commentaries on Colonial and Foreign Laws* (London, 1838), I, 737, note, and W. B. Stevens, *History of Georgia*, I, 286. The text of this act does not seem to be extant.

[63] The acts of the Colonial assemblies affecting the slave trade are listed chronologically in W. E. B. Du Bois, *The Suppression of the African Slave Trade to the United States of America, 1638-1870* (New York, 1896), Appendix A. *Cf.* St. George Tucker, *Blackstone's Commentaries* (Philadelphia, 1803), note H, pp. 45-53, where he discusses twenty-three slave trade laws of Colonial Virginia. April 1, 1772, the Virginia House of Burgesses petitioned the Crown to "remove all those restraints on your Majesty's governors of this colony, which inhibit their assenting to such laws as might check so very pernicious a commerce" on the grounds that: "The importation of slaves into the Colonies from the coast of Africa, hath long been considered as a trade of great inhumanity, and under its present encouragement, we have too much reason to fear will endanger the very existence of your Majesty's American dominions." *Ibid.*, pp. 51-52.

[64] Burge, *loc. cit.*

slave. In time of war they were a source of weakness to the Colony defensively. Moreover, it was known that pestilential diseases were brought into the Colonies through the medium of the slave trade.[65] The chief objective behind the slave trade legislation was the regulation and limitation of the number of slaves that might be admitted in order to preclude these evils. In furtherance of the same general purpose, acts were passed to encourage indentured servants to immigrate and thereby to maintain a safe and wholesome balance between the two races.[66] These are the reasons given in the preambles for the passage of the acts. They indicate that the acts were not directed at an overthrow of domestic slavery but rather aimed at the protection of the institution against alien influences.[67] Suffice it to conclude here that the phraseology and history of the slave trade acts do not suggest that natural rights was one of the motives that led to their enactment.

Nor is there much evidence of the natural rights motive to be found in the slave resolutions passed by local meetings during the year 1774, urging a non-importation association of the Colonies. A typical example of such resolutions, with

[65] See Acts cited in Du Bois, *loc. cit.* Similar ideas were expressed in "An Act for Rendering the Colony of Georgia more Defensible by Prohibiting the Importation and Use of Black Slaves," *The Colonial Records of Georgia* (A. D. Candler, ed.), I, 50-52, and in "An Act for Repealing An Act . . ." (1750), *ibid.*, pp. 56-62.

[66] See Du Bois, *loc. cit.*; Tucker, *loc. cit.* The South Carolina Statute of 1751 is typical: "Whereas, the best way to prevent the mischief that may be attended by the great importation of Negroes into this Province, will be to establish a method by which such importation should be made a necessary means of introducing a proportionate number of white inhabitants." *Statutes at Large*, III, 739. And of like import were the Statutes of 1698, *ibid.*, II, 153, and the Statute of 1716, *ibid.*, p. 646.

[67] Years later, during the controversy in South Carolina over the reopening of the slave trade, it was argued by the opponents that a distinction had always been drawn in the South between opposition to the slave trade and to the domestic institution. J. J. Pettigrew in his *Report of the Minority of the Special Committee on Slavery and the Slave Trade* (Columbia, 1857), *passim*, quoted from preambles of the Acts of 1714, 1716, 1717, 1744, 1751, 1764, 1787, 1788, 1792, 1796, 1798 to establish this distinction in the slavery theory of the South.

reasons stated, was passed in Prince George County, Virginia: "Resolved that the African trade is injurious to this Colony, obstructs the population of it by freemen, prevents manufacturers and other useful emigrants from Europe from settling amongst us, and occasions an annual increase of the balance of trade against this Colony."[68]

When the Colonists came to frame statements of grievances against the British Crown use was made of natural rights, in objecting to the disallowance of the slave trade acts. An instance of this use is found in the list of instructions for the delegates in Congress submitted by Thomas Jefferson to the Virginia Convention of 1774. A follower of Locke and the natural rights school of thinkers, Jefferson by this time favored abolition. The assertion of this view perhaps accounts for the rejection of his proposal which was as follows:

The abolition of domestick slavery is the greatest object of desire in these Colonies, where it was unhappily introduced in their infant state. But previous to the enfranchisement of the slaves we have, it is necessary to exclude all further importations from Africa. Yet our repeated attempts to effect this by prohibitions, and by imposing duties which might amount to a prohibition, have been hitherto defeated by his majesty's negative. Thus preferring the immediate advantages of a few African corsairs to the lasting interests of the American States, and to the rights of human nature, deeply wounded by this infamous practice.[69]

Undaunted by the refusal of the Virginia Convention to accept this proposal, Jefferson made a similar indictment in

[68] *American Archives* (Peter Force, ed.), Ser. IV, I, 494. Similar resolutions were passed in the following Virginia counties: Nansemond, *ibid.*, p. 530; Caroline, *ibid.*, p. 541; Surry, *ibid.*, p. 593; Hanover, *ibid.*, p. 616; Princess Anne, *ibid.*, p. 641. In Fairfax County, however, the meeting declared "our most earnest wishes to see an entire stop forever put to such a wicked, cruel and unnatural trade." *Ibid.*, p. 600.

[69] "A Summary View of the Rights of British America," *ibid.*, p. 696. *Writings* (Bergh, ed.), I, 201. The first clause of the first Virginia Constitution listed "the inhuman use of the royal negative" in refusing permission to exclude slaves from Virginia by law as one of the reasons for separation from Great Britain.

listing the grievances of the Colonies in his first draft of the Declaration of Independence.

He has waged cruel war against human nature itself, violating its most sacred rights of life and liberty in the persons of a distant people who never offended him, captivating and carrying them into slavery in another hemisphere, or to incur miserable death in their transportation thither.[70]

This part of the general excoriation of the King was struck out in the revision due to objections from Southern members in Congress. Use was made of it, however, at a later date when the slaveholders constructed the theory of entailment as an excuse for the continuance of an institution that they had unsuccessfully attempted to check in Colonial times. A more definite application of natural rights to domestic slavery appeared in the resolutions adopted at Darien, Georgia, January 12, 1775.

To show the world that we are not influenced by any contracted or interested motives, but a general philanthropy for all mankind, of whatever climate, language, or complexion, we hereby declare our disapprobation and abhorrence of the unnatural practice of Slavery in America (however the uncultivated state of our country, or other specious arguments may plead for it), a practice founded in injustice and cruelty, and highly dangerous to our liberties (as well as lives), debasing part of our fellow-creatures below men, and corrupting the virtue and morals of the rest; and is laying the basis of that liberty we contend for (and which we pray the Almighty to continue to the latest posterity) upon a very wrong foundation.[71]

[70] *Writings*, I, 34.
[71] *American Archives*, Ser. IV, I, 1136. In 1739 the inhabitants of Darien had petitioned Governor Oglethorpe against the introduction of slaves into Georgia, giving among other reasons that: "It is shocking to human nature that any race of mankind, and their posterity, should be sentenced to perpetual slavery; nor in justice can we think otherwise of it, than that they are thrown amongst us, to be our scourge one day or other for our sins; and as freedom to them must be as dear as to us, what a scene of horror it must bring!" Reprinted in Hugh McCall, *The History of Georgia* (Savannah, 1811-1816), I, pp. 91-93.

Thomas Paine, one of the leading expounders of the natural rights theory, arriving in America while the Colonists were stating their case to the world, published an essay attacking slavery and proposing abolition. Paine asserted that "as these people are not convicted of forfeiting freedom, they have still a natural, perfect right to it; and the Governments whenever they come should, in justice set them free, and punish those who hold them in slavery."[72] Believing that the slavery of the parents was unjust, he thought that that of the children was more so. For, he said, even "if the parents were justly slaves, yet the children are born free; this is a natural, perfect right of all mankind."[73]

Natural rights permeated the writings on slavery of the Revolutionary period. Expressions of it may be duplicated many times. These produced a tremendous effect upon the popular mind and anti-slavery opinion rapidly crystallized. The natural rights argument against slavery inevitably suggests itself as a corollary to the general principle asserted in the Declaration of Independence: "We hold these truths to be self-evident, that all men are created equal; that they are endowed by their Creator with certain unalienable rights; that among these are life, liberty, and the pursuit of happiness." Anti-slavery leaders during the coming generations assumed that the signers consciously accepted such an application of their statement.[74] They argued that the Repub-

[72] "African Slavery in America," *Writings* (Conway, ed.), I, 7. The Article was originally published in the postscript to the *Pennsylvania Journal and the Weekly Advertiser*, Philadelphia, March 8, 1775.

[73] *Ibid.*

[74] There is no evidence to support the theory of a conscious embodiment of the emancipation principle to be found in the records of the drafting and adoption of the Declaration. Many of the signers were slave holders and it is reasonable to assume that they would have made the same objection that the records show they made in reference to the inclusion of the indictment of the King for keeping the slave trade open. Jefferson had a doubt that was never fully resolved as to the equal intellectual capacity of the Negro and the white. He discusses this matter under Query 14, "Notes on Virginia," *Writings*, II, 191-208. See also

lic was founded on a principle, which, if applied as the founders intended, would extend freedom to the enslaved Negroes; and that this higher law of nature appeal, written into the Declaration, was later incorporated into the fundamental law of the land, in the clause of the Constitution which guarantees to every State a republican form of government. Such implications were made by the anti-slavery group on each occasion that the issue of slavery was drawn in the Congress, and reverberated wherever the institution of slavery was subjected to attack within the South. As pro-slavery thinkers prepared their defense, much of their attention was directed at meeting the natural rights appeal to the fundamental law of nature. In one way or another, in order for them to defend slavery logically, they had to break down the force of the argument that all men have a natural right to freedom. Indeed an anti-slavery writer, a contemporary with the Declaration, indicated the answer that later developed to meet this apparent incongruity in American political principles.

If these solemn *truths,* uttered at such an awful crisis, are *self evident:* unless we can show that the African race are not *men,* words can hardly express the amazement which naturally arises on reflecting that the very people who make these pompous declarations are slave holders, and, by their legislation, tell us, that these blessings were only meant to be the *rights of white men,* not of all *men:* and would seem to verify the observation of an eminent writer: 'When men talk of liberty, they mean their own liberty, and seldom suffer their thoughts on that point to stray to their neighbors.'[75]

his letter to Benjamin Banneker, Aug. 30, 1791, *ibid.,* VIII, 241. Therefore, he probably did not intend to include the Negro in the self-evident truth that "all men are created equal." On the other hand he did believe that slavery was unjust and violated natural rights.

[75] [Anthony Benezet], *A Serious Address to the Rulers of America, on the Inconsistency of Their Conduct Respecting Slavery* (Trenton, 1783), p. 14.

Closely fused with the natural rights attack on slavery was the contention that slavery was inconsistent with the theory and policy on which the Americans fought the Revolution. As the Colonists began to examine their own rights they could not avoid seeing the incompatibility of contending for liberty while they were holding members of their own species in abject bondage. National Niles in a discourse on liberty delivered in Boston in 1774 warned against the effects of this inconsistency.

We have boasted of our liberty and free spirit. A free spirit is no more inclined to enslave others than ourselves. If then it should be found upon examination that we have been of a tyrannical spirit in a free country, how base must our character appear! . . . God gave us liberty and we have enslaved our fellow men! May we not fear the law of retaliation is about to be executed on us? . . . What excuse can we make for our conduct? What reason can we urge why our oppression shall not be returned in kind? Should the Africans see God Almighty subjecting us to all the evils we have brought on them, and should they cry to us, Oh, daughter of America, who art to be destroyed, happy shall be he that rewardeth thee as thou hast served us . . . how could we object? Then shame, let us either cease to enslave our fellow men, or else let us cease to complain of those, that would enslave us.[76]

Tory writers, likewise, availed themselves of the argument of inconsistency against the Whigs of 1775.

Negroe slaves in Boston! It can not be! It is nevertheless very true. For though the Bostonians have grounded their rebellions on the immutable laws of nature, and have resolved in their Town Meetings, that 'It is the first principle in civil society, founded in nature and reason, that no law of society can be binding on any individual, without his consent given by himself in person, or by his representative of his own free election; yet notwithstanding the

[76] Quoted in Coffin, *op. cit.*, p. 340.

immutable laws of nature, and this public resolution in Town Meetings, they actually have in town two thousand Negroe slaves, who never by themselves in person, nor by representatives of their own free election ever gave consent to their present bondage.[77]

Anthony Benezet pointed out the effect of the Revolutionary disquisitions and reasonings on the rights of man when he declared that the eyes of multitudes had been opened "who clearly see, that, in advocating the rights of humanity, their slaves are equally included with themselves, and that the arguments which they advance to convict others, rebound with redoubled force back on themselves."[78]   No longer, he thought was it necessary to turn to Europe for authorities that blacks are equally free with whites, for "it is declared and recorded as the sense of America."   He cited the resolve of Congress: "That the inhabitants of the English Colonies in America, by the immutable law of nature, are entitled to life, liberty and property with our lordly masters, and have never ceded to any power whatever a right to deprive us thereof."[79]   The author then arrayed in parallel columns a record of the resolves of Congress asserting American liberty which were at variance with the conduct of its members in continuing to hold others in slavery.

Thomas Paine bringing with him the European opinion of American practice entreated Americans to consider: "With what consistency or decency they complain so loudly of attempts to enslave them, while they hold so many hundred thousands in slavery; and annually enslave many thousands more, without any pretense of authority, or claim upon them?"[80]   Dr. Benjamin Rush, one of the founders of the American Anti-Slavery Society, inquired: "Where is the difference between the British Senator who attempts to enslave

---

[77] Moore, op. cit., p. 145, quoting from Sagittarius' Letters, pp. 38-39.
[78] A Serious Address, p. 19.
[79] Ibid., p. 11.   [80] Loc. cit.

his fellow subjects in America, by imposing taxes upon them contrary to law and justice; and the American Patriot who reduces his African Brethren to slavery, contrary to justice and humanity?"[81]   On many occasions through oratory and with the pen, the inconsistency between the American theory of liberty and the practice of slavery was pointed out.   It seemed contradictory for the American patriot to sign the Declaration of Independence with one hand and with the other to brandish a whip over an affrighted slave.   George Buchanan, in an Independence Day address, shouted this protest to the nation:

Cruel and oppressive she wantonly abuses the Rights of Man and willingly sacrifices her liberty at the altar of slavery.   What an opportunity is here given for triumph, among her enemies?   Will they not exclaim, that upon this very day, while the Americans celebrate the anniversary of Freedom and Independence, abject slavery exists in all her states but one?[82]

The argument that a logical extension of the Revolutionary principles would cover slavery made an impression on the thinking of many Southerners as well as Northerners. William Pinkney, later to become a strong defender of slavery, with the ardor of youthful enthusiasm, arose in the Maryland House of Delegates to advocate a bill to permit manumission and expressed surprise at the opposition.

Sir, it is really matter of astonishment to me, that the people of Maryland do not blush at the very name of Freedom. . . . that they should step forward as the zealous partizans of freedom, cannot but astonish a person who is not casuist enough to reconcile antipathies. . . . It will not do thus to talk like philosophers, and act like unrelenting tyrants; to be perpetually sermonizing it with

[81] *A Vindication of the Address to the Inhabitants of the British Settlements, on the Slavery of the Negroes in America* (Philadelphia, 1773), p. 24.

[82] *An Oration upon the Moral and Political Evils of Slavery, delivered at a public meeting of the Maryland Society for Promoting the Abolition of Slavery* (Baltimore, 1793), p. 13.

liberty for our text, and actual oppression for our commentary. What a motley appearance must Maryland at this moment make in the eyes of those who view her with deliberation! Is she not at once the fair temple of freedom, and the abominable nursery of slaves; the school for patriots, and the foster-mother of petty despots; the asserter of human rights, and the patron of wanton oppression?[83]

St. George Tucker, who proposed a plan of gradual abolition to the Virginia Legislature in 1779, was amazed that: "A people who have declared 'That all men are by nature equally free and independent' and have made this declaration the first article in the foundation of their government, should in defiance of so sacred a truth, recognized by themselves in so solemn a manner, and on so important an occasion, tolerate a practice incompatible therewith."[84] And so, when Congress in 1793 refused to accede to his petition to abolish slavery, Warner Mifflin, a Quaker enthusiast for the rights of the Negro, indignant in defense of his position, cited the record, listing the occasions, from the non-importation association to the Northwest Ordinance, when Congress had applied a legislative policy of liberation.[85] Slavery was repugnant to the genius of the American government.

[83] Speech reprinted in Henry Wheaton, *Some Account of the Life, Writings, and Speeches of William Pinkney* (New York, 1826), p. 12.

[84] *A Dissertation on Slavery* (Philadelphia, 1796), p. 30. Tucker was here referring to Art. I of the Virginia Bill of Rights. The force and efficacy of this provision of the fundamental law on the institution of slavery was debated in the Virginia Convention of 1829, and in the debates over abolition in the Virginia Legislature in 1831-32. The Courts in Virginia never construed the provision to have any application or effect on the slave.

[85] *Op. cit.* At p. 28 he says he was "acting only consonant with the principles of the late Revolution, in peaceably indicating the natural Rights of Men, on the grounds of humanity and obligations of the Christian Religion." Both the religious and the natural right, sanction appear in the Quaker petitions to Congress for abolition. See *supra*, note 31. The natural rights impulse is prominent in the Quaker petition signed by Benjamin Franklin and submitted "from a persuasion that equal liberty was originally the portion, and is still the birthright of all men." *Annals of Congress*, 1st Cong. 2nd Sess., p. 1239.

THE GENESIS OF PRO-SLAVERY THOUGHT IN AMERICA

Expressions of pro-slavery thought appeared in America immediately after the first anti-slavery publication. Pro-slavery theory being characteristically defensive in nature followed attacks on the institution throughout the Colonial period rather than preceded the attacks. There was no occasion for defending an institution that appeared to be well entrenched in the customs and usages of the times until some aggressor called its validity into question. *Pari passu,* as the attacks were launched against slavery, the defense unfolded.

The first defense of slavery published in America that has been preserved was a pamphlet written by John Saffin, *A Brief and Candid Answer to a Late Printed Sheet, Entitled The Selling of Joseph* (1701), which was issued in reply to the attack made by Judge Sewell.[86] One by one Saffin analyzed and refuted Sewell's arguments for emancipation. He then justified slavery on the broad ground of the Mosaic law in terms consonant with the theocratic political theory of the Puritan State. Thus early the defender of slavery denied the general principle of natural equality of men and argued that divine revelation showed inequality to be the order of the universe. Saffin's pamphlet seems to be the only positive statement of the pro-slavery theory for the early Colonial period extant.

Indications of the nature and content of the defense that was gradually forming during the first half of the eighteenth century, however, can be found reflected in the anti-slavery writings. Hepburn included in his dialogue between a Christian and a slaveholder, for purposes of refutation, the current pro-slavery arguments.[87] The slaveholder relied upon the historical sanction, that slavery was a natural phenomenon of society, which had existed in all ages, among all peoples,

---

[86] *Op. cit., supra,* note 9.   [87] *Op. cit.*

in some form; and upon the Biblical sanction, emphasizing the prophetic curse on Canaan (Genesis IX: 20-27), the Levitical ordinance (Leviticus XXV: 44-46), and the Pauline mandate in the Epistle to Philemon (verses 8-15). Likewise, Woolman mentioned certain arguments that he had to contend with in his crusading against slavery.[88]   Anthony Benezet, in like manner, attempted to refute the current pro-slavery contentions, directing special attention to the slaveholder's idea of the inferiority of the Negro.[89]   It appears that those who argued that an inferior capacity fitted the Negro for a status of slavery went so far as to contend that he was of a separate species from the white.[90]

Another of the pro-slavery arguments was brought out in a pamphlet by Arthur Lee, a Virginia slaveholder. He emphasized that the social condition of the slaves compared favorably with the peasant classes in other parts of the world: "I have traveled through most parts of Scotland and Ireland; and I can safely assert, that the habitations of the negroes are palaces and their living luxurious, when compared with those of the peasants of either of those countries. There is, I confess, an irrepressible misery, to the generous mind, in the very idea of slavery; but abstracting this, the condition of those slaves is far happier than that of the Scotch or Irish vulgar."[91]   Moreover, it was customary to justify slavery during the Colonial period, on the plea of necessity. Montesquieu's view that tropical countries could not be developed without Negro slaves was often used to support this argument.[92]   Pufendorf's admission that there were two law-

---

[88] *Journal*, pp. 58-60.   [89] *Observations*, p. 59.

[90] [Theodore Parsons and Eliphalet Pearson], *A Forensic Dispute on the Legality of Enslaving the Africans* (Boston, 1773), p. 37. Reference is made to certain attempts to prove that the Negro was of a separate species.

[91] *An Essay*, p. 25.

[92] Passages from *The Spirit of Laws* (1748), were cited many times by writers on slavery during the Colonial period. See Boucher, *op. cit.*, p. 39; Lee, *An Essay*, p. 36; Bernard Romans, *A Concise Natural History of East and West*

ful origins of slavery, namely, consent and force, was also frequently cited;[93] and arguments drawn from Aristotle[94] and Grotius[95] were occasionally used to sanction slavery by Colonial writers.

Georgia, the only Colony whose charter prohibited slavery, was the home of the first offense launched by the protagonists of slavery. Georgia had been founded less than a decade when petitions began to be sent to the Trustees praying for an introduction of Negroes.[96] The principal argument relied upon to persuade the trustees that slavery was for the best interests of the Colony was the necessity plea. As one writer phrased it, "in spite of all endeavors to disguise this point, it is as clear as light itself, that Negroes are as essentially necessary to the cultivation of Georgia as axes, hoes, or any other utensil of agriculture."[97] James Habersham, William and Thomas Stephens, and George Whitefield were the leaders in the movement for the introduction of slaves. Whitefield, one of the early apostles of Methodism, explained why he advocated slavery: "The Providence of God has appointed this Colony rather for the work of black slaves than for Europeans, because of the hot climate, to which the Negroes are better used than white people."[98] He

---

Florida (New York, 1775), p. 105; Otis, *The Rights of the British Colonists,* p. 43, thought that no better reason could be given for slavery than "such as Baron Montesquieu has humorously given."

[93] Lee, *An Essay,* p. 32.   [94] *Ibid.,* p. 36.   [95] *Ibid.,* p. 35.

[96] Petition of citizens of Savannah, Jan. 3, 1739, reprinted in McCall, *op. cit.,* pp. 84-90. This petition called forth the Darien petition against the introduction of slavery, *ibid.,* pp. 90-92, and the Ebenezer petition, *ibid.,* pp. 92-97. See reference to pro-slavery petitions in a letter of William Stephens to the Trustees, Nov. 27, 1740, *Georgia Colonial Records,* XXII, Pt. II, 449, and in "An Account Showing the Progress of the Colony of Georgia in America" (London, 1841), *Georgia Historical Society Collections,* II, 300.

[97] [Thomas Stephens], "A Brief Account of the Causes That Have Retarded the Progress of the Colony of Georgia in America" (London, 1843), *Georgia Historical Society Collections,* II, 93.

[98] This quoted argument was answered by John Bolzius in a letter to Whitefield, Ebenezer, Dec. 24, 1775, *Georgia Colonial Records,* XIV, 434-444.

elaborated upon his theory in justification of slavery in a letter to John Wesley in 1751.

Thanks be to God, that the time for favoring the colony of Georgia seems to be come. Now is the season for us to exert our utmost for the good of the poor Ethiopians. We are told, that even they are soon to stretch out their hands to God; and who knows but their being settled in Georgia may be overruled for this great end? As for the lawfulness of keeping slaves, I have no doubt, since I hear of some that were bought with Abraham's money, and some that were born in his house. I also can not help thinking, that some of these servants mentioned by the apostles in their epistles were, or had been, slaves. It is plain that the Gibeonites were doomed to perpetual slavery; and, though liberty is a sweet thing to such as are born free, yet to those who may never know the sweets of it, slavery perhaps may not be so irksome. However this be, it is plain, to a demonstration, that hot countries can not be cultivated without Negroes. What a flourishing country might Georgia have been, had the use of them been permitted years ago! How many white people have been destroyed for the want of them, and how many thousands of pounds spent to no purpose at all? Though it is true, that they are brought in a wrong way, from their own country, and it is a trade not to be approved of, yet as it will be carried on whether we will or not, I should think myself highly favored if I could purchase a good number of them, in order to make their lives comfortable, and lay a foundation for breeding up their posterity in the nurture and admonition of the Lord.[99]

After the middle of the century written defenses of slavery began to appear in greater numbers. The African slave trade was supported in one book as essential to the British policy of mercantilism.[100] In 1764, a French work was published, outlining a defense of slavery on Biblical and

---

[99] Reprinted in L. Tyerman, *op. cit.*, II, 132.

[100] [Malachy Postlewayt], *The African Trade, the Great Pillar and Support of the Plantation Trade in America* (London, 1745).

ethical grounds, in which the writer contended that the Golden Rule did not require, by command or implication, the emancipation of the slaves, that, in fact, by bringing Christianity to the Negroes, slavery made effective the law of love.[101]   In 1773 a pamphlet appeared in Philadelphia defending the system of slavery in the West Indies on the Biblical sanction, the necessity plea, and the inferiority argument.[102]   The author of an ironical tract criticized in detail recent anti-slavery writings of Woolman, Benezet, and others.[103]

During the year 1775 Bernard Romans published his *Natural History of East and West Florida* in which a strong case was made out for the institution of slavery, it being called forth by "the narrow system of morality adopted by some of our contemporary enthusiastical philosophers [to] restrain us from properly using this naturally subjected species of mankind."   He showed that slavery was sanctioned by Scripture and that it was lawful, being supported on the fivefold origins, crime, war, sale, birth, and consent.   Romans also argued that the Negro was by nature suited for the hot climate and the production of staple commodities and that the country was progressing under his labor.[104]   During the 1780's James Ramsay published several slavery tracts.[105]

---

[101] [J. Bellon de Saint Quentin], *Dissertation sur la Traite et le Commerce des Nègres* (Paris, 1764).

[102] [Richard Nisbet], *Slavery not forbidden by Scripture, Or a defense of the West India planters from the aspersions thrown out against them by the author of a pamphlet entitled, "An Address to the Inhabitants of the British Settlements in America upon Slave Keeping"* (Philadelphia, 1773).

[103] [Machiavelus Americanus], *Personal Slavery Established by the Suffrages of Custom and Right Reason, being a full answer to the gloomy and visionary reveries of all the fanatical and enthusiastical writers on that subject* (Philadelphia, 1773).

[104] *Op. cit.*, pp. 103-110.

[105] *Essay on the Treatment and Conversion of African Slaves in the British Sugar Colonies* (London, 1784).   The author summarizes on pp. 39-40 Andrew

In 1788 a very elaborate scriptural defense of slavery was published in London and circulated in the Colonies.[106]

An indication of the character of the philosophic defense that formed to meet the natural rights attack of the Revolutionary period may be found in the discussion over emancipation in Massachusetts. In that State public opinion appears to have been fairly evenly divided on the issue. At the Harvard commencement exercises in 1773, a debate was held on the question of the legality of enslaving the Africans, and the argument of the affirmative speaker probably reflected the prevailing pro-slavery thought of the period. The question debated was whether or not slavery was agreeable to the law of nature.[107] Defining the law of nature in utilitarian terminology rather than in terms of natural rights, the speaker argued that any principle of society was "in its nature fit and proper, just and right" and therefore conformable to the law of nature if "concomitant circumstances being considered," it "tends to the happiness of the whole" community. For, he observed, "such is the nature of society, that it requires various degrees of authority and subordination; and while the universal rule of right, *the happiness of the whole*, allows greater degrees of Liberty to some, the same immutable laws suffer it to be enjoyed only in less degrees by others"; and as "nothing in nature can possibly be of the least consequence but happiness or misery, so the difference in the tendency of

Fletcher of Saltoun, *Second Discourse on the Affairs of Scotland* (1698), where he advocated the enslavement of the Scottish beggars; also *Objections to the Abolition of the Slave Trade, with answers to which are prefixed, strictures on a late publication, entitled "Considerations on the Emancipation of Negroes, and the Abolition of the Slave Trade, by a West India Planter"* (London, 1788).

[106] Rev. Raymond Harris, *Scriptural Researches on the Slave Trade, showing its conformity with the principles of natural and revealed religion* (London, 1788).

[107] Parsons and Pearson, *op. cit.* In the following pages I have summarized the argument of the affirmative speaker which runs throughout the pamphlet.

the practical principles of any society to the production of
these, is the only thing that can possibly render some eligible,
fit and proper rather than others." The truth of this principle had been recognized, he thought, "as well by the gen-
earlity of ethnic writers, as by the wisdom of all good governments."

The speaker then undertook to demonstrate "the agreement of the law of nature with the idea of slavery in general, in opposition to that principle of natural equality, which
is so zealously contended for by the advocates for universal
liberty." He meant by slavery in general "the involuntary
subordination of the will of one to that of another; whereby
independent of all compact, the actions of the former are in
all things to be directed by the will of the latter." He
thought that the right of authority in one being, involving
subordination in another being, was universally acknowledged
in "the right of the Governor of the universe to govern and
direct the conduct of all finite existence," and in "the right
of parents to govern and direct the conduct of their children."
The question, then, reduced itself to whether or not the
"reason and foundation of the absolute authority of the Governor of the universe over the creation, and the limited authority of parents over their children, be found to operate
with equal strength in favor of a right of some individuals
among mankind to exercise any degrees of authority over
others"?

The answer to this question became obvious, because the
right to authority in the first two cases was founded on "the
greatest good of the whole." Just as the right of absolute
authority of the Creator was not based solely upon the relation of Creator and created, but also upon "the natural im-
perfection and dependence of the creature and the natural
perfection of the Creator" in accomplishing the greatest hap-

piness for the creation; so the limited authority of the parents over their children was not based on the notion of derived existence, but on "the different qualifications of parents and children to exercise this immutable law" and insure more happiness to both. He concluded, therefore, that the principle of authority and subordination between individuals was justifiable because of "the vast inequality observable between different individuals of the human species, in point of qualification for the proper direction of conduct." It mattered not whether this inequality arose from "difference in natural capacity, difference in the means of improvement, or in disposition properly to employ such means," that is, from nature or education. So long as some excelled others "in respect of wisdom and benevolence, both in the knowledge and principles of propriety and a disposition to practice such principles, that the general end, happiness, would be better promoted" this right to authority of the master in the slave was justified.

The speaker concluded with a challenge to the political equalitarian. "I think it demonstrable, that the principle of absolute equality could not be supported, even though we had no argument from fact by which [inequality] might be illustrated. And in truth, I think, before the principle of absolute equality can be maintained, it must be made to appear, that all mankind, in point of capacity and disposition to conduct properly, are equal."

It would seem, therefore, that at this early period in the philosophical discussion over the slavery issue the equalitarian's speculative appeal to a natural rights law of nature was answered by a realistic statement of the observable facts which demonstrated an actual inequality in nature.

In summary, it appears that slavery thought of the Colonial period, both pro-slavery and anti-slavery, had developed into a fairly systematic and organized body of theories. In embryo its features were clear enough to forecast its future lines of growth as the controversy progressed through American history. The foundation for each branch of the pro-slavery theory was laid during this formative period, and in the years to come the many hackneyed arguments were applied over and over again in varied form.

CHAPTER II

THE GROWTH OF PRO-SLAVERY THOUGHT IN THE OLD SOUTH

THE PERIOD OF QUIESCENCE

PRO-SLAVERY theory throughout the period 1790-1820 may be characterized generally as being in a state of quiescence. During these three decades the prevailing opinion throughout the South was in support of slavery, but its defense normally remained dormant, only occasionally being aroused from a passive condition to become articulate. The apathetic and apologetic attitude of slaveholders in this period was in striking contrast to the aggressive and even belligerent utterances in defense of their institution during later decades.

In the South the weight of public opinion had always been in support of slavery. The weighty opposition that developed in Colonial times to the continuance of the slave trade had not been directed at the overthrow of domestic slavery. The natural rights philosophy of the Revolutionary era contributed to the growth of an emancipation sentiment in the South, as it had in the Northern and Middle States, but its influence in the South was confined to a comparatively few speculative thinkers and was not diffused widely among the slaveowners. In order to support the view that the prevailing sentiment during the early decades of the Republic continued to be in justification of slavery, we need only peruse the records of the occasions when the institution was subjected to attack, either locally or in the national councils. Although the number of systematic pro-slavery treatises that appeared were few, on each of these occasions the pro-slavery impulse was evident. Whether the specific defense made by the slaveholding interest was apathetic or militant depended largely upon the general policy of expediency and to a degree upon the exigencies of the particular occasion that called forth the defense. Slavery had defenders whenever defenders were needed; the exact nature of the defense was determined to a great extent by the degree to which and by the way in which the welfare of slavery was endangered.

The slavery issue took on a national significance in the Constitutional Convention. Although the general question of domestic slavery was not debated openly, the debates on the slave trade had a definite bearing on that issue. The strategic policy of the slaveholding delegates in the Convention was to demand, as a *sine qua non* of entering into the compact, that control over slavery be permanently reserved to the States, and guarantees be included that its future welfare would not be imperiled by the powers delegated to Congress. In order to maintain security it was necessary that the slave States retain control of the slave trade for a period of years, as a sort of safety valve that might be opened when the institution needed new life and closed when the evils incident to excessive importations threatened. Such evils were freely admitted and reprobated. As a matter of strategy the slaveholders were apologetic in attitude, and the debates evidence the entailment excuse, the plea of economic and social necessity, and even hold out the hope that, if left alone, the slave States would in due time do away with slavery. Nevertheless, not all of the delegates in the Convention and by no means all of those in the ratifying conventions deprecated slavery. There were statements in the conventions vindicating slavery as an institution of positive merit.

In the Congress under the Constitution there were only a few occasions before 1820 when slavery was openly debated. Hardly had the new Congress assembled in its first session when the Quakers and allied anti-slavery groups began the bombardment of petitions that never entirely abated until abolition was finally accomplished by constitutional amendment. It was in response to these petitions calling for some form of Congressional action on the subject that the first debates occurred during the decade of the nineties. The defensive position then taken by Southern Congressmen, and consistently maintained by them thereafter, was that slavery was not a subject for Congressional deliberation. Since Congress had no power to legislate in the matter, it was an unconstitutional proceeding even to consider petitions calling for action. They insisted that assumption of jurisdiction by Congress over any detail of the slave problem would be an entering wedge to pry open the security of the entire system.

The under surface readiness of the South to defend slavery at this time may be found in the statements of Southern Congressmen. They warned that the slaveholders were so apprehensive for the welfare of their institution that a suggestion amongst them of its insecurity would result in danger to the Union. Baldwin of Georgia, himself a framer, recalled the pain and difficulty the subject had caused in the Convention:

The members from the Southern States were so tender upon this point, that they had well-nigh broken up without coming to any determination; however, from the extreme desire of preserving the Union, and obtaining an efficient Government, they were induced mutually to concede; and the Constitution jealously guarded what they agreed to.[1]

Jackson of Georgia explained the effect that Congressional action would have upon the Southern mind:

I apprehend, if through the interference of the General Government the slave trade were abolished, it would evince to the people

[1] *Annals of Congress*, 1st Cong., 2nd Sess., p. 1242 (Feb. 12, 1790).

a disposition toward a total emancipation, and they would hold their property in jeopardy. Any extraordinary attention of Congress to this petition may have, in some degree, a similar effect. . . . If Congress pay any uncommon degree of attention to their petition, it will furnish just ground of alarm to the Southern States.[2]

In the same debate Tucker of South Carolina inquired: "Do these men expect a general emancipation of slaves by law? This would never be submitted to by the Southern States without a civil war."[3] And again Jackson, in like vein, questioned the policy of bringing up a problem that would "light up the flame of civil discord; for the people of the Southern States will resist one tyranny as soon as another? . . . they will never suffer themselves to be divested of their property without a struggle."[4] William Smith of South Carolina spoke in defiant tenor:

When we entered into this confederation, we did it from political, not from moral motives, and I do not think my constituents want to learn morals from the petitioners; I do not believe they want improvement in their moral system, if they do, they can get it at home.[5]

At a later time he thought "the gentlemen had gone too far to make use of the word *emancipation*. . . . He feared lest the use of it should spread an alarm through some of the States."[6]

Not always disposed to acquiesce in the hostile attacks on slavery, Southern members occasionally were stirred to deliberate and overt defenses. Such an one was made by Jackson in reply to castigations of anti-slavery advocates:

The gentleman said, he did not stand in need of religion to induce him to reprobate slavery, but if he is guided by that evidence upon

[2] *Ibid.*, p. 1228 (Feb. 11, 1790).   [3] *Ibid.*, p. 1240 (Feb. 12, 1790).
[4] *Ibid.*, p. 1242.   [5] *Ibid.*, p. 1244.
[6] *Ibid.*, 4th Cong., 2nd Sess., p. 1734 (Dec. 29, 1796).

which the Christian system is founded, he will find that religion is not against it, he will see, from Genesis to Revelation, the current setting strong that way.   There never was a Government on the face of the earth, but what permitted slavery.   The purest sons of freedom in the Grecian Republics, the citizens of Athens and Lacedaemon, all held slaves.   On this principle the nations of Europe are associated; it is the basis of the feudal system.[7]

A more elaborate pro-slavery argument was made by William Smith.   After endeavoring to show the impracticability and the folly of the suggested plans for emancipation, he undertook to remove "the force of the observations which have been advanced against the toleration of slavery, by a misguided and misinformed humanity."[8]   To rebut the argument that all men are equal by nature, he quoted from Jefferson's *Notes on Virginia*, "proving that negroes were by nature an inferior race of beings."[9]   To the assertion that public opinion reprobated slavery, he pointed out that none of the emancipation petitions came from the slave States, and that the best informed part of the citizens of the Northern States knew that "slavery was so engrafted into the policy of the Southern States, that it could not be eradicated without tearing up by the roots their happiness, tranquility, and prosperity; that if it were an evil, it was one for which there was no remedy, and, therefore, like wise men, they acquiesced in it."[10]   He did not believe that it brought down reproach upon the slave States:

We found slavery ingrafted in the very policy of the country when we were born, and we are persuaded of the impolicy of

[7] *Ibid.*, 1st Cong., 2nd Sess., p. 1242 (Feb. 12, 1790).

[8] *Ibid.*, p. 1463 (Mch. 17, 1790).

[9] *Ibid.*, pp. 1455-1456.   The *Annals* do not state what passage Smith read from, but it is probable that it was Query 14 where Jefferson discusses the question of the mental capacity of the Negro.   See *Writings*, II, 191-208.   *Cf. supra*, Chap. I, note 74.

[10] *Ibid.*, p. 1458.

removing it; if it be a moral evil, it is like many others which exist in all civilized countries and which the world quietly submits to.[11]

He would not admit that it was a moral evil, for "humanity first gave origin to the transportation of slaves from Africa into America" by order of the benevolent Las Casas.[12]

Turning now to a consideration of the few occasions when the policy of slavery was brought into question in the South locally, it appears that pro-slavery opinion proved dominant over anti-slavery sentiment, and no considerable disrelish of the institution was manifest. In Virginia, St. George Tucker, a teacher of law at William and Mary, greatly influenced by the natural rights thinking of Blackstone and sympathetic with the earlier scheme of Jefferson, prepared a plan of gradual emancipation. He presented this, along with a defending essay, to the Virginia Legislature in 1796. He thought that his endeavor needed no apology to an enlightened legislature, for "the Representatives of a free people, who in a moment of becoming such, have declared that all men are by nature equally free and independent, can not disapprove an attempt to carry so incontestable a moral truth into practical effect."[13] The fate of the proposal was told by a friend who described its reception: "Such is the force of prejudice, that in the house of delegates, characters were found who voted against the letter and its inclosure lying on the table." Although making the purport and object of the bill as public as possible, "I despair of being able to obtain leave to bring it in." The consequence of a motion to take the ayes and nays on the bill's introduction "among men of whom too many regard more the popularity of the moment than the investigation of truth and the permanent interests of their constituents, may easily be forseen."[14]

[11] *Ibid.*, p. 1460.   [12] *Ibid.*
[13] Letter from Tucker to the Speaker of the Senate, Nov. 30, 1796. MS. in a private collection.
[14] G. K. Taylor to Tucker, Dec. 2, 1796. MS. in a private collection.

Such was the strength of pro-slavery opinion in Virginia at the turn of the century that Bishop Asbury pessimistically recorded in his diary:

I am brought to conclude that slavery will exist in Virginia perhaps for ages; there is not a sufficient sense of religion nor of liberty to destroy it; Methodists, Baptists, Presbyterians, in the highest flights of rapturous piety, still maintain and defend it.[15]

In Kentucky, on the eve of the Convention that framed the State's first Constitution, David Rice, a Presbyterian divine, essayed in favor of a system of gradual emancipation.[16] With little debate, nevertheless, the dominant pro-slavery faction rushed through article ix which provided for a permanent slave code.

A hint of the public attitude toward slavery in the lower South is found in a letter written from Georgia in 1796:

Domestic slavery is generally reprobated throughout the Northern States. It is not a prudent subject of discussion in Georgia, whether it be proper or improper. I shall, therefore, waive it, and confine myself to the conduct of numbers who have slaves in their possession and care.[17]

At the turn of the century sparring again took place in Congress on the slavery issue. Thatcher of Massachusetts asserted that Congress had the power to legislate on the subject because slavery was a political evil. He declared that the 700,000 slaves were public enemies, and "a greater evil than the very principle could not exist; it was a cancer of immense magnitude, that would some time destroy the body politic, except a proper legislation should prevent the evil."[18] The answer of Jones of Georgia is indicative of the Southern attitude as to the evil of slavery:

[15] Tipple, *op. cit.*, p. 439, Jan. 9, 1798.

[16] *Slavery Inconsistent with Justice and Good Policy* (Philadelphia, 1792).

[17] Letter signed Monitor in *Columbian Museum and Savannah Advertiser*, March 11, 1796.

[18] *Annals of Congress*, 6th Cong., 1st Sess., p. 232 (Jan. 2, 1800).

The gentleman farther says that 700,000 men are in bondage. I ask him how he would remedy this evil as he calls it? but I do not think it is an evil; would he have these people turned out in the United States to ravage, murder, and commit every species of crimes? I believe it might have been happy for the United States if these people had never been introduced amongst us, but I do believe that they have immensely benefitted by coming amongst us.[19]

Throughout the decade Southern Congressmen, with a polite acquiescence, usually submitted to the charge that slavery was a political evil in contrast to a moral evil. Many of them admitted this charge and offered the traditional excuses for its continuance, that is, entailment and social and economic necessity.[20] But apology is one form of defense, and so long as there was no danger of federal interference or encroachment, it might have been the most expedient form. Occasionally, however, when excoriation became too severe, the veil of apology was thrown aside and the true picture of the Southern mind was revealed. A significant statement to this effect was made by Early of Georgia in the discussion over the bill to prohibit the slave trade in 1806:

The gentleman (Mr. Smilie) has said that in the Southern States, slavery is felt and acknowledged to be a great evil and that therefore we will execute a severe law to prevent an increase of this evil. Permit me to tell the gentleman of a small distinction in this case. A large majority of the people in the Southern States do not consider slavery as a crime. They do not believe it immoral to hold human flesh in bondage. Many deprecate slavery as an evil; as a political evil; but not as a crime. Reflecting men apprehend, at some future day, evils, incalculable evils, from it; but it is a fact that few, very few consider it as a crime.

[19] *Ibid.*, p. 235.
[20] For a good statement of the necessity argument for slavery see the "Petition of Remonstrance of the People of Louisiana to the prohibition of the importation of slaves," *ibid.*, 8th Cong., 2nd Sess., Appendix, p. 1606 (Dec. 31, 1800).

It is best to be candid on this subject. If they considered the holding of men in slavery as a crime, they would necessarily accuse themselves, a thing which human nature revolts at. I will tell the truth. A large majority of the people in the Southern States do not consider slavery as even an evil. Let the gentleman . . . go from neighborhood to neighborhood, and he will find that this is a fact.[21]

Holland of North Carolina in a similar vein admitted that "in the Southern States slavery is generally considered as a political evil, and in that point of view nearly all are disposed to stop the trade for the future" but he insisted that "the people of the South do not generally consider slavery as a moral offence."[22] He deplored the fact that "gentlemen always appear on this subject to blend the question of immorality with that of political expediency."[23] As the Negroes imported are brought from a state of slavery, "there is only a transfer from one master to another: and it is admitted that the condition of the slaves in the Southern States is much superior to that of those in Africa. Who, then, will say that the trade is immoral?"[24]

For a decade after the closing of the foreign slave trade in 1808 the slavery controversy was submerged beneath more absorbing political problems. Not until after the difficulties of the war of 1812 had passed was the question again injected into the deliberations of Congress. In 1818 incidental to the discussion of several bills a number of anti-slavery Senators aired their views. Indicative of the brewing storm that would break with full force two years later in the debates

---

[21] *Ibid.,* 9th Cong., 2nd Sess., p. 238 (Dec. 31, 1806). A few days before he had not been so frank in revealing the Southern attitude when he said, "Yes, sir, though slavery is an evil, regretted by every man in the country, to have among us in any considerable quantity persons of this description, is an evil far greater than slavery." *Ibid.,* p. 174 (Dec. 17, 1806).

[22] *Ibid.,* p. 239 (Dec. 31, 1806).

[23] *Ibid.*   [24] *Ibid.,* p. 240.

over the admission of Missouri, Burrill of Rhode Island, King of New York, and Morril of New Hampshire manifested a very hostile attitude to domestic slavery. Smith of South Carolina undertook to repel their attacks. In a caustic counter attack he charged that the anti-slavery group was motivated by self-interest:

Whilst it was their interest to hold slaves, so long they kept them. Whenever the interest coupled with it ceased, slavery ceased, but not before. . . . And there are no persons more apt to remonstrate against that crying sin, slavery, than such as have just sold off their stock of negroes, and vested the price in bank stock. Slavery, then, becomes very odious.[25]

Referring to the participation by New England merchants when South Carolina reopened the slave trade in 1803, Smith perceived that "whenever interest is concerned, and a little profit is to be made, all this delicacy about slavery is laid aside."[26] And in spite of their hostility to slaveholding, he thought that "they employ their free blacks in all their drudgery, and obtain their labor on better terms than masters do."[27]

It was time, he thought, for the South to awaken and offer its defense, for he was convinced "that a general emancipation is intended . . . if they can find means of effecting it. The abolition societies are avowedly for it, what else can the very name itself indicate? . . . Look at the language of the petitions. If they had applied directly for emancipation, they could not have spoken plainer."[28] The Colonization Society was another step in the grand scheme, for "it is said it will pave the way for a general emancipation."[29] And a perpetual source of misrepresentation, which served to place slavery in an odious light, was "the number of catchpenny

[25] Ibid., 15th Cong., 1st Sess., p. 234 (Mch. 6, 1818).
[26] Ibid.   [27] Ibid.
[28] Ibid., p. 235.   [29] Ibid.

prints and pamphlets that are published by persons who know no more of the condition of the slave than they do of the man in the moon."[30]   These matters were sufficiently annoying, but he singled out the charge that slavery was "contrary to our holy religion" to answer specifically. Presenting the Bible defense of slavery, he emphasized the argument of prophecy and quoted as authority from the New England scholar Newton's *Prophecies* where he says that the Africans are descendants of Canaan, "and are still expiating in bondage the curse upon themselves and their progenitors."[31]

THE CONSERVATIVE REACTION TO RADICAL THEORY

During the period when the pro-slavery argument was quiescent, a definite conservative reaction to the radical principles of the Revolutionary era became observable in Southern thought. The expression of this general tendency assumed several forms, one of which was a denial of the state of nature concept and the compact theory of government. Timothy Ford, a Charleston planter, wrote a series of articles in 1792 on amending the South Carolina Constitution in which he attacked this general theory of society and government: "Now it is manifest that such a state as is called a state of nature never in fact existed since the creation of Adam and Eve. Man was no sooner born, than he was associated under some common tie, which bound the human race together."[32] Ford's statement may stand alone at the time but it points the way to the future when pro-slavery thinkers generally accepted its reasoning. By 1829, in the Virginia

[30] *Ibid.*, p. 236. He mentioned specifically Jesse Torrey, *A Portraiture of Domestic Slavery* (Philadelphia, 1817) and John Kenrick, *Horrors of Slavery* (Cambridge, 1817). Someone had placed this latter pamphlet on the desk of every Senator.

[31] *Ibid.*, p. 238.

[32] *The Constitutionalist, or an inquiry how far it is expedient and proper to alter the Constitution of South Carolina* (Charleston, 1794), p. 4. This was first published in 1792 in the *City Gazette and Advertiser*, by Americanus.

Constitutional Convention, representatives of the slaveholding interest were openly challenging the validity of the compact theory.[33] Synchronous with the attack on the compact and natural rights theory in the South there was an undersurface forming of the organic theory of society, which eventually gained positive expression as an element of the political theory of Calhoun and other systematic expounders of pro-slavery thought.

Another phase of the conservative trend was directed at the principles implicit in the Declaration of Independence. This was expressed either by a denial of their binding force as a part of the fundamental law of the nation, or else by questioning their intrinsic validity. In regard to the former, the slaveholder pointed out that the Constitution was the only organic law. It embodied the theory of federalism which left the reconciliation of liberty and slavery to the locality, or the State.

Examples of the latter are cumulative as a part of the current pro-slavery reasoning of the period. In the slave trade debate in Congress in 1806, Nathaniel Macon of North Carolina asserted that the power to prohibit was purely commercial.[34] Smilie of Pennsylvania insisted that the subject was connected with the higher order principles of the Declaration.[35] Then Clay of Pennsylvania warned:

The Declaration of Independence is to be taken with a great qualification. It declares those men have an inalienable right to life; yet we hang criminals—to liberty, yet we imprison—to the pursuit of happiness, yet we must not infringe upon the rights of

---

[33] See the speeches of A. P. Upshur, *Proceedings and Debates of the Virginia State Convention of 1829-30* (Richmond, 1830), pp. 65-79; B. W. Leigh, *ibid.*, pp. 151-173; Chapman Johnson, *ibid.*, pp. 257-294. For a clearer statement of Upshur's views, written in 1841, see "The True Theory of Government," *Southern Literary Messenger*, XXII (1856), p. 401.

[34] *Annals of Congress*, 9th Cong., 2nd Sess., p. 225 (Dec. 29, 1806).

[35] *Ibid.*, pp. 225-226.

others. If the Declaration of Independence is taken in its fullest extent, it will warrant robbery and murder, for some may think even those crimes necessary to their happiness.[36]

Again, in the Missouri debates in 1820 the anti-slavery group appealed to the principles of the Declaration, and the repudiation of those principles permeated the speeches of the pro-slavery group. As William Pinkney expressed it: "The self-evident truths announced in the Declaration are not truths at all, if taken literally, and the practical conclusions contained in the same passage of that declaration prove that they were never designed to be so received."[37] Tyler of Virginia showed that the equality principle could have no application to individuals in a state of society:

Does not its fallacy meet you in every walk of life? Distinctions will exist. Virtue and vice, wealth and poverty, industry and idleness, constitute so many barriers, which human power cannot break down, and which will ever prevent us from carrying into operation, *in extenso*, this great principle. . . . No, sir, the principle, although lovely and beautiful, cannot obliterate those distinctions in society which society itself engenders and gives birth to.[38]

In the debate over sending a delegate to the Panama Congress in 1826 John Randolph branded the freedom principle of the Declaration as untrue: "a falsehood, and a most pernicious falsehood, even though I find it in the Declaration of Independence, . . . if there is an animal on earth to which it does not apply—that is not born free, it is man—he is born in a state of the most abject want, and a state of perfect helplesssess and ignorance, which is the foundation of the connubial tie."[39] Time after time slaveholders

[36] *Ibid.*, p. 227.

[37] *Ibid.*, 16th Cong. 1st Sess., p. 405 (Feb. 15, 1820).

[38] *Ibid.*, p. 1381 (Feb. 17, 1820).

[39] *Register of Debates in Congress*, 19th Cong., 1st Sess., pp. 125-126 (Mch. 2, 1826).

pointed to phenomena in nature that demonstrated the falsity of the maxim that all men are born equal.

Pro-slavery theorists often explained the Declaration and excused the framers on two grounds: that the abstract principles asserted were not intended to be applied in practice, and that the authors were asserting a principle of national independence and not a maxim of personal equality. A similar maxim in the Virginia bill of rights was appealed to by the anti-slavery group in the Virginia Convention of 1829 and again in the debates on emancipation in the Virginia Legislature, 1831-1832. In both cases the pro-slavery group treated the maxim as a high sounding phrase and a flourish of the pen which had no practical force in a state of society.

A broader phase of the reaction was the protest against systems of abstract political theory. William Smith gave vent to the current attitude of the slaveholder in this regard in an Independence Day oration at Charleston in 1796:

Among the wonders which no human research can fathom, even in these days, with all the miseries of anarchy before our eyes, there [are] still to be found political speculatists, who deriving their ideas of government from abstract theorems, and estimating man more by what he ought to be, than what he is, [wish] to erect an Utopian constitution on a sandy basis.[40]

Jefferson, speculative thinker, admirer of Paine and Condorcet, suggested a plan of emancipation in his *Notes on Virginia*. Because of his abstract theorizing, the force of the conservative attack, at times, was directed against him personally. A South Carolinian writing on the eve of the election of 1800 objected to his availability for the Presidency on this ground:

But there is one objection peculiar to the Southern States, and which it behooves them to consider maturely, before they elevate

[40] *An Oration Delivered July Fourth at Charleston* (Charleston, 1796), p. 10.

him to the chief magistry of the country. Mr. Jefferson is known to be a theorist in politics, as well as in philosophy and morals. He is a *philosophe* in the modern French sense of the word. In that character he entertains opinions unfriendly to property, which forms the efficient labor of a great part of the Southern States:— The evidences of this are numerous . . . in plain English it means that he wishes the 500,000 blacks in America should be emancipated.[41]

And about the same time a similar allusion appeared in another pamphlet:

Of Mr. Jefferson's theoretical and speculative disposition in politics, no other proof is necessary than his own writings. . . . His professed admiration of the writings of Thomas Paine, a testimonial whereof was prefixed to one of his editions of the rights of man, may also be adduced as a proof of this point; for, I believe, that at this period, no man of correct judgment can appropriate the wild theories of this enthusiast, a conformity whereto, or to the theories familiar to them, has plunged the French nation into a series of calamities.[42]

John Taylor of Caroline also wrote of the influence of radical French philosophy upon Jefferson.[43] In later years it became the habit of pro-slavery debaters to excuse the early views of Jefferson. As William Smith explained in 1820:

[41] *Address to the Citizens of South Carolina, by a Federalist* (Charleston, 1800), p. 15. As evidence the author cites Jefferson's Emancipation scheme which he intended to introduce in the Virginia Legislature, his *Notes on Virginia*, the letter to Benjamin Banneker, his close relationship with Condorcet and *Les Amis des Noirs*.

[42] [Charles Pinckney?], *Answer to a Dialogue between a Federalist and a Republican* (Charleston, 1800), p. 15. Note on page 13 refers to Jefferson's letter to Sir J. Sinclair: "He will there find a number of benevolent sentiments, . . . which discovered a deficiency of sound political sagacity, and knowledge of the nature of man, as it has been found to exist in civilized society. He will there see the visions of an amiable theorist, but will search in vain for the sound judgment of the practical statesman."

[43] See *Arator; being a series of agricultural essays, practical and political* (Baltimore, 1817), p. 44.

These observations of Mr. Jefferson could not have been founded on facts. They were wrote to gratify a foreigner, at his own request, when every American was filled with enthusiasm. They are the effusions of the speculative philosophy of his young and ardent mind, and which his riper years have corrected. He wrote these notes near forty years ago; since which his life has been devoted to that sort of practical philosophy which enlarges the sphere of human happiness, . . . and, during the whole time, his principal fortune has been in slaves, . . . It is impossible, when his mind became enlarged by reflection and informed by observation, that he could entertain such sentiments, and hold slaves at the same time.[44]

As the extravagances of French theory, instead of bringing on an Utopian state, were followed by a despotism, a practical illustration was furnished the Southerner of the dangerous results of such speculative systems of thought. While the application of those theories to the blacks of the West Indies brought forth the desolation of Santo Domingo, an object lesson unfolded before the eyes of the slaveholder to bring the danger close home to him. As St. George Tucker expressed it around 1800: "The recent scenes transacted in the French colonies in the West Indies are enough to make one shudder with the apprehension of realizing similar calamities in this country."[45] The proponents of slavery continued to use the example of Santo Domingo as the chief objective argument to show the impossibility of emancipation whenever it was proposed within the South or by outsiders.

Throughout the entire ante-bellum period the political principles of the French Revolution were anathema in the

[44] *Annals of Congress*, 16th Cong., 1st. Sess., p. 269 (Jan. 26, 1820).

[45] *Blackstone's Commentaries*, II, Appendix, p. 73. In writing to Dr. Belknap, June 29, 1795, Tucker had said: "The Calamities which have lately spread like a contagion through the West India Islands afford a solemn warning to us of the dangerous predicament in which we stand." *Massachusetts Historical Society Collections*, XLIII, 405.

mind of Southerners. Rutledge of South Carolina in opposing an anti-slavery petition in Congress in 1800 observed
that "already had too much of this new-fangled French
philosophy of liberty and equality found its way and was too
apparent among these gentlemen."[46] They attempted to establish the intimate relationship of French philosophy with
the theories of the anti-slavery movement. When Rufus
King appealed to certain "original principles" in the Missouri debates, William Pinkney branded them as "sentiments
the most destructive, which, if not borrowed from, are identical with, the worst visions of the political philosophy of
France when all the elements of discord and misrule were let
loose upon that devoted nation. I mean 'the infinite perfectibility of man and his institutions,' and the resolution of
everything into a state of nature."[47] Again, in the Panama
debates John Randolph warned that Southern institutions
would be endangered as a result of relations with the South
American countries where the principles of the French Revolution had been carried out to the extreme.[48] And Hayne
of South Carolina thought that the independence of Haiti
should never be recognized because they have "proclaimed
the principles of 'liberty and equality' and have marched to
victory under the banner of universal emancipation."[49]

As a concomitant of the opposition to abstract theory,
Southern thought assumed an objective character. Observation rather than speculation became the technique of pro-
slavery thinking. The slaveholder became a realist rather
than an idealist in politics. History and experience were his
guides in government; practical utility was the best test of
the merit of an institution. Here is a picture of life as the
slaveholder viewed it:

[46] *Annals of Congress*, 6th Cong., 1st Sess., p. 230 (Jan. 2, 1800).
[47] *Ibid.*, p. 391 (Feb. 15, 1820).
[48] *Debates of Congress*, 19th Cong., 1st Sess., p. 112.
[49] *Ibid.*, p. 165.

This is what may be seen on the theatre of human life; continually chequered with good and evil, happiness and misery. The philanthropist may seek perfection and happiness among the human race; but he will never find it complete. The philosopher may plan new laws, and new systems of government, which practice too often declares but the effervescence of fancy, and unequal to the end proposed. Nature, governed by unerring laws, which command the oak to be stronger than the willow, and the cyprus to be taller than the shrub, has at the same time imposed on mankind certain reflections, which can never be overcome. She has made some to be poor, and others to be rich; some to be happy and others to be miserable; some to be slaves and others to be free.[50]

The reaction against speculative theory made a permanent impress upon the slaveholding mind. Its permanent effect was to mold his philosophy into pragmatism and to make of him a realist.

THE DEVELOPMENT OF THE POSITIVE GOOD THEORY OF SLAVERY
1820-1835

During the decade beginning in 1820 came an awakening in the South. The defense of slavery which had remained, for the most part, in a dormant and inarticulate state since the compromise effected in the Constitutional Convention, was now enunciated in overt form. A number of factors contributed at this time to arouse the slaveholder to the expediency of making an open justification of the institution. Due to the fight over the admission of Missouri into the Union, the Charleston Insurrection of 1820,[51] the enlarged

---

[50] John Drayton, *A View of South Carolina, as Respects Her Natural and Civil Concerns* (Charleston, 1802), p. 148.

[51] Evidence was brought out at the trial of the insurrectionists tending to prove that they had been influenced in their actions by the speeches of Rufus King and abolition propaganda sent into the South. See [James Hamilton], *An Account of the Late Intended Insurrection among the Blacks of the City* (Charleston, 1822), p. 42. In 1841 Ingersoll of Ohio in replying to J. Q. Adams asserted that King's

scope of activity of the Colonization Society, and the increased propaganda of the abolitionist groups, the South, for the first time, felt an imminent danger to the welfare of the slave system. The first stage brought on an oscillation between the "shuts" and the "opens," the former faction contending for a policy of continued reticence and the latter urging the launching of an aggressive defense. The final outcome was a decided swing to the latter policy and with it the selection of the high ground of defense, the "positive good theory."

Evidence of the early vacillation of Southern leaders was noted by the keen observer, John Quincy Adams. In a conversation with John C. Calhoun in 1820 over the Southern attitude toward slavery, Calhoun admitted that he considered it "the best guarantee to equality among the whites," and that "it produced an unvarying level among them." Adams concluded:

The discussion of this Missouri question has betrayed the secret of their souls. In the abstract they admit that slavery is an evil, they disclaim all participation in the introduction of it. . . . But when probed to the quick upon it, they show at the bottom of their souls pride and vain glory in their condition of masterdom.[52]

The Missouri debates were epochal in the history of the slavery controversy. An analysis shows that they were significant on the development of the pro-slavery argument, because Southern members became unusually aroused due to two causes. These causes grew out of two phases of the debates. The first was the constitutional phase which involved arguments of a technical and legalistic nature. Here the anti-slavery speeches carried the implication that Congress possessed powers that could be exercised to emancipate the slave.

---

speech had inspired the revolt. *Congressional Globe*, 27th Cong., 1st Sess., Appendix, p. 70.

[52] *Memoirs of John Quincy Adams, comprising portions of his diary from 1795 to 1848* (Charles Francis Adams, ed.), V, 10.

The effect was to disturb the traditional complacency of the slaveholders, which rested on the Constitutional Compromise. Holmes of Massachusetts stated in the House that the restrictionists claimed six sources of power: laying and collecting taxes, regulation of commerce, prohibiting migration and importation of persons, admitting new States, governing territories, and making treaties.[53]   A seventh source claimed, the subject of extended discussion, was the guaranty to every State of a republican form of government.   Many of the anti-slavery speakers expressly disclaimed that the power extended to the original slave States, but the disturbing implication logically made by Southerners was that, if the power existed at all, its exercise in the old States became a matter of policy for Congress to decide.   The pro-slavery position was that the compromise in the Convention impliedly limited every delegated power of the Federal government so that it could not be construed to extend to the subject of slavery.

The second phase of the debates was philosophical and moralistic in character, bringing into question the lawfulness of a system of human bondage.   This phase was for the most part submerged but broke out in full fury at times.   The attack on the legality of slavery took on some three forms: that it was contrary to the law of nature, that it was incompatible with the Declaration of Independence, and that it was contrary to the genius of a republican government.   Probably the full force of this attack came with the speech in the Senate of Rufus King of New York.   He appealed to the higher law of nature to deny emphatically that "one man can make a slave of another."[54]   The explosion set off by King is re-

[53] *Annals of Congress,* 16th Cong., 1st Sess., p. 970.

[54] There was no reporter present to take down the speech. The *Annals* merely record that King addressed the Senate for two hours on Feb. 11th. *Annals of Congress,* 16th Cong., 1st Sess., p. 372. King later stated that he had not preserved on paper what he had said. King to J. Mason, May 4, 1820. *The Life and Correspondence of Rufus King* (C. R. King, ed.), VI, 336. See also *The*

corded in a letter from Senator Walker of Alabama written a few hours after the speech was delivered.

Missouri engulfs everything. Nothing of importance will be done till that question is decided, and when that will be no one can tell. [The prospect has been good for a compromise]. But since the arrival of Mr. King of New York these *humanity men* have changed their minds, and their consciences are awakened and forbid them to tolerate such a damning sin. . . . He has raised this tempest, which threatens the peace and existence of this Union, merely to ride on it into power. This same Mr. King made a speech today, . . . with a bold avowal of doctrines which astonished me. He unhinges the Union at a dash. He has emancipated the whole of our slaves by one potent *ipse dixit*. By the Declaration of Independence all men are created equal! The law of nature—that is the law of God—that is the Christian dispensation—forbids slavery. The law of God is supreme to the law of man. Therefore no human law, compact, or compromise can establish or continue slavery. They are all null and void, being contrary to the law of God. No man can rightfully enslave his fellows. Society is a collection of men. What the constituent

---

National Intelligencer, Feb. 15, 1820, referring to the indisposition of their reporter. But see letter of King to C. Gore, Feb. 17, 1820, in which he summarizes the line of thought in his speech: "I referred the decision of the Restriction on Missouri to the broad principles of the law of nature, a law established by the Creator, which has existed from the beginning, extends over the whole globe, is everywhere, and at all times, binding upon mankind: a law which applies to nations, because their members are still men; a law which is the foundation of all constitutional, conventional and civil laws, none of which are valid if contrary to the law of nature; that according to this law all men are born free, . . . Hence that man could not enslave man; and that states could not make them slaves, since they could not possess any authority except that which naturally belongs to man." *Op. cit.*, VI, 276-277. Senator Smith of South Carolina in replying to King on Feb. 14th quoted him as follows: "Mr. President, I have yet to learn that one man can make a slave of another. If one man cannot do so, no number of individuals can have any better right to do it. And I hold that all laws or compacts imposing any such a condition upon any human being, are absolutely void, because contrary to the law of nature, which is the law of God, by which he makes his ways known to man, and is paramount to all human control." *Annals of Congress*, 16th Cong., 1st Sess., pp. 380-381. King's biographer accepts this statement as authentic. *Op. cit.*, VI, 276.

cannot do the society cannot do. Therefore slavery cannot exist —consequently there is no such thing as a slave. These are his principles and his arguments. So follows that all our Southern Constitutions are of the devil's own making—which indeed that enthusiastic simpleton, Jonathan Roberts,[55] had told us before. I do not exaggerate the doctrines of Mr. King. I heard them distinctly. His impudence astonishes me. Every man may draw the inferences for himself. [King's speech will not be printed.] The stenographer did not take it; and . . . King will not dare to publish it *as it was delivered.*[56]

The great preponderance of the slaveholder's argument revolved around constitutional questions. Their principal task was to deny the existence in Congress of any power to legislate on the subject of slavery. From time to time, however, a positive defense cropped out in their speeches. This defense took on several forms and it is doubtful that any of the traditional arguments were omitted from the debate.

[55] Roberts was a Senator from Pennsylvania. He became enthusiastic in the anti-slavery cause at an early time, introducing many abolition petitions. Jan. 17, 1820, he addressed the Senate, asserting that slavery was outlawed by the Declaration of Independence and the Ordinance of 1787. *Annals of Congress*, 16th Cong., 1st Sess., p. 119. In his second address, Feb. 1st, he contended that slavery was contrary to the genius of a republican government. *Ibid.*, p. 335 ff.

[56] John W. Walker to Charles Tait, Feb. 11th, 1820, MS. in the Alabama Department of Archives. John Quincy Adams, who also heard King's speech, recorded its effect upon Southern Congressmen: "He laid down the position of the natural liberty of man, and its incompatibility with slavery in any shape. . . . He spoke, however, with great power, and the great slaveholders in the House gnawed their lips and clenched their fists as they heard him." *Memoirs*, IV, 522. Adams later attended a party at Calhoun's and "heard of nothing but the Missouri question and Mr. King's speeches. The slaveholders cannot hear of them without being seized with cramps." *Ibid.*, p. 524. Thomas Hart Benton a few years later in the Panama debates referred to King as an agitator, "who proclaimed to our faces, that slavery did not exist! could not exist! was condemned by God and man! by our own Declaration of Independence! by the nature of our government! and that the Supreme Court would so declare it!" *Debates in Congress*, 19th Cong., 1st Sess., pp. 330-331. King's speech made a lasting impression on Southerners. R. M. T. Hunter referred to it in the Senate in 1850 as "the declaration of that war upon slavery, which, with some intermissions, has been waged ever since by the North against the South." *The Congressional Globe*, 31st Cong., 1st Sess., Appendix, pp. 375-376.

One group of Southerners defended the system by presenting a portraiture of slave society in which they extolled its
virtues and pointed out the benefits to all parties concerned.
They entered into a contrast and a comparison of conditions
in slave and free society. This group was temperate and
moderate in its advocacy of slavery, and in one sense, merely
carried forward the apologetic tendency of the period of
quiescence.

Another feature of the pro-slavery argument appearing
many times in the debates was the spread theory, that is, that
it was necessary to extend and spread the institution into new
territory so as to lighten its burden on the old slave communities. In order to understand the full significance of
this theory, as a pro-slavery argument, it is pertinent to hold
in mind a factor that was almost constant in the history of
pro-slavery thought. To the Southern mind, the institution
of domestic slavery afforded the best relationship under which
a superior and an inferior race could live together provided
that a proper ratio of those races was maintained. Intolerable
evils would result to society if the proportion of the races
became unbalanced. The slave trade theory of the Colonial
period was predicated upon this idea. It appeared again in
the compromise of the Constitutional Convention on the importation provision. The spread theory was the natural expression of the same idea at a time when the peculiar danger
to the welfare of slave society was the closing of the safety
valve through which the excess Negro population would flow
to the western territories. It appears, therefore, that the
spread argument, instead of being evidence of a deprecation
of slavery, was a way of defending it.[57]

[57] The spread theory continued for a long time as a part of the philosophy of
the slaveholder. It played a significant rôle in the debates on emancipation in the
Virginia Legislature, 1831-1832. See *infra*, p. 81. It was incorporated in the
report on slavery adopted by the Tennessee Convention of 1834. "The Convention
are persuaded, that while slavery exists in the U. S., it is expedient, both for the

Finally, there were those who justified slavery as a thing good in itself, in a militant and aggressive manner without apologetic tenor. The speech of William Smith in the Senate, January 26th, was the most militant on the pro-slavery side of the question.[58] Ruggles of Ohio said that Smith had "justified slavery on the broadest principles, without qualification or reserve. This was taking entirely new ground; it was going farther than he had ever heard any gentleman go before. Heretofore, in discussions upon this subject, slavery had not been considered as a matter of right, but as an evil, as a misfortune entailed upon the country, for which no complete remedy could be suggested."[59] Roberts of Pennsylvania was impressed that Smith "pronounces it right, views it as a benefit and looks for its perpetuity."[60]

Following the Missouri debates, a number of pamphlets issued from the lower South. These manifested the awakened spirit in defense of slavery. The North was warned that the rights of the slave States must not be trampled upon and informed that the abolition sentiment developing in the North had become very distasteful. One writer relied upon

---

benefit of the slave and the free man, that the slaves should be distributed over as large territory as possible; as thereby the slave receives better treatment, and the free man is rendered more secure." *Journal of the Convention of the State of Tennessee convened for the purpose of revising and amending the constitution thereof, held at Nashville* (Nashville, 1834), p. 90. As late as 1849 the theory was given lip-service in Mississippi. "But laws to confine slavery to narrow limits, hemming it in, and surrounding the slave States with a cordon of assailing States on all sides, seeking their destruction, by preventing its extension into the territories tend to render it always unsafe and forever impossible to emancipate slaves in slave States. Such extension does not add to the number of slaves, it only spreads the same number over a greater surface, dispersing them among a greater number of free white inhabitants, lessening the danger of emancipation from proximity of numbers." *Proceedings of a Meeting of Citizens of Central Mississippi, in Relation to the Slavery Question: Also the proceedings of the State convention, on the same subject* (Jackson, 1850), p. 14, "The address of the Convention to the Southern States."

[58] *Annals of Congress*, 16th Cong., 1st Sess., pp. 259-275.

[59] *Ibid.*, p. 279.   [60] *Ibid.*, p. 338.

the historical argument and the climate argument in making a defense,[61] while another pamphlet brought out an elaborate scriptural argument that slavery was not unchristian.[62] Probably the most significant pro-slavery statement of the early twenties was that of Dr. Richard Furman made in an exposition of the views of the Baptists on the subject. He entered into an elaborate justification, declaring that the South should take a stand on moral grounds and not on the plea of necessity. He thought that liberty consisted not in the name but in the reality. "While men remain in the chain of ignorance and error, or under the dominion of tyrant lusts and passions they cannot be free."[63] This pamphlet found its way into the North and caused some speculation as to whether the views expressed were generally concurred in or not. One writer commented through the *Boston Recorder:*

But whatever were the motives of our Baptist brethren and whether tney came forward called or uncalled, to the vindication of slavery and the slave trade, they have placed themselves on the popular side of the question. . . . Should any individual consider the principles contained in the Exposition unscriptural, and inconclusive, still it would be difficult for him, if not impractical, to print and circulate his opposite sentiments at the South, and by some it would be regarded as bringing into hazard the safety of the community.[64]

One of the most vigorous writers who endeavored to arouse the South from her lethargy in defending her insti-

[61] [E. C. Holland], *A Refutation of the Calumnies Circulated against the Southern and Western States Respecting the Institution and Existence of Slavery among Them* (Charleston, 1822).

[62] [Frederick Dalcho], *Practical Considerations Founded on the Scriptures Relative to the Slave Population of South Carolina* (Charleston, 1823).

[63] *Exposition of the Views of the Baptists Relative to the Colored Population of the U. S. in a Communication to the Governor of South Carolina.* (Charleston, 1823), p. 14.

[64] [Samuel Melanthon Worcester], *Essays on Slavery, republished from the "Boston Recorder and Telegraph" for 1825, by Virgornius and Others* (Amherst, 1826), p. 40.

tution was Whitemarsh B. Seabrook. In a pamphlet published in 1825 he reviewed the numerous attacks upon slavery and challenged Southerners to resent the false and revolting colors in which outsiders were painting the institution.[65] Edward Brown in a more lengthy book published shortly afterward said that the South was highly indebted to Seabrook for "exposing the secret machinations and open hostilities displayed toward these States." This latter writer himself expressed strong pro-slavery views, and evidenced the advanced position that was being taken at that time:

Slavery has ever been the stepping ladder by which countries have passed from barbarism to civilization. History, both ancient and modern, fully confirms this position. It appears, indeed, to be the only state capable of bringing the love of independence and of ease, inherent in man, to the discipline and shelter necessary to his physical wants. . . .[66]

Hence the division of mankind into grades, and the mutual dependence and relations which result from them, constitutes the very soul of civilization; and the more numerous these grades are, in a country, the more highly civilized may we expect to find it.[67]

A year later the eminent Dr. Thomas Cooper of South Carolina College published his first pro-slavery pamphlet. He argued that the Bible nowhere forbade slavery and that it had existed in some form universally throughout the history of civilization. Furthermore, he asserted that the condition of the Southern slave compared very favorably with that of the poor of other countries.[68]

[65] *A Concise View of the Critical Situation, and Future Prospects of the Slave-Holding States, in Relation to Their Colored Population* (Charleston, 1825).
[66] *Notes on the Origin and Necessity of Slavery* (Charleston, 1826), p. 6.
[67] *Ibid.*, p. 38.
[68] See for an analysis of Cooper's views, Dumas Malone, *The Public Life of Thomas Cooper, 1783-1839* (New Haven, 1926), pp. 288-289. In note 19, p. 288, the author comments on Professor W. E. Dodd's, *The Cotton Kingdom*, p. 149, which describes T. R. Dew's *Review of the Debates in the Virginia Legis-*

As a part of the pro-slavery thought of the twenties came a reaction in attitude to the Colonization Society. This Society had grown out of the Jeffersonian school of philanthropists and, consequently, was never enthusiastically accepted by a preponderance of slaveholders. The scheme was acquiesced in by some who desired to get rid of the free Negro and the surplus slave population which were generally recognized evils of the slave system. When the colonization movement went beyond this initial purpose, however, and proposed the emancipation and ultimate overthrow of the slavery system, it ran directly counter to the ideas of those who desired the perpetuation of the institution. The group in the South who actually desired to destroy slavery through the medium of the Society was at all times inconsiderable outside of the border States.

Whether or not the Society had in fact intentionally entered upon a program that looked toward emancipation, it, along with the other movements of the twenties, was so credited. Seabrook bitterly castigated the activities of the Colonization Society, charging that it had instigated the King and Tucker resolutions in Congress, which would have provided funds from the federal government to aid in an extended program of colonization.[69] Another expression of

lature of 1831 and 1832 as "the ablest of all the works treating slavery from historical and social points of view." Malone points out that Cooper's *Essay on the Constitution of the United States and the Questions that Have Arisen under It* was published six years earlier in 1826 and further states that Dew knew of Cooper's defense of slavery and "may have been emboldened by it." He suggests a similar influence of Cooper upon Harper and Hammond. So far as the writer has been able to see there is nothing in Cooper's essay that had not been declared many times before. The arguments were not original, but can be duplicated in many other pamphlets at that time and earlier.

[69] *Op. cit.*, p. 3. In a series of articles published in the *Richmond Enquirer* from October, 1825, to August 8, 1826, Gracchus definitely charged that the Society was connected with the Missouri restrictionists as well as the Tucker-King resolutions. These articles were published later as *A Controversy between Caius Gracchus and Opimius, in reference to the American Society for the Colonization of Free People of Color of the U. S.* (Georgetown, 1827). See p. 12.

antipathy to the Society came from Virginia under the signature of Caius Gracchus. The writer, contending that the Society had departed from its original purpose, the colonization of free blacks, pleaded that Southern men divest themselves of every feeling of fanaticism on slavery and regard colonization as a practical political problem fraught with grave difficulties.

Yet in relation to the emancipation part of your scheme, the great difficulty still exists. How are you to invert the order of human nature, and to render that ruling passion, self-interest, and the love of wealth so wholly inoperative as to secure the voluntary surrender of $300,000,000? . . . but even this obstacle, as formidable as it certainly is, offers not a hundredth part of the difficulties you will have to encounter in your attempt to revolutionize the whole character and habits of the people of the South. . . . Even our bodies, as well as our minds have been moulded under the influence of the principle of labor among us; and that which was first a habit has become constitutional . . . there is a peculiarity in the love which most masters entertain for their slaves, that does not apply to any other species of property. . . . To all these conditions may be super-added the peculiar caste of character in the South, which the ownership of slaves has certainly had a great tendency to produce. Proud, high spirited and independent, the love of freedom and jealousy of invasion of their rights, either individually or politically, have ever, I think, been characteristic of the Virginian and the South. With such a population, with such habits, feelings, and interests, what miracle itself could work the desired change? None, I am sure which obtains in the management of human affairs.[70]

Many other examples might be cited to illustrate the antagonistic attitude to the Colonization Society that was becoming current in the South. C. C. Pinckney, once a strong supporter, characterized the movement as cruel and absurd.[71]

[70] *Op. cit.*, p. 16.
[71] See E. L. Fox, *The American Colonization Society, 1817-1840* (Baltimore, 1919), p. 85.

In 1827 Brutus denounced it in his pamphlet on the usurpations of the federal government: "An insidious attack on the tranquillity of the South, as the nest egg placed in Congress by Northern Abolitionists, that therefrom might be hatched and raised for the South anxiety, inquietude and troubles to which there could be no end."[72]   *The Charleston Mercury* stigmatized it as "a society reprobated at the South, and justly regarded as murderous in its principles, and as tending inevitably to the destruction of the public peace."[73]

Returning now to the positive statement of pro-slavery thought, C. C. Pinckney declared before the South Carolina Agricultural Society in 1829: "That slavery, as it exists here, is a greater or more unusual evil than befalls the poor in general, we are not prepared to admit."[74]   He saw no necessity for its extermination.   Probably the most definite and clear statement that slavery was a benefit, and not an evil to be eradicated, was made by Governor Stephen D. Miller in his message to the legislature of South Carolina in 1829.   It is significant not only because of its official nature, but, moreover, because it stands at the end of the decade as the culmination of the movement for an open and aggressive defense.

Slavery is not a national evil; on the contrary, it is a national benefit.   The agricultural wealth of the country is found in those states owning slaves, and a great portion of the revenue of the government is derived from the products of slave labor—Slavery exists in some form everywhere, and it is not of much consequence in a philosophical point of view, whether it be voluntary or involuntary.   In a political point of view, involuntary slavery has the advantage, since all who enjoy political liberty are then in fact free.

[72] Quoted in R. A. Gurley, *Remarks on the South Carolina Opinions of the American Colonization Society from the African Repository of 1830* (n. p., 1830), p. 16.

[73] *Ibid.*, quoting *The Mercury*, April 24th, 1829.

[74] *Address before the South Carolina Agricultural Society, August 18, 1829* (Charleston, 1829).

Wealth gives no influence at the polls; it does where white men perform the menial services which slaves do here. *Upon this subject it does not become us to speak in a whisper, betray fear, or feign philanthropy.*[75]

Additional examples could be given, but these are sufficient virtually to establish the fact that the "positive good theory" was an outgrowth of the twenties. Its statement antedated the Garrisonian movement, instead of coming, as historians have commonly concluded, as the answer to abolition propaganda. One may question the weight of opinion in the South that had reached the advanced position at this early date, but the entertainment and statement of the theory by a large group of slaveholders is evident.

By 1833 the two leading Charleston papers were contending that the South was ready to justify slavery as a social benefit. The *Courier* took the following stand:

We must be permitted to say to the Boston editor, that he is utterly mistaken in supposing that the people of the South regard domestic slavery, as it exists among them, in the light of a curse; on the contrary they hold it to be absolutely necessary to the proper cultivation of the soil, and to be the great source of their prosperity, wealth and happiness; without it their fertile fields would become a wilderness and a desert—their real curse being not slavery but a climate. . . . Nor do the people of the South deem slavery "a curse" to the Negroes themselves—it exists with us in a mild and parental form.[76]

The editor of the *Mercury* replied to an editorial of the *Philadelphia Inquirer*, asserting that he was expressing the sentiment of nineteen-twentieths of the people of the Southern States:

We were fully aware of the admissions of Southern writers and speakers on this subject, and we did not forget the doings of the

[75] Printed in *Charleston Courier*, November 28, 1829. Italics in the original copy.

[76] *Ibid.*, July 25, 1833.

Virginia Convention; but allowing for the operation of northern influence on the frontier States of the South, and for the influence which Virginia has always exercised over N. C., we confidently assert that even including these two States, "the great mass of the South" now sanction no such admission, as that Southern slavery is an evil to be deprecated. We wish the Southern press would speak out on the subject, and not only enlighten the *Inquirer*, and those who labor under the same mistake, but also defeat the efforts of others, who have wilfully promoted the deception, by misrepresenting the public of the South.[77]

Two years later Governor McDuffie of South Carolina delivered his famous message in which he contended that slavery was a blessing to both white and black races. Instead of being a political evil, it was "the cornerstone of our republican edifice."[78] These statements indicate that the lead in the aggressive movement to defend slavery came from the lower South. The enunciation of the "positive good theory" was first made locally within the slave States rather than in Congress by the representatives of those States.

Following the Missouri debates, Southern Congressmen lapsed back into a shut policy, resuming the position that the slavery discussion was improper. They had become, however, since the shock of the Missouri assault, much more sensitive to the slightest implication of hostility to their interest. Imbued with such a feeling, Garnett of Virginia arose in the House of Representatives in 1824 to warn Southerners of the danger to slavery from a loose construction of the constitutional powers of Congress:

Sir, we must look very little to consequences if we do not perceive in the spirit of this construction, combined with the political fanaticism of the period, reason to anticipate, at no distant day, the

[77] "Remarks," *The Charleston Mercury*, Nov. 13, 1833.
[78] Reprinted as "Message on the Slavery Question," (1835), in A. B. Hart (ed.), *American History Leaflets*, No. 10.

usurpation, on the part of Congress, of the right to legislate on a subject which, if you once touch, will inevitably throw this country into revolution.[79]

The very touchy feelings of Southerners on this subject were again evidenced when they objected to sending delegates to the Panama Congress because it would tacitly sanction the principles of emancipation carried out by some of the Hispanic American countries.

Not until 1829, however, did a slaveholder in Congress take a very positive stand in justification of slavery. At that time Weems of Maryland called "the attention of the nation, through the House, to that view of slavery, which, as a slaveholder, I have received for myself, and am ready to defend, whenever assailed by reasons only half as well supported by proofs such as I shall now offer."[80] He chided slaveholders for their apologetic attitude and insisted that the institution should be defended abstractly as well as on the grounds of policy.[81]

It was in the debates over the reception of the abolition petitions that Southern Congressmen finally swung over to the open defense policy. At that time they enunciated the positive benefit argument and thereby reflected the advanced position already generally held at the South. James Henry Hammond energetically asserted his belief in the social benefit theory in 1838:

But it is no evil. On the contrary, I believe it to be the greatest of all the great blessings which a kind Providence has bestowed upon our glorious region. For without it, our fertile soil and our fructifying climate would have been given to us in vain. And as to its impoverishing and demoralizing influence, . . . the history of the short period during which we have enjoyed it has rendered

[79] *Annals of Congress,* 18th Cong., 1st Sess., p. 2097 (April 2, 1824).
[80] *Debates in Congress,* 20th Cong., 2nd Sess., p. 183 (January 7, 1829).
[81] *Ibid.*

our southern country proverbial for its wealth, its genius, and its manners.[82]

Almost simultaneously with Hammond's assertion, John C. Calhoun in the Senate was advancing his theory that slavery was a high trust for the slave States to preserve for posterity.[83] In his speeches during the next few years Calhoun did much to elaborate and clarify the "positive good theory." The following year he expressed himself in no uncertain terms:

But let me not be understood as admitting, even by implication, that the existing relations between the races in the slaveholding States is an evil:—far otherwise; I hold it to be a good, as it has thus far proved itself to be to both, and will continue to prove so if not disturbed by the fell spirit of abolition.[84]

The element of good in the system was portrayed more clearly in a later speech:

We now believe it has been a great blessing to both of the races—the European and African, which, by a mysterious Providence, have been brought together in the Southern section of this Union. The one has greatly improved, and the other has not deteriorated; while, in a political point of view, it has been the great stay of the

[82] *Ibid.*, 24th Cong., 1st Sess., p. 2456 (Feb. 1, 1836). This speech was printed in *Selections from the Letters and Speeches of the Hon. James H. Hammond of South Carolina* (New York, 1866), p. 34. See also E. Merritt, "James Henry Hammond, 1807-1864," *Johns Hopkins University Studies*, XLI (1923), 36 note 18 where she states: "It would perhaps be rash to assert that this is the very earliest defense of slavery, not as something to be endured because it was present, but as a genuine good; . . . it may well be the first statement to that end by a man of any prominence."

[83] Speech on the reception of abolition petitions, March 9, 1836. *Ibid.*, p. 766. "It has entered into and modified all our institutions, civil and political. None other can be substituted. We will not, cannot, permit it to be destroyed. If we were base enough to do so, we would be traitors to our section, to ourselves, our families, and to posterity. It is our anxious desire to protect and preserve this relation . . ." *Ibid.*, p. 777.

[84] Speech printed in full in *The Works of John C. Calhoun* (Crallé, ed.), II, 630, and a sketchy report in *Debates in Congress*, 24th Cong., 2nd Sess., p. 718 (Feb. 6th, 1837). Calhoun was not leading Southern opinion but was merely reflecting it.

Union and our free institutions, and one of the main sources of the unbounded prosperity of the whole.[85]

Instead of being recognized as a political evil, slavery was considered to be an element of social welfare, a feature of good government that should be nourished and passed on to posterity. It was "the most safe and stable basis for free institutions in the world."[86] The true position of the South was now definitely stated to the nation; pro-slavery leaders in Congress had taken the high ground of defense.

THE EMANCIPATION DEBATE IN VIRGINIA

It now becomes pertinent to view the situation in Virginia. Pro-slavery thought in the lower South was unquestionably far in advance of pro-slavery opinion in that State, where conditions were different. The institution of slavery was going to seed in Virginia, and she was faced with the double problem of lands speedily becoming exhausted and of a black population rapidly growing out of proportion to the white. Furthermore, the future outlet of her surplus blacks was threatened when several States of the far South contemplated closing the domestic slave trade.[87] Moreover, the

[85] *Congressional Globe*, 25th Cong., 3rd Sess., p. 177 (Feb. 18, 1839). ("Have" changed from "has" by the author).

[86] Speech of Calhoun, Jan. 10, 1838, *ibid.*, 25th Cong., 2nd Sess., Appendix, p. 62. Calhoun had had this idea for a long time, as he explained to J. Q. Adams in 1820, *supra*, p. 66. As a matter of fact it was a traditional part of the philosophy of the slaveholder and not at all original with Calhoun.

[87] The Constitution of Mississippi provided for such a power and the legislature had recently passed such a law. See *infra*, chapter IV, note 38. See also the speeches of Roane of Hanover in the House of Delegates of Virginia, Jan. 16, 1832, *Richmond Enquirer*, Feb. 4, 1832, and Moore, Jan. 16, 1832, *ibid.*, Jan. 19, 1832. The latter thought that in the future the western lands would be closed to the blacks, cited the case of the recent law passed in Louisiana providing a severe punishment for the importation of blacks. He said that Georgia, Alabama, and other states were about to pass similar laws.

The writer is indebted to the late Professor U. B. Phillips of Yale University for the loan of his photostat copies of the Virginia debates, from the files of the *Richmond Enquirer*. In the following discussion of the debates many of the speakers will be mentioned only by their surnames, the initials not being reported

free black population had become an economic and social problem. Consequently, to many Virginians, the evils of slavery were beginning to outweigh the benefits; and, instead of coming forward to defend slavery as a good, they remained reticent and sought some ameliorating scheme, not that they would have abolished the institution, but that they would have eradicated the evil and dangerous elements attendant.

The period up to 1830 was marked by a conflict between the "opens" and the "shuts," the faction that desired openly to seek a solution of the problem and the faction that considered all debate on the subject inexpedient. In the Constitutional Convention of 1829, although neither emancipation nor colonization was considered, the basic factor that divided the Convention on the suffrage and the representation features of the new Constitution was the slavery interest. The fight over those two issues showed that the slavocracy was determined to insure protection for the future life of its institution and was not anxious to find a means of eradicating it. Suddenly, at the beginning of the thirties, occurred the Southampton insurrection, and the wave of excitement that overran the state forced the legislature into an open debate on the public policy of continuing or abolishing slavery. It has often been said that the opinions expressed in the great debate of 1830-1831 in the Virginia House of Delegates are proof sufficient that, at this late period, the South looked upon slavery as an evil to be done away with, and that the only question was the solution by which this should be accomplished. It, therefore, becomes apropos to point to a few facts that have generally been overlooked, which tend to throw doubt on such a conclusion.

---

with the speeches. A number of the speeches were later collected and printed in pamphlet form. There is a collection of these in the Virginia State Library, and another in the North Carolina State Library.

In the Virginia debates occurred the unique case within the South when pro-slavery and anti-slavery theory openly clashed over a solution of the slavery question on the grounds of public policy. During the discussion the anti-slavery theories were stated in all their ramifications, this side being the aggressor throughout. Many of them declared the institution of slavery to be an evil.[88] S. D. Moore said, "I think that slavery as it exists among us, may be regarded as the heaviest calamity which has ever befallen any portion of the human race."[89] Another member felt, "that slavery in Virginia is an evil and a transcendent evil, it would be idle . . . for any human being to doubt or deny . . . all would remove it, if they could."[90] Another felt that it was a "grinding curse upon this state."[91] There can be no doubt about the extreme character of these statements of anti-slavery men.

On the other hand, opinion shaded off until the very opposite view was taken. Throughout the entire debate there was manifest a distinct cleavage between the slaveholding section and the non-slaveholding. The western representatives were practically unanimous in opposing slavery as an evil, contending that its natural increase was rapidly threatening to engulf their section.[92] Their attitude was well expressed in this passage:

Sir, tax our lands, vilify our country—carry the sword of extermination through our now defenseless villages; but spare us, I implore you, spare us the curse of slavery—that bitterest drop from the chalice of the destroying angel.[93]

[88] See the speeches of Charles J. Faulkner, Jan. 20, 1832, *Richmond Enquirer*, Jan. 31; G. W. Summers, Jan. 17, *ibid.*, Feb. 14; Moore, Jan. 16, *ibid.*, Jan. 19; J. G. Bryce, *ibid.*, W. H. Brodnax, Jan. 19, *ibid.*, Jan. 24; Henry Berry, Jan. 16, *Speeches in the Virginia Convention* (a collection of pamphlets).

[89] Speech of Moore, Jan. 16, *Richmond Enquirer*, Jan. 19.

[90] Speech of Brodnax, Jan. 19, *ibid.*, Jan. 24.

[91] Speech of Henry Berry, Jan. 16, *Speeches.*

[92] See the speeches of Faulkner, Jan. 20, *Richmond Enquirer*, Jan. 13; Summers, Jan. 17, *ibid.*, Feb. 14; McDowell, Jan. 21, *Speeches*; Henry Berry, Jan. 16, *ibid.*   [93] Faulkner, *ibid.*, p. 10.

The eastern members replied that the slave was the most suitable laborer for the plantation, and that to abolish slavery would be to destroy the whole life of their section. Their defense was based upon necessity and upon the rights of property.[94] J. H. Gholson believed that the eastern section would oppose any scheme of abolition: "Mr. Speaker, what portion of this commonwealth is it that demands this measure at our hands? Not the East, Sir, for they rise up, almost as one man, against it."[95]

Aside from the sectional attack, there was another group who pictured the inherent evils of slavery to the white race, to the slave, and to the state.[96] Thomas Marshall said: "Wherefore, then object to slavery? Because it is ruinous to the whites—retards improvements—roots out an industrious population—banishes the yeomanry of the country—deprives the spinner, the weaver, the smith, the shoemaker, the carpenter, of employment and support."[97] Many denied these arguments outright as being untrue.[98]

A second group based their idea of the evils on the existence of the free Negro element and the surplus slave population.[99] This group, it is believed, represented the true feeling of the people at large. Then finally, there were individuals who went so far as to declare slavery contrary to the principles of the age and to American institutions. Moore asked: "Can we be justified in the eyes of man, or of Heaven,

[94] See speeches of J. T. Brown, Jan. 18, *ibid.*, pp. 12, 13, 14; W. H. Roane, Jan. 16, *Richmond Enquirer*, Feb. 4. He pointed to the compromise of the Constitution of 1829 where property rights were guaranteed to the East. J. H. Gholson, Jan. 18, *ibid.*, Jan. 21; W. D. Sims, Jan. 26, *ibid.*, Jan. 28.

[95] Speech, Jan. 18, *ibid.*, Jan. 21.

[96] Speeches of T. J. Randolph, Jan. 21, *Speeches;* Moore, Jan. 16, *Richmond Enquirer*, Jan. 19; P. A. Bolling, Jan. 25, *Speeches;* W. B. Preston, Jan. 16, *Richmond Enquirer*, Feb. 9, J. G. Bryce, *ibid.*, Jan. 19, Philip Berry, Jan. 16, *Speeches.*

[97] Speech of Thomas Marshall, Jan. 14, *Speeches*, p. 6.

[98] Speeches of J. C. Bruce, Gholson, *Richmond Enquirer*, Jan. 21.

[99] Speech of Roane, Jan. 16, *ibid.*, Feb. 4.

in withholding from our negroes rights which we have solemnly declared to be the common property of the human
race and that too in violation of the sound principles of our
government?"[100]

In the course of the debate, discussion shifted to the
question of what form, if any, the plan of action should take.
Many schemes were proposed, all of which were in the nature
of colonization. There were those that would colonize beyond the Rockies and those that would establish the colony
in Africa; there were those that would colonize through the
medium of the federal government, the State government,
or the Colonization Society, supplemented by funds from the
State or nation. Thomas Marshall proposed that an amendment to the Constitution be passed providing for the appropriation of funds from the sale of western lands for this purpose.[101]

Upon another aspect of the question, there was a sharp
disagreement. Who was to be colonized? One group advocated that the whole Negro population should be sent
away; they were the abolitionists. They subdivided into the
immediatists who would colonize all the slaves, and the gradualists, or the *post-nati* group, who would colonize all Negro
children born after a certain date. The other group desired
to send away only the free Negroes and the surplus Negro
population. W. H. Roane explained the views of the last
mentioned group.

As a member of the committee to whom this whole subject was
referred, I contributed my humble mite towards the formation of
a scheme to be presented to the House for removing, in the first
place, all free blacks from the commonwealth. That done, Sir,
pari passu, if means can be provided . . . I am in favor, to the
extent of those means, of a slow, gradual, certain, and energetic

[100] Speech of Moore, *ibid.,* Jan. 19; Summers, *ibid.,* Jan. 17, Preston, *ibid.*
[101] Speech of Thomas Marshall, Jan. 14, *Speeches,* pp. 10-11.

system for the removal of all emancipated or purchased slaves from the commonwealth, till the ratio of population, beween them and the whites, attains, at least, that equilibrium, which, in all future time, will give to every white man in the state, that certain assurance that this is his country; which every slave holder should feel and ever shall feel, as far as I am concerned, that his slave is his own property.[102]

Many felt that the domestic interstate slave trade would provide a sufficient outlet in order to reduce the black population and to relieve the pressure on the institution.[103] Taking the speeches as a whole, it appears quite evident that the majority of members, if they desired any scheme at all, advocated colonization only to the extent that it would not endanger domestic slavery. Whenever colonization approached abolition, it had few professed advocates.

Just how large the group was who whole-heartedly defended slavery it is difficult to estimate. In at least one case, it was defended "as a good in itself."[104] In another case, the orator speaking on the abstract question declared:

I am not one of those who have ever revolted at the idea or practice of slavery, as many do. It has existed and ever will exist, in all ages, in some form, and some degree. I think slavery as much a correlative of liberty as cold is of heat. History, experience, observation, and reason, have taught me, that the torch of liberty has ever burnt brightest when surrounded by the dark and filthy, yet nutritious [influence] of slavery. Nor do I believe in that

---

[102] Speech of Roane, Jan. 16, *Richmond Enquirer*, Feb. 4. See also speeches of Wm. Wood, Jan. 16, *ibid.*, Feb. 7; Thomas Marshall, Jan. 14, *Speeches*, p. 10; Gholson, Jan. 18, *Richmond Enquirer*, Jan. 21.

[103] Speech of Wood, Jan. 16, *ibid.*, Feb. 7.

[104] See the *Constitutional Whig* (Richmond), Jan 28, 1832, referring to the speech of W. D. Sims. See also speech of Sims, Jan. 26, *Richmond Enquirer*, Jan. 28. "Mr. Sims was so unfortunate as to differ from every gentleman who had spoken on this subject. He gave it as his deliberate opinion that slavery was not an evil in Virginia . . . and that whenever slavery becomes an evil, the owner would no longer continue to own slaves. Whenever that time arrives, the *suprema lex* would regulate the evil without the interposition of the Legislature."

[fanaticism] about the natural equality of man. I do not believe that all men are by nature equal, or that it is in the power of human art to make them so.[105]

These statements are open and definite defenses but the slaveholders as a group did not adopt such strategy. Instead, they refused to view the "obtuse abstractions" and looked upon the question in a practical light.[106] Brown said:

For my part, sir, I am not an advocate of slavery in the abstract, and if the question were upon introducing it, I should be the very last to agree to it; but I am yet to be convinced, that slavery, as it exists in Virginia, is either criminal or immoral.[107]

He appealed to the Scriptures for substantiation. By other members the apologetic argument of entailment was employed. The truth seems to be that the slaveholders were unwilling to give up their institution, and by masterful evasion and selection of position they were able to out-manoeuver the advocates of amelioration; for not only did they defeat plans to emancipate and colonize, but under the plea of property rights and of necessity, without taking a bold positive stand, they prevented any action at all being taken.

The result of the great debate was a practical illustration that there was no hope in the colonization scheme. Shortly following the debate, appeared the essay of Professor Thomas R. Dew of William and Mary College, in which he clearly showed that the only alternatives for the South were abolition, with the Negro remaining as an element

[105] Speech of Roane, Jan. 16, *Richmond Enquirer*, Feb. 4.

[106] Speech of Faulkner, Jan. 20, *Richmond Enquirer*, Jan. 31. He said that no one had arisen the avowed advocate of slavery. . . . "And yet, who could have listened to the very eloquent remarks of the gentleman from Brunswick (Gholson) without being forced to conclude, he at least considered slavery, however not to be defended on principle, yet as being divested of much of its enormity, as you approach it in practice." See also speech of Roane, *ibid.*, Feb. 4, and Wm. Daniel, *ibid.*, Jan. 31.

[107] Speech of J. T. Brown, Jan. 18, *Speeches*, p. 20.

of local society, or a continuance of the system of slavery.[108]
This essay did much to lead opinion in Virginia to the position already arrived at in the lower South. From now on the
South as a whole became united in the active defense of its
institution.[109] After the middle ground of colonization was

[108] Review of the Debate [on the Abolition of Slavery] in the Virginia Legislature of 1831 and 1832 (Richmond, 1832). Republished in The Pro-Slavery
Argument; as maintained by the most distinguished writers of the Southern States
(Charleston, 1852), pp. 287-490, also in DeBow's Review of the Southern and
Western States (New Orleans), X (1851), 658-665; XI (1851), 23-30; XX
(1856), 118-140, 175-189, 271-290, 468-487. It is interesting to note that a
number of recent writers in American political theory erroneously give Dew's first
initial as F. instead of T. I have been unable to trace the origin of this error.
For example, see J. Mark Jacobson, The Development of American Political
Thought, a documentary history (New York, 1932), p. 348, and B. F. Wright,
American Interpretations of Natural Law, a study in the history of political
thought (Cambridge, 1931), p. 236. In Wright's earlier work, A Source Book
of American Political Theory (New York, 1929), p. 462, he correctly gives the
first name as Thomas.

[109] The Tennessee Convention of 1834 adopted the report of its select committee to which a number of memorials on the subject of slavery had been referred. The committee refused to enter into a discussion of slavery because the
plans suggested for its overthrow were impracticable and inexpedient. Journal,
pp. 87-93. The report is interesting because of the admission that slavery was
an evil. "The committee do not understand the Convention as denying the truth
of the proposition which asserts that slavery is an evil. To prove it to be a
great evil is an easy task, but to tell how that evil can be removed, is a question
that the wisest heads and the most benevolent hearts have not been able to answer
in a satisfactory manner." Ibid., p. 88. After this prefatory apology, the report then
goes on to make a practical justification for the continuance of slavery on three
grounds. It was the only relation under which diverse races could live together.
The attempt at emancipation in Santo Domingo had proved to be folly. The
condition of the slaves compared favorably with that of the laboring classes in
free society. Ibid., pp. 88-90. The report made a gesture at pacification of the
memorialists. Gradualism was the hope and the Colonization Society the agency
through which slavery "will be extinguished as certainly and as speedily as the
friends of humanity have any reason to expect." Ibid., p. 93. The Colonization
plan would ultimately succeed because: "The ministers of our holy religion will
knock at the door of the hearts of the owners of the slaves, telling everyone of
them to let his bondmen . . . go free, . . . and the voice of these holy men
will be heard and obeyed." Ibid. A minority of the committee filed a protest
contending that it was the duty of the Convention to find an immediate solution
to the problem. The protest insisted that slavery was subversive of the true
principles of republicanism, violated the natural rights of man, and was contrary to the spirit of the gospel. Ibid., pp. 102-104. The majority replied to the
protest: "It is very obvious that the great end for which a republican govern-

discredited, and the only plan proposed was abolition, then the attack upon the institution lost all its appeal to the Southern people, and was viewed as a sectional encroachment. There remained some few lingering supporters of the idea of colonization within the South, up to the war, but the movement no longer had vital force and steadily lost ground.

THE CULMINATION OF PRO-SLAVERY THOUGHT
1835-1860

The period from 1835 to 1860 marked the culmination of the trends of pro-slavery thought in the finished statement of the pro-slavery argument. Throughout the period pro-slavery theory flourished, full bloom in its expansive character. The South, in a challenging temper, without apology, presented her completed case to the world tribunal, confident that the verdict would be an entire vindication of her course in perpetuating her peculiar institution.

The assertion of the positive good ground of defense made necessary a thorough reëxamination of the virtues of the slave system as a social institution. This brought on the first phase in the preparation of the slaveholder's case: namely, a comprehensive and intensive study of the institution viewed from every possible angle. Calhoun speaking in January, 1838, thought that "this agitation has produced one happy effect at least. It has compelled us to the South to look into the nature and character of this great institution, and to correct many false impressions that even we had entertained in relation to it. Many in the South once believed that it was a moral and political evil; that folly and delusion are gone; we see it now in its true light, and regard

---

ment is instituted, is to promote peace, protect property, and to preserve all the rights and principles of every member of the community. Therefore, whatever has a tendency to the attainment of these ends, is in perfect accordance with the principles of a republican government. *Ibid.*, p. 129.

it as the most safe and stable basis for free institutions in the world."[110]

The preparation of the case was an intricate process and led the slaveholder into many fields of scientific investigation and scholarly inquiry. Materials and evidence with which to construct the case were gathered from varied sources. History, both natural and social, ethnology and allied natural sciences, the political and social sciences, and even Biblical exegesis, as they were exploited by the investigator, played a part in the refinement and polishing of the traditional arguments, and contributed to the building up of the finished case. The slaveholder did his endeavor not only through his own researches, but he drew freely upon outside sources. He was sensitive to and influenced by the schools of thought current in free society.

Presentation of the case naturally followed upon its preparation. No longer need one search for casual expressions of pro-slavery theory made in legislative halls or in an occasional pamphlet. The entire literature of the period is fairly permeated with it. The newspapers and periodicals, both religious and secular, are filled with articles on the many aspects of the general subject. The sermons preached from the pulpit, the lectures delivered in the classroom, and the speeches made from political and literary rostrums revolve about the general theme. It formed the chief topic for the long letters in the interchange of ideas through private correspondence between the slaveholders. Indeed, a survey of the literature of the period produces the impression that the entire product of the collective mind of the South was colored by this one absorbing interest.

Another feature of the presentation of the case was the great increase in the publication of systematic treatises on

[110] *Congressional Globe,* 25th Cong., 2nd Sess., Appendix, pp. 61-62 (Jan. 10, 1838).

slavery. Prior to this time such works had been rare and few in number. Now many books appeared treating the slavery issue, in all its ramifications, critically and exhaustively. The energies of some of the students of slavery reached fruition in the publication of monumental studies on specialized aspects of the subject. Literally a flood of pamphlets appeared. Finally, the presentation of the case took the form of republishing collections of pro-slavery writings that had come to be recognized as classics.

Through the culmination period the critics of slavery may be classified as the immediatists, the gradualists, and the expulsionists.[111] All of these had the common element of aiming at complete abolition of slavery. Immediatism held that it was the slave's natural right to instant freedom without expatriation from the land or without compensation to the owner. This form had its most extreme and consistent support from the Garrisonian abolitionists and a large portion of Southern thought was directed at its refutation.

The second form was gradualism, which shaded into various grades of opinion. They differed with the immediatists, taking the ground that abolition should be accomplished by degrees and steps. Instead of emphasizing the natural right of the slave, they recognized the property right of the master and the practical results of abolition to society. Some of them belonged to the *post-nati* school who would emancipate at birth. Others believed that generations, and in some cases centuries, would be necessary to attain complete emancipation. Whereas immediatism had practically no support within the South, gradualism, in some phases of its theory, had many advocates. The Southern advocates usually believed that exportation should accompany freedom: whereas

---

[111] Each of these terms was applied at various times to various factions of anti-slavery advocates, but the writer believes that the present classification has not been made before.

many of the Northern gradualists were willing for the freed-men to remain in the South and even to have political rights.

The third form that the criticism took was expulsionism. They agreed with the immediatists that prompt action should be taken and that the entire race should be freed, but reached the opposite opinion as to its future residence. Instead of being the friends of the Negro, they were bitter haters of that race. This type of thought was confined almost entirely to the South, and apparently grew out of the attitude of the poor whites to slavery, a result of their economic conflict with the Negro. There were few overt manifestations of this atti-tude. Probably the clearest of early ones was contained in the pamphlets of J. J. Flournoy of Georgia and Alabama.[112] He claimed to be the founder of a new sect, "The Efficient and Instantaneous Expulsion Association of Philosophic and Fearless Patriots."[113] The basis of his theory was that God had not blessed Ham's descendants as he had other men— "Constitutionally ignorant and uncouth, malicious when in power, and proud without beauty—blasphemous and full of obloquy, this race of men are not destined for our society, or helps in any [. . .] aspect or capacity."[114] He declared that the Abolitionist and the slaveholder "agree to a nicety and tally exactly in their arguments that the negroes are necessary to the South . . . cannot be expelled, disagreeing only as to their condition here."[115] He reached the conclusion that it would not do "for negroes to live among white folks in any shape or sense. The evil of it is too intolerable." He pointed out various evils of mingling two extremes of human nature,

[112] *A Reply to a Pamphlet Entitled "Bondage a Moral Institution"* (Athens, Ga., 1836), *An Essay on the Origin, Habits, etc., of the African Race, incidental to the propriety of having nothing to do with Negroes* (New York, 1835), *Much Prefatory Declarations, tending to throw further light upon the annexed second edition of scriptural examination into the question of whom or what are evil genii, of the objects portrayed by the Apostle St. John* (Athens, Ga., 1838).

[113] *An Essay*, p. 4.

[114] *A Reply*, p. 22.   [115] *Ibid.*, p. 52.

declaring that it was not possible for the master to love the Negro and that the endeavor to develop such an affection would lessen his capacity for love of his brother whites.[116] Flournoy believed that the South was retarded by slavery, and felt that as the Negroes increased she would inevitably be faced with abolition. He offered the cure of expelling the entire Negro population from the country.[117]

In order to establish the fact that Negroes were an inferior race and not fit to associate with the whites, Flournoy had perceived the pertinency of refuting the theory of the unity of the human races. He undertook to refute the chief American proponent of the unity theory, Dr. Samuel Stanhope Smith, President of Princeton University, who had advanced his ideas in *An Essay on the Causes of the Variety of Complexion and Figure in the Human Species* (1787). Believing that the reasoning of Smith was calculated to equalize the Negro in every respect with the white man, Flournoy wrote: "I question the authenticity of his positions, and rescue my countrymen from the future inevitable amalgamation with the negroes, if Dr. Smith stands unrefuted."[118]

The ideas of Flournoy had their culmination in the 1850s in the writings of Hinton Rowan Helper, a North Carolinian, who caused quite a storm of resentment from the slaveholders by the publication of the *Impending Crisis* (1857). In this book in which he became the advocate of the poor whites, he laid blame for their impoverished state, and the backward condition of the South generally, upon slavery. He advocated abolition and immediate colonization of the Negroes, for whom he had the greatest antipathy.[119] While expressing

---

[116] *An Essay*, p. 49.   [117] *Ibid.*, p. 33.

[118] *An Essay*, p. 12. His refutation of Smith runs from p. 10 to p. 17.

[119] Helper some years later scribbled the following note in a copy of his book now in the Library of the University of North Carolina, Chapel Hill, N. C.: "Opinions and arguments of the Author, in irreconcilable opposition to slavery, are apparent on every page of this book, and his natural, and as he believes

private disbelief in the unity of the races, Helper unlike Flournoy, thought that it was "a matter, however, which has little or nothing to do with the great question at issue." He ridiculed the "types of mankind" theory that was being advanced by the pro-slavery school of ethnologists because they used it as proof: "That it was right for the stronger race to kidnap and enslave the weaker—that because Nature had been pleased to do something more for the Caucasian race than for the African, the former, by virtue of its superiority, was perfectly justifiable in holding the latter in absolute and perpetual bondage! No system of logic could be more antagonistic to the spirit of true democracy." Aside from the theory of the original parentage of the different races, he believed slavery to be "a great moral, social, civil, and political evil—an oppressive burden to the blacks, and an incalculable injury to the whites . . . an impediment to progress . . . and a dire enemy to every true interest."[120]

Finally, pro-slavery theory furnished the impulse to two significant domestic movements within the South in the 1850s. These movements came as the logical consummation of the idea that slavery must be defended as a "positive good." The first was motivated by the reform spirit and was an attempt to purge the slave system of attendant evils. It was both an answer to the outside critic of the institution and a bid for the support of a large group within who insisted that the only justification for slavery was its humanitarian element. There were two aspects of the reform movement, a religious aspect and a legal one. The first was manifested by the interest of the churches, which, under an evangelical zeal, undertook to improve the spiritual condition of the slaves. The second

---

rightful, antipathies to the negro, are also perspicuously expressed or plainly implied on all of the following twenty odd pages, as likewise on many other pages." *The Impending Crisis of the South* (enlarged ed., New York, 1867).

[120] *Op. cit.*, p. 145. See *infra*, Chapter VI, for the pro-slavery theory of the ethnological school.

aspect appeared in a campaign for revision of the slave codes with the purpose of more adequately protecting the rights of the slave's person and improving his social status. The ultimate purpose of the reformers was to make the facts of the slave system conform to the theory of positive good.[121]

In the 1850s occurred also the movement to reopen the foreign slave trade. A cleavage developed in pro-slavery thought over this question. The principal division was between the school of moral philosophers and the ethnological school. The former, believing that the true basis of justification of slavery was moral in character, opposed the reopening; whereas the latter, minimizing the moral factor involved, generally favored reopening the trade. The Southern divines and the religious periodicals, emphasizing the great humanitarian possibilities of a slave system free from barbarian influences, almost without exception stood out against the trade.

Occasionally the slave trade had been defended in the South before the fifties. Matthew Estes, for example, justified it in 1846: "I do not hesitate for a moment in maintaining that the slave trade has been the source of incalculable blessing to mankind. Just so far as African Slavery in the United States is superior to African Slavery as it exists in Africa—just so much good has resulted from the slave trade."[122] The real impetus to the movement to reopen the trade was given, however, in 1856 by the message of Governor Adams to the legislature of South Carolina when he argued that a revival of the trade was necessary to maintain Southern institutions.[123] The special committee to whom the message was referred divided, the majority handing in a

---

[121] The reform movement is discussed more fully, *infra*, pp. 153-54.

[122] *A Defense of Negro Slavery as It Exists in the United States* (Montgomery, 1846), p. 92.

[123] *Message No. I of His Excellency James H. Adams to the Senate and House of Representatives at the Session of 1856* (Columbia, 1856).

report favorable to the reopening of the trade[124] and the minority an unfavorable report.[125]   These reports are probably the best statements of the arguments, pro and con, on the question.   Following this legislative discussion a small but very active group throughout the South became interested in reviving the slave trade.   Most active in the movement were L. W. Spratt, editor of the *Charleston Standard*,[126] and Edward B. Bryan.[127]   *DeBow's Review* espoused the cause, and the subject was discussed in the Southern commercial conventions.   The Savannah Convention of 1856 appointed a committee to gather facts bearing upon the reopening of the African slave trade composed of: L. W. Spratt, South Carolina; Thomas Clingman, North Carolina; Robert Toombs, Georgia; William L. Yancey, Alabama; General Quitman, Mississippi; Governor James E. Brown, Florida; Hon. John Perkins, Louisiana; Dr. J. G. M. Ramsey, Tennessee; Hon. Albert Rust, Arkansas; Dr. Brewer of Montgomery County, Maryland; and Roger A. Pryor of Virginia.[128]   Spratt made a report to the Montgomery Convention in 1858 in which he presented a strong case for revival of the trade.[129]

The arguments over the slave trade may be classified as moral, economic, political, and social.   On the moral question the rationale of the proponents was that recognizing slav-

---

[124] *Report of the Special Committee of the House of Representatives of South Carolina on Governor James H. Adams' Message as Relates to Slavery and the Slave Trade* (Charleston, 1857).

[125] J. J. Pettigrew, *Report of the Minority of the Special Committee of Seven, to whom was Referred So Much of His Late Excellency's Message No. 1 as Relates to Slavery and the Slave Trade* (Columbia and Charleston, 1858).   Also in *DeBow's*, XXV (1858), pp. 166-185, 289-308.

[126] His most widely circulated pamphlet was *The Foreign Slave Trade.   The source of political power—of material progress, of social integrity, and of social emancipation to the South* (Charleston, 1858).

[127] *Letters to the Southern People* (Charleston, 1858).

[128] *Proceedings*, p. 8, published as an appendix to *The Official Reports of the Debates and Proceedings of the Southern Commercial Convention Assembled at Knoxville, Tennessee, Aug. 10, 1857* (Knoxville, 1857).

[129] "Report on the Slave Trade," *DeBow's*, XXIV (1858), pp. 473-491.

ery as a good in itself "our position drives us to two things . . . the reopening of the slave trade and the closing of the colonization movement."[130] If slavery was a benefit to the slave, then the logic was compelling that it would be humanitarian to bring more Africans under the pale of the institution. The advocates contended that the moral justification of slavery and the slave trade must stand or fall together. As Bryan emphasized: "Slavery and the slave trade are indissoluble in the minds of thinking men all over the world. In the words of the distinguished Robert Hall, 'they are integral parts of the same system'. . . . One is not more defensible than the other. . . . We have both to defend."[131] And to the same purport Spratt insisted that "if we affirm this union of unequal races, we must affirm the means to its formation."[132] He believed that slavery itself was an affirmance of all the proper means to its extension.

The opponents, on the other hand, thought that there was a vast moral distinction between upholding slavery and upholding the slave trade. As Robert G. Harper, a leader in opposition to the reopening movement, saw the matter:

Slavery, as it exists among us, is a subject upon which the sentiment of the Southern people, at least, is well and deeply grounded, both as a moral and religious question. Its defense before the world is such that we are willing to rest upon. But the slave trade in native Africans is a different thing altogether. It is a thing in relation to which we have not been educated and taught by the same lights and demonstrations that have been brought to bear upon domestic slavery. Even in the South there is a strong sentiment of moral horror and opposition to it. . . . No friend of slavery should be willing to place the fate of our institutions upon the same basis of moral and religious opinion and sentiment, and feeling, as the slave trade stands upon in the Southern mind, much

[130] "Editorial Note," *DeBow*, XXII (1857), 445. The editor agreed with the position stated in a letter from W. S. Grayson.

[131] *Op. cit.*, p. 9.   [132] "Report," *loc. cit.*, p. 476.

less to submit it to the same fate of the same public opinion through-out the civilized world which is entertained concerning this odious traffic.[133]

Pettigrew in his report to the South Carolina House of Representatives labored to show that there existed a tradi-tional distinction in the Southern mind between domestic slavery and the slave trade.[134]   The opponents argued that a moral foundation for reopening the trade did not exist.   As the moral sentiment of the people abhorred it, to reopen would drive a large group of moral defenders into the camp of the critics of slavery.   For, as J. B. Adger pointed out, the moralists of the South were led to defend slavery because of the great progress that had been made in civilizing the Negro and ameliorating the rigors of the institution since the barbarian influences had been shut out by the closing of the trade.[135]

The advocates of revival drew a parallel between the foreign and the domestic slave trade.   If the domestic trade could be justified then why could not the foreign?   But the opponents saw a material difference between the two.   As Pettigrew phrased it: "It can be easily shown that there is a vast difference between bringing a Virginia Negro to Caro-lina, where he finds nothing changed except the sky above him, and catching one in Africa to sell him into a land in every respect foreign."[136]   It was the detrimental effect of the African barbarian upon the civilized slave that the opponents chiefly objected to.

[133] *An Argument against the Policy of Reopening the African Slave Trade* (Atlanta, 1858), pp. 75-76.

[134] *Op. cit.*, Bryan in rebuttal cited Rawlins Lowndes' speech in the South Carolina ratifying convention in which he justified the slave trade "on the prin-ciples of religion, humanity, and justice." *Op. cit.*, p. 8. See *Elliott's Debates*, IV, 265.

[135] "Revival of the Slave Trade," *Southern Presbyterian Review* (Columbia), XI (1858), 100.

[136] *Op. cit.*, p. 38.

The economic argument in favor of reopening the slave trade was premised upon the belief that the South was in need of an additional labor supply.   There were a number of reasons why more slaves were needed.   Primarily it arose in order to continue the monopoly on plantation products.   The advocates, however, argued that additional slave labor might be used as the means of a greater industrial and commercial development within the South.   Governor Adams struck this note and gave the reason for extending slave labor beyond the field of agriculture:

It is much better that our drays should be driven by slaves—that our factories should be worked by slaves—that our hotels should be served by slaves—that our locomotives should be manned by slaves, than that we should be exposed to the introduction, from any quarter, of a population alien to us by birth, training and education, and which, in the process of time must lead to that conflict between capital and labor, which makes it so difficult to maintain free institutions in all wealthy and highly civilized nations where such institutions as ours exist.[137]

Incidentally an increased supply would reduce the price of slaves.   This would enable the poorer classes to purchase them and become slaveowners.   The result would be to do away with the undesirable economic conflict between hirelings and slave labor within the South.   More slaves were needed in order to break up the concentration of ownership in a small group and diffuse it among the large number of potential masters.   It was necessary for the large group of poor whites to share directly in the benefits of slavery in order for them to be brought fully to support the institution. Bryan saw clearly the significance of this fact.   He thought that "it would be well for those in whose hands this property is becoming concentrated, to avoid a perpetual exclusion of slaves from the farms or the workshops of their poor

[137] *Op. cit.*, p. 11.

fellow-citizens, by refusing to monopolize slave labor . . . and thereby repudiate the erection of a slave aristocracy in the very heart of the South." Since it was as much as the South could do "to keep our external enemies at bay; let us occasionally glance within."[138]

In the last analysis, additional slaves were needed so that the institution might be extended into new territories. Thus the movement for slave imperialism was closely tied up with the movement to reopen the trade, and there was a consequent interaction between the theories of the two.

The attempt to reopen the slave trade, of course, ran into the prohibition in the Congressional statute. There was a group of Southern statesmen who believed that the States had the right to reopen the trade, if Congress would repeal the laws prohibiting importations. Some of them even doubted the constitutionality of the slave trade acts of 1807 and 1818. Of such an opinion was Jefferson Davis who thought that "it would be more consonant with the genius of our government and the rights of the States to leave the subject to the control of the several States, as a domestic interest, which each community can best decide for itself."[139] Robert G. Harper, on the other hand, took the view that the repeal of the acts by Congress would not enlarge the powers of the States on the subject of the slave trade, that a constitutional

---

[138] *Op. cit.,* p. 35.

[139] "Speech to the Democratic State Convention, Jackson, Mississippi, July 6, 1859"; *Works* (Rowland, ed.), IV, 65. See the explanation of John A. Quitman in the House of Representatives for voting against the resolutions opposing the revival of the slave trade. He did not look upon the trade as shocking "for I believe it has resulted in practical benefit to the Negro." He thought that revival was inexpedient at that time but that it should be left an open and not a settled question of policy for the future. *Congressional Globe,* 34th Cong., 3rd Sess., Appendix, p. 120, Dec. 18, 1856. See also the report of the committee of the Texas House of Representatives calling upon the Texas Congressmen to urge upon Congress the repeal of the laws and the abrogation of all treaties prohibiting the importation of African slaves. *A Report and Treatise on Slavery and the Slave Trade* (Austin, 1857), p. 7.

amendment would be necessary to enable the States to reopen the trade.[140]

In order to get around the constitutional obstruction to the revival of the trade, a faction in the South, interested in securing the African as a source of labor, developed a movement to bring them in as legal apprentices or contract laborers. To show that the plan could be worked harmoniously with the slave system, they argued that "the immigrant Africans that may be introduced . . . though indentured for a term of years, and in this not having the political status belonging to involuntary and unlimited servitude, still, their color, their instincts, habits, and the character of their service, will place them precisely on a level with the black population already established among us."[141] To meet the exigencies of the new labor system Henry Hughes expounded his theory of warranteeism.[142] Hughes conceived of three labor systems possible in civilization, a free labor system, slavery, and warranteeism. The Constitution of the United States contemplated only the first two, and he admitted that the framers had looked to the eventual abolition of the slave system. But the form that had evolved in the South since the framing of the Constitution, warranteeism, was essentially different from either slavery or free labor. As he viewed Southern society: "Between freedom at one extreme and slavery at the other, the golden mean is liberty, that liberty is the order of slavery without its tyranny, and the immunity

---

[140] *Op. cit.,* p. 30.

[141] See "Report of the Committee of the Louisiana Legislature on the Importation of African Laborers," *DeBow,* XXIV (1858), 421. A bill to permit African contract labor passed the Louisiana House in 1858 but was killed in the Senate.

[142] He first enunciated warranteeism as being the true form of society in the South in *Treatise on Sociology, Theoretical and Practical* (Philadelphia, 1854). The theory was later developed and urged as a practical means of evading the slave trade acts in *State Liberties or the Right to African Contract Labor* (Port Gibson, 1858) and *A Report on the African Apprentice System, read at the Southern Convention held at Vicksburg, May 10, 1859* (Vicksburg, 1859).

of freedom without its license, that in short liberty is freedom inside order."[143]   Hughes undertook to differentiate between the three forms of society by means of a very elaborate composition formula. Suffice it to point out here his conclusion that the immigrant warrantee, having an entirely different legal status from that of a slave who was a person without any rights and therefore property, fell outside of the power of Congress to control the slave trade.[144]

One of the chief arguments for reopening the slave trade was that it would advance the political power of the South. Political power in the Union depended upon population. The South needed population so as to extend the slave system into new territories, which would become slave States and thus restore the equilibrium between the sections.[145]   Fascinated with the possibilities of imperialism, the slave propagandists, believing that only a cheap and plentiful supply of Negroes was necessary for slave labor to compete success-

[143] *Report*, p. 2.

[144] Hughes framed a model statute for the States to enact and give legal standing to warranteeism. "Be it enacted that hereafter, our negro labor system shall be held, taken, and adjudged to be warranteeism, in which the masters shall be magistrates, property in man shall be abolished, labor obligations shall be capitalized, caste shall be maintained for the progress and purity of races, the negroes never shall be citizens, the rule of distribution as of the system shall be justice, the agent of the distribution shall be the State, and the act of distribution shall be the order of work and wages." *Ibid.*, p. 14.

[145] Of interest was the vacillating stand of James Henry Hammond. He was an early imperialist and came out for reopening the trade at the Savannah Convention in 1856. But by January, 1858, he opposed any further extension of slave territory: "That our 850,000 sq. mi. are enough for us: that with our soil, climate, coasts, rivers, and staples we have ample ground to make ourselves the ruling power of the World without one foot more soil: that our vocation should be to develop our resources and consolidate the South. . . ." Hammond to W. G. Simms, Jan. 20, 1858, MS. in the Library of Congress. Later the same year in his Beach Island speech he reversed himself on the slave trade. Governor Adams wrote him blaming him, along with Orr and Boyce, for beginning the agitation over the slave trade and admonishing him for his duplicity. Adams to Hammond, Sept. 22, 1858, MS. He undertook to explain his reversal on the grounds that the South was divided on the policy and a vast majority opposed it. *Speech, Delivered at Barnwell Courthouse, October 29, 1858* (Charleston, 1858), p. 12.

fully with free labor, argued that the institution "is not condemned to any latitude, but that it is catholic as humanity in its character, and is capable of extension to the utmost limits of the habitable globe." Spratt declared that with a cheap supply of slaves the institution could be spread over all the west "and perhaps drive hireling labor back to its sterile fastnesses in New England. . . ."[146]

The group of imperialists visualized the great contest of the ages ensuing between slave and free society. They believed that had the slave trade never been closed slave society would have already won the contest in this hemisphere. They realized, moreover, that the contest would continue, even within the South, after Southern independence. Spratt pointed out after the dissolution of the Union that the causes that tended to defeat slavery still existed. The slaves were still being drawn off to the west by high prices, and the border States, and even South Carolina, were being supplied with pauper labor and developing an element opposed to slavery. He, therefore, renewed his efforts to revive the trade when the South was in the formation of a slave republic.[147] He regarded the slave trade as the test of the integrity of slave society. The new republic founded on the slavery principle could not reprobate the means to its extension.

In last analysis, it was argued that reopening the slave trade would afford a reintegration of society in the South. Since the closing of the trade it had been impossible to preserve a due proportion of masters and slaves for the proper constitution of slave society. With the reopening the process of natural formation of the social constitution would be resumed.[148]

[146] *The Foreign Slave Trade*, p. 1.

[147] See his article, "The Slave Trade in the Southern Congress," *Southern Literary Messenger*, XXXII (1861), pp. 409-420.

[148] It is interesting to note that Jefferson Davis gave as the one reason for opposing reopening that it would destroy the due proportion of masters and

In concluding the discussion of the historical phase of pro-slavery thought it will be well to view in retrospect the nature of its development. The defense of slavery always followed an attack. Thus during the first two decades of the nineteenth century pro-slavery opinion was passive. Few persons in public life, or through private writings, rose to defend an institution that apparently remained securely surrounded by constitutional safeguards. The slaveholder, feeling that the question had been settled once for all in the compromises of the Federal Constitution, did not care to reopen the question, and was content that no one else did so. On the few occasions in which the question was brought up in Congress, the Southern representatives denied jurisdiction in that body to act.

The first defenses that appeared, and there was an occasional one from the very earliest period, were apologetic. This may be explained on the ground that it was the easiest way to put aside the question. It must also be held in mind that, while there had always existed a strong faction that desired to perpetuate slavery, yet many lesser elements within the South looked to its final overthrow. These elements had to be brought in line with the perpetualist before the apologetic attitude could be thrown off.

One of the favorite apologies was that of entailment.[149] The South was not responsible for the introduction of slavery; it was an inherited problem. England was responsible for introducing slavery and had prevented the Colonies checking it when they desired to do so. Another attempt to shift re-

---

slaves already existing. He did favor, however, "a policy that could promote the more equal distribution of those we now have." *Loc. cit.*

[149] Robert Walsh, *An Appeal from the Judgments of Great Britain Respecting the United States of America* (Philadelphia, 1819). This was probably the most elaborately developed of the entailment arguments. Entailment lingered on as an apologetic pro-slavery argument in the South as late as 1850. See *The Address of the Mississippi Convention.*

sponsibility was the argument that the Northern States prof-
ited by the slave trade as long as possible and did not begin
to oppose slavery until that source of income was cut off.
Therefore, it was just that the South should be given time to
work out the problem in her own way.

Next came the arguments of necessity. First it was necessary because of climate and staple products. The white man
could not work in the heat and swamps of the South, while
the Negro was by nature fitted to do so. This was the only
way, it was held, that that section of the country could have
been successfully settled. Secondly, it was necessary because
of the inferiority of the Negro race. Two races, the one by
nature inferior, could not exist side by side without extermination of the one or the other, unless the inferior be subordinated to the superior. Finally, the apologetic defense took
the position that slavery was a local problem and that it concerned no one but the slaveholder himself.

As has been shown, the positive defense became pronounced in the twenties. The first type of argument was the
scriptural argument. If the Bible sanctioned slavery then
how could it be a moral evil? Then followed the historical
type of argument. Slavery existed in all ages, in some form,
in all countries. Therefore, the institution was not novel to
the South. Related to the historical approach were certain
object lessons, such as the results of abolition in the West
Indies, the condition of the free Negro, and the comparison
between the condition of the slaves and the free laboring class.
All these lines of reasoning aided in completing the "positive
good theory."

During the thirties on account of the agitation over the
abolition movement, Southern men began to study the institution in all its aspects and to formulate systematic arguments.
As time went on, the church developed its theory of slavery

on principles of moral philosophy, the scientist undertook to prove that inferiority was the natural condition of the Negro; and the political economist pictured the system as an important cog in world economy. Finally, the nature of the defense resulted in a desire for imperialism and perpetuation of the institution. The course of pro-slavery theory takes us from the apologist of the early period to the propagandist of slavery, from an attitude of passivity to one of militancy, from toleration to glorification of the institution.

CHAPTER III

THEORIES OF THE SLAVE INSTITUTION

ONE of the most interesting results of the slavery controversy was that it forced the slaveholder to become consciously articulate with reference to slavery as an institution of social, economic, and political life. Placed under the necessity of defending this element of his environment he could no longer accept it unconsciously as a phenomenon such as the peculiar quality of the climate or the special composition of the soil; nor was he able simply to meet it as a problem of his daily life. Subject from attack from without at this point, he was forced to become a casuist, an historian, a jurist, a philosopher, and even a prophet with reference to it. What was the nature of this "peculiar institution"? What its component elements? How and at what time in the history of civilization did it originate? In what laws did it find its sanction? Within the American Union, what were the legal incidents of its relation to the State, and at what points did it come into contact with the jurisdiction of the federal government? What, finally, was its future to be? Was it a transitory or a permanent institution of society? To the slaveholder's answers to these questions we may now turn our attention. They supply the material for a discussion of the philosophic and legalistic reasoning in the slavery thought of the Old South.

THEORIES AS TO THE NATURE OF SLAVERY

A chief cause of the conflict between slavery theorists arose out of the different concepts that they had of the thing itself. To the mind of the critic, the institution was in essence something entirely different from what the slaveholder conceived it to be. The antagonist defined slavery after the manner of Locke as "absolute, arbitrary, despotical power" in one person over another;[1] or after Montesquieu who thought that "slavery, properly so called, is the establishment of a right which gives to one man such a power over another as renders him absolute master of his life and fortune."[2] The system of Roman slavery, as long as the master had the power of life and death over his slave, was the best example of their idea. Influenced by such thinkers, the American antagonists of slavery developed a concept of unmitigated and unrestrained bondage. To them the essence of Southern slavery was an arbitrary will of the master which regulated the physical, intellectual, and moral actions of the slave. That will, upheld by force, reduced the slave to the condition of a thing without rights. It destroyed his personality.

In contrast, the defender of Southern slavery accepted the idea of Grotius. According to him, "that is perfect slavery, when a man gives his whole labour forever for the sustenance and other necessaries of life."[3] The slaveholder denied that his power over the slave was absolute as in the case of the Roman master. The slave of the South was held for specific purposes only, and the power of the master was limited to certain property rights that he held in the services of the slave. The property rights of the master did not destroy the personality of the slave nor make of him a chattel. No other right than that of a right to his own labor was alienated from the slave. He retained his rights to life, livelihood, happiness, marriage, religion, everything that was consistent with the service that he was obligated to render.

[1] "Two Treatises of Government," *Works* (Rivington, ed., London, 1824), IV, 351.

[2] *The Spirit of Laws* (Prichard, ed., 1900), I, 253.

[3] *De Jure Belli ac Pacis* (Whewell, ed. and tr., Cambridge, 1853). Passage taken from II, v, xxvii.

There was no such thing as the master owning the corpus or the animus of the slave. He held no such property as the owner of an ox or a swine.[4] James Henley Thornwell, the brilliant Presbyterian expounder of pro-slavery theory, philosophically explained the nature and extent of slave property: "The property of man in man is only the property of man in human toil. The laborer becomes capital, not because he is a thing, but because he is the exponent of a presumed amount of labor."[5] Edward B. Bryan phrased the same theory of property in these terms:

With us this property does not consist in human "flesh" . . . Our property in man is a right and a title to human labor. And where is it that this right and title does not exist on the part of those who have the money to buy it? *The only difference in any two cases is the tenure. . . . Our slave property lies only incidentally in the person of the slave but essentially in his labor.* Who buys a slave except he has work for him? His person is held as the only sure means of obtaining his labor. The proprietorship of his person extends only so far as the derivation of a fair amount of labor. The value of the slave is determined by the sort and amount of labor he is capable of and it is according to these that he is bought and sold; and it is undeniable that these are the same conditions which determined the hireling's wages. *In fact we own our slaves for their labor. We govern them as men.*[6]

Viewed in such a light the property right of the master in the slave was analogous to the claim of an employer in the service of a freeman, under contract, enforceable at law. In other words the right to the slave's person, physically speaking, came from the right to exact labor from the slave, and it stood in place of the power to enforce the contract in

[4] See an article by R. S. Buck, "Duties of Masters," *Southern Presbyterian Review*, VIII (1854), 266 in which he explains the theory of the Church.

[5] From a sermon, "Our National Sins," *Fast Day Sermons, or the Pulpit on the State of the Country* (New York, 1861), p. 46.

[6] *Op. cit.*, p. 10. Italics in the original.

the case of the freeman. C. G. Memminger expressed it in this way: "The essential difference between free and slave labor is, that one is rendered in consequence of a contract, the other is rendered in consequence of a command. The laborers in each case are equally moral, equally responsible, equally men, . . . but they work upon different principles."[7] In other words, it was not an ownership of the servant's moral personality but a property in his involuntary labor. Again the Southern theory of slavery was brilliantly expressed by Thornwell in these words:

The two ideas that he is a person, and as a person, held to service, constitute the generic conception of slavery. How is his obligation to service fundamentally differenced from that of other laborers? By this, as one essential circumstance, that it is independent of the formalities of a contract. Add the circumstance that it is for life and you have a complete conception of the thing.[8]

So important was the labor element in the institution that Thornwell concluded: "In its last analysis, slavery is nothing but an organization of labor, and an organization by virtue of which labor and capital are made to coincide."[9]

The idea that the slave's labor was involuntary was generally accepted. Some theorists maintained that, while slavery had existed in different forms in different nations, this was a fundamental requisite. George S. Sawyer, a prominent member of the Louisiana bar, expressed the idea by saying: "Slavery is any system of involuntary servitude by which the time, service, and toil of one person becomes the property of another by compulsion."[10] George Frederick Holmes, student of Aristotle and classical teacher in several Southern colleges, held much the same idea as to the essential nature of

[7] *Slavery Consistent with Moral and Physical Progress* (Augusta, Ga., 1851), p. 6.

[8] *The State of the Country* (Columbia, 1861), p. 16.

[9] "Our National Sins," *op. cit.*, p. 46.

[10] *Southern Institutes* (Philadelphia, 1858), p. 249.

slavery: "We think, therefore, that the more accurate view of slavery is to regard it as continuous and involuntary dependence—leaving the degree of dependence and its form undefined, as they vary with the varying modes of the master and the fluctuating conditions of society."[11]

The eminent intellectual, Dr. Thomas Cooper of South Carolina College, thought that in substance no other definition could be given of slavery than "that state or condition in which a man is governed without his consent."[12]   One prominent thinker arrived at the fundamental principle of the institution through a definition of the terms "master" and "slave": "As the abstract idea of master is governing by one's own will, and that of slave is submission or subjection to such control; and as a system of slavery is a condition into which these ideas enter in correlation—it follows that *the abstract principle of slavery is the general principle of submission or subjection to control by the will of another.*"[13]   Here the idea of submission on the part of the slave is expressed.   Many emphasized the idea of his tacit consent as an element of the relationship.   John Fletcher, in his great work on slavery, in answer to the famous definition of Dr. Paley, which held to the non-contractual nature of slavery, declared that "in all the claims of morality, here is a contract and consent, and the statute might make it legal."[14]   Governor Hammond actually compared it with the compact:

[11] Observations on a Passage in the Politics of Aristotle Relative to Slavery, MS. in the Library of Congress.

[12] *Op. cit.,* p. 24.

[13] W. A. Smith, *Lectures on the Philosophy and Practice of Slavery* (Nashville, 1856), p. 40.   Italics in the original.   Thornton Stringfellow in his book, *Slavery: Its Origin, Nature, and History, considered in the light of Bible teachings, moral justice, and political wisdom* (New York, 1861), p. 3, thought that the leading principle of slavery, that is, "submission to and control by the will of another," was the essential principle in all forms of government.

[14] *Studies on Slavery* (Natchez, 1852), p. 59; for Paley see *The Works of Wm. Paley* (Wayland, ed., London, 1837), I, 145.

If we travel back with the philosophers who refer all human institutions to an original compact, I will still engage to find a place for slavery there. Let it be regarded as a compact between the master and the slave, and I assert that no saner or more just agreement was ever made working to the mutual benefit of both and charitably inclined in favor of the weaker party. The master exacts of the slave obedience, fidelity, and industry; and places him under just so much restraint as insures compliance with his regulations. The slave in return has far more certainly insured to hi·. *peace, plenty, security,* and the proper indulgence of his social propensities—freed from all care for the present, or anxiety for the future with regard either to himself or his family.[15]

A large group of slavery defenders argued that the institution had a quasi-contractual character. Samuel Seabury considered that an implied contract existed because "the obligation to service for life, on condition of protection and support, is the essence of American slavery."[16] Edmund Bellinger believed that "food, cloathing and protection are ample equivalents for the loss of freedom."[17] Professor Washington of William and Mary College in discussing the slave relationship in the South pointed out "how little foundation there is in fact, and in the condition of a large portion of the human race, for the celebrated maxim of the common law that there can be no equivalent for liberty, that every sale implies a *quid pro quo,* and that, therefore, no man can sell himself into slavery."[18] This school of thought on the nature of slavery had no difficulty in finding the consideration essential to a contract in the slave relationship. Somewhat in line with them was the theory of Albert Taylor Bledsoe, Professor of Mathematics at the University of Virginia. He

---

[15] Hammond to L. Tappan, Aug. 1, 1845, MS. in the Library of Congress.

[16] *American Slavery Distinguished from the Slavery of English Theorists and Justified by the Law of Nature* (New York, 1861), p. 202.

[17] *A Speech on the Subject of Slavery, September 7, 1835* (Charleston, 1835), p. 23.

[18] Note book MS. in a private collection.

contended that slavery did not deprive the slave of a natural right. Admitting that liberty in the true sense, being the enjoyment of one's rights, was inalienable, he argued:

In the true sense of the term *liberty*, slavery is not its opposite. Its opposite, its antagonistic principle, is license. By the institution of slavery for the blacks, license is shut out, and liberty is introduced. It is introduced for the slaves themselves. For they have a natural right to that government, to that supervision and control, which, on the whole, is best for them; and such is slavery. Hence slavery secures them in the enjoyment of their natural right; and, according to the measure of their capacity to receive it, bestows upon them real liberty. Let this institution be abolished, and they will no longer enjoy their natural rights.[19]

In contrast to those who saw the incidents of a contract in the slave relationships, others viewed it as a status, existing independently of the consent of the parties, which the law recognized and acted upon. The status of slavery was one of many others in society. Incident thereto the law enforced upon the parties correlative rights and duties. The master had no rights in the slave without corresponding duties to him. That the slave had rights was demonstrable; those rights, however, were consistent with his position in society. The legal basis of the slave relationship was analogous to that of the common callings and the public service enterprises, under the common law, where the law recognized a status and thrust upon the parties engaged therein reciprocal rights and duties regardless of their will working upon them.[20]

[19] "Review of His Reviewer," *Southern Literary Messenger*, XXIII (1856), 25. Bledsoe developed his theory of slavery in *An Essay on Liberty and Slavery* (Philadelphia, 1856), republished in *Cotton Is King, and Pro-Slavery Arguments: comprising the writings of Hammond, Harper, Christy, Stringfellow, Hodge, Bledsoe, and Cartwright on this important subject* (E. N. Elliott, ed., Augusta, 1860), pp. 271-458. He was reviewed by G. F. Holmes in *DeBow*, XXI (1856), 132-143, and by R. in *The Southern Literary Messenger*, XXII (1856), 382-388.

[20] See note by C. K. Burdick, "Origin of Public Service Duties," *Columbia Law Review*, XI, 514, where he shows that tort suits, in case, arose against the

Another analogy was in the law of domestic relations where the source of liability of the parties was relational rather than volitional.   It was in this sense, too, that the claim was often made that the law of slavery was harmonious with the common law of England.   Slavery was just another status that had grown up in society, and the common law was satisfied to fix the rights and duties of the parties to the relation.   Thus the common law foundation for slavery had to be sought in the body of tort and domestic relations law rather than in the branch of contract law.

This view of the reciprocal quality of the slave relationship led many to contend that Southern slavery, therefore, was not the pure form.   According to one writer the difference between the two forms lay in the fact that, in the South, "the Negro has in many cases an appeal from the judgments of his master who is responsible to the law for cruel oppression"; whereas "perfect slavery implies authority without appeal, in the one individual, and subjection, without right of resistance, in the other."[21]   T. R. R. Cobb, the eminent authority on the law of slavery, also explained the basic difference between the two forms.   As he saw it, under a system of absolute slavery, the slave was totally deprived of the three great common law rights guaranteed to every citizen, namely, the right of personal security, the right of personal liberty, and the right of private property; and infringement upon those rights, even by third parties, could be remedied and punished only by suits brought by the master for loss of the service or diminution of the value of the slave.   But in the Southern States the system had been so modified and these personal rights so protected "partly by natural law,

---

common callings for a violation of duties imposed by law rather than contract cases, in assumpsit, for the violation of a promise.

[21] Louisa S. McCord, "Carey on the Slave Trade," *Southern Quarterly Review*, XVII (1854), 163.

partly by express enactment, and more effectively by the influence of civilization and Christian enlightenment, that it is difficult frequently to trace to any purely legal sources many of those protecting barriers, the denial of whose existence would shock an enlightened public sense."[22] Sawyer, with a similar purpose, undertook to demonstrate that the law in speaking of chattel slavery did not destroy the rights of personality of the slave and make of him a thing:

The sole object and meaning, which has been so grossly and blindly perverted, is not to brand the slave as a chattel, in contradistinction from a person, but to mark that species of property, which the master holds in his slave, as a *chattel personal,* in contradistinction from real estate. All this, so far as regards the person of the slave, or reducing him from a person, under the law, to a mere chattel, is but a fiction; in a literal sense it renders the law inconsistent with itself and is absurd. There is not a State in the Union where slaves are not deemed, taken, and held to be persons within the meaning of the law, amenable, and protected by the same. To maim, mutilate, or take the life of one of them, is, in every State, a criminal offence, visited with various penalties. . . . Homicide with malice, etc. is as much murder with regard to a slave as any other person. But it would be a singular freak of criminal law to condemn a man to be hung for murdering a chattel, or piece of property. Such a crime can be committed only upon a person within the power of the State.[23]

Thus Henry Hughes was led to apply the name warranteeism instead of slavery to the system in the South; the warrantees being persons who had all of their rights pro-

[22] *Op. cit.,* pp. 83-84.

[23] *Op. cit.,* pp. 314-315. Chief Justice Marshall in Boyce *v.* Anderson (1829) 2 *Peters* 150, gave sanction to the personality character of the slave under the law when he distinguished in the nature of property between slaves and cattle. According to the law of common carriers, the carrier was under a non-fault liability for damage to cattle but not to passengers. At 155, in speaking of slaves, he held: "It would seem reasonable, therefore, that the responsibility of the carrier should be measured by the law which is applicable to passengers, rather than by that which is applicable to the carriage of common goods."

tected, whereas slaves had no rights under the law.[24]   Another view, holding that the Negro in the South was not properly called a slave, considered slavery to be the subjection of a race equally endowed with the subjecting race.   The relation of the black and white races was regulated by a natural law, as definite as the law of gravitation.[25]

By way of concluding the analysis of definitions, we reach the slavery principle.   This was a theory holding that the very idea of government implied slavery.   This correlative relation—control on the part of one and submission on the part of another—was the same whether it be exercised by the state upon the subject, by the parent upon the child, or by the master upon the slave.   In each case, the one had acquired authority while the other had incurred dependency.   As Professor Robert L. Dabney of Virginia expressed it: "Domestic servitude, as we define and defend it, is but civil government in one of its forms.   All government is restraint; and this is but one form of restraint."[26]   And Sawyer insisted that the same principle that would abolish the relation of master and slave and remove the restraint imposed by the relation upon the slave population would also, if logically carried out, "abolish all restraint imposed by penal codes, prison discipline, and poor laws, upon the rest of the population."[27]   Many went so far as to assert that it would abolish all social relations and resolve society into an anarchistic state.

Again, the slavery principle was defined as being the service of one person to another, leaving the degree, the form, character, and extent of the service undefined.   Thus the ultimate logic of the slavery principle transcended the

[24] *Treatise on Sociology*, p. 227.

[25] J. W. Mills, *The Relation of the Races at the South* (Charleston, 1861), p. 35.

[26] *A Defense of Virginia* [*and through Her of the South*] (New York, 1867), p. 259.

[27] *Op. cit.*, p. 234.

race element as an essential of the institution, and held that slavery was the basis of all social union and progress. George Fitzhugh went so far as to assert that "the defense of Southern slavery involves, necessarily, the defense of every existing human institution." He thought that the defense of Negro slavery as an exceptional institution was "absurdly untenable," for "the slavery principle is almost the only principle of government, the distinctive feature of man's social and dependent nature, and the only cement that binds society together and wards off anarchy."[28]

THEORIES OF THE ORIGIN OF THE INSTITUTION OF SLAVERY

In the Old South, there was a considerable body of theory dealing with the inception of the institution of slavery. Writers on the history of the institution were concerned with the various causes that had led to the forming of the slave relation under the law of past civilizations. In Jewish, Greek, and Roman societies slavery came into being in several ways, which might be classified as debt, crime, birth, sale, contract, and war. Many of the philosophers discussed the justice of these modes of origin. Pufendorf, for instance, thought that slavery based upon consent or contract was valid, and he contended that the relation had always arisen in that way. To him slavery was merely an implied agreement: "I promise to give you constant sustenance, upon condition you assist me with your constant work."[29] In the same manner, Grotius thought that there was nothing shocking in the slavery of consent, for "the obligation to labor was compensated by the perpetual certainty of food."[30] In another connection, he recognized the justice of reducing prisoners of war to slav-

---

[28] "The Conservative Principle or Social Evils and Their Remedies," *DeBow*, XXII (1856), 422-424.

[29] *The Law of Nature and of Nations*, III, iv, vi, quoted in S. B. How, *Slaveholding Not Sinful* (New Brunswick, 1858), p. 66.

[30] Grotius, *op. cit.*, II, v, xxvii.

ery.[31] In fact, many of the philosophers recognized the right
to reduce prisoners of war to slavery; its origin in this case
was in mercy, as an option for death.   Vattel took occasion
to recognize this practice in cases where the prisoner could
be put to death by the recognized laws of nations.[32]   And
Locke, who contended that according to the law of nature,
that is, by contract, there could be no slavery, recognized that
in the case of prisoners the condition was a continuation of the
state of war and was, therefore, beyond the realm of the law
of nature.[33]   Dr. Paley, the great moral philosopher of the
latter part of the eighteenth century, thought that slavery
could arise consistent with the law of nature in three ways,
from crime, from captivity, and from debt.[34]

Apparently, Montesquieu was the first to repudiate the
justice of any mode of origin of slavery.   He denied that a
free man could sell himself, and again he contended that the
relation had no ethical basis in war.[35]   Reasoning in the
same manner, Blackstone said that "slavery cannot originate
in compact because the transaction excludes an equivalent";
and that war was not a legitimate source, for there the claim
rested on the necessity of destroying the prisoner, and such
necessity clearly did not exist.[36]

In the American writings on the origin of slavery appears
the entire series of causes, but only that of war required justification as American slavery had its origin in the internal wars
of the African tribes.   Consequently, Professor Dew replied
to Blackstone pointing out that he had conceived of slavery
in its pure, unmitigated form, which in fact did not exist;
and secondly, that he had misunderstood the argument of
the civilians, who held that the horrors of war sprang from

[31] *Ibid.*, III, vii.
[32] *The Law of Nations* (Chitty, ed., Philadelphia, 1844), III, viii, 152.
[33] *Works*, IV, 352.
[34] "Moral and Political Philosophy," *Works*, I, 145-148.
[35] *Op. cit.*, I, 253-260.   [36] See Tucker's *Blackstone*, II, 423.

retaliation and not from necessity.[37]   Judge Beverley Tucker added to the suggestion of Dew that there was a triple alternative in the disposal of a prisoner, "to kill, to enslave, or to set at large."   The victors could not maintain security from danger under the third; consequently, there had arisen the practice of deporting the prisoner to foreign lands.[38]   In this manner the legitimate source for American slavery was found in the internal wars of the African tribes.   Few Southern writers went beyond this argument to account for the mode by which slavery had originated.

Beyond the theories as to the modes by which the institution had come into being at different periods in history, there were theories attempting to explain the ultimate origin of the institution in the history of mankind.   Many thinkers accepted the theory that war not only was the chief source but was, also, the first.[39]   Likewise, a great many considered it sufficient to place the origin in the Biblical curse on Canaan.[40]   A kindred theory of divine origin traced it to the fall of man in the Garden of Eden.   Judge Upshur declared that "when the Almighty decreed that man should eat bread by the sweat of his face, he laid the foundation of all the differences which we see in the order of society.   It is a necessary consequence of this decree that one portion of mankind shall live upon the labor of another portion."[41]   The divine origin theory was not entirely based on the idea of sin; some writers

[37] "Essay," *Pro-Slavery Argument*, p. 310.

[38] "Note to Blackstone's Commentaries," *Southern Literary Messenger*, I (1835), 227.

[39] Sawyer, *op. cit.*, p. 28, passim.

[40] Jefferson Davis considered this a sufficient explanation to offer the Senate of the U. S., Speech, April 12, 1860, *Works*, IV, 230. Often a further step was taken tracing the origin to Cain as a punishment for his sin, and holding that Ham had married a descendant of Cain, thus placing a double curse upon Canaan, his son. See Fletcher, *op. cit.*, p. 249.

[41] A. P. Upshur, "Domestic Slavery," *Southern Literary Messenger*, V (1839), p. 685. See also Beverley Tucker, *loc. cit.*, p. 28; Thornton Stringfellow, *Slavery and Government* (Washington, 1841), p. 36.

traced the slavery principle to the subordination resulting from the first domestic relation—God had given authority to Adam to rule over his household.

Other theorists departed from any thought of divine causation and found the origin to be in nature itself. These adopted the ideas of Aristotle as the basis of their thought. Aristotle had said that the principle of domination and subjection pervaded all nature and that the attainment of human progress necessitated a combination of command and obedience. Moreover, realizing that some were by nature fitted for command and others for obedience, he thought that the slavery of certain races was natural.[42] Professor Dew, affirming that "the relations of the different classes of society depend almost exclusively upon the state of property," and that the owners of property had always been the rulers of mankind, found that slavery began with the private right of property.[43] With him its development was synchronous with society. To others the institution was anterior to and the cause of the development of civilization. Edmund Ruffin held the view that compulsion was necessary to force labor to produce wealth.[44]

Finally, the origin of slavery was traced by some to the division of labor necessary in the early family,[45] and by others to the necessity of the weak to sacrifice their liberty in order to preserve life.[46] These ideas led logically to the belief that slavery had its ultimate origin in the inequalities of nature. They might, therefore, be classified as the natural

---

[42] *The Politics of Aristotle* (Welldon, ed., London, 1888), I, iii, vii. Holmes took occasion to make his "Observations" on a passage from Book I, Chapter V: "Nature has already designed some for freedom, and others for slavery, to whom slavery is both just and beneficial." MS.

[43] *Loc. cit.*, p. 294.

[44] *The Political Economy of Slavery* (Richmond, 1857), p. 10.

[45] Edward Brown, *op. cit.*, p. 10.

[46] See "Thoughts on Slavery," by a Southron, *Southern Literary Messenger*, IV (1838), 732.

origin school. The natural origin theory of slavery was, of course, a part of the organic thought that was developing in the South, which repudiated the whole compact philosophy and held to the natural origin of all political and social organization.[47] There was, moreover, a third school, as we might assume from our consideration of the theories of the nature of slavery, who considered the institution's ultimate origin to have been contractual.[48]

THEORIES CONCERNING THE LEGAL BASIS OF SLAVERY

The discussion over the legal basis of slavery resolved into two broad questions. The first was a philosophical inquiry as to whether the institution conformed to the law of nature and the second took on more of the character of a legalistic dispute as to whether there was a positive law sanction for the institution. From the genesis of the slavery controversy, both the antagonists and the proponents of slavery had appealed to the law of nature to support their opposite positions. In American slavery history the anti-slavery group argued, from the very beginning, that the institution was contrary to nature's law; and at times, they appealed to nature as a higher law that overrode all man-made sanctions for slavery. Pro-slavery, thinkers, therefore, were led to study the great writers on the law of nature and to set forth interpretations of it with which slavery might harmonize.

To be sure, many of the philosophers had condemned slavery under the law of nature. Jean Bodin, the great French political theorist of the latter part of the sixteenth century, appears to have been the first of the moderns to refute openly the logic of Aristotle, which had found a place for slavery in nature.[49] Francisco Saurez, the eminent

---

[47] See *supra*, p. 59, and *infra*, p. 135.

[48] See *supra*, pp. 111-13.

[49] *De Republica*, I, v, referred to by W. A. Dunning, *A History of Political Theories* (New York, 1923), II, 91.

Spanish jurist and theologian of the same period, likewise could not reconcile human bondage with the law of nature.[50] According to the thinking of John Locke, there could be no slavery under the law of nature; rather, enslavement resulted from the withdrawal of the protection of that law.[51] The natural rights school of philosophers, of which Locke and Paine were members, had great influence upon the development of American anti-slavery theory. In large measure, the anti-slavery theorist conceived of the law of nature in terms of individual natural rights. Natural law, to them, was the positive sanction by which man in his social state was guaranteed the inherent and inalienable rights that he had acquired in his state of nature.[52]

To meet the attack from the natural rights interpretation of natural law, the defenders of slavery divided into two schools; the first attempted to reconcile slavery and natural rights, whereas the second discarded natural rights entirely. J. K. Paulding was among the small group of thinkers that tried to retain natural rights as a part of the pro-slavery argument. In order to accomplish a reconciliation of the two, he classified rights under the law of nature into those that are inalienable, such as that of self-defense, those that may be voluntarily surrendered, and those that may be forfeited by crime, captivity in war, or debt. "Unquestionably," he thought, "all men are born equal, and born free, and yet many forfeit that freedom. To deny this is to impeach the right of self defense, which justifies the necessity of putting captives in war beyond the reach of doing us further injury, as well as those laws which inflict imprisonment and hard

---

[50] *Tractatus de Legibus ac Deo Legislatore*, II, viii, 4, referred to by Dunning, *op. cit.*, p. 140.

[51] *Loc. cit.*

[52] See *supra*, Chapter I, pp. 22-38, for the significance of natural rights in the early slavery controversy.

labour."⁵³   Moreover, all men have a natural right to live as long as they can, but they may be deprived of life as a punishment, or to secure the safety of society.   Man also has a right to pursue his own happiness, so long as he does not illegally or immorally interfere with the happiness of others. And to interpret the Declaration of Independence in any other manner, he insisted,

would be to pervert its principles into a warrant for the violation of all human statutes, under the sanction of the inalienable rights of nature. It was not an elaborate metaphysical discussion of human rights, but a mere assertion of great general principles; and to have enumerated all the exceptions would have been giving the world a volume in folio, instead of a simple declaration of rights. The charge of inconsistency between our principles and practice is, therefore, entirely unfounded.⁵⁴

Paulding concluded that "upon the same principle of self defense" if it could be proved that emancipation of the slaves would "be destructive to the property, fatal to the peace, and dangerous to the lives of the whole white population" they were rightfully kept enslaved, and that it was not inconsistent with natural rights.⁵⁵

A much more labored attempt to make use of natural rights in the justification of slavery was that made by Bledsoe in his *Liberty and Slavery*. He, too, admitted that all men have certain inalienable rights:

No man has a right to alienate his rights. All natural rights are, indeed, in so far as they are real and existing, *inalienable*. That is to say, no man can rightfully transfer them to society, nor can society rightfully divest him of them. To say that a man has a right to anything, and, at the same time assert that society may take it from him, is to affirm that society may do injustice, or deprive the individual of his dues.⁵⁶

⁵³ *Slavery in the United States* (Philadelphia, 1836), p. 42.
⁵⁴ *Ibid.*, p. 43.   ⁵⁵ *Ibid.*, p. 48.
⁵⁶ Quotations taken from Bledsoe's review of his reviewer where he gives a concise exposition of his ideas. *Loc. cit.*, p. 22.

But he denied that life and liberty were among the inalienable rights of all men, "for the simple, sole, and sufficient reason that some men have no such right at all; the murderer, for instance, has no right to life, nor has the highway robber to liberty." The right to life and liberty existed in some men and not in others; therefore, it was a conditional right; but there was a right in all men to do their duty, which was absolute and, therefore, inalienable. For those men who possess the right to liberty, he conceded it was inalienable, and society could not take it from them. But in all cases where men do not possess such a right, he contended:

both life and liberty may be taken away by society for its own highest good. It is on this ground that I justify the institution of slavery. Not on the ground that society may divest the slave of his natural *right* to personal freedom, but on the ground that he possesses no such natural right, and the good of all is incompatible with his personal freedom.[57]

Liberty and freedom as the abolitionists meant them, "the power to act as one pleases," were certainly alienable. But, in the true sense of the word, liberty, "the enjoyment of one's own rights," was inalienable. Hence, he argued, that "in compelling the colored population of the South to work, *the law does not deprive them of liberty in the true sense of the word; that is, it does not deprive them of the enjoyment of any right.* It merely requires them to perform a natural duty."[58] Thus, it would seem, in final analysis, that Bledsoe, although not admitting it, in effect discarded the traditional theory of individual natural rights and took up a concept of natural law, based on the public good, which was restrictive of individual liberty.[59]

[57] *Ibid.*, p. 24.   [58] *Ibid.*, p. 24. Italics in the original.

[59] This is the conclusion reached by B. F. Wright, *op. cit.*, p. 233. Pages 228-241. Wright has an excellent treatment of the natural law concept of the pro-slavery theorists.

By far the preponderant pro-slavery thought, however, entirely discarded the traditional natural rights theory, and, in its place, constructed other concepts of the law of nature upon which was based the justification of slavery. As we have already seen in an earlier chapter, the attack on natural rights, in the South, began as a part of a general reaction to the speculative philosophy of the Revolutionary period. Based on observation of the facts in nature, it grew synchronously with the forming of the organic concept of the nature of institutions, and was fully developed by the time the South had advanced to the position of justifying slavery as a "positive good."[60] Thomas Cooper gave expression to the prevailing thought about natural rights when he wrote in 1835:

We talk a great deal of nonsense about the rights of man. We say that man is born free, and equal to every other man. Nothing can be more untrue: no human being ever was, now is or ever will be born free. Where is the freedom of an infant in swaddling clothes? No two men were ever born equal to each other or ever will be. Are they equally strong, equally talented, born to equal pretensions and chances? If nature has ordained inferiority, that inferiority will tell its own story through life, and such is the fact.[61]

The same tendency to flout natural rights appeared in the classical pro-slavery essays of Thomas R. Dew, William Harper, William Gilmore Simms, and James Henry Hammond published in *The Pro-Slavery Argument* and also ran through the pro-slavery literature quite generally. Calhoun in his *Disquisition* probably contributed the most profound thought in refutation of the whole natural rights notion.[62] Liberty, to Calhoun, was not a right of every man equally. It was, rather, a noble and high reward to be earned by the intelligent and deserving. It was its greatest praise that an all wise

---

[60] See *supra*, Chapter II, pp. 58-59.
[61] "Slavery," *Southern Literary Journal*, I (Charleston, 1835), 188.
[62] *Works*, I, 55-59.

Providence had reserved it for the high development of the individual's moral and intellectual faculties. He thought that this was a fixed law of nature and that every attempt to advance a people in the scale of liberty beyond the point to which they were entitled would prove abortive.

Nor did Calhoun think that equality was a natural right. Inequality of condition was both a necessary consequence of liberty and at the same time indispensable to progress. This was true because the mainspring to progress is the desire of individuals to better their condition, and its strongest impulse the freedom of the individual to exert himself according to his peculiar abilities. As individuals differ greatly from each other in "intelligence, sagacity, energy, perseverance, skill, habits of industry and economy, physical power, position and opportunity,—the necessary effect of leaving all free to exert themselves to better their condition, must be a corresponding inequality between those who may possess these qualities and advantages in a high degree, and those who may be deficient in them."[63] Calhoun placed the natural rights error on the unfounded and false assumption, which was contrary to universal observation, that all men are born free and equal in a state of nature. But such a purely hypothetical state never did nor could exist, because it was inconsistent with the preservation and perpetuation of the race. Instead of its being man's natural state, the social or political state, "the one for which his Creator made him, and the only one in which he can preserve and perfect his race," was man's natural state; and instead of being born free and equal in it, he was "born subject, not only to parental authority, but to the laws and institutions of the country where born, and under whose protection they draw their first breath."[64]

James Henry Hammond was another who thought deeply upon the question of natural rights and the law of nature

[63] *Ibid.*, p. 57.   [64] *Ibid.*, p. 58.

as being essentially involved in a philosophical discussion of the slavery problem. In writing his rationale of the subject to Professor Beverley Tucker of William and Mary, he warned that he was taking ground that would startle many, "but not I am inclined to think a reasoner so bold and searching as yourself."[65] In an accompanying manuscript, Hammond in a profound and incisive manner undertook to maintain the position that man had no natural rights and that an appeal to the law of nature was not the proper justification for man's actions.[66] In answer to the many judges, philosophers, demagogues, and reformers that had descanted on the law of nature and natural rights, Hammond observed:

But they have never told us very distinctly what these Laws and Rights are. For one I confess myself quite ignorant of them. That all bodies shall gravitate toward a common center—that the earth shall move around the sun and revolve on its own axis in exact periods of time, are indeed Laws of Nature. And these Laws I can comprehend. But they have no bearing on the Rights of Man. It is also a Law of Nature that sexual intercourse is indispensable to the propagation of all species both of animals and vegetables. It is possible that from such a Law as this man might attempt to set up Natural Rights—and I believe it has been done. It might be argued from this known necessity that each individual is entitled to the unbounded indulgence of his lusts and that any attempt to restrain him would be a violation of the Laws of Nature and Natural Rights.

But the abolitionists did not affect to advocate such a right as this. On the contrary, they most strenuously denounced unbridled sexual intercourse as one of the peculiar evils of slaveholding. Then, after all, they admitted that nature

[65] Dec. 19, 1846. MS. in a private collection.
[66] "Laws of Nature—Natural Rights—Slavery," MS. in a private collection. So far as I have been able to determine this manuscript was never published. I have paraphrased Hammond's argument in the following pages. Italics and capitalization in the original.

must not be allowed to reign supreme; and, consequently, that some natural rights may justly be curtailed. In admitting this, he thought, they yielded the whole ground, for "in certain cases where according to their judgment it would be for the best, they would restrain the enjoyment of Natural Rights." The slaveholder only asked to do the same; therefore, the parties did not differ in principle but only in detail. The whole discussion was made to turn on expediency.

He realized, nevertheless, that the abolitionists would not agree that this was the correct view or a fair illustration to make. Then, how could the laws and rights ordained by nature be determined? If it were possible to see a man in a state of nature, "that is an isolated savage, holding no rational communion with his species, yet not an idiot, or madman," then it might be possible to discover those mysterious laws and to obtain a clue to those rights, by merely observing his actions. But as no such man has ever existed, or, if he had, he had not fallen under the observation of any intelligent human being:

I am not at all ashamed to confess myself wholly in the dark as to any Laws affecting him save physical ones common to the whole animal and vegetable creation; and those laid down in the word of God, or established by human Governments and Associations. On any Rights but such as he holds under God from his fellow man. In fact, strange as it might be thought, I do not regard Man as having strictly speaking any Rights at all.

After all what was a right? It was difficult to define. It was usually regarded as something belonging to man of which he could not with justice be deprived. But this was not a correct definition, because:

it turns upon our various and discordant views of justice, and fails to convey a perfect idea of a possession certain, complete and undivided. Philosophers, unable to define, attempt to describe our

Rights and commence by dividing them into Absolute and Relative. Absolute Rights are said to consist in what is denominated
Natural Liberty. And Natural Liberty is explained to be the
power of what one sees fit to do without any restraint but that imposed by the Laws of Nature. Again the question recurs what
are these Laws of Nature? But our common sense is at once convinced that all this is an affair of words, incomprehensible, only
suited for metaphysical dialecticians to exercise their subtle intellects about, or for impostors to delude the vulgar with.

"The moment a man opens his eyes in this world," Hammond believed, he leaves the realm of nature and is divested
of all rights he may have enjoyed there. From the instant
he exists here, "he exists as *one among many* of his kind,
who at once impose upon him Laws from which he has no
possible escape, but by ceasing to be and returning to whence
he came. Rights shrink into privileges which they permit
him to enjoy, limit and withdraw at their good pleasure."
If man could bring with him a single right, it would seem
to be the right to live; and yet, if he should transgress the
laws fastened upon him, he would be taught that there is
nothing sacred or inalienable about the right to live. If nature had bestowed upon him any peculiar right, it must have
been the right to act in conformity with his instincts. But
what are the most universal and strongest instincts of man?
They are ambition, avarice, lust. These are the instincts
which it is his natural right to indulge to exhaustion or satiety.
But this right can not be indulged save at the expense of
others. To enforce this right as to some is to violate it as
to others. "Thus," he wrote, "at the very outset the right
to act in conformity with the laws of nature must be surrendered, or some men must be subjected to the entire
dominion of their fellows . . . to slavery the most abject and
horrible—they must be the doomed pander of ambition and
avarice."

He refused, however, to uphold the system of slavery on any such grounds, for the law of nature, and its concomitant natural rights, were the creations of those who held themselves as the apostles of perfect liberty and universal equality. They were the worst enemies of progress, who making

eccentric excursions into the fields of Natural Law and Natural Rights, collect brilliant but poisonous wild flowers with which to dazzle the eyes and drug the senses of the multitude until they become truly "Children of Wrath"—"Shapen in iniquity"—"desperately wicked" and in demoniac madness overturn the altars, trample down the Laws, and scatter to the winds the Social Bonds which God and Time and Human Wisdom have erected and ordained for the happiness of Man.

Throwing overboard the whole natural law concept, Hammond rested the defense of slavery "on the revealed Will of God—on custom—on utility—on the happiness of the greatest number—in one word on Law—but the Law of God and Man, on which also rests . . . all the true and rational freedom we enjoy." Man, in point of fact, as we know him, was without inherent rights. He possessed really only privileges, which consisted in "permitting each member of society to act as he sees fit except so far as he is restrained by Laws enacted for the benefit of Society at large." If these views were correct, then, he concluded, the true and sole question in reference to slavery is "whether its existence is in conformity with the ascertained will of the community where it is found." Certain it was that the slave had no right from nature or any other source to be free "unless his freedom would advance the interests of the Society of which from position he is a member, or his Slavery proves detrimental to it."

Turning now from the answer of the pro-slavery theorist to the natural rights attack, we come to consider the concepts of natural law to which he appealed as the true foundation for the institution. The term "law of nature" was sometimes used to express the deductions drawn from an observation of the natural world. It was often asserted that slavery was contrary to natural law because no counterpart or analogous operation could be found in the natural world. One answer to such a claim was that by a parity of reasoning cannibalism and many other crimes could be justified; because, among the lower animals, the destruction of their own species was a common occurrence. Support for the claim, nevertheless, was drawn from the Roman law. Under the Justinian Code slavery was said to be that by which one man is made subject to another, according to *jus gentium*, though contrary to *jus naturale*.[67] According to Ulpian, "*jus naturale* is what nature has taught to all animals, for this law is not peculiar to man but common to all animals, whether brought forth upon the earth, in the sky, or in the sea."[68] In order to include human slavery under the *jus naturale*, therefore, it was necessary to find an analogous relationship among the brute creation. The ancient Roman observed none, but the ingenious Southern slaveholder pointed to recent discoveries of the entomologists to prove that a form of slavery did actually exist among the lower animals. He pointed out that

[67] See *Institutes* I, ii. Professor McIlwain shows that at the time of Gaius the *jus naturale* and the *jus gentium* were considered to be one and the same in content, character, and origin, and that slavery was an admitted right under that law because all nations employed it. He shows, however, that Gaius recognized that the abuse of the right to the slave could be limited by the *jus civile*. He thinks that this inconsistency was a small breach in the older legal theory which widened into the settled belief by the time of Justinian that *jus gentium* and *jus naturale* were totally separate in origin, character, and content, and that slavery, a part of the first, was inconsistent with the latter. *The Growth of Political Thought in the West* (New York, 1932), p. 123, citing Gaius, *Institutiones*, I, 52.

[68] *Ibid.*, p. 126, translating Ulpian, *Institutiones*, D, i, i, 2-3. Upon the principle that the law of nature was the law that nature taught all living creatures, St. Ambrose declared that the copulation of asses and mares, by which mules are produced, was forbidden, the same being an unnatural connection. Cited in Cobb, *op. cit.*, p. 7, note.

it was a well established fact that the red ant would go forth to conquer and subjugate the black ant.[69] Consequently, he believed that had the Roman known of this phenomenon of nature he would not have denied slavery its place under natural law.

Another view conceived of law as applying only to rational creatures who have reason and will to perceive an obligation and to adapt their acts accordingly. The law of nature was that which reason appoints for all men. Viewed in this light, it was closely identified with the Roman *jus gentium*, which Gaius defined as whatever natural reason establishes among all men and is observed uniformly among all peoples.[70] With the same idea in mind, Grotius defined it as "the dictate of reason, by which we discover whether an action be good or evil, by its agreement with the rational social nature of man."[71] Similar in meaning was the definition of Pufendorf that it was "that most general and universal rule of human actions to which every man is obliged to conform, as he is a reasonable creature."[72] This natural reason found its positive expression in the laws of the nations; which were, therefore, merely declarative of the law of nature. In this sense, the slaveholder could appeal to the authority of the *jus gentium*, Pufendorf, Grotius, and many other writers in the field of jurisprudence who had made in their expositions of natural law a place for slavery. According to their use of natural law, a meaning attached synonymous with justice, "not that imperfect justice which may be discerned by

[69] T. R. R. Cobb, *An Inquiry into the Law of Negro Slavery in the United States of America* (Philadelphia and Savannah, 1858), pp. 8-9, cites the discoveries of Huber and M. Latrielle in *Considérations Nouvelles*, p. 408. See also Seabury, *op. cit.*, pp. 118-125, for a similar discussion of this aspect of the appeal to natural law.

[70] See McIlwain, *op. cit.*, p. 122, translating *Institutiones*, I, i.

[71] Cobb, *op. cit.*, p. 10, quoting *De Jure Belli*, II, 18, 3. For a full explanation of Grotius' idea of the law of nature, see Dunning, *op. cit.*, II, 164-171.

[72] Cobb, *op. cit.*, p. 11, quoting *Law of Nature and Nations*, I, i, v.

the savage mind, but those ethical rules, or principles of right, which, upon the grounds of their own fitness and propriety, and irrespective of the sanction of Divine authority, commend themselves to the most cultivated human reason." Accepting this social justice interpretation, the able lawyer, J. P. Holcombe, addressing the Virginia State Agricultural Society, insisted that "African Slavery in the United States is consistent with Natural Law, because if all the bonds of public authority were suddenly dissolved, and the community called upon to reconstruct its social and political system, the relations of the two races remaining in other respects unaltered, it would be our right and duty to reduce the negro to subjection."[73]

At this point as at many others in the pro-slavery argument, the influence of Thomas Carlyle was profoundly felt. The law of nature, according to the societarian concept of this great contemporary philosopher, embraced the principle of slavery. With reference to it, he announced that it was "the eternal law of nature for a man, that he shall be permitted, encouraged, and *if need be compelled*, to do what work the Maker of him has intended, by the making of him for this world."[74] Carlyle's ideas about natural rights were also used in support of the argument of the slaveholder. "Of all the rights of man," Carlyle thought that the most indispensable ordained by nature was "the right of the ignorant man to be guided by the wiser, to be gently and firmly held in the true course," and, furthermore, that "if freedom have any meaning, it means enjoyment of this right, in which all other rights are enjoyed."[75] So, looking at the law of nature,

---

[73] "Is Slavery Consistent with Natural Law," *Southern Literary Messenger*, XXVII (1858), 408.

[74] "Letter on West India Emancipation," *DeBow*, VIII (1850), 531. The same passage is used with approval in reconciling slavery and the law of nature by Cobb, *op. cit.*, p. 12.

[75] Quoted by Holcombe, *loc. cit.*

also from the standpoint of protection to individual liberty, Carlyle's thought fit in with the Bledsoeian school of pro-slavery theorists.

Another group of pro-slavery theorists held that the law of nature was the general conduct of mankind upon a given state of circumstances. In order to determine what nature demanded of man in a particular circumstance, it was necessary to inquire into what he had always actually done in that situation. Thus the whole question resolved itself into a study of the history of man. By the historical test, the normality of slavery, and, therefore, its conformity to natural laws, appeared from the fact that it had had a primitive, spontaneous, and universal development in society. After a careful study, Thornwell observed that "if there be any property that can be called natural in the sense that it spontaneously springs up in the history of the species, it is property in slaves."[76] Holmes also concluded from his study of ancient slavery that the essential features of the institution were its spontaneous origin and its universal existence in some form.[77] A full exposition of the theory of the universality of slavery was made by a representative in Congress from Maryland:

... it has been a necessary condition of civilized man from earliest periods; that all the most polished nations of antiquity recognized and protected it; that the barbarian practiced it, and was master or slave according to circumstances; that you find it everywhere an element of society, but nowhere can you find the time or the manner in which it became such; and, therefore, they argue, it must spring from an ordinance of nature, universally recognized and universally binding.[78]

Holmes stated the theory more philosophically. The mode of determining what was natural in social and political philos-

---

[76] *The State of the Country*, p. 20.

[77] "Ancient Slavery," *DeBow*, XIX (1855), 559-578.

[78] Speech of J. R. Franklin, March 28, 1854, *Congressional Globe*, 33rd Cong., 1st Sess., Appendix, p. 420.

ophy, he thought, was to discover what things were habitually
attached to political organization in the various steps of its
development; whatever was of constant occurrence in the
development of nations was natural and whatever was natural was just.   Now as slavery existed "in a very considerable degree under all forms of civilized society, we may consider it a necessary consequence of social organization (or
may even go further and with Aristotle regard it as a necessary constituent thereof) and as this is admitted to be natural, so we may consider its consequence to be consonant with
the laws of nature."[79]

It is apparent that this aspect of the natural law appeal
of the slaveholder was a part of his organic thinking.   The
idea of the naturalness of slavery because of its normality in
society was a counterpart of the theory of the organic nature
of the state, that was being expounded by political theorists
in the South.   In fact slavery offered the best pragmatic illustration for such speculation.   The influence of Edmund
Burke also was apparent at this point, because of the great
weight given in his thinking to the historical factor and the
experience of mankind in the justification of political institutions.

Another point of view, important in pro-slavery concepts
of natural law, made a distinction between the law of nature
and the state of nature.   Many institutions such as marriage,
property, servitude, and government were absent from the
pre-social state of nature, yet they did no violence to natural
law when they developed in society.   A distinguished Scotch
commentator applied this distinction philosophically to slavery:

It is indeed contrary to the state of nature, by which all men were
equal and free; but it is not repugnant to the law of nature,

---

[79] Observation on a Passage in Aristotle's *Politics*, MS.

which does not command men to remain in their native freedom nor forbid the preserving persons at the expense of their liberty.[80]

This view of the naturalness of institutions drew support from the writings of the church fathers. It was the peculiar contribution of Bishop England to review the patristic thought in support of the pro-slavery argument and to conclude that the church regarded slavery "not to be incompatible with natural law, to be the result of sin by Divine dispensation, to have been established by human legislation."[81]   According to St. Augustine, men were equal and free in their state of innocence, and there was no domination of any kind by one over another. But the fall of man altered this situation and sin became the prime cause of slavery as of all forms of domination. Slavery, therefore, was just one of the institutions ordained by God to cope with wickedness in man's fallen state.[82]   St. Thomas Aquinas also undertook to differentiate in regard to slavery between the two usages of naturalness. In one sense, he points out, a thing is natural or in accord with nature if its contrary does not exist in nature, as when we say that a man is naked according to the law of nature because nature gave him no clothes. In the same sense liberty and the common possession of all things are a part of the law of nature. But the state of nature may be added to or altered by human laws among the nations to meet legitimate needs as man advances in the social state. These additions àre not departures from the law of nature nor repugnant to the state of nature: "The distinction of possession and slavery were not by nature but by reason of man, for the benefit of human life, and thus the

---

[80] Cobb, *op. cit.*, p. 13, quoting from McDouall's *Institutes*, I, 2, 77.

[81] "Letters to John Forsyth," *Works* (Reynolds, ed., Baltimore, 1849 , III, 106-190.

[82] See McIlwain, *op. cit.*, pp. 160-161, explaining the theory of the *De Civitate Dei*, XIX, xv.

law of nature is not changed by their introduction, but an addition is made thereto."[83]

The last view to be considered in the philosophical discussion of the naturalness of slavery had its source in the thought of Aristotle. Slavery, to him, was another of the manifestations of the general rule of nature that whenever several parts combine to form a whole, the inevitable result will be the subordination of some of the parts to others, and a subject-ruler relationship. This appeared in the rule of man over man, of man over the body, and the reason over the appetite. But for the slave-master relationship to be just, the slave had to be a natural inferior. He assumed that men differed from one another in capacity to perform the functions of life, but he did not clearly indicate how a true slave was to be known from a freeman.[84] The Aristotelian influence upon Southern thought was strong and may be traced through much of the pro-slavery literature. Probably to no other thinker in the history of the world did the slaveholder owe the great debt that he owed Aristotle.[85] He used his philosophical principles to build upon, and undertook to prove that the Negro was actually inferior in capacity and was fitted for a true slave. We have earlier noted the Colonial heritage of the inferiority argument. From the earliest times the slaveholder had testified to his observation of the phenomenon of nature. As time passed, the energies of a large group of scientific investigators were directed toward establishing this natural inferiority. The anatomist, the ethnologist, and the ethnographer worked out the scientific coun-

[83] Fletcher, op. cit., p. 266, quoting from Summa Theologica, Prima, Secundae Partis, Quaestio XCIV. See also McIlwain, op. cit., pp. 334-335.

[84] See McIlwain, op. cit., pp. 69-72, for an excellent analysis and criticism of Aristotle's slavery theory, which I closely follow.

[85] Specific examples of Aristotle's influence are too numerous to need citation, but see Calhoun's letter to A. D. Wallace, Correspondence, p. 469, where he acknowledges his debt to Aristotle.

terpart to the Aristotelian philosophy of slavery. Thus ultimately the philosophy of the slaveholder becomes empirical
in character.

Empiricism led the slaveholder to the conclusion that inequality was the natural order of the universe. Here he
rested ultimately the natural law foundation for slavery.
Nature was governed by unerring laws "which command the
oak to be stronger than the willow; and the cypress to be
taller than the shrub." The couplet from Pope's *Essay on
Man* was often quoted as beautifully expressive of the idea:

> Order is heaven's first law, and this confest,
> Some are, and must be, greater than the rest.[86]

William Gilmore Simms commenting on these lines profoundly added: "All harmonies, whether in the moral
or physical worlds, arise wholly from the inequality of
their tones and aspects; and all things, whether in art or
nature, social or political systems, but for this inequality,
would give forth only monotony or discord."[87]   Indeed, as
the slaveholder viewed creation, variety and inequality were
stamped upon every work of the Great Creator. It was so in
the material universe, and here he quoted at length from
that sublime epistle of St. Paul in which he said: "One star
differeth from another star in glory" (I Cor. XV:41).[88]
The same inequality was seen in all animated creation, as one
slaveholder described life to another:

. . . the trees of the forest—the flora of the valleys and the products of the farm and garden—the beasts of the field and the fowls

---

[86] See William Gilmore Simms, "The Morals of Slavery," *The Pro-Slavery
Argument*, p. 256; W. G. Brownlow, *A Sermon on Slavery* (Knoxville, 1857), p.
14; and Drayton, *op. cit.*, p. 148, who in 1802 used Pope freely.

[87] *Loc. cit.*, p. 257.

[88] Letter of J. G. M. Ramsey to L. W. Spratt, April 16, 1858, MS. in the Mc-
Clung collection, Lawson McGhee Library, Knoxville, Tennessee. Alexander H.
Stephens made use of this simile in arguing the inferiority of the Negro. *Speech*,
Dec. 14, 1854, *Congressional Globe*, 33rd Cong., 2nd Sess., Appendix, p. 38.

of the air. The rational creation, the genus homo itself, bears too the impress of the same variety and inequality, in their physical, moral, and intellectual manifestations and developments. Compare the idiotic features of the Hottentot with the colour of the cultivated European—the forehead and eye of the educated Irishman with the lustreless and vacant countenance of the Asiatic drone, the genius and brilliance of Newton and Fulton with the dullness and stupidity of the aboriginal American. Inequality exists everywhere. It is one of God's laws extending throughout inanimate-animate, irrational-rational, and probably the angelic, seraphic-cherubic and the purely spiritual creation.[89]

But where was the warrant, the authority, the source of power for using the inferior genera of creation to promote the growth and progress of the superior genera?

It is by a fixed law of nature, and by the necessary operation of natural causes that the rich mould of the hill side gradually disappears from its primary location and is as gradually removed to the valley below to enrich and fertilize it. *Nature* itself takes from that "which hath and giveth to that which hath not" . . . the monarch of the forest derives its growth and aliment and vigor from the decay and decomposition of the inferior . . . co-vegetables which surround him . . . the smaller animals by a necessity of nature constitute the necessary food of the larger . . . it is a fixed law of nature that the "Big fishes eat up the little ones."[90]

So the philosophical argument that slavery conformed to the law of nature eventuated in an identification of the law of nature with the laws of the physical world.

The law of nature, however perfect a rational foundation for the institution, was not a positive law sanction. During the past, important contributions had been made toward the recognition of slavery in legal codes: Roman law had recognized it under the *jus gentium* and under the *jus civile*.

---

[89] Ramsey to Spratt, MS.   [90] *Ibid.*

Bodin, although denying its natural basis, admitted that it was approved by "the great argument and consent of almost all nations."[91] Suárez, the great Spanish lawyer, definitely contrasting the law of nature with the law of nations, placed slavery under the latter. Grotius, Pufendorf, Vattel, and in fact almost all of the great writers on the law of nations recognized its existence and gave sanction to it in their works.

With the weight of these authorities, the Southern slaveholder united the facts he had derived from history. Slavery had existed in all ages and at all times in some form. It owed its being, therefore, to universal custom, the common consent of mankind. Based upon the common law of nations, that is upon universal custom and usage, the institution had received the sanction of the legal codes and judicial decisions, or of the municipal law, of individual nations. Sawyer said that the relation of master and slave was as old as the human family, that it had existed anterior to all human law and institutions of government, that it was founded upon "immemorial custom, incorporated into the ancient and modern codes of nations," and that its abolition was the exception abrogating universal custom.[92] Reasoning in this way, the slaveholder reached the conclusion that the institution did not depend for its support upon the *lex loci,* or the municipal law of a state. Its legality arose by force of international law simultaneously with its first introduction into a state, no positive enactment of the sovereign authority being necessary. Dr. Thornwell clearly stated this theory of the legal basis of slavery:

In the first place, slavery has never, in any country so far as one knows, arisen under the operation of statute law. It is not a municipal institution, it is not the arbitrary creature of the State, it has not sprung from the mere force of legislation. Law defines,

[91] *De Republica* (Knowles, ed.), I, v, 32, quoted by J. C. Hurd, *op. cit.,* I, 165.
[92] *Op. cit.,* pp. 308-309.

modifies and regulates it, as it does every other species of property, but *law* never *created* it. The law found it in existence, and being in existence, the law subjects it to fixed rules. On the contrary what is local and municipal is the abolition of slavery. The states that are now non-slaveholding, have been made so by positive statute. Slavery exists, of course, in every nation in which it is not prohibited.[93]

An opinion contrary to this legal theory had been handed down in England in the famous Somerset case, of 1772, by Lord Mansfield. Refusing to return Somerset to his master, who had brought him from a British colony, and from whom he had escaped, Mansfield granted a habeas corpus on the ground that he became a freeman *ipso facto* upon coming into England, because there could be no slavery under the common law of England. In a dictum he declared:

The state of slavery is of such a nature, that it is incapable of being introduced on any reasons, moral or political; but only positive law, which preserves its force long after the reasons, occasion, and time itself from whence it was created is erased from memory: it's so odious, that nothing can be suffered to support it, but positive law.[94]

The significance of this decision can readily be seen as destroying the authority of the master beyond the limits of his own state, and as giving the institution a standing dependent solely upon local law. Throughout the slavery controversy, anti-slavery jurists argued that the Mansfield decision was authority for the contention that slavery could not exist under the common law. Since the common law of England was inherited by the American States as the basis of their legal systems, the slaveholders had to meet this contention. This they did in several ways. One group dis-

[93] *The State of the Country*, p. 13. Italics in the original. For similar views see Cobb, *op. cit.*, p. 82; Dabney, *op. cit.*, p. 61.

[94] 20 *State Tr.* 80, *Lofft* 1, 98 *Eng. Dec.* 499, 510.

puted Mansfield's opinion outright, contending that he was wrong in holding that slavery had never been recognized by the English courts. Arguing purely from an historical study of earlier English cases, they pointed out that the English courts had recognized the status of a slave on two grounds. One of these grounds had been the infidelity of the unbaptized Negro, the reason being that infidelity negatived legal personality and permitted the law of property to operate as upon an animal.[95] The second ground was that in enforcing the comity of nations the courts had recognized the general practice throughout the world of holding persons to service, and had given the master an action sufficient to enforce the service of his slave if brought into England from a slave nation.[96] Under the Southern theory of the nature of the master's property rights in the slave, this second ground was a sufficient base for an answer to the Mansfield opinion.

Another group limited the definite authority of the Somerset case to England. They contended that it had no force to establish the principle that slavery was the creature of positive law for all common law nations. The Mansfield doctrine, being judge-made law, became a part of the common law of England, but at too late a date to have been inherited in the American States. Support for this view came in 1827 when Lord Stowell in deciding the case of the slave Grace in admiralty court recognized custom as a proper foundation for slavery within the British Empire and, con-

[95] For a review of this legal theory see *supra*, Chap. I, notes 48, 49, and 50. The English cases are also discussed in Cobb, *op. cit.*, pp. 159-175, and Sawyer, *op. cit.*, pp. 319-326. See also Neal *v.* Farmer, 9 *Ga.* 576-580.

[96] Cobb, *op. cit.*, p. 162. See especially Madrozo *v.* Willis (1820), 3d *B. & A.* 353 106 *Eng. Dec.* 692, holding: "A native of a country where slavery is not prohibited by law may recover in a court of England, at common law, the value of slaves wrongfully seized by a British officer, on board of a ship of a country allowing slavery. And the master can recover damages, generally at common law, for the loss of services, when his slaves have been taken from him."

sequently, limited the effect of the Mansfield doctrine to the isle of Great Britain.[97]

A third group was willing to admit with Mansfield that the law of slavery was never a part of the common law of England; and, consequently, that the common law did not *proprio vigore* bring slavery to the American colonies. But they differed with his opinion that slavery was the creature of positive law. Their theory was that the body of English common law did not have an exclusive operation when brought into the Colonies. They accepted it in so far as it was applicable to their conditions, which were different in many particulars from conditions in the mother country. They accepted it as slaveholding communities supplemented by their own customs, which local common law was in harmony with a higher common law, the law of nations.[98]

There was another theory that attempted to reconcile slavery with the common law. According to it, the institution was not foreign to the law inherited from England. It was the theory that the common law recognized the existence of any status found in society; that it attached to and operated on the slave relation in the same way as it operated upon marriage, etc. As Representative Keitt of South Carolina said, "it did lay hold of slavery, as it did of every other social fact, when it came to settle the relations of society."[99] The common law had certainly operated upon villenage which it was claimed was almost a protype of American slavery.

American legal opinion, however, remained divided between the Mansfield doctrine that slavery was the creature of positive law and the Southern theory that it was based on

[97] 2 *Hagg. Adm. Rep.* 94, 107. Stowell went so far as to charge that Mansfield had gone contrary to precedent in England and had made new law.

[98] The leading case developing this theory of the legal basis of slavery was Neal *v.* Farmer, 9 *Ga.* 555.

[99] Speech, Jan. 15, 1857, *Congressional Globe*, 34th Cong., 3rd Sess., Appendix, p. 141. See also *supra*, pp. 113-14.

international law and remained in full force and vigor everywhere until abolished by a sovereign power. The principal was involved in a number of practical government problems. The federal judiciary had to decide it in relation to the slave trade. Chief Justice Marshall in the case of the Antelope applied international law to return to the owners a number of slaves captured from a Spanish ship by an American revenue cutter. Although directly upholding the slave trade as sanctioned by the usages and general assent of the nations, Marshall stated the principle as applying to slavery as well in these words: "Slavery, then, has its origin in force; but as the world has agreed that it is a legitimate result of force, the state of things which is thus produced by general consent, cannot be pronounced unlawful."[100]

The principle was involved also in the return of fugitive slaves. It was argued by the free States that the clause in the constitution (Art. IV, sec. 2, cl. 3) was the slaveholders' only protection; whereas the slave States contended that the Constitution did not confer the right of reclaiming the fugitive, that it merely secured and insured a right recognized as a part of the comity of international law. The question was never directly decided by the Supreme Court.[101]   In the dispute over the extension of slavery into the territories this legal principle was continually involved. The slaveholders contended that the institution went into all territory acquired by the United States as a matter of course and remained until the sovereign power destroyed it. International law was sufficient to provide a legal basis for slavery everywhere, un-

[100] 10 *Wheaton* 121.

[101] In the leading case on the fugitive slave act of 1793, Justice Story's *dicta* accepted the Mansfield doctrine. He said that had it not been for the fugitive slave clause in the Constitution a free State would have been at liberty to set the runaway slave free. Prigg *v.* Commonwealth (1842), 16 *Peters*, 610. Justice Baldwin on circuit court gave the opinion that the Constitution did not confer but only secured the right to reclaim the fugitive. Johnson *v.* Tompkins *et al* (1833) 1 *Baldwin C. C.*, 571, *Fed. Cases* 7416.

til local law abolished it, even though there was not a slave upon which the law could operate.[102]

They ran into a difficulty, however, in applying the theory to the territory acquired from Mexico. There slavery had already been abolished by positive act of the Mexican government; and it was pointed out that the rules of international law would keep the laws of the ceded territory in force until they were abrogated by positive act of the new government. The Southerners admitted the rule to be correct in the field of private or civil law which affected the relations of one individual to another within the ceded territory; but they contended that when the law affected the relation of people to their sovereign, the force of the public or political law ceased *eo instanti* with the transfer of the territory. In order to establish the fact that slavery was a political institution it was necessary only to inquire into the relation in which slavery stood to the Constitution. Under that instrument slavery was a basis for both representation and direct taxation. The Mexican law of slavery ceased, therefore, with the cession of the territory to the United States, and the rules of international law sprang up immediately as the only law applicable.[103]

In last analysis the Southern theory of the legal basis of slavery provided a purely extra-constitutional support for the institution. It had arisen everywhere entirely apart from the force of that instrument. As we shall see the corollary advanced by the slaveholder was that there was no power under the Constitution to interfere with the operation of the rules of international law upon the institution of slavery.

[102] See the Speech of Representative Millison of Virginia, Feb. 21, 1850, contending that slavery existed in California and New Mexico even though there was not a single slave there. *Congressional Globe*, 31st Cong., 1st Sess., Appendix, p. 187.

[103] For an excellent exposition of the *eo instanti* doctrine, see the Speech of Senator Berrien of Georgia, Feb. 11, 1850, *ibid.*, pp. 202-209.

THEORIES OF THE FUTURE OF SLAVERY

Finally, having reviewed the theories of the origin and legal status of the institution, we now come to a brief consideration of the theories about the future of the institution. Here we find many and diverse ideas expressed. One large group considered slavery as a temporary state that would pass away in the natural course of events, just as villenage had passed in Europe. By some it was pictured as a stage in the government of man, analogous to Russia which was passing through a stage of despotism.[104]   Others thought of it as a training school for an inferior race, which should last only until that race was prepared for civilization. It might be brought to an end through the agency of gradual legal amelioration. Others looking at the economic and climatic aspects, contended that slavery in the South would last until the white man was able to cultivate safely the Southern savannah and prairie, and successfully compete with slave labor in staple production.[105]   Another view held that slavery would not cease until the earth and all things upon its surface had reached a state of physical maturity, a time beyond human calculation.[106]   Then there was a group who believed slavery to be retreating into the tropics, its natural habitat, being pushed ever southward by the encroachment of free labor.[107] Taken as a whole, these groups considered the life of the institution as being transitory, although to many of them the end was not in sight before the Messianic dawn.

On the other hand, there was a group who openly avowed a belief in perpetualism. One element of this group said that the relation of the races could never change regardless of the passage of time and the humanitarian endeavors

[104] F. A. Ross, *Slavery Ordained of God* (Philadelphia, 1857), p. 186.
[105] T. R. R. Cobb, *op. cit.*, p. 221.   [106] Matthew Estes, *op. cit.*, p. 186.
[107] J. H. Van Evrie, "Slavery Extension," *DeBow*, XV (1853), pp. 1-14.

of individuals.[108]   The other group held that the slavery principle had always existed and would exist throughout all eternity, regardless of the race element.[109]

The perpetualists composed a large part of the Southern propagandists, and as a result, there occurred during the fifties an agitation looking toward expansion and imperialism. This imperialism, under the impact of missionary zeal, economic prosperity, and nationalism, sought to extend the institution of slavery under the principle of federalism. Many manifestations of this spirit are found in the writings of the slaveholders.   One of them wrote:

We anticipate no terminus to the institution of slavery.   It is the means whereby the white man is to subdue the tropics all around the globe to order and beauty, and to the wants and interests of an ever expanding civilization.[110]

Some of them contended that slavery was adapted to the North and Northwest and that only legal restrictions kept it out.[111]   Another said, "the Lone Star of our Empire attracts our political needle to the tropics; there with our Africans will we expand."[112]   Again it was expressed that "our origin, our manifest destiny, summon us to win a name, the noblest in history."   One of the clearest statements showing the extent to which some Southern thinkers went is found in a letter of Beverley Tucker of Virginia to Governor Hammond of South Carolina.

Let us get a Southern Confederacy, emancipate the Southern colonies of Great Britain—take them in and establish the slave trade

[108] This was the group that believed in the separate origin of the Negro.   See *infra*, Ch. VI.

[109] George Fitzhugh was the leading exponent of this group.

[110] W. H. Holcombe, *The Alternative* (New Orleans, 1860), p. 7.

[111] Percy Roberts, "African Slavery Adapted to the North and Northwest," *DeBow*, XXV (1858), 379-395.

[112] W. O. Prentiss, *Sermon, St. Peter's Church, Charleston, November 21* (Charleston, 1860), p. 18.

under proper regulations. Settle a colony of blacks on the Spanish Main or Hispanolia under a *territorial* government and let them colonize themselves. . . . As I read the writing on the wall this is what it imports and the savagery of Africa is to be diluted by civilization carried from America, as a return cargo for slaves. The circuit is large, but not more than the gulf stream makes. . . . God works on this scale and we pigmies set ourselves to thwart his plans.[113]

Thus the result of these imperialistic desires led to the agitation for a reopening of the foreign slave trade so that sufficient labor might be secured to expand the institution of domestic slavery throughout the western hemisphere and insure its future security and progress.

[113] ?, 1850, MS. in the Library of Congress.

CHAPTER IV

THE RELATION OF SLAVERY TO GOVERNMENT

THE STATUS OF THE INSTITUTION WITHIN THE STATE

HAVING done with the theories of the legal basis of slavery, we now turn to a consideration of its status within the State and under the Federal Constitution. As an institution slavery had its primary relation to the State. Since its place was not created by positive act of the State, however, it becomes important to inquire into the exact legal control that the State exerted over the institution by means of protective, regulatory, or prohibitive powers.

In the separate States it was often claimed that the declarations or bills of rights in the constitutions, which declared inalienable the natural rights of man to life and liberty operated to free the Negro. One answer to this contention, made by strict constructionists, limited the protection of the bill to the posterity of those who had entered into the political society. As the African had formed no part of the original social compact he remained alien to the body politic.[1] Under another construction, the bill was regarded as being the declaration of the "natural rights of man," not a declaration of the "powers of government," or of the "social obligations" or "rights of society."[2] Men might be born equally free in a state of nature and yet not remain so in a state of society. Finally the argument was made that the framers did not intend the declaration to be so broad as to include slaves since they themselves were slaveholders. Contemporary opinion

---

[1] "Locke, The Debate, No. II," Article in the *Richmond Enquirer*, Mar. 27, 1832. See also the Speech of Summers, *ibid.*, Feb. 16.

[2] Speech of J. H. Gholson, *ibid.*, Jan. 21.

was the best rule for judicial interpretation of the organic law. But some went so far as to concede that it did apply to the slaves and guaranteed them their rights. However, they insisted that slavery was necessary in order that these rights of the Negro be secured. Moreover, the duty of the masters had also to be weighed in reference to all other rights and duties springing from the social state.[3]

Interpreting the bills of rights in such manner that they did not affect slavery, the question arose as to the competency of the powers of the State government to affect the institution. The whole problem was thoroughly discussed during the great debate on slavery in the Virginia House of Delegates of 1831-1832. At that time the discussion resolved itself into a controversy over property rights and legislative powers. Did the legislature have any power to destroy the institution by destroying property in slaves? By some it was contended that such property was a danger to the State and that under the plea of public necessity, a power superior to all laws, the legislature could abolish it.[4] They pointed out that certainly a plenary power in the legislature on this subject was in no manner restricted by the Constitution of the United States, for the fifth amendment, requiring just compensation in case of confiscation of property, was a restriction on the national government and not the State legislatures. The other side insisted, however, that such power, while existing in all communities, was not delegated to the legislature, but remained in the State as a political community and could be exercised only by a convention. Since no grant was made in the Constitution, it was fallacious to claim that it was an inherent power of the legislature. On such ground it was

[3] See for this view, "Liberty and Slavery," Review by "R," *Southern Literary Messenger*, XXII (1856), 382.

[4] J. A. Chandler brought out this theory, Speech, Jan. 17, *Richmond Enquirer*, Feb. 24, 1832.

as logical to claim that the judiciary could emancipate by *habeas corpus*.[5] Secondly, in answer to the argument that the legislature might confiscate for public use under its delegated power of eminent domain, they pointed out that the exercise of this power depended upon public necessity and just compensation.[6] Only upon the fulfillment of these requirements was its exercise possible for the purchasing by the State of the slave property.[7]

From this the discussion shifted to one concerning the nature of slave property. Some of the delegates held that it was property *sui generis* and did not come under the constitutional guarantee, that it was a form of property determined by statute; consequently, that it might be destroyed by statute.[8] The slaveholder replied that it was impossible to specify in the Constitution everything that was comprehended by property; but as slavery was an established form of property at the time of the adoption of the Constitution, it was included under the constitutional guarantee.[9] Again they openly denied that any property was statutory, but rather, that anything might become property that a man appropriates to himself, without violating the law of the land.

Then the emancipationists argued that the rules of property such as the laws of descent and of primogeniture were determined by statute and might be repealed at any time. On this ground, they contended that a State might modify the rules of descent and thus liberate the *post nati* slaves; for the master's right in this case was not absolute, as in the case of a slave in being, but was dependent upon a contin-

[5] "Locke, the Debate, No. IV," *ibid.*, April 3.

[6] Article III, Clause 9 of State Constitution of Virginia.

[7] See the speech of Thomas Marshall, Jan. 14, *Speeches.*

[8] W. B. Preston, Jan. 16, *Richmond Enquirer*, Feb. 9, 1832.

[9] J. T. Brown in his Speech Jan. 18 held that the statute declaring slaves to be property was in force at the adoption of the Constitution and was to be recorded as supplementary to and explanatory of the article in the Constitution. *Speeches.*

gency, that the slave be born. It was a right in expectancy and did not vest until birth; therefore, it could be legislated on prospectively and the right *in futuro* would never come into being. In answer, the pro-slavery theory was that the rule of *partus sequitur ventrem* (that the child shall follow the condition of the mother) had come down through both the civil and the common law, and that a right to change the rules of property *inter vivos* was not to be used as the power of confiscation or appropriation of private property. An abrogation of the rules of descent would be tantamount to declaring it property no longer, for the value of the female slaves depended upon the value of the offspring. The master had the same ethical right to the offspring as he had to the produce of his land or to the increase of his animals. Furthermore, applying a strictly legal argument, the doctrine of contingency was destroyed: "If you cannot own a child until born, you cannot emancipate a child unborn"; but at the instant of birth, the right of property vests, and an act divesting cannot be antecedent in its operation.[10]

The view appears from this debate that the prohibitive function of the State government was so circumscribed by limitations that it was not competent to abolish slavery. It was the accepted theory in the South that it would take an act of the sovereign power expressed through the constituent function of the State in order formally to abolish slavery.

The powers of the State legislature were significant, nevertheless, when used as a protective and regulatory function. Here was the source of the legal incidents that attached

[10] See for this argument Brown's Speech, Jan. 18, *ibid.* Dew, *loc. cit.*, objected to the *post nati* doctrine on the ground that it changed an estate in fee simple into an estate for years. For the entire discussion see the proceedings of the debate published in the *Richmond Enquirer*, January to June, 1832, also *Speeches*, being a collection published in pamphlet form. See also "Locke, The Debate," a series of Essays in the *Richmond Enquirer* and [B. W. Leigh], *The Letter of Appomatox* (Richmond, 1832).

to the slave-relationship. The rights and duties of the parties to the relation were determined by statutes. In every one of the slaveholding States the homicide of a slave was declared to be a murder, and the security of limb and the general comfort of body were provided for, with penalties for cruelty of masters.[11] On the other hand, the slave was given certain rights and incurred certain liabilities under the law. For instance, he was individually held amenable to the law; and when he violated it, he was taken from the master and tried. If found guilty, he was punished by the State.

Besides certain rights that the slave had secured through enacted law, he had acquired many others through usage and custom. As an able lawyer of the South remarked:

> Though the slave's right to property is not known *de jure*, yet it exists, and is practically recognized *de facto*—as much so as the property of a free person; and in their intercourse with the world it is universally observed and respected. Like the Roman slaves they have their *peculium*, to which the master lays no claim.[12]

Viewing the institution in this light, the slaveholder contended that the slave had the status of a person under the law as well as the status of property. The fact that the slave was specified as a chattel was merely a fiction of the law. The meaning was not to mark the slave a thing in contrast to a person, but a *chattel personal* in contradistinction to real estate.

The point was often made that the evils of slavery so frequently charged by the abolitionists were not inherent in the system, but were mere incidents of it and were susceptible to legal reform. Moreover, it was freely admitted that much of the slave code, being remnants of British Colonial legislation, was obsolete and therefore unenforced. The

[11] See J. B. O'Neall, *The Negro Law of South Carolina* (Columbia, 1848), Ch. II, sec. ii; Cobb, *op. cit.*, p. 84; Sawyer, *op. cit.*, p. 211, *passim*.

[12] Sawyer, *op. cit.*, p. 212.

need for police regulation following the abolition propaganda was the reason assigned for not having repealed many obsolete statutes. With the idea of mitigating the system under the reforming hand of the law, a movement was begun in the fifties urging the enactment of legislation to this end. The main feature of this movement was the desire to extend to the slaves protection of their domestic relations, first by making legal their marriages and secondly by preserving the relations between parent and child in the sale of slaves. A third feature was the desire to repeal the laws prohibiting slaves from being taught to read and write. These ideas of reform were very generally approved by the planters so that it would seem that a period of amelioration was about to begin.[13] By some it was even advocated that masters be prevented from using slaves as security for their debts. George Fitzhugh suggested that a system of entails and primogeniture was due to the slaves to prevent them from being sold under execution or to be separated at each descent.[14]

There were a number of problems which the legislative authority had to deal with that had an indirect bearing upon the institution of slavery. Of first importance, as measures protective of the institution, were the laws passed against the free Negroes. They were denied the ballot under the theory that they were not members of the body politic; they were prohibited from entering the State and were denied residence in the State on penalty of enslavement. Of similar purpose was the limitation upon the master's power to manumit. In several of the States it was advocated that the free Negroes be prohibited from employment in the mechanical trades because of the economic pressure upon the poor whites.

[13] See article, "Slavery in the United States," *Southern Quarterly Review*, XII (1846), 91. Apparently there was a plan providing for such legislation agitated before the Legislature of North Carolina. See article, "Slave Marriages," *DeBow*, XIX (1855), 130.

[14] "Modern Civilization," *DeBow*, XXIX (1860), 65.

One incident that is illustrative of the theory of State power over the free Negro is the report submitted to the Maryland legislature of 1844 on the removal of the free Negro element from a section of that State:

They do not derive their rights from the Constitution. They had no part in the formation of our Government. They are not members of our community. They enjoy no rights as citizens; . . . the free Negroes have their *independent existence*, by the consent of the Government of Maryland; and that Government has the right at any time to repeal the law giving them their separate existence, or their special privileges. . . .

The free negroes are creatures of the law, the beings of special statutes. . . . We constantly pass acts taking away a portion of their privileges—and it would be extraordinary, if we can not take away the whole when we take away a part. . . .[15]

This report provided that the Negroes be taken by the State and worked out until sufficient funds were made to pay for transportation.

This leads into the problem of the domestic slave trade. It was generally conceded that the trade could be destroyed by the States and some sentiment existed for doing so. However, the internal traffic was usually defended on the ground of being a necessary incident of the institution. The reformer felt that the evils of the trade could be abolished through careful regulation. The defense of the trade was based on the right of property; that being established, the right of transfer naturally grew out of it. Furthermore, the transfer was intended to provide a master more capable of caring for the slave. Finally, it was merely a rearrangement and readjustment of the slave's position, without affecting the condition in which he was born.

[15] *Document M., Jan. 25, 1844, House of Delegates, Report of the Select Committee on Removal of the Free Colored Population from Charles County.*

THE STATUS OF SLAVERY UNDER THE CONSTITUTION

From the State to which slavery had its primary relationship, we proceed to consider its status in the Union. As in the case of the State bills of rights, the American Declaration of Independence expounded principles incompatible with slavery. The anti-slavery group inferred that the Declaration was intended to imply that slavery was a natural evil incapable of being legalized. They claimed that the document had the organic force of constitutional law to the Union. The slaveholders countered with the contention that it was a justificatory statement to the outside world and not an act of organic legislation ascertaining the rights of the citizens within. Its only enactment of organic nature was the independence of the American States.[16]   Nathaniel Macon remarked during the Missouri debates: "Is it not wonderful, that, if the Declaration of Independence gave authority to emancipate, that the patriots who made it never proposed any plan to carry it into execution?" He furthermore insisted that the fact that the words of the Declaration were no part of the Constitution "is as true as that they are no part of a book."[17]   Another explanation held that the Declaration referred to States and nations when asserting the equality of mankind, and not to individuals. "All men in their national or state capacity were equally at liberty, to rid themselves of oppression, and act for themselves—a right which as individual citizens they did not possess and could not exercise as against an established government."[18]   Others advanced the view

---

[16] For this view, see Dabney, *op. cit.*, p. 72. For the early attack on the Declaration in the South, see *supra*, p. o.

[17] Speech, Jan. 20, 1820, *Annals*, 16th Cong., 1st Sess., p. 227.

[18] "Channing's Duty of the Free States," *Southern Quarterly Review*, II (1842), 156. With this idea J. H. Hammond wrote L. Tappan, Sept. 1, 1850: "Jefferson . . . was maintaining the justice of a combination of the political societies of America to throw off the yoke of England." MS. in the Library of Congress. See also [Dalcho], *Practical Considerations:* "The American Revolution was a family quarrel among equals. In this the negroes had no concern; their condition

that the slaves of the United States were not included in the Declaration or any constitutional provision except when expressly designated; neither "man" nor "citizen" applied to them, but "all other persons."[19]

Slavery as an institution under the Constitution offered many problems for disagreement between the anti-slavery and the pro-slavery factions. According to the Southern theory there was no necessity of finding a positive constitutional sanction; it was sufficient as a corollary to the delegated authority theory of the federal state to demonstrate that there was not an abolition power in that instrument. Thus the theory of the slaveholder held that the Constitution was a compact between sovereign States by which a government came into being with certain specifically delegated powers, beyond the scope of which the States reserved control over municipal affairs. Secondly, that "the Southern States, upon entering into this compact brought with them, as a part of their social system, as the substratum of their industrial pursuits, the institution of slavery," and demanded its security as a *sine qua non* before acceding to the compact. In the Constitution Convention, a compromise was effected by which the Northern States recognized the legality of and guaranteed the secure enjoyment of that institution.

The three clauses involved in the compromise were the one keeping the slave trade open until 1808 (Art. I, sec. 9, cl. 1), the one providing that three-fifths of the slaves should be counted as a basis for taxation and for representation in the House (Art. I, sec. 2, cl. 3), and the one requiring the return of persons "held to service or labor," escaping into other states (Art. IV, sec. 2, cl. 3). Beyond the obligations arising

---

remained, and must remain unchanged. They have no more to do with the celebration of the day [4 July] than with the landing of the Pilgrims on the Rock at Plymouth."

[19] Sawyer, *op. cit.*, p. 208, note.

from these clauses, the citizens of the free States had no more to do with slavery than had the subjects of Great Britain.[20] As for the policy of the government, it must always remain impartial and neutral upon any question relative to slavery, for upon that question it had no power to act.[21] Following out this theory, it is easy to see how the Constitution did no violence to the first contention of the slaveholder, that is, that slavery existed in the territories without positive legislation providing for its introduction.

To insure the carrying out of this doctrine, that the central government had no power over slavery, there developed the theory that slavery had a definite sectional status, and that it was necessary to maintain a parity of sections in order to preserve the Union in its true form and to prevent an accretion of power in the central government. It was argued that a balance of power would successfully restrict the government to the limits of the Constitution. Calhoun saw clearly that upon no other ground could the South remain in the Union with slavery; and, as he saw his section gradually losing, he sought to find some check that would, despite the lost ground, maintain the equilibrium.[22]

With the same thought, Langdon Cheves declared in the Southern Convention that the Union had already been dissolved: "What was the Union? A government wisely and

[20] For this idea see: *Journal of the State Convention Held in Milledgeville, Ga.* (1850), p. 34, also Senator Toombs, "Slavery, Its Constitutional Status," *Debow*, XX (1850), pp. 581-605.

[21] Dr. Thomas Cooper wrote Hammond Jan. 18, 1836, desiring that he take the stand that if the slavery question was ever brought up in the Halls of Congress the Southern representatives should declare the Union dissolved and retire. "If the Northern members claim the right of discussion, it implies *a claim to act on the question*; for why discuss a subject you are prohibited to act on? . . . You should as I think, force the honest Southern members into a private caucus to lay down the plea on what you must finally act. I forsee it will end in a dissolution of the union, for we have no safety in any other measure." MS. in the Library of Congress.

[22] See his Speech on the Slavery question, March 4, 1850, *Works*, IV, 542.

practically balanced—balanced by a distribution of power which protected all interests and all sections of the country. . . . Property [in the South] is no longer protected, on the contrary war is made on it."[23]   Hence, it was said that the compromise of 1850 virtually repealed the Constitution and that new terms of union had been submitted to the Southern States.[24]   Dr. Palmer, the great Presbyterian divine, said on the eve of the Civil War that the guarantees of the Constitution had been abolished politically and that there was no chance for a renewal.[25]   The parity of the sections, of course, depended not only upon keeping the common territory open to slavery and admitting new Slave States as often as needed, but also it depended upon a sufficient supply of slave labor to settle that common territory.   Consequently, it was argued that the laws closing the foreign slave trade were contrary to the spirit of the Constitution in that they discriminated against the Southern form of labor and gave the Northern section advantage in the settlement of territory.[26]

[23] *Speech in the Southern Convention* (1850), p. 17.

[24] Thornwell, *The State of the Country*, p. 9.

[25] "Slavery a Divine Trust," *Fast Day Sermons*, p. 69.

[26] See *A Report on Slavery and the Slave Agitation* (printed by order of the H. of R. of Texas). Also *DeBow* XXV (1858), 121, quoting the report on re-opening the slave trade before the Southern Commercial Convention at Montgomery by W. L. Yancey. Senator Hammond wrote in 1858 that the South should accept realities, that she did not have slaves to colonize new territory, and all that would be acquired would be colonized by Yankees and foreigners, and come in as free states. "I propose also today that I am not in favor of any further extension of slave territory; that our 850,000 sq. mi. are enough for us. . . . Let us consolidate our Great Empire, develop it, ignore all aids and stand ready to rule the Union or send it to the devil." Hammond to W. G. Simms, Jan. 20, 1858, MS. in the Library of Congress. In a reply from a friend he was advised against the policy, not on the grounds that it was absurd, but that "if the north will let us alone and allow us to develop in civilization in our own way, I would be willing to allow them to colonize as many new States as they pleased, the great secret is to find out a preventive for this interference. . . . It is not whether this state [Kansas] should be admitted into the Union with a Pro-Slavery constitution, but whether the States now in, having slave labor, shall be permitted to go in

Although the general plea was that the Federal Government had absolutely no power over the institution of slavery, yet it was contended, at times, that the Constitution protected the institution. By implication it did so by withholding all power of injury and, expressly, by the fugitive slave clause (Art. IV, sec. 2, cl. 3), by the guarantee against domestic violence upon the application of a State (Art. IV, sec. 4), and by the power of Congress to call forth troops "to execute the laws of the Union, to suppress insurrections and repel invasions" (Art. I, sec. 8, cl. 15).[27] However, the implications that might be drawn from this interpretation were far-reaching and out of harmony with the general strict construction of Congressional powers. Yet there were many in the North who declared that the Constitutional guarantees were the great bulwark of Southern institutions. Daniel Webster in a speech at Capon Springs in Virginia shortly before his death declared that the North was willing to maintain the compact and execute the guarantees.

The whole anti-slavery faction of the North repudiated the idea of living under a Constitution that fostered slavery. To them the spirit of the Constitution was not more than a toleration of it for the time being. Consequently, they thought it incumbent upon the government to hinder the spread of slavery and to exert all its powers toward its eventual destruction. Therefore, to them the problem became one of finding powers in the Constitution that could be applied directly or indirectly upon slavery. They searched for the power in individual clauses and not in a general interpretation of the nature of the entire instrument.

In the discussion over the admission of Missouri as a State the entire question was for the first time thoroughly investi-

---

the enjoyment of their rights. . . ." O. P. Aldrich to J. H. H., Feb. 14, 1858. MS. in the Library of Congress.

[27] This argument is stated in Toombs, *loc. cit.*, p. 585.

gated. At that time the problem was to find some means of checking the spread of the institution. It was asserted, on the one side, that Congress might impose certain restrictions upon a State entering the Union; and, on the other, that such restrictions would either destroy the equality of the States or would become a nullity after the State entered the Union. Then it was argued that Congress had complete sovereignty over the territories and could therefore abolish slavery during the territorial state. This power was derived from the following clause: "The Congress shall have power to dispose of and make all needful rules and regulations respecting the territory or other property belonging to the United States" (Art. IV, sec. 3, cl. 2). The slaveholder replied that this clause authorized Congress to make rules and regulations for "the territory itself, that is, the domain, the land, the actual soil belonging to the United States; and not the inhabitants of the territory." The word "territory" being immediately followed by the words "or other property" was sufficient proof to establish this meaning.[28] The clause contained no grant of power to legislate over persons and private property within a territory.[29] Again, it was said that a denial of the right to hold slaves in the territories was not a needful regulation; and, moreover, that the power was limited by the words "and nothing in this Constitution shall be so construed as to prejudice any claims of the United States or any particular State" (Art. IV, sec. 3, cl. 2), which protected the slavery rights of the Southern States.

The second source from which indirectly the complete

[28] See Speech of Leake of Mississippi, Jan. 19, 1820, *Annals of Congress*, 16th Cong., 1st Sess., p. 198. Madison interpreted the clause in this light that the power "cannot well be extended beyond the territories as property and a power 'to make the provisions really needful or necessary' for the Government of settlers until ripe for admission as States in the Union." See Letter to Robert Walsh, 1819, *The Writings of James Madison* (Hunt, ed., New York, 1910), IX, 4.

[29] Smyth of Virginia, Jan. 28, *ibid.*, p. 1003.

sovereignty of Congress over the territories was drawn was the treaty making power (Art. II, sec. 2, cl. 2). The power to acquire, and as a necessary consequence, to govern territory was held to be ancillary to the power to make treaties. Here again it was pointed out that the right to acquire territory under the treaty making power was itself an implication and not a specific grant. The right to govern, being claimed as an incident to the power to acquire, was a second implication; and, finally, the power to exclude slavery under the power to govern became a third implication from express power. Granting the first two implications, under strict construction the third fell because it was neither necessary nor proper to the execution of the former, that is, to acquire and govern. In other words, the slaveholder admitted that the power of Congress over the territories was exclusive but not absolute.[30] The following paragraph summarizes his argument:

The power to govern is, therefore, merely derivative and subordinate to the express powers delegated over the territories, as may be necessary and proper for those purposes of protection. It cannot be construed to extend to destroy domestic relations or title to property validly acquired under the laws of the Slave States, by setting up territorial laws to destroy such rights; and thus to deprive the Slave States of their equal rights to settle the territories with their slave property.[31]

There were two other clauses in the Constitution in which the opponents of slavery sought power to restrict the spread of the institution. First, it was claimed under the clause pro-

[30] Toombs, *loc. cit.* An interesting question arose in relation to the sovereignty of the ceded territory. Where was the sovereignty after the surrender of it by the ceding nation? The territory was governed by Congress and yet Congress' powers were limited by the Constitution. A similar problem arose over abolition in the District of Columbia. In this case, however, Congress was directly granted exclusive legislative power over it, and, it might be inferred, remained the sovereign power regardless of the spirit of the remainder of the Constitution.

[31] *Address of the Committee of the Mississippi Convention to the Southern States*, p. 9.

hibiting Congress from closing the slave trade before 1808 (Art. I, sec. 9, cl. 1). In this case, it was argued that the grant of power to Congress over the general subject of commerce was merely suspended in regard to the slave trade, for a period; and that the suspension recognized the competency of the general commerce power over the importation and migration of slaves. The clause was construed at other times to operate with the force of a negative pregnant, that is, the implication of a positive power derived from negative language. From the restrictive language before 1808 was implied a positive grant of power after 1808.[32] Here was a power that might be applied in restricting the removal of slaves from State to State, or from a State to a territory, because it was said, that importation meant the bringing into this country from a foreign country, and that migration meant the taking from one State to another or from a State to a territory within this country. The two terms did not refer to the same thing because a tax could be placed upon the former, "importation," but not the latter, "migration." Migration did not apply to citizens because of the comity clause (Art. IV, sec. 2, cl. 1), "The citizens of each State shall be entitled to all privileges and immunities of citizens of the several States."[33]

The proponent of slavery replied that the clause was not a grant of power, nor did it enlarge any power already granted, and that to construe it as doing so would change the government of limited powers into one of absolute authority.[34] It was explained why the two terms were necessary:

[32] See Speech of Cook of Illinois in the House of Representatives, Feb. 4, 1820. *Annals*, 16th Cong., 1st Sess., p. 1094, and Pinckney of South Carolina, Feb. 14, *ibid.*, pp. 1316-1317.

[33] For examples of this reasoning, see Speech of Foote of Connecticut in the Senate, Jan. 27, *Annals*, 16th Cong., 1st Sess., 969, and Morril of New Hampshire in the House, Jan. 17, *ibid.*, p. 137.

[34] See Leake of Mississippi, Jan. 19, *ibid.*, p. 198; Barbour of Virginia, Feb. 1, *ibid.*, p. 317.

"importation" applied to "slaves" while "migration" applied to "free persons." Consequently, it was permitted Congress to place an import duty on the imported slaves but not on the immigration of free persons. Moreover, it was said that "migration" implied free agency which could not be predicated to a slave. But even if "migration" referred to slaves, still, as associated with "importation," it meant a coming in from a foreign country. The consequence was that Congress had power to abolish the external trade, but the internal trade was exempt from the power to prohibit.[35]

The second claim arose under the definite grant of power to regulate interstate commerce (Art. I, sec. 8, cl. 3). At the time of the Missouri Compromise a great portion of the discussion hinged around this power. The slaveholder pointed out that the suppression of the slave trade had not depended upon the power to regulate commerce alone, but also was inferred from the prohibitory clause (Art. I, sec. 9, cl. 1).[36] Moreover, the power to regulate commerce did not extend to the power to destroy commerce. Again, the power was specifically restricted by the words: "No tax or duty shall be laid on articles exported from any State" (Art. I, sec. 9, cl. 5); "no preference shall be given by any regulation of commerce or revenue to the ports of one State over those of another; nor shall vessels bound to or from one State be

---

[35] Walker of Georgia, Jan. 19, *ibid.*, p. 167, and Van Dyke of Delaware, Jan. 28, *ibid.*, p. 306. Luther Martin in his "Letter on the Federal Convention of 1787" said that this clause related solely to the importation of slaves from abroad and that the words "migration" and "importation" were "synonymous." *Elliott's Debates*, I, 372-375, quoted by Smith of Virginia, *Annals*, 16th Cong., 1st Sess., p. 994. For a similar view, see Madison, *Works*, IX, 4-8, and speech of James Iredell of North Carolina in *Elliott's Debates*, IV, 119.

[36] See the Speeches of Smyth of Virginia, Jan. 28, *Annals*, 16th Cong., 1st Sess., p. 996. Following out this logic the advocates of reopening of the slave trade said that all the laws passed by Congress upon the slave trade were unconstitutional, because there was no grant of power contained in a limitation of power. They even went so far as to deny the validity of treaties with foreign nations on the subject of the slave trade.

obliged to enter, clear, or pay duties in another" (Art. I, sec. 9, cl. 6). Certainly Congress had no power to prevent a person from taking his property from one State to another. In other words, if the transfer was to be prohibited under this clause, then slaves must be commerce, and there was no power to prohibit carrying of an article of commerce from State to State. Congress could not prevent the cotton of the South from being sent to New York. If they were to be prohibited as persons, then the power extended to white persons as well as to Negroes; and in such a case they were no longer articles of commerce and the commerce power would not support a regulation.[37] This question remained open as the Court never determined how far the power of Congress extended.[38] The matter, however, received an

[37] See Speeches of Smith of Maryland, Jan. 26, *ibid.*, p. 942; Holmes of Massachusetts, *ibid.*, p. 991; Smyth of Virginia, *ibid.*, p. 996; Harding of Kentucky, *ibid.*, p. 1079.

[38] This introduces the question whether an individual State had the power to prohibit the introduction of slaves from other States and thereby break up the interstate slave trade? The constitutions of Mississippi of 1817 and 1832 provided that the legislature could pass a law prohibiting slaves being brought into that State as merchandise. It was argued by Webster and Clay that the clause was in conflict with the commerce clause of the Constitution of the United States. In Groves *v.* Slaughter (1841), 15 *Peters* 449 the court held that the clause was merely directory to the legislature and did not operate *proprio vigore;* therefore, the point of conflict was not involved. But Taney at p. 508 declared that this power was exclusive in the separate States and that Congress could not control it under the commerce power, or any other power. Justice McLean, p. 506, concurred on the ground that slaves were persons. Justice Baldwin, p. 513, dissented on the ground that slaves were recognized as property under the Constitution. In the Passenger Cases (1848), 7 *Howard* 283, these principles were again involved. Chief Justice Taney, p. 467, reasoned that a State had the right to expel or keep out any "description of persons whom it regards as injurious to its welfare," and Justice Grier, p. 457, said that the State could act on principles of self defense which no power of Congress could restrain. Thus it would seem that the problem resolved itself into a conflict between the commerce power of Congress and the police power of the State. Consequently Berrien 2 *Op. U. S. Att'y Gen.*, 426, 817 justified the law of South Carolina in regard to free Negroes as within the police power and Wirt 1 *Op. U. S. Att'y Gen.* 659 as interfering with the power to regulate commerce. In the Dred Scott decision 19 *Howard* 519 Justice Campbell said "This Court has determined that the inter-migration of slaves was not committed to the jurisdiction of Congress." However, it must

increased importance after the general anti-slavery convention that met in London in 1840 passed a resolution condemning the domestic slave trade and suggesting that means
be taken to prevent it.

Aside from these two clauses that might be interpreted to
give Congress the power to restrict the growth and spread of
slavery, two others were suggested that might support Congressional interference with the existence of the institution
within the Slave States themselves. The power might have
been derived from a general welfare clause and the guaranty
clause. We will consider the latter in a later section dealing
with the general subject of the republican form of government. The fear that the clause delegating to Congress power
"to lay and collect taxes, duties, imposts and excises, to pay
the debts and provide for the common defense and general
welfare of the United States" (Art. I, sec. 8, cl. 1), might
endanger slavery was first discussed in the convention that rat-
ified the Federal Constitution in Virginia. Patrick Henry
pointed out that Congress might sometime exercise this in relation to slavery.[39]

Richard Hildreth, the historian, felt that an exercise of
the power to tax was the most plausible way by which Congress could interfere with slavery. By construction he gave
the clause a very broad and comprehensive character. The
power to tax for the common defense and the general wel-

---

be seen that the conclusion was reached reasoning from the premise that the
slave was a person under the Constitntion. It would seem that the opinion expressed in the Dred Scott case, that the slave was property under the Constitution,
applied to this problem, might have brought forth the opposite conclusion.

[39] *Elliott's Debates*, III, 334. Henry said: "Have they not the power to provide for the general defence and welfare? May they not think that these call
for the abolition of slavery? May they not pronounce all slaves free, and will
they not be warranted by that power?" Earlier in the debate George Mason had
said that under the power to tax Congress might effect a manumission, *ibid.*, p.
408. He was answered by Madison who showed that this was impossible under
the mode of taxing, *ibid.*, p. 418. See also the reply of Randolph, *ibid.*, p. 541.

fare was the power to do anything the end of which could be accomplished by the expenditure of money. If Congress had power to purchase Florida, Louisiana, and California under the clause, it could also vote money towards the liberation of slaves. The one question for Congress to determine was that the termination of the system of slavery was for the defense and welfare of the United States, "their defense against invasion from abroad, and insurrection at home; their welfare, moral, social, and economical, . . . and, in this point of view, it seems to matter but little whether we consider that system an illegal usurpation or a legal institution of those states in which it exists."[40]

In the last analysis, this became a question of extent of power. The slaveholder contended that the general welfare phrase was merely a limitation on the power of taxation: " 'To lay and collect taxes,' this is the power—'to pay the debts and provide for the common defense and general welfare' this is the object. 'But all duties shall be uniform'— this is the restriction. As if they had said 'Congress shall have power to lay and collect taxes, for the purposes of paying the debts, providing for the common defence and general welfare, taking care that these taxes shall be uniform.' "[41] Furthermore, he said that to interpret the power as a general welfare grant would give plenary powers to Congress, it would be completely dictatorial, and absolute.[42] Rather the power for the general welfare existed only incidental to the specific and implied powers given to the government. On one occasion, at least, the argument was made that the preamble of the Constitution granted complete power for the

[40] Despotism in America: An inquiry into the nature, results, and legal basis of the slave-holding system in the United States (Boston, 1854), pp. 241-242.

[41] See Speech of Holmes of Massachusetts, Annals, 16th Cong., 1st Sess., p. 971.

[42] Speech of Smyth of Virginia, ibid., p. 994, and Smith of Maryland, ibid., p. 942.

general welfare. It was immediately denied that the pre-amble granted any power at all.[43]

The question arose as to abolishing the institution through formal amendment to the Constitution. The pro-slavery po-sition was that an amendment could not extend to an altera-tion of society or fundamentally change the form of govern-ment. Just as to constitute the republic a monarchy would be in opposition to the compact so would it equally be in op-position to destroy the basic compromise.[44]

Aside from these several clauses that might be interpreted to give Congress the power to interfere with slavery, prob-lems relating to slavery arose under other parts of the Consti-tution. What was the status of a slave under the Constitu-tion? Was he a person or was he property? Madison had said that the true state of the case was that he partook of both qualities, "being considered by our laws in some re-spects as persons, and in others as property."[45] This was il-lustrated by the clause in the Constitution which made the slave both the basis for taxation and for representation.[46] Throughout the judicial history of slavery there existed a conflict of opinion amongst the judges on this point. Justice McLean, for one, maintained that under the Constitution slaves were persons.[47] The Justices divided in the Dred Scott case as to whether they should be considered primarily

---

[43] See Speech of Jones of Tennessee in the House of Representatives, Feb. 23, 1820, *ibid.*, p. 1459, and letter of J. H. Hammond to L. Tappan, Sept. 1, 1850, MS. in the Library of Congress. In Jacobson *v.* Massachusetts (1905), 197 *U. S.* 11, the Supreme Court handed down a decision in accord with Hammond's argu-ment. Justice Harlan said: "Although that preamble indicates the general pur-poses for which the people ordained and established the Constitution, it has never been regarded as the source of any substantive power conferred on the govern-ment of the United States, or on any of its departments."

[44] Seabrook, *op. cit.*

[45] *The Federalist*, No. 54 (Lodge, ed.), p. 340.

[46] J. K. Paulding, *op. cit.*, p. 100.

[47] See Jones v. Van Zandt (1843), 2 *McLean* 602, *Fed. Cases* 7501; Groves v. Slaughter (1841), 15 *Peters* 502; Dred Scott *v.* Sanford (1856), 19 *Howard* 393.

as persons or as property. The Dred Scott case did decide that the Negro could not become a citizen under the Constitution. According to Chief Justice Taney and Justice Daniel the Negro was not a citizen of the United States, for citizenship was limited to the white race who had entered into the body politic. Consequently, Negroes could not sue in a federal court, since that privilege was conferred only upon citizens of the United States.[48]

Another constitutional problem arose over the question whether the privileges and immunities clause (Art. IV, sec. 2, cl. 1) operated to guarantee the free Negro, who had become a citizen in one State, the rights and privileges of citizenship in the other States.[49] Many of the Southern States passed laws prohibiting the immigration of the free Negro citizens of other States. South Carolina passed a law in 1820 which subjected free Negro seamen to imprisonment upon entering the State.[50] The State claimed authority to legislate, under the police power, a power of protecting its internal peace and domestic property, which was paramount to all powers of Congress, and secondly under a concurrent power

[48] See Cobb, op. cit., p. 316, for a discussion of the citizenship of Negroes.

[49] See the Speech of Pinckney of South Carolina in the House of Representatives, Feb. 13, 1821, Annals, 16th Cong., 1st Sess., p. 1134, claiming authorship for the comity clause and asserting that it did not apply to Negroes as they could not become citizens.

[50] The law was declared unconstitutional by Judge Johnson in Circuit Court, but remained in force. Elkison v. Deliesseline (1823), 2 Wheeler Cr. Cas. 56, Federal Cases 4366. Berrien 2 Op. U. S. Att'y Gen., 426, 659, declared the law was within the police power of South Carolina; see also The Report of the Committee of the South Carolina Legislature on the Communication of the British Consul Relative to the Law Concerning Colored Seamen; see also Report of Committee of Massachusetts Senate Doc. 92 (1936) and Committee on Treatment of Senator Hoar by South Carolina, Doc. 31 (1845). In the latter the protection of the privileges and immunities clause is claimed as a citizen of Massachusetts and not of the United States; Virginia proposed to pass such a law in 1840. See Report of Select Committee of Delegates on the Controversy with New York. Here it was argued that the clause applied only to fundamental rights such as that to property, and again that the bill would not deprive a citizen of New York of any right that a citizen of Virginia might not be deprived of.

over commerce. The quarantine laws were said to cover an analogous situation.

Again over the problem of incendiary publications there arose a conflict between the police power of the State to regulate the mails and the guarantee of the freedom of the press. It was contended that the freedom of the press meant the right to publish without previous permission but did not include the publication of licentious material or freedom from responsibility after publication. Neither did it apply to a discussion of the domestic institutions of other States.[51]

Another constitutional problem incident to the slavery dispute arose over the proper interpretation of the right of petition, which was guaranteed by the first amendment to the Constitution. The Southerner argued that the right of petition extended only to questions arising under the scope of the Constitution and not to a discussion of local institutions.[52] Where the right of petition conflicted with the Houses' rules of order, it was said that the right of petition extended only to an acceptance of the petition and no discussion of the subject need follow.

Aside from the conflicts between the States and the Federal authority under the Constitution there were certain questions that were beyond the Constitution altogether and affected one State in its relation to another State. The question of incendiary literature, where citizens of one State attacked the slave institution of the Southern States was a case involved. Some contended that there was a constitutional remedy under the right of the State executive to demand rendition of fugitives from justice (Art. IV, sec. 2,

[51] See *Preamble and Resolutions on the Subject of Incendiary Publications 19 Dec., 1835* passed by the South Carolina Legislature and Replies from Virginia, North Carolina, Georgia, Alabama, and Massachusetts.

[52] Paulding, *op. cit.*, p. 104-105. See also the Speeches of Calhoun in the Senate, March 9, 1836, *Works*, II, 465, and Hammond "On the Justice of Receiving Petitions for the Abolition of Slavery," *Letters and Speeches*, p. 15.

cl. 2). To this it was replied that the citizens of one State were not amenable to the laws of other States because they were not protected by those laws. But it was argued that the privileges and immunities clause threw the protection of the laws of each State around citizens of all the other States, and this gave each State the right to punish infraction of the laws within its limits, by citizens of another State, the idea of the constructive presence of the publisher being relied upon.

The constitutional remedy was repudiated entirely by most lawyers, and an extra-constitutional remedy sought.[53] It was argued that the States remained independent nations in respect to their domestic affairs; that is, in relation to the whole field of reserve powers, beyond the delegated powers in the Constitution. International law applied *proprio vigore,* and independently of a constitutional recognition, to the co-States internally and to the foreign States externally, unless expressly, or by implication, altered or modified by the Constitution.[54] Furthermore, the institution of slavery had entered into society in the slave States to such an extent that an attack upon it was tantamount to an attack upon their government. It was claimed that the activities of the abolitionists would be sufficient cause for war between nations, but that the friendly bond of the Union suggested other remedies. Two remedies were suggested, a demand upon the States to pass penal laws providing for the punishment of incendiaries remaining within their borders,[55] and the right to make a demand for extradition of the libeler.[56]

[53] For example see Thomas Cooper, "Slavery," *loc. cit.,* p. 188.

[54] On this point it was argued that the Supreme Court would enforce international law.

[55] See *Report of Joint Committee of South Carolina Legislature on Governor McDuffie's Message on Slavery, 18 Dec., 1825.*

[56] Vattel was cited for authority, also the case of Peltier where the English Court of the King's Bench tried an Englishman for a libel published in London in the English language against Bonaparte, First Consul. For a discussion of the whole affair, see Richard Yeadon, *The Amenability of Northern Incendiaries, as*

Another question of the application of international law, or comity, arose in respect to the status of the slave under the law of domicile. If the master traveled in a free State with his slave, or if he went through a free State in order to take up residence in another State, would his slave become free by the action of the positive law of that State? According to the Mansfield doctrine it would seem that the slave relation would be abolished. The slaveholder, however, gave another answer to this problem of conflict of laws. First, he contended the domicile of the slave was determined by that of the master. Then the general principle was laid down that the status of a person was determined by the law of his domicile, that a person carries the law of his domicile with him—if the law of his domicile recognized slavery, the relation continued so long as the person did not change his domicile. Where the residence in a free State was temporary, that is, where the master did not intend to take up permanent residence, the relationship of master and slave was protected by the comity of nations, and the courts were bound to recognize the laws of his domicile.

The rules of international law worked in this manner. But in case a State refused to abide by international comity and interposed its own authority in the matter, then what remedy did the Constitution itself offer to the slaveholder? The levying of war or a tariff for retaliation was specifically prohibited. The only possible remedy arose under the clause which declared that "full faith and credit shall be given in each State to the public acts, records and judicial proceedings of every State" (Art. IV, sec. 1, cl. 1). Congress being em-

---

Well to Southern as to Northern Laws (Charleston, 1835). W. Rice, Vindex: On the Liability of the Abolitionists to Criminal Punishment, and on the Duty of Non Slave-Holding States to Suppress their Efforts (Charleston, 1835), and "Governor McDuffie's Message on Slavery 1835," in American History Leaflets, No. 10. O. H. Brownson accepted the principle that international law should apply to such cases. See Works (H. F. Brownson, ed., Detroit, 1906), XV, 55.

powered to prescribe by general laws the carrying out of this clause, it was argued that the purpose of the framers was to give strength and support to the rules of comity and incidentally to guarantee the slaveholder's right to property.[57]

THEORIES OF SLAVERY AND REPUBLICAN GOVERNMENT

The subject of slavery and republican government falls into two divisions. The first dealt with constitutional theories involved in the construction of the clause whereby the United States guarantees to every State a republican form of government (Art. IV, sec. 4). The second division dealt with the compatibility of slavery and republicanism as a problem of political science. There were two main questions involved in the first phase of the discussion. What was the force of the guaranty as a grant of power to the federal government? Secondly, what was the constitutional meaning of a republican form of government? These two questions were so intimately interwoven in the discussion that it is impossible to separate them entirely in our exposition of the general subject. Rather it will be necessary to oscillate from one to the other as we progress.

There is little contemporary evidence extant as to the intention of the framers in regard to the guaranty clause. We have already seen that the view was maintained by many during the founding period that slavery was contrary to the genius of a republic. Luther Martin in his *Letter on the Federal Convention of 1787* said that a large faction in the Convention had urged "that slavery is inconsistent with the genius of republicanism, and has a tendency to destroy those principles on which it is supported, as it lessens the sense of the equal rights of mankind and habituates us to tyranny and oppression."[58] He suggested that this sentiment was

[57] For a full discussion, see Cobb, *op. cit.*, pp. 189-200.
[58] *Elliott's Debates*, I, 374.

recognized in the guaranty clause in that "by this system of government, every State is to be protected from foreign invasion and from domestic insurrection." From this he argued that Congress should have power to prohibit the slave trade in order that the States would not be weakened and exposed to invasion and thereby become a burden to the Union.[59] Madison in *The Federalist* made no hint that slavery might come under the ban of the guaranty clause. Rather, he implies that slavery and a constitutional republican form were consistent in that the guaranty "supposes a pre-existing government to be of the form which is to be guaranteed."[60] In other words, all of the State governments existing at the framing of the Constitution were presumed to be republican and their maintenance guaranteed.

It does not appear that a definite connection was made between the guaranty clause and slavery in the ratifying conventions. General Heath in the Massachusetts Convention and James Wilson in the Pennsylvania Convention implied that slavery was unrepublican and that Congress would be able to keep it out of the new States. But they based their opinion on the commerce power of Congress rather than upon the guaranty.[61]

The history of the Congressional debate over the application of the guaranty to exclude slavery dates from the admission of Illinois into the Union in 1818. Tallmadge of New York, feeling that the Constitution submitted by Illinois did not sufficiently prohibit slavery, made the point that the duty was enjoined upon Congress to admit the State under the condition that slavery never be introduced there. He thought it was well understood that should a State, admitted into the Union with a republican government, later change its form to a monarchy, it would immediately cease

---

[59] *Ibid.*
[60] No. XLIII (Lodge, ed.), p. 271.   [61] *Elliott's Debates*, II, 129 and 423.

to be a member. And the same result would follow, he presumed, "if a State were to violate the condition on which it was admitted into this Union, by admitting the introduction of slavery."[62]

The many ramifications of the guaranty clause were brought into full light for the first time in the Missouri debates. On February 13, 1819, Tallmadge proposed an amendment to the bill admitting Missouri prohibiting the future introduction of slavery there. This amendment brought on an extended discussion in both houses of Congress concerning the compatibility of slavery and the republican form and concerning the duty of Congress under the guaranty. The point was made by the restrictionists that the guaranty became operative when Congress acted to admit a new State. At that time the duty enjoined upon Congress was to inquire into the Constitution of the territory petitioning for statehood in order to ascertain its republican form. And such a duty in the case of Missouri required the inclusion of the restriction in her Constitution because slavery was incompatible with the republican form.

The anti-slavery group expounded two theories as they sought to define the constitutional meaning of republican form. One of these defined it in terms of the history of the American Republic. The principles inherent in the republican form were those incident to the winning of American independence. The framers had incorporated into the Constitutional phrase the same principles expressed in the Declaration of Independence. Thus Fuller of Massachusetts gave as his reason for recurring to the Declaration that he could

[62] *Annals*, 15th Cong. 2nd Sess., p. 310. Roberts of Pennsylvania made the claim in 1820 that he first proposed the restricting of slavery from the territory north of the Ohio when the bill to establish a territorial government was under consideration in 1811, but because of the war the matter was deferred until a more convenient season. *Ibid.*, 16th Cong., 1st Sess., p. 337. I have been unable to find any record of his proposal in the *Annals*.

"draw from an authority admitted in all parts of the Union a definition of the basis of republican government."[63]   Ruggles of Ohio insisted that slavery was "a violation of the fundamental principles of Republican government" because it was "repugnant to the great and essential rights contained in the Declaration of Independence."[64]   The framers had merely transplanted into the Constitution through the guaranty clause the principle declared in the Declaration that all men are born free and equal.   Natural rights thus became an element of the republican form under the organic law of the nation.   According to this theory slavery was unrepublican because it deprived persons of their natural rights of liberty and equality.   For, as Fuller insisted, since all admitted that slaves are men, "it follows that they are in a purely republican government born free, and are entitled to liberty and the pursuit of happiness."[65]

Indeed, some of the anti-slavery group went so far as to assert that the principle of natural rights was so fundamental as to be a limitation upon the sovereign whenever it acted, either in the State or the nation.   According to the view of some, in order to give effect to the principle it would have been unnecessary for the framers of the Declaration even to have expressly recognized it.   Roberts argued that no State could ever authorize or establish slavery; for "such a power in the constitutions of all these States is held to be incompatible with the nature of legislative trust, and is excepted out of the powers of government."[66]   And Sergeant contended that should slavery ever be extirpated from the Union there was no "moral or political competency under the Constitution to restore it among us."[67]   The anti-slavery group

---

[63] *Ibid.*, 15th Cong., 2nd Sess., p. 1181.

[64] *Ibid.*, 16th Cong., 1st Sess., p. 279.

[65] *Ibid.*, 15th Cong., 2nd Sess., p. 1180.

[66] *Ibid.*, 16th Cong., 1st Sess., p. 128.   [67] *Ibid.*, p. 1190.

without exception, nevertheless, admitted that this restrictive principle operated only when the sovereign acted in aid of slavery. It had no effect to abolish slavery in the old States because the positive character of the principle had been qualified by the compromise in the Convention.

The second theory followed the Madisonian definition of republicanism. In *The Federalist* he had said that the peculiar characteristic of such a government was that it "derives all its powers directly or indirectly from the great body of the people, and is administered by persons holding their offices during pleasure, for a limited period, or during good behavior."[68] According to the representative definition the exclusion of a large class of the population from the base of political power destroyed the republican character of the government. From which Roberts insisted that a republican government did not mean one where one half of the people had the power to make the other half slaves. He thought that a government might as well make a king as slaves, for in the one case it was putting a person above the law and in the other below the law.[69] On the ground that representation and election were the essentials of a republic, Fuller undertook to demonstrate that "the exclusion of the black population from all political freedom . . . is an equally palpable invasion of right and abandonment of principle." Morril of New Hampshire went so far as to identify republican government with a democracy. Slavery being incompatible with a pure democracy, he thought "in the same degree that you admit slavery, you contaminate the Republic. It degenerates to a demi-democracy, to aristocracy, monarchy, and perhaps, despotism itself."[70] The second theory made slavery inconsistent with republican government

[68] No. XXXIX, p. 233.
[69] *Annals,* 16th Cong., 1st Sess., p. 339.
[70] *Ibid.*, p. 150.

because a large portion of the population was outside the pale of political power and privileges.

On the other hand, the pro-slavery group undertook to show that slavery was an element of the constitutional republican form. To meet the theory that the phrase should be construed in terms of the natural rights principles of the founders, they argued that it should be interpreted in the light of the entire document; that all parts of the instrument should be considered together. They pointed to the three clauses in the Constitution which recognized slavery. In order for the "republican form" to harmonize with these parts of the Constitution, tacitly it had to comprehend the slavery principle.[71] Since the federal Constitution recognized the slavery principle, certainly the framers did not intend the States to be more republican than the United States government. A variant of this reasoning construed the phrase in the light of the understanding of those who adopted the Constitution. Since the people in all of the States but Massachusetts legally owned slaves at the adoption of the Constitution they could not have felt that their own constitutions were thereby vitiated.[72] Another tactic of the pro-slavery group was to look to the history of the world to find the elements of the republican form rather than to the history of America. Slavery, it was shown, had been a constant characteristic of the republics of the ancient world, both the Grecian and the Roman.[73]

Pinkney made the best reply to the argument that a republican government was one in which all men participated in its power and privileges. He pointed out that in no State was there either universal suffrage or universal el-

[71] *Ibid.*, p. 1028.

[72] See Speech of Smyth of Virginia, in the House, Jan. 28th, 1820, *ibid.*, p. 993.

[73] Speech of William Pinkney in the Senate, Feb. 15th, 1820, *ibid.*, pp. 410-411, and William Smith in the Senate, Dec. 8, 1820, *ibid.*, 16th Cong., 2nd Sess., pp. 51-77.

igibility. All the States had age, citizenship, or property qualifications for voting and for office holding, and the persons who could not meet them were just as much disfranchised with regard to the government and its power as if they were slaves. Such persons had civil rights, as indeed slaves had in a less degree, but they had no more participation in the government than the slaves. Their province was merely to obey the laws, not to assist in the making of them. He thought, however, that according to the true theory of a republican government "rights, political and civil, may be qualified by the fundamental law, upon such inducements as the freemen of the country deem sufficient."[74] There were a thousand examples of qualified civil rights, such as those of minors, aliens, the female sex. As a matter of principle "if it be true that all men in a republican Government must help wield its power, and be equal in rights," then, he inquired, "why not all the *women?*" Why was it that the exclusion of the women from the power of a popular government did not destroy its republican form?[75] But Pinkney could not comprehend how the law of slavery could affect the form of a government. He conceived of form as applying to the structure of the governmental organs. He said:

But it has not been very clearly explained what the *laws* which such a government may enact can have to do with its *form.* . . . The introduction or continuance of civil slavery is manifestly the mere result of the power of making laws. It does not in any degree enter into the form of the government. It presupposes that form already settled and takes its rise not from the particular frame of the government but from the general power which every government involves. Make the government what you will in its organization and in the distribution of its authorities, the introduction or continuance of involuntary servitude by the legisla-

[74] *Ibid.,* 16th Cong., 1st Sess., p. 412.
[75] *Ibid.,* p. 413.

tive power which it has created can have no influence on its pre-
established form, whether monarchical, aristocratical, or republican.   The form of government is still one thing, and the law,
being a simple exertion of the ordinary faculty of legislation by
those to whom that form of government has entrusted it, another.
The gentlemen, however, identify an act of legislation sanctioning
involuntary servitude with the form of government itself, and they
assure us that the latter is changed retroactively by the first, and is
no longer republican.[76]

The pro-slavery group also disagreed with the anti-slavery
group as to the meaning of the guaranty and the power conferred on Congress by it.   In answer to the contention that it
gave the power to coerce a State, Pinkney thought:

It is passing strange that any man, who thinks at all, can view this
salutary command as a grant of power so monstrous; or look at
it in any other light than as a protecting mandate to Congress to
interpose with the force and authority of the Union against the
violence and usurpation by which a member of it might otherwise
be oppressed by profligate and powerful individuals, or by ambitious
and unprincipled factions.[77]

The Southern view of the guaranty was that it gave a power
to sustain and maintain the existing governments and not the
power to supervise or to create new governments.   As Elliott
of Georgia said, "it is to be considered as an evidence of the
patronage of the Constitution rather than as an authority to
impose restrictions on the States."[78]   The pro-slavery group
often construed the guaranty clause in the light of the succeeding clause: "And shall protect each of them against invasion, and on application of the legislature, or of the executive (when the legislature cannot be convened), against
domestic violence."   Viewed in this light intervention of
Congress would depend upon request and might be for the
purpose of upholding the slave institution.

[76] *Ibid.*, pp. 409-410.
[77] *Ibid.*, p. 413.   [78] *Ibid.*, p. 130.

Campbell of Ohio insisted that the guaranty of a republican government was merely the guaranty to a State of its sovereignty, or the right of self government.[79] P. P. Barbour of Virginia thought that it guaranteed a government derived from the people to be governed and one liable to be altered, reformed, or abolished by themselves.[80]

The anti-slavery group without exception disclaimed the right to interfere with slavery in the original States. There, they admitted, it was protected by the compromise of the Constitution and the guaranty would not operate against it. The pro-slavery group, on the other hand, believed that acceptance of the principle of restriction on a new State would later lead to coercion of the old slave States. Pinkney drove home the logical conclusion of the anti-slavery argument: "Do gentlemen perceive the consequences to which their arguments must lead, if they are of any value? Do they reflect that they lead to emancipation in the old United States— or to the exclusion of Delaware, Maryland, and all of the South . . . from the Union."[81] Smyth of Virginia called upon all the slaveholding States to make common cause with Missouri. He believed that if Congress could make a new State insert a clause against slavery in its Constitution, under the same authority it could make an old State add such a clause to its Constitution.[82] If Congress could erect such a standard of republicanism for Missouri, then as Johnson of Kentucky stated, she could dictate to the old States better principles for revision of their Constitutions. Congress might even strike out the freehold qualification in the Virginia Constitution and proclaim universal suffrage and annual elections for that State.[83] Under such a Constitution, Smith of South Carolina feared that Congress might at any time issue its writ of *quo*

---

[79] *Ibid.*, 16th Cong., 2nd Sess., p. 1013.
[80] *Ibid.*, 16th Cong., 1st Sess., p. 1226.
[81] *Ibid.*, p. 411.   [82] *Ibid.*, p. 1004.   [83] *Ibid.*, p. 357.

warranto and require a State to show by what warrant it claimed to have a republican government.[84]

Repercussions from the Congressional debates over the guaranty clause were felt in the South. This is evident from the debates in the Virginia Convention of 1829. In taking up the question of the proper principle of representation for the new legislature to be created, the pro-slavery group argued that it should not be grounded upon numbers only, but that the proper base should be a compound of numbers and property. To surrender the traditional element of property in representation and go to that of pure numbers, would be to admit that the basis of federal representation was unrepublican. This would endanger slavery in all the Southern States and would be an invitation for Congress to act. As Stanard put it:

If this assembly pronounce that the infusion of this principle [property representation] converts any Government from a republic to an aristocracy, can you consistently, when that declaration shall be invoked against you, refuse to abide by your own decree? You must consent either to exhibit an open, undisguised, and glaring inconsistency, or you must surrender your rights as soon as you are confronted by your own declaration.[85]

Judge Upshur wondered what answer Virginia could make to a proposition to strike out of the Federal Constitution the three-fifths clause after embracing the basis of numbers in her own Constitution: "Would she not be told by those who abhor this species of property, and who are restive under the power which it confers, 'You have abandoned this principle in your own institutions, and with what face can you claim it in your connections with us.' "[86] Upshur undertook to show that property must necessarily be protected both in the form and in the fundamental principles of all republican govern-

[84] *Ibid.*, 16th Cong., 2nd Sess., p. 55.
[85] *Debates*, p. 304.   [86] *Ibid.*, p. 75.

ments. This was true because it was a constituent element of society, without which society could not exist; and because "in the operations of Government, as they are conceived in legislation, the most numerous and most interesting class of subjects on which the power is to be exerted, are all derived from property, and intimately connected with it."[87] He drew support for such a theory of republicanism from the revolutionary maxim of no taxation without representation.

The fear seemed to hang over the Southern mind that Congress might attempt to exercise the guaranty toward them. In 1833 Calhoun replying to Forsyth of Georgia, who had said that South Carolina at that time because of nullification furnished a case calling for the exercise of the guaranty, replied by warning the Senator of the results of such a loose construction of the clause. He feared that it was:

A power which, hereafter, if not rigidly restricted to the objects intended by the Constitution, is destined to be a pretext to interfere with our political affairs and the domestic institutions, in a manner infinitely more dangerous than any other power which has ever been exercised on the part of the General Government. . . . There exists in every Southern State a domestic institution, which would require a far less bold construction to consider the government of every State in that quarter not to be republican, and of course, to demand on the part of this government a suppression of the institution to which I allude in fulfillment of the guarantee. . . . With the rapid strides with which this Government is advancing to power, a time will come, and that not far distant, when petitions will be received from the quarter to which I allude, for protection; when the faith of the guaranty will be at least as applicable to that case as the Senator from Georgia now thinks it is to Carolina.[88]

Nine years later a petition was presented to the House of Representatives by John Quincy Adams from a group of citizens

[87] *Ibid.*, p. 72.
[88] *Debates in Congress*, 22nd Cong., 2nd Sess., p. 774.

of Massachusetts which confirmed Calhoun's prediction. Naming each of the thirteen slaveholding States, it branded its government as "despotic, onerous, and oppressive in its actions on a great number of its citizens" and called upon Congress to exercise the guaranty to restore its republican form.[89]

The apprehension of Southern Congressmen was again raised as to the potentialities of the guaranty in 1844 when the House had under consideration an investigation into the republican character of rival governments in Rhode Island. The new revolutionary government requested that the guaranty be invoked to support it, because it did away with the monarchical and aristocratic features of the old charter government. Caleb Smith, however, appealed to the slaveholding representatives to uphold the old government on the ground that any other interpretation of the guaranty than that it was the power to sustain an existing government against revolutionary change would be to aim a blow at the institution of slavery. He inquired "where did the gentlemen find the authority to exclude from political rights the Negroes of South Carolina and Virginia," if the people of Rhode Island can overthrow their government and adopt another one? If the reason was that the charter government did not extend the suffrage to all whites, then the next step would be to argue that the governments of the slave States were unrepublican because the large class of blacks was excluded from the suffrage. If the guaranty could be invoked in the one case, it could be also in the other.[90]

The relation of the guaranty clause to slavery came up again in Congress when objection was made to the admission

[89] *Congressional Globe,* 27th Cong., 2nd Sess., p. 158, Jan. 21, 1842.

[90] *Ibid.*, 22nd Cong., 2nd Sess., p. 384. See also the Speech of John A. McClernand of Illinois, referring contemptuously to Smith's appeal. *Ibid.*, appendix, p. 331.

of three slave States: Arkansas, 1836; Florida, 1845; and Texas, 1845. The question involved in each of these cases differed from that of Missouri in that their Constitutions expressly recognized slavery as a settled principle of the fundamental law of the State, their legislatures being prohibited from emancipating the slaves. In the case of Missouri the anti-slavery group had urged that Congress act prohibitory for the abolition of slavery. In the other three cases they argued that the question was whether Congress would act confirmatory of its perpetuation. In the Arkansas debate, Hard of New York delivered a lengthy speech developing the natural rights theory of republican government:

The term "republican" as applied to the science of government with us, does not borrow its import from the schools of antiquity. Its legitimate application was ascertained and established by the political philologists of the Revolution. The doctors of those days knew best how to apply terms of government to their appropriate ideas. They affixed names to a set of principles that laid the foundation of our happy and much-admired form of government . . . they became familiarly acquainted with the use of those principles, and were enabled to assign them their appropriate objects in the various departments of human society. [Quoting the axioms of the Declaration] These are the political axioms upon which our beautiful and noble constitution was founded. These compose the elements from which it derived its existence, its spirit, and by which it is sustained; and when it speaks of a republican form of government, it contemplates one that embodies and supports these axioms—one that combines all and is repugnant to none of them.[91]

In all three cases the pro-slavery group took the position that the guaranty meant the right of a political community to self-government and not the rights of personal liberty. Calhoun contrasted the two views in this way: "It is proposed, from a vague, indefinite, erroneous, and most danger-

[91] *Debates in Congress*, 24th Cong., 1st Sess., p. 4271.

ous conception of private individual liberty, to override this great common liberty which the people have of framing their own constitutions."[92]   Thomas L. Clingman of North Carolina delivered a long speech in the Senate, December 22, 1847, in which he used the historical method to refute the theory that the essential element of a republic was the perfect political equality of all persons.   He concluded from his study of the philosophers that there was no term in the English language more difficult to define with preciseness, but according to the most sagacious of the political theorists a republic was composed of a mixture of the features of monarchy, aristocracy, and democracy.[93]

In the Congressional debates during the 1850s, the guaranty was definitely linked with the problem of slavery in the States. Cabell of Florida, March 5, 1850, in replying to Thaddeus Stevens wondered if the latter had not hinted at an exercise of the guaranty to coerce when he had declared that the governments of the slave States were not republican but despotisms.   He asked:

When we compare abolitionism, now, with what it was fifteen years ago, is the fear unreasonable, that the northern people may be induced to believe it their duty to "guarantee a *republican form of government* to every State in the Union" as required by the Constitution, and abolish the despotism of slavery?   Perhaps the gentleman is "showing the hand of the North" too soon in this case.[94]

R. M. T. Hunter about the same time expressed the opinion that history justified the Southern apprehension that the

[92] *Congressional Globe,* 29th Cong., 2nd Sess., p. 454, Feb. 19, 1847.

[93] *Ibid.,* 30th Cong., 1st Sess., Appendix, p. 43.

[94] *Ibid.,* 31st Cong., 1st Sess., Appendix, p. 241.   See also the Speech of Senator Brown of Mississippi, Dec. 22, 1856, inquiring to what purpose Senator Seward had declared that the slaveholding class in the South was only one hundredth part of the population of the country and that this privileged class in the South was dangerous to republican institutions. *Ibid.,* 34th Cong., 3rd Sess., Appendix, p. 94.

federal government might yet become the instrument of serious and dangerous assaults upon the institution of slavery in the States. "Suppose that this government should ever be committed, fully and unequivocally, to the proposition that there can be no property in slaves," he inquired, "how long afterward before the institution is abolished in the States?" If the government should regard the slaves as persons and not as property, it would not be long before it would recognize their right, in States where they constituted the majority, to form a government under the protection of the guaranty of the Constitution.[95]   There was a strong opinion in the South that accepted the representative theory and upheld the republican character of their governments only on the ground that the slaves were property, not legal persons, and consequently outside the body politic.[96]

In at least one instance an anti-slavery Congressman, Gerrit Smith, openly declared on the floor of the House that it was the emphatic duty of the General Government to exercise the guaranty in order to interfere with the internal arrangements and policy of the slave States. Since the nation had been "brought into great peril by the slavocratic element in its councils," and since in those States, "the white, as well as the black masses, are crushed by that political element," he insisted, "the nation is entitled to liberation from this peril; and, surely, these masses have a perfectly constitutional, as well as most urgent claim on the nation for deliverance from

[95] *Ibid.*, 31st Cong., 1st Sess., p. 378.

[96] See especially the argument of Geo. S. Sawyer who reversed the reasoning and contended that slaves must be property because the governments of the slave States had become recognized as valid through precedent and custom, *op. cit.*, p. 300. In view of the many expressions of the representative theory of the guaranty from the time of the Missouri debates on, it is remarkable that Professor Dunning should have considered the interpretation of "republican form" to include Negroes in the suffrage as running counter to the facts of history and previous interpretations of the fundamental law, and have regarded it as revolutionary. *Essays on the Civil War and Reconstruction* (New York, 1910), p. 132.

the worst of despotisms, and for the enjoyment of a 'republi-can form of government.' "[97]

There was a more considerable and a very respectable body of opinion outside Congress that expressed itself in favor of enforcing the guaranty. In 1844, the historian, James G. Palfrey, raised the question "whether the nation is true to its solemn guaranty to South Carolina of 'a republi-can form of government,' when more than one-half of her people are under the despotic sway of the rest."[98]   Many of the formal treatises on the constitutionality of slavery dealt with the potentialities of the guaranty clause. G. W. F. Mellen, for instance, concluded that because the slave was thrown outside the pale of citizenship, he was denied a re-publican form of government, and that "the laws of these States, which impose these disabilities are null and should be of no effect."[99]   Lysander Spooner in his book on constitu-tional aspects of slavery, insisted that the clause was not idle verbiage but that it was full of meaning, its meaning being fatal to slavery. In a thorough exposition of the whole prob-lem, he urged many reasons why it was to the interest of the nation to awaken to "the legal import of so open, explicit and peremptory a guaranty of freedom, equality and right."[100]   William Goodell went so far as to assert that by the failure to exert the guaranty the federal government was "sustaining and being responsible for slavery."[101]

Probably the best statement of the anti-slavery interpreta-tion was made in 1858 by Theodore Parker in a speech before the New England Anti-Slavery Society. He declared that there was but one great question before the American peo-

---

[97] Congressional Globe, 33rd Cong., 1st Sess., Appendix, p. 523, April 6, 1854.
[98] Op. cit., p. 85.
[99] An Argument on the Unconstitutionality of Slavery (Boston, 1841), p. 87.
[100] The Unconstitutionality of Slavery (Boston, 1847), p. 106.
[101] Slavery and Anti-Slavery; a history of the great struggle in both hemispheres (New York, 1843), p. 587.

ple, namely, "is slavery consistent with the Republican form of Government which the Revolution was fought to secure, and the Union established to found?"[102] In answer to the question he asserted that the people had enacted the guaranty clause in order to carry out the principles of the Declaration and the purposes of the Constitution. As he expressed it, the people had laid down in the Declaration maxims, the norm of institutions, which in the Constitution, the norm of statutes and customs, became purposes utterly destructive of property in man. Branding the slave governments kakistocracies, he called upon the State of Massachusetts to insist upon the enforcement of the guaranty.

Other anti-slavery societies became impressed with such a practical mode of abolishing slavery. By it Congress would use the same measures to displace slavery that it would employ in case a State should establish an order of nobility or a hereditary monarch for a representative government.[103] In the great debate between Parson Brownlow and Abram Pryne in Philadelphia in 1858, Pryne expressed the opinion that the States had no sovereignty that would override the guaranty power of Congress and that it might be utilized successfully to sweep slavery from the nation.[104]

Implicit in the anti-slavery writings is the idea that the guaranty clause might have been used as the means of nationalizing the federal bill of rights. Under it, the protection of life, liberty, and property in the due process clause of the fifth amendment restricting the federal government might have been extended as a protection to the individual against the State's encroachment. This would have transferred to the federal courts the protection of the personal

[102] *The Relation of Slavery to a Republican Form of Government* (Boston, 1858), p. 17.

[103] *The Constitutional Duty of the Federal Government to Abolish American Slavery, an exposé of the Abolition Society of New York* (New York, 1855), p. 14.

[104] *Ought American Slavery to be Perpetuated* (Philadelphia, 1858), p. 230.

rights against State encroachment; and on petition for habeas corpus, the Court might have declared the institution illegal and thereby freed the slave as a judicial rather than a Congressional exercise of the guaranty.[105]

Passing now from the constitutional aspects of republican government as related to the guaranty clause, we turn to the philosophical discussion over the compatibility of slavery with a republic as a problem of political science. This aspect of the subject leads into an analysis of the ideas of the slaveholder about liberty and equality under government. With the idea that equality and liberty were basic ingredients of a republic, the slaveholder believed that they flourished fully only in the presence of slavery. In one sense, he was capitalizing upon the Revolutionary philosophy and the principles of the Declaration of Independence. He always acknowledged that there was essential truth in the axioms of the Declaration, properly understood. He refused to view that truth in terms of abstract principles, however, and insisted upon applying the test of substance. He was positive that slavery produced the most perfect equality and nurtured the most substantial liberty that could be expected or desired in a state of society.

Calhoun pointed to the basic reason why slavery was the best guarantee of equality among the whites of the South when he told John Quincy Adams in 1820 that "it produced an unvarying level among them." Representative Campbell of South Carolina argued on the floor of Congress in 1842 that the institution of slavery instead of "being uncongenial

---

[105] The nearest approach to such a direct suggestion that I have found, was made in the exposé of the New York Abolition Society, *op. cit.*, p. 14. An analogous situation is the recent development where the Court has used the liberty phrase in the fourteenth amendment to nationalize freedom of speech, Stromberg *v.* California (1931), 283 *U. S.* 359 and freedom of press, Near *v.* Minnesota (1931) 283 *U. S.* 697 both of which are in the first amendment, and the procedural right to counsel in Powell *v.* Alabama (1932), 287 *U. S.* 45 in the Sixth Amendment.

with a republican government" was more useful in such a government than in any other, because "as paradoxical as it may appear on a superficial view" to him it was "nevertheless capable of demonstration that domestic slavery produces equality and nurtures a spirit of liberty among the citizen population of a country." He explained this phenomenon on the ground that, in a country where domestic slavery did not exist, the menial and domestic offices were performed by a portion of the citizen population, and such a degradation of a few affected the respectability of the entire class to which they belonged. The result was that the rich and the poor divided into classes and the "freeborn and laboring poor, although perhaps more virtuous than their rich neighbors, are treated as inferiors." Such a state of society as this could not be congenial to the principles of republican government, he thought, because "equality among its citizens is the corner-stone of a republic; and the spirit of independence which equality produces and cherishes is the vestal that fans the fire that burns on the altar of Liberty."[106]

Henry A. Wise of Virginia observed about the same time that wherever black slavery existed, equality among the white population was to be found, but that where it had no place such equality was never found. "Break down slavery," he insisted, "and you would with the same blow destroy the great Democratic principle of equality among men." Because the principle of slavery was a levelling principle, he believed that it was friendly to equality.[107] Richard M. Johnson at an earlier date in the Senate had drawn a contrast between the slave and the free States as to the existence of equality among the population. In the slave States, he contended, all white men were on a plane of equality, for "we have no classes—no patrician or plebeian rank. Honesty and honor form all the

---

[106] *Congressional Globe*, 27th Cong., 2nd Sess., Appendix, p. 337.
[107] *Ibid.*, p. 173.

distinctions that are felt or known.   Whatever may be the condition of a citizen with us, you must treat him as an equal." He found that such a condition was not true of the free States, for there "ranks and distinctions, the precursors of aristocracy, already begin to exist."[108]   Jefferson Davis as late as 1859, in order to support the Southern theory of equality, felt called upon to reply to the charge that white laborers in the South were degraded. He branded such a charge as untrue:

I say it is there true that every mechanic assumes among us the position which only a master workman holds among you. Hence it is that the mechanic in our Southern States is admitted to the table of his employer, converses with him on terms of equality— not merely political equality, but an actual equality—wherever the two men come into contact. The white laborers of the South are all of them men who are employed in what you would term the higher pursuits of labor among you. It is the presence of a lower class, those lower by their mental and physical organization, controlled by the higher intellect of the white man, that gives this superiority to the white laborer. Menial services are not there performed by the white man. We have none of our brethren sunk to the degradation of being menials. . . . One of the reconciling features of the existence [of African slavery] is the fact that it raises white men to the same general level, that it dignifies and exalts every white man by the presence of a lower race."[109]

Senator Brown of Mississippi declared that nowhere except in the slaveholding States was there "a living, breathing exemplification of the beautiful sentiment that all men are equal." Slavery made white men equal in the South, and "the wives and daughters of our mechanics and the laboring men stand not an inch lower in the social scale than the wives and daughters of our Governors, secretaries, and judges." In

[108] *Annals of Congress*, 16th Cong., 1st Sess., pp. 348-349.
[109] Speech in the Senate, March 2, 1859, *Works*, IV, 49.

the South one beheld "a whole Community standing on a perfect level, and not one of them a tithe of a hair's breadth higher in the social scale than another." The cause for this he believed was that the line separating menial from honorable labor was marked by a caste or a distinct color. In the South, as in the North, the mechanic arts were treated as honorable, but there were certain menial employments in the South which belonged exclusively to the Negro and therefore furnished "a field of labor that the white man never invades." Brown concluded that the beneficial effect of equality at the South was that it "represses thereby many of the evil passions which rise up and drive men to madness in communities where white men are not equal."[110]

T. R. R. Cobb also commented upon the fact that it was the element of equality that made slavery a conservative institution politically. According to his reasoning:

The mass of laborers not being recognized among citizens, every citizen feels that he belongs to an elevated class. It matters not that he is no slaveholder; he is not of the inferior race; he is a freeborn citizen; he engages in no menial occupation. The poorest meets the richest as an equal; sits at his table with him; salutes him as a neighbor; meets him in every public assembly, and stands on the same social platform. Hence, there is no war of classes. There is truthfully republican equality in the ruling class.[111]

The Southern idea of republican equality was not one of an equal status as between all persons under government. It was the idea that slavery insured equality of condition between those that were substantially equal in capacities. As John Randolph Tucker pointed out, the Southerner thought that it would be a violation of the true principle of equality, "the greatest inequality of right, to enforce an equality of

[110] *Congressional Globe*, 33rd Cong., 1st Sess., Appendix, p. 230.
[111] *Op. cit.*, p. 213.

condition" among those that were unequal by nature.[112]   In order to apply the principle of equality in government, the slaveholder insisted that unequal classes of persons had to be given different treatment.   So Robert Toombs said that two principles, "the perfect equality of the superior race, and the legal subordination of the inferior are the foundation on which we have erected our republican system."[113]   The slaveholder's idea of republican equality was an equality among equals, based on a classification of persons for purposes of treatment according to substantial differences in their capacities.   It was a classified equality.[114]

Not only did slavery have the effect of producing republican equality, it also generated a high spirit of liberty among the whites of slave communities.   As a matter of fact, Professor Dew of William and Mary College believed that it was the spirit of equality that was "both the generator and preserver of the genuine spirit of liberty."   He appealed to history to establish the fact that liberty was more ardently desired by slaveholding communities than by any other:

In the ancient republics of Greece and Rome, where the spirit of liberty glowed with most intensity, the slaves were more numerous than the freemen.   Aristotle, and the great men of antiquity, believed slavery necessary to keep alive the spirit of freedom.   In Sparta, the freemen were even forbidden to perform the offices of slaves lest [they] might lose the spirit of independence.[115]

[112] *Republicanism and Slavery; An address delivered at William and Mary College, July 3, 1854* (Richmond, 1854).

[113] *Loc. cit.*, p. 581.

[114] The Supreme Court in construing the "equal protection of the laws" provision of the 14th Amendment has conformed to a degree to the pro-slavery theory of a classified equality instead of to the anti-slavery theory of the essential right of every individual to equality with every other individual under the law.   The Supreme Court permits the classification of persons within the State for the purpose of legislation wherever a substantial basis of classification can be found, but the Court, of course, has never accepted the Southern idea that race is such a substantial basis.

[115] *Loc. cit.*, p. 461.

Professor Washington, also of William and Mary, taught that not only had all "the great Republics of ancient and modern times been slaveholding, but those great stands that have been made in the world in defense of liberty and human rights have been by slaveholders." Moreover, from a study of philosophy, he concluded that "the great intellects of the world, looking deep into the true relations of things, have discovered the most intimate connection between slavery and liberty."[116]

Such was the view of all the ancient schools of philosophy and as a modern example the slaveholder cited Burke. In the speech on conciliation with the Colonies in 1775, Burke had observed that the Colonies to the southward "are much more strongly, and with a higher and more stubborn spirit, attached to liberty, than those of the northward." He accounted for this fact on the ground that "freedom is to them not only an enjoyment, but a kind of rank and privilege."[117] When Nathaniel Macon quoted from the speech on conciliation in the Missouri debates in order to prove that the spirit of liberty had always been high and haughty in the Southern States, he called Burke "that celebrated master of human character."[118] Burke was greatly admired in the South and probably no piece of literature was so much used in the pro-slavery argument as his speech on conciliation. It was after the same observation as Burke had made that Robert Barnwell Rhett declared "the very existence of slavery around him" gave the Southerner "a loftier tone of independence and a higher estimate of liberty."[119]

Analyzing the slaveholder's idea of liberty, its charm and chief value was the security that it gave to property. But the

[116] Notebook, MS.
[117] Quoted by Dew, *loc. cit.*, p. 461.
[118] *Annals of Congress*, 16th Cong., 1st Sess., p. 228.
[119] *Address to the People of Beaufort and Colletin Districts upon the Subject of Abolition* (Charleston, 1838), p. 8.

freedom given to the white man in a slave community had another value. It afforded the leisure essential for the development of the mental and moral capacities that fitted him as a noble specimen for the task of self government. As Beverley Tucker taught his students:

Gentlemen: freedom, in its simplest, social form, is an affair of government. The philosophy of social freedom is the philosophy of *self-government.* If this were all, this alone were enough to show the difficulty of the problem. Who of us is equal to the task of self-government, even on the narrow theatre of private life, and in the discharge of its simple duties? Yet it is in that sacred regard to these, and all the other duties of life, which we dignify by the name of virtue, that political philosophers place the foundation of republican government.[120]

Slavery had the effect of fitting a community for republican government. Its effect was "to make the temper of the ruling caste more honourable, self-governed, reflective, courteous, and chivalrous, and to foster in them an intense love of, and pride in, their free institutions."[121] Thus Jefferson Davis, on the eve of the war, in commenting upon the institution of slavery, gave it as his "deliberate conviction, that it is promotive of, if not essential to, the preservation of the higher orders of republican civilization."[122]

Aside from the virtue of promoting the ideals of equality and freedom, slavery had another utility in a republic. It acted as a great conservative force for order and stability. Chancellor Harper thought that instruction of inestimable value on this point could be gathered from a study of the ancient republics, because "they teach us that slavery is compatible with freedom, stability, and long duration of civil government, with denseness of population, great power, and

[120] *A Series of Lectures on the Science of Government, intended to prepare the student for the study of the Constitution of the United States* (Philadelphia, 1845), pp. 352-353.

[121] Dabney, *op. cit.*, p. 297.   [122] *Works*, IV, 49-50.

the highest civilization."[123]   In like vein, Rhett declared that "no republic has ever yet been long maintained without the institution of slavery."[124]

With the same idea in mind, Governor Hammond undertook to explain why slavery was the "'corner-stone' and foundation of every well-designed and durable 'republican edifice.'" No society could exist without a natural variety of classes, the rich and the poor, the educated and the ignorant. The poor had less time to prepare themselves for the proper discharge of public duties than the rich, and the ignorant were unfit for such. Universal suffrage being a necessary appendage to a republican system the ignorant and poor could not be excluded from the ballot by law as they were under other forms of government. But since they constituted the numerical majority, in non-slaveholding communities the government would be in their hands. He thought it was bound to be a wretched and insecure government that was administered by the ignorant and those who had the least at stake under it. These reckless and unenlightened numbers, he believed, were "rapidly usurping all power in the non-slaveholding States" and were threatening "a fearful crisis in republican institutions there at no remote period." In the slaveholding republics, on the other hand, the poorest and most ignorant half of the population had no political influence because they were slaves. Of the other half those that unfortunately were not educated were still elevated far above the mass, were "higher toned and more deeply interested in preserving a stable and well-ordered government, than the same class in any other country."[125]

Beverley Tucker also considered the institution of slavery as the remedy for the distemper of the body politic, which was a prevailing epidemic under free governments, that is,

---

[123] "Memoir on Slavery," *The Pro-Slavery Argument*, p. 71.
[124] *Op. cit.*, p. 8.   [125] *Loc. cit.*, pp. 110-111.

the struggle between the property class and numbers, where "property is driven by the desire of security, to war against freedom, and numbers are excited by rapacity, or the fear of oppression, to war against property." He explained this curative effect of slavery on the ground that in slave States there was no class of men who had a distaste for the institutions of their community, because there was no class who did not "feel itself secure, not only in the possession, but in the fullest enjoyment of all its rights, whether original or acquired." This was so "because of the existence of an institution, which makes it impossible that the strife for political power should ever be exasperated by hunger, and makes all men in all conditions alike safe." As a consequence, universal suffrage failed to produce the same effect in slave communities as elsewhere, because it introduced to the polls but "a small number of those who have not a feeling sense of the importance and sanctity of the rights of property, and do not cherish a prevailing desire for their security." The cause of this effect Tucker believed to be the presence of the institution of domestic slavery.[126]

Robert L. Dabney, after the war, in a reflective mood attempted to explain how slavery had solved for the South the dilemma of republics and had secured a condition of stability and order. It was because the moneyless labor class, which carries in its bosom the elements of disorder and anarchy, had been wholly disfranchised of political powers and thus deprived of the power of mischief. It had been accomplished without injustice to them as they were made parts of the families of the ruling class and were thereby insured an active protection and a competent maintenance. At the same time the tendency of slavery had been to diminish the numbers and the destitution of the moneyless whites and

[126] *Lectures,* pp. 345-346.

thereby rendered them a harmless element in the State. This had been accomplished by broadening the industrial pursuits available for them, by increasing the total of property, and by making its acquisition by them easier.[127]

The conservative influence of slavery in sustaining republican institutions did not consist solely in the fact that it curtailed universal suffrage, but also in the fact that it united capital and labor and thereby precluded the danger of an economic class war. As one writer observed, "it is this peaceful trait in the institution of slavery that constitutes it a leading ingredient in the best social state."[128] The Southerner felt, moreover, that the effect of slavery as a stabilizer of republican institutions extended beyond the limits of the South and was felt in other parts of the Union. Calhoun thought that it made the South "the balance of the system; the great conservative power which prevents other portions, less fortunately constituted, from rushing into conflict."[129] With the same idea in mind, Cabell of Florida warned Northern Congressmen in 1850 that "the *conservatism of slavery* may be necessary to save you from the thousand destructive *isms* infecting the social organization of your section."[130] Thus the rationale of the slave republic culminated in the contention that the influence of the institution was essential to preserve free institutions from the revolutionary spirit current in the world.

[127] *Op. cit.*, pp. 299-300.

[128] [Iverson L. Brookes], *A Defense of Southern Slavery against the Attacks of Henry Clay and Alexander Campbell* (Hamburg, S. C., 1849), p. 44.

[129] Speech, Jan. 10, 1838, *Congressional Globe,* 25th Cong., 2nd Sess., Appendix, p. 62.

[130] *Ibid.,* 31st Cong., 1st Sess., Appendix, p. 242.

CHAPTER V

THE MORAL PHILOSOPHY OF SLAVERY

FROM the realm of legal and constitutional theories of the slave institution we now pass into that of moral philosophy. The moral rationale of slavery made up a distinct division of the philosophy of the slaveholder. From the beginning of the controversy, the principle of right and wrong involved in the slavery relationship was fundamental in both anti-slavery and pro-slavery thought. When the relation was first attacked as a moral evil, the reaction of the slaveholder was objective. He observed actual conditions and replied that it could not be an evil when so much good resulted to the parties. Thus the first stage in the moral justification was the argument of the realist in answer to the idealist who would judge all human relations by a set of abstract principles. But when the attack advanced to the position that the relationship of master and slave was a sin *per se*, everywhere and under all conditions, then he began to construct a moral philosophy under which slavery could be authoritatively supported. Ultimately pro-slavery thought in the field of ethics led to the statement of a rational system under which slavery was brought into conformity with the moral foundation of the universe. For an authoritative code of morality that would govern all human relations, the slaveholder went to the Bible, where divine revelation contributed the basic element in preparing the moral defense.

THE SCRIPTURAL ARGUMENT

The scriptural defense of slavery was prepared with exhaustive research and probably attained the most elaborate

and systematic statement of any of the types of pro-slavery
theory. Instead of presenting it with its mass of detail, it
will suffice for our purpose to sketch it in general outline.
Broadly, the Biblical arguments may be divided chronologically into those taken from the Old Testament and those
found in the New Testament. First came the argument of
divine decree. God had decreed slavery before it had actually come into existence: "And he said, Cursed be Canaan;
a servant of servants shall he be unto his brethren" (Genesis
IX:25). Then followed the argument of divine sanction.
God had ordained and sanctioned the practice of holding
slaves throughout the Patriarchal period. The Patriarchs
from Abraham to Moses were large slaveholders who counted
their slaves among their goods, as they did their oxen, their
horses, and their camels. Abraham held many slaves and he
had been exalted to be the father of the chosen people (Genesis XIV:14). The same was true of Jacob (Genesis
XXX:43). God, moreover, had ordained the relation of
slavery in the covenant entered into with Abraham: "And
he that is eight days old shall be circumcised among you,
every man child in your generations; he that is born in the
house, or bought with money of any stranger, which is not
of thy seed" (Genesis XVII:12). God sanctioned it through
his angel when the runaway slave, Hagar, was commanded
to return to her mistress Sarah (Genesis XVI:9).

During the period of the legal dispensation extending
from the time of Moses to the time of Christ, the Jews lived
under a written constitution of government given to them
by the Lord. Under it the practice of slaveholding was not
only recognized but its protection provided for. The Mosaic
law distinguished between the servitude of a Hebrew and
that of an alien. The Jew was a servant to the Jew for six
years only or until the sabbatical jubilee when he was to go

out free (Exodus XXI:2-8; Leviticus XXV:39-43; Deu
teronomy XV:12). His status was different also in that he
was treated rather as a hired servant than with the full rigor
of the treatment accorded a slave. There was a definite
authorization, however, for holding persons in slavery who
were taken from among non-believers:

Both thy bondmen, and thy bondmaids, which thou shalt have,
shall be of the heathen that are round about you; of them shall ye
buy bondmen and bondmaids.

Moreover, of the children of the strangers that do sojourn
among you, of them shall ye buy, and of their families that are
with you, which they begat in your land: and they shall be your
possession.

And ye shall take them as an inheritance for your children after
you, to inherit them for a possession; they shall be your bondmen
for ever: but over your brethren, the children of Israel, ye shall
not rule one over another with rigour (Leviticus XXV: 44-46).

This passage of scripture was the rock of Gibraltar in the Old
Testament case; it was used in all of the Biblical defenses
from the earliest to the last. The edict was a most important
cog in the pro-slavery argument because it authorized buying,
selling, holding and bequeathing slaves as property. Hitherto the relation rested on the custom of the Patriarchs. Here
it received positive law sanction. Joshua, the successor of
Moses, applied the Levitical law when he made the conquered Gibeonites "hewers of wood and drawers of water"
(Joshua IX:27).

If the Levitical law was a dispensation for the Hebrew
nation alone, the Decalogue was God's revelation to all men
for all time, rising above temporary and positive precepts and
pronouncing the sum of duties in human relationships. In
the Fourth Commandment the authority of the master over
the servant was enjoined in the same manner as that of the
parent over the child. In the Tenth Commandment the

servant or slave was catalogued along with the other types of property in which the rights of the owner were protected against the covetous. So much for the affirmative sanctions found in the Old Testament. Negatively it received sanction in that nowhere was there a passage of scripture condemning or opposing slavery. God had raised up his prophets for two thousand years and none of them had seen fit to condemn the practice.

Arguments drawn from the New Testament, or the Christian dispensation strengthened the scriptural justification of slavery. Christ came to fulfill and not to destroy. Therefore, He sanctioned the institutions and relationships existing at His time which He did not expressly condemn. Notwithstanding the fact that slavery flourished in every known part of the world and that Christ and the Apostles were continually coming into contact with it, He did not condemn it in the Sermon on the Mount or in any other formal enumeration of sins given by Him or the Apostles. Certainly had they considered it an evil they would have stated so. On the other hand, Christ tacitly approved it on the occasion when he healed the slave of the Roman centurion while he spoke no word of freedom (Luke VII:2-10). Finally, in the precepts of the New Testament, the Apostles taught submission of the slave to his master, and by so doing recognized the relation as being compatible with Christianity. The example made most use of was taken from the epistle of St. Paul where he tells the story of sending back the runaway slave, Onesimus, to his master Philemon.[1] On many other occasions the Apostles exhorted the slave to be obedient and abide peacefully by his lot.[2]

[1] For a lengthy commentary upon the Pauline philosophy of slavery, see A. B. Longstreet, *Letters on the Epistle of Paul to Philemon* (Charleston, 1845). See also Dabney, *op. cit.*, pp. 176-185.

[2] References most often cited were: *I Corinthians* VII:20-23; *Titus* II:9-10; *I Peter* II:18; *Colossians* III:22-25; *I Timothy* VI: 1-9.

Thus briefly the Biblical case of the slaveholder may be summarized. Essentially it stated that the relation of master and slave could not be sin, since it conformed to the highest moral code known to man, that based upon divine revelation. Aside from the facts of history drawn from the Bible, another important scriptural evidence of the morality of Negro slavery was found in the prophecy connected with the curse on Canaan. The curse was the ultimate basis on which the religious element in the South justified slavery. They considered the condition to be God's punishment and remedy for moral degradation. Bondage was His ordained form of restraint instituted because of moral depravity in man. In other words, it had been the factor of sin that had caused the relationship to originate.[3] Those holding the sin theory, however, did not all believe that the bondage of the Negro was predicated upon the curse. John Fletcher, for instance, expressed the theory that a long continued disregard of any of the moral laws of God by a race would sufficiently deprave them to require the curative force of the slavery restraint.

But we present the doctrine that sin—that any want of conformity to the laws of God touching our health and happiness, our physical and mental improvement and condition, has a direct tendency to deteriorate the animal man, and that a general abandonment and disregard of such laws, through a long series of generations, will be found sufficient to account for the lowest form of degradation found to exist. We believe there is truth in the saying, 'The fathers have eaten sour grapes, and the children's teeth are set on edge'; that, when the progenitors for a series of ages manifest some particular quality or tendency of action, the same may be found, even in increased degree, in their descendants; and that this principle holds true to some extent through the whole animal world. Further, that such progressive tendency to some

---

[3] See *supra*, Ch. I, note 45 and Ch. III, pp. 119-20, for the idea of the church fathers that sin caused slavery.

particular mental or physical condition may be obviated, and its action reversed, by a sufficient controlling force.[4]

The great number of Biblical exegetes, nevertheless, beginning with the curse as the origin of the Negro's depravity developed the prophetic argument from the succeeding verses:

And he said, Blessed be the Lord God of Shem; and Canaan shall be his servant.

God shall enlarge Japheth, and he shall dwell in the tents of Shem; and Canaan shall be his servant. (Genesis IX:26-27).

Many of the Southern writers traced the curse through the complete course of history and proved American slavery to be a fulfillment of this prophecy. One writer explained the discovery of the New World and its later settlement as its fulfillment:

By the discovery of America Japheth became enlarged as had been foretold 3800 years before. He took the whole continent. He literally dwelt in the tents of Shem in Mexico and Central America. No sooner did Japheth begin to enlarge himself, and to dwell in the tents of Shem, than Canaan left his fastnesses in the wilds of Africa, where the white man's foot had never trod, and appeared on the beach to get passage to America, as if drawn thither by an impulse of his nature to fulfill his destiny of becoming Japheth's servant.[5]

Jefferson Davis in one of his greatest speeches said that "the good Bishop Las Casas with philosophical humanity inaugurated the importation of the race of Ham; they came to relieve from an unnatural state the dwellers in tents and to fulfill their own destiny, that of being the 'servant of serv-

---

[4] *Op. cit.*, p. 161.

[5] S. A. Cartwright, *Essays, being inductions from the Baconian philosophy, proving the truth of the Bible and the justice and benevolence of the decree dooming Canaan to be a servant of servants* (Natchez, 1843), pp. 7-8.

ants.' "[6]   Another writer believed that the whole philosophy of ethnography could be explained under this prophecy of God. The continents, the rivers, and the mountains had been formed as they were with the idea that the higher race should rule the inferior, and God had directed each race to its ordained continent.[7]

The theory of prophecy ran into the difficulty of establishing the connection between the curse and the Negro race. To solve this problem much care was taken to trace the descendants of the sons of Noah. Etymology aided those attempting to establish the connection. Dr. S. A. Cartwright of Mississippi contended that the Biblical names were all prophetic, that Ham meant "the progenitor of hot and black," and that Canaan meant "the self-submissive knee bender." But after tracing all the black races to Ham, the second difficulty arose in the fact that the curse was delivered only upon Canaan. This was explained on the ground that Canaan was mentioned to denote all of Ham's posterity, as it was the conduct of Ham in disrespect of Noah that had offended the Lord rather than the conduct of Canaan.[8]

The value of the Bible argument to the defense of slavery may be briefly stated. It was the earliest type of pro-slavery argument that appeared. Throughout the entire controversy it was made use of more often than any other. Practically every one of the several treatises on slavery had a section devoted to the scriptural arguments, and a large number of special scriptural studies were published. A prominent Southern clergyman wrote in 1854: "Our table is crowded with pamphlets and sermons, with speeches in Congress and dissertations by clergymen and laymen, on the subject of slav-

---

[6] Speech before the Democratic State Convention, Jackson, Mississippi, July 6, 1859," *Works*, IV, 71.

[7] F. A. Ross, *op. cit.*, pp. 50-51.

[8] See Howell Cobb, *A Scriptural Examination of the Institution of Slavery in the United States* ([Perry],Georgia, 1856), pp. 26-27.

ery.   The teachings of the Bible are the most effective weapons that are used. . . . Our representatives in Congress used the argument contained in the scriptures, and their opponents dared not tell them that the historical parts (and all that refers to slavery is historical) were uninspired and untrue."[9]   Not only was the Bible argument the cornerstone upon which the religious element in the South built the moral defense of slavery, but pro-slavery men in the political sphere as well were constantly resting their justification upon the high ground of scriptural revelation.

THE THEORY OF THE CHURCH'S RELATION TO SLAVERY

The theory of the nature and office of the church in its relation to slavery had to be formulated as a part of the moral philosophy of the slaveholder.   It was important to clarify the position of the church both as to slavery as a civil institution and as a moral relationship between individuals.   The theory of the Southern church received its most philosophical statement probably by Dr. Thornwell in a report to the Presbyterian synod of South Carolina.[10]   He viewed the church as a society or organization which had a fixed and unalterable constitution in the inspired word of God.   It did not derive its "authority and obligation from the consent of its members" nor were "its doctrines, discipline, and order" the "creatures of human will."   The power of the church, accordingly, was "only ministerial and declarative."   Its sphere of activity was restricted to the bounds of the Holy Book; to announcing its principles, to enforcing its commands, and to prohibiting what it condemned, but never

[9] John Bachman, a Lutheran minister who lived in Charleston, quoted in L. Bacon, *loc. cit.*, p. 644.

[10] *Report on the Subject of Slavery Presented to the Synod of South Carolina, at their sessions in Winnsboro, November 6th, 1851* (Columbia, 1852).   The following is merely a summary and paraphrase of the report.   See also, Thornwell "An Address,'" *Southern Presbyterian Review*, XIV (1862), 541, and an unsigned article, *ibid.*, IX (1856), 345.

transcending the revealed word of God. The church dis-
charged its entire office when it declared what the Bible
taught, that alone was "her rule of faith and practice."

On the other hand, the church was not "a moral institute
of universal good, whose business it is to wage war upon
every form of human ill, whether social, civil, political or
moral, and to patronize every expedient which a romantic
benevolence may suggest as likely to contribute to human
comfort and to mitigate the inconsequences of life." He did
not believe it was the purpose of God under the present dispensation of religion that "all ill shall be banished from this
sublunary state and the earth be converted into a paradise,
or that the proper end of the church is the direct promotion
of universal good." The church had "no commission to construct society afresh, to adjust its elements in different pro-
portions, to rearrange the distribution of its classes, or to
change the forms of its political constitutions"; just as it was
not "the distinctive province of the church to build asylums
for the needy and insane." Regarding slavery as a civil institution, therefore, the church in its ecclesiastical capacity
had no more warrant to preach its extermination than it had
to advocate the establishment of a monarchy or the overthrow of the republic. The slavery problem in its political,
social and civil aspects transcended the proper sphere of the
church's interests; because under "the rule of faith which
gives the church its being, the relation of master and slave
stands on the same footing with the other relations of life."
The church could not undertake to disturb the relation;
it was bound by the decision of the state. The theory led to
a complete separation of church and state on the question of
the policy of the institution.

Although the church had no authority to interfere with
slavery as a political institution, yet it did have a definite duty

to perform in regard to the personal relationship of master and slave. In carrying out its ministerial duties the church had certain obligations enjoined upon it by its constitution. Accepting the Biblical argument in its entirety, the theory of the church taught that there were duties of both master and servant, which were just as definitely commanded as the right of slaveholding was sanctioned. The commission of the church was to teach and enforce upon its members these duties arising under the divinely appointed relation. In this moral question, moreover, it was not the province of the state to interfere and the church should be given a free hand to carry out its work.[11] The duties of both master and slave were recorded in the Bible and when followed the relation became a mutual benefit. As the servant was directed to "obey in all things your masters" so the master was commanded "to give unto your slaves that which is just and equal." The instant, however, the moral duties were neglected then the scriptural argument lost its force, for God approved of slavery in that manner alone.

The Bible taught the necessity of restraint, and slavery was simply a form of government which must be administered with equity for the good of the governed. In this respect the relation resulted in benefit for the slave and for the public order. In another respect, the relation of master and slave was recognized in the Bible as carrying the same implications of authority and dependence as that of husband and wife or of parent and child. Thus the church pictured the Biblical form of slavery as the patriarchal. Nothing appeared clearer than that the sacred scriptures considered slaves to be a part of the household. The head of the house owed as definite duties to the slave as to his children; both came

[11] For a definite claim of the separation of state and church in this sphere see "A Review, 'The Religious Instruction of the Blacks'," *Southern Presbyterian Review*, I (1846), 108.

under the same benevolent discipline of the family. It was often pointed out that Southern slavery was a projection down through the ages of the old Hebrew form. The following passage is an example of the patriarchal theory:

The Slave Institution at the South increases the tendency to dignify the family. Each planter in fact is a Patriarch—his position compels him to be a ruler in his household. From early youth, his children and servants look up to him as the head, and obedience and subordination become important elements of education. Where so many depend upon one will, society assumes the Hebrew form. Domestic relations become those which are most prized— each family recognizes its duty—and its members feel a responsibility for its discharge. The fifth commandment becomes the foundation of Society. The state is looked to only as the ultimate head in external relations while all internal duties, such as support, education, and the relative duties of individuals, are left to domestic regulation.[12]

Thus Bishop Stephen Elliott, of Georgia with the patriarchal picture in mind said on the eve of the war that "we are fighting to protect and preserve a race who form a part of our household and stand with us next to our children."[13]

The church in following out this idea of the patriarchal form of slavery felt that its mission was twofold in relation to it. First, it must expound the duties and obligations commanded of the master. In this manner the master would be led to maintain a system of justice and mutual benefit for himself and the slave. There were many scriptural texts but the Epistle to Philemon was most often used in teaching these duties. The second part of the church's mission was in behalf of the slave. Christian instruction of the slave, as to his duties and for spiritual enlightenment, became the great missionary work of the church. A strong missionary move-

[12] C. G. Memminger, *op. cit.*, p. 14.
[13] *Sermon, Christ Church, Savannah* (Savannah, 1861).

ment for religious instruction of the slave began during Colonial times. The desire to benefit the slave originated long before any program for abolishing the system was proposed, the purpose being to destroy the evils without abolishing the relation. This program of benefiting the slave was urged by the church as the true humanitarian policy that the slave-holder should carry out toward the slave, and was the South's answer to the more drastic humanitarian plea for abolition. Missionary zeal became the chief moral barrier to abolition.

During Colonial times the church had made efforts to carry out these ideas, but was faced with a definite obstruction in the opposition of the masters themselves.[14] At that period, the Negroes, fresh from Africa, were little advanced beyond the state of savages and there arose the practical problem of regulating and restraining them. This problem was mitigated, however, as generations passed and the Negro began to absorb the civilization of the whites. The road was opened for more effective work of the church. During the early twenties we find many evidences of an awakening movement within the churches, with all the denominations interested, a movement which assumed as an obligation of religion the instruction of master and slave in their reciprocal duties. The position of the Baptists was well stated in 1823 by their eminent leader, Dr. Furman, as follows:

If, also, by their own confession, which has been made in manifold instances, their condition, when they have come into the hands of humane masters here, has been greatly bettered by the change; if it is, ordinarily, really better, as many assert, than that of thousands of the poorer classes in countries reputed civilized and free; and if, in addition to all other considerations, the translation from their country to this has been the means of their mental and religious improvement, and so of obtaining salvation, as many of themselves have joyfully and thankfully confessed—then may the

[14] See *supra*, pp. 17-22.

just and humane master who rules his slaves and provides for them, according to Christian principles, rest satisfied, that he is not in holding them, chargeable with moral evil, nor with acting in this respect, contrary to the genius of Christianity.[15]

The churches were not given a free hand at first. The whole question had a political significance as well as a religious one. A certain conflict was evident in regard to the policy of the state which had enacted laws prohibiting the teaching of slaves to read and write. The state justified the laws on the ground that the teachings of the abolitionists had made them necessary, yet denied that they hindered the interests of true religion, for they were intended merely to prevent the acquisition of such knowledge that tended to render the slave dissatisfied with his lot.[16]   On the other side, the church clarified its position by denying that religious instruction included any attempt to interfere with slavery. As one of the prominent leaders of the movement explained, "human happiness does not so much depend upon the cultivation of the intellect as on the improvement of the disposition and the heart." When the slave was informed on points essential to his salvation, the whole duty of the instructor was fulfilled.[17]

Another objection often raised was that the field was largely filled by outside missionaries, who did not understand the true conditions and often taught principles of abolition. To relieve this situation, the Southern churches began to stimulate interest in the missionary work. Bishop Nathaniel Bowen of the Episcopal church issued a pastoral

---

[15] *Op. cit.*, p. 12.   Frederick Dalcho, an Episcopal minister, also advocated religious instruction in 1823. See *Practical Considerations*.

[16] For a statement of the position of the state, see W. B. Seabrook, *Essay on the Management of Slaves* (Charleston, 1834), and E. R. Lawrens, "Address before the Agricultural Society of South Carolina," *Southern Agriculturist*, V (1832), 617.

[17] C. C. Pinckney, *op. cit.*

letter in 1836 in which he said that the clergy was ready and anxious to undertake the task, but recognized that it was a delicate problem. He feared that unless the ministry of his church began the work, however, the Methodist missionaries would teach ideas inconsistent with slaveholding.[18] Following this move there was a rapid growth of interest in the work in the home churches.[19] It steadily grew so that in 1845 a great meeting of all denominations was held in Charleston to discuss methods of instruction and coöperation between the denominations.[20] By the fifties, the Southern churches had sufficiently awakened to their responsibility so that a virtual crusade ensued, the purpose being to fulfill their mission with regard to slavery.

It will be necessary to analyze this crusade. The two-fold function of instructing the master in his duties and of carrying the gospel to the slave was followed out. Many sermons were preached on the duties of masters to servants. The church periodicals were filled with articles expounding that subject.[21] Probably the more definite side of the work, however, was carried on by the missionaries who went to the plantations preaching and teaching the slave. For this purpose, a number of collections of sermons was compiled to-

[18] *A Pastoral Letter on the Religious Instruction of the Slaves of Members of the Protestant Episcopal Church* (Charleston, 1835).

[19] Several religious periodicals advocated religious instruction as early as the thirties: *The Gospel Messenger* (Episcopal), *The Charleston Observer* (Presbyterian), *The Christian Index* (Baptist), *The Southern Christian Advocate* (Methodist), *The Western Seminary* (Kentucky), *The New Orleans Observer, The Southern Churchman*, quoted in C. C. Jones, *op. cit.*, p. 67.

[20] *Proceedings of the Meeting in Charleston, South Carolina, May, 1845* (Charleston, 1845).

[21] Of wide circulation and influence were the following published sermons: G. W. Freeman, *Rights and Duties of Slaveholders; two discourses delivered on Sunday, November 27, 1836, in Christ Church, Raleigh* (Raleigh, 1836), J. H. Thornwell, *The Rights and Duties of Masters* (Charleston, 1850), H. N. McTyeire, *Duties of Masters to Servants* (Charleston, 1851), Being Three Prize Essays, J. B. Adger, *The Doctrine of Human Rights and Slavery* (Columbia, 1849).

gether with specially devised catechisms to explain Christianity in the simple terms of the slave and exhort him faithfully to occupy his position in society.[22]   Furthermore, many churches were built for them and some encouragement given toward the organization of separate congregations, although the latter was generally discouraged.   The general policy was to give them a place in the church building used by the whites. Consequently, the slave portion of each congregation became a special interest to the minister and required special methods. We shall not enter into the technique of the work here.

Undoubtedly, the movement so enthusiastically entered upon and so courageously carried on by the ministry had important results.   The slave was taught humility and submission.   The Negro was civilized and his condition ameliorated from that of the savage who was imported from Africa. Christianity gave to him moral hopefulness and an emotional outlet that his nature demanded.   On the side of the master, Christianity was the one great bond which taught sympathy for the slave.   As Dr. Thornwell remarked: "We feel that

[22] There were a number of these collections issued by the different churches. One of the earliest of these was published by Rev. John Mines of Leesburg, Va., *The Evangelical Catechism, or a Plain and Easy System of the Principal Doctrines and Duties of the Christian Religion*, (1822); Rev. B. M. Palmer of Charleston, *A Plain and Easy Catechism, Designed Chiefly for the Benefit of Colored Persons, with Suitable Prayers and Hymns Annexed* (1828); Rev. W. Capers published for the Methodists Mission, *A Short Catechism for the Use of Colored Members on Trial of the M. E. Church in South Carolina* (1832); Rev. Samuel J. Bryan, *A Plain and Easy Catechism Designed for Benefit of Colored Children, with Several Verses and Hymns* (1833); *The Colored Man's Help; or the Planter's Catechism* (Richmond, 1834); and Mrs. Horace S. Pratt, *Biographies of Servants Mentioned in the Scriptures, with Questions and Answers* (1834); Rev. C. C. Jones, *A Catechism for Colored Persons* (1834); Bishop Meade of Virginia, *Sermons, Dialogues and Narratives for Servants* (1836).   The Diocese of S. C. had published through Dr. Christopher Gadsden, T. Frazier and Wm. Barnwell, *A Catechism to Be Used by the Teachers of Religious Instruction of Persons of Color* (1837); Rev. A. F. Dickinson, *Plantation Sermons, or Plain and Familiar Discourses for the Instruction of the Unlearned* (1850); and Rev. Alexander Glennie, *Sermons Preached on Plantations to Congregations of Negroes.* Referred to in C. C. Jones, *op. cit.* the best work on the history of religious instruction.

the souls of our slaves are a solemn trust and we shall strive to present them faultless and complete before the presence of God."[23] Finally, the movement acted as an effective check to antagonistic teachings and became a bulwark in the defense of the slaveholder. In so far as the church was successful in stating and applying its theory, the charge that slaveholding was immoral lost its force.

Having done with the theory of the church as to its office and with the means of carrying it out, we may now analyze the church's ideas of the essential nature of slavery and the ideas as to the future of the institution. Accepting the authority of the Bible, the church had determined that morally slaveholding was not sinful. This decision did not imply, however, that it was an ideal state to be perpetuated. That conclusion depended upon circumstances of time and place. The church merely went so far as to uphold the system as the most perfect relation of the races in the South. As a matter of fact, the position of the church was that slavery existed because of the state of sin in the world, and not that it would remain in a state of perfect holiness and purity. Dr. Thornwell explained his idea of the nature of slavery as follows:

Slavery is a part of the curse which sin has introduced into the world and stands in the same general relations to Christianity as poverty, sickness, disease, or death. In other words, it is a relation which can only be conceived as taking place among fallen beings— tainted with a curse. It springs not from the nature of man as man, nor from the nature of society as such, but from the nature of man as sinful, and the nature of society as disordered.[24]

In the fallen state of misery and sin in which man lived, slavery became necessary as the lesser of evils and as the only means of progress. Slavery was an evil in the same sense as servitude, of any degree, or even hired labor, for viewed in

---

[23] "Address," *Southern Presbyterian Review,* XIV (1862), 541.
[24] *Rights and Duties of Masters,* p. 31.

an ideal sense even to gain one's bread by the sweat of one's brow was an evil. Thus slavery was placed in a category with all sin and the query ultimately became that of why God had permitted any sin to come into the world.

This conception of slavery fitted well into the Calvinistic theology and the prominent Presbyterian divines of the South carried the logic of the theory to its extreme. Dr. Palmer explained it as follows:

In the imperfect state of human society, it pleases God to allow evils which check others that are greater. As in the physical world, objects are moved forward, not by a single force, but by the composition of forces, there are checks and balances whose intimate relations are comprehended only by himself.[25]

Considering slavery a result of sin without considering the slaveholding relation essentially sinful the final question was as to its future. Here again was manifested a division between perpetualists and gradualists. The first group, it would appear, were in the minority. Such men as Parson Brownlow said that "slavery having existed ever since the first organization of society, it will exist to the end of time."[26] This view was held in a modified form by Dr. Thornwell:

That the design of Christianity is to secure the perfection of the race, is obvious from all its arrangements; and that when this end shall have been consummated, slavery must cease to exist, is equally clear. This is only asserting that there will be no bondage in heaven. Among beings of the same nature, each relatively perfect, there can be no other inequalities than those which spring from superior endowments—the outward advantages of all must be of the same kind, though they may vary in degrees proportioned to the capacities of the individuals to enjoy them. If Adam had never sinned and brought death into the world, with all our woe, the bondage of man to man would never have been instituted;

[25] *Op. cit.*, p. 69.
[26] *Ought American Slavery To Be Perpetuated?*, pp. 18-19.

and when the effects of transgression shall have been purged from the earth, and the new heavens and the new earth, wherein dwelleth righteousness, given to the saints, all bondage shall be abolished. In this sense, slavery is inconsistent with the spirit of the Gospel, that it contemplates a state of things, an existing economy, which it is the design of the Gospel to remove.[27]

Here Thornwell stated the theory that the influence of Christianity was to mitigate the severity of bondage. Nevertheless, he felt that the complete liberation would not occur until the millennium, as there would not be a condition of holiness upon the earth until then. A great many other divines thought that the theory of religious instruction, which in fact was necessary to reconcile slavery with Christianity, would lead to a gradual destruction of the system. Since the relation existed because of the benefit to the slave, then as generations passed, the condition of the slave would become such that he no longer would have need of the relation. From this idea, developed the theory that God never intended slavery to be perpetual, but merely a stage in the development of society, whereby the slave was raised from barbarism to a degree of civilization that would in the end make safe the abolition of the institution. In other words religious thought in the South conceived of slavery as a condition of tutelage in which the principles of Christianity would be instilled into the slave, and he would be prepared for a heavenly equality. Bishop Elliott, of Georgia, was one of those who believed in the power of Christianity to effect, some day, a change in the status of the slave.

However the world may judge us in connection with our institution of slavery, we conscientiously believe it to be a great missionary institution—one arranged by God, as he arranges all the moral and religious influences of the world so that the good may be brought out of seeming evil, and a blessing wrung out of every

[27] *Rights and Duties of Masters*, p. 31.

form of the curse. We believe that we are educating these people as they are educated nowhere else; that we are elevating them in every generation; that we are working out God's purposes, whose consummation we are quite willing to leave in his hands.[28]

Finally, it would seem that the religious element held that slavery was a divine trust maintained for the time being in order to Christianize and civilize the slave. As a result the church group almost as a unit opposed the reopening of the slave trade, because the influx of a large barbarian element in the population would tend to destroy the work already accomplished and would postpone the final consummation of the divine mission. Consequently, we find that the church distinguished between the morality of slavery and of the slave trade. The latter could not fit in its scheme of justification. On the other side, the advocates of the African slave trade drew heavily upon the theory of the church in an attempt to extend its benevolent influence to the entire black race. Regardless of their contention that their desire was consistent with the teaching of the church, they were never able to gain the support of any of the churches. Upon this issue there remained a definite cleavage in pro-slavery theory, each side contradicting the other and both affirming Christian motives.

THE CLASH BETWEEN ANTI-SLAVERY AND PRO-SLAVERY
MORAL PHILOSOPHY

The third phase of the ethical defense of slavery grew out of the conflict betwen two systems of moral philosophy. The anti-slavery and pro-slavery schools ran into conflict over a number of principles of morality. The slaveholder's case based on the Bible stood until refuted. In order to rebut its conclusiveness and make out a contrary case, the anti-slavery

---

[28] *Address to the 39th Annual Convention of the Diocese of Georgia* (Savannah, 1861), p. 9.

moralist had to depart from a strict construction of the literal text. Applying liberal rules of textual criticism, the anti-slavery exegete denied the correctness of the slaveholder's conclusions, and by using the general principles of Christianity, he attempted to destroy the Bible defense. Criticising the general principle technique of the abolitionist, Representative Keitt of South Carolina declared in 1858 that the South was "to be damned into a change of its institutions by virtue of pseudo-scriptures, edited with notes, and exegeses tacked to them by Yankee exponents of bogus Gospel law."[29] Thornwell was struck by the fact that in the scriptural arguments against slavery the principles from which conclusions were drawn were of "the abstrusest speculations," based on "strained application of passages from the Bible" and "forced inferences from doctrine."[30]

One attempt made was to deny that the word "servant" used in the Saint James version had a synonymous meaning with the word "slave," but that it meant a "hired servant." Upon this point, a dispute ensued which led into exhaustive etymological researches. The slaveholder argued that the term "servant" was used to express the original Hebrew term, which was the concept "slave."[31] Another attack upon the conclusiveness of the scriptural argument was the assertion that the slavery of the Bible was not the same as the Ameri-

[29] *Congressional Globe*, 35th Cong., 1st Sess., Appendix, p. 409.

[30] *A Report on Slavery*, p. 11.

[31] James Smylie, *A Review of a Letter from the Presbytery of Chillicothe, to the Presbytery of Mississippi, on the Subject of Slavery* (Woodville, 1836), devoted a portion of his work to this argument. Later Albert Barnes became the chief exponent of the theory that "servant" did not mean "slave." See *An Inquiry into the Scriptural Views of Slavery* (Philadelphia, 1846). He was especially interested in proving this in regard to the Epistle to Philemon. Charles Sumner made much of the same argument. They were answered by Bledsoe, *Liberty and Slavery*, pp. 182-225. See also W. A. Smith, *op. cit.*, pp. 141-142; and John Fletcher, *op. cit.*, in Study VII, probably goes most thoroughly into the derivations and orthography of the words. The great Biblical commentator, Adam Clark, was often cited as authority by the slaveholder to support his contention.

can form, and that God gave no countenance to the latter. It was argued that the Old Testament slavery was sanctioned only for the Hebrew polity, and that the slavery which existed during New Testament times was of the white race and not of the Negro race.[32] In reply, the pro-slavery theorists said that it was the thing itself, the principle of slavery that was sanctioned, and that it might take various forms at different times. In moral science a relation once given divine sanction remained moral under all conditions until prohibited, or modified, by the same authority.

But the more important attack upon the scriptural argument was that the spirit of the scriptures opposed any idea of slavery and that Christ established certain principles of morals, which would gradually destroy the relation wherever it existed. Viewed as a whole, the spirit of the Bible was progressive. The Old Testament taught the principle of exact justice, "a tooth for a tooth," while the New Dispensation set forth the principle of mercy and forgiveness. Again, only on such a progression theory in the realm of morals could the existence of polygamy and concubinage among the early Jews be explained. On like grounds it might be said that slavery which had been permitted to a primitive civilization would become a sin in a developed state of society. Dr. Channing felt that the argument for slavery on the ground that it was permitted in the Old Testament and not condemned in the New proved too much: "If usages, sanctioned in the Old Testament and not forbidden in the New, are right, then our moral code will undergo a sad deterioration. Polygamy was allowed to the Israelites. . . . But the Apostles nowhere condemn it."[33]

[32] This argument was proposed by Dr. W. E. Channing, *Slavery* (Boston, 1836), p. 120, and by Henry Drisler, *Bible View of Slavery Examined* (n., p. 1862), pp. 3-9.

[33] *Op. cit.,* p. 119.

On the pro-slavery side, it was claimed that the cases of polygamy and slavery were not parallel, because the first was never expressly sanctioned by God, as slavery was. There was no law, ordinance, or decree supporting polygamy; and in the last analysis, it remained with the Israelites merely as a private vice. Moreover, Christ did condemn it openly.[34] The real import of this argument was brought out in the debate between two eminent Baptist divines, Dr. Wayland, of Brown University, and Dr. Fuller, of South Carolina. Dr. Wayland acknowledged that slavery existed under the Jewish theocracy, being regulated by divine law. Consequently, Dr. Fuller contended that slavery could be no sin, since sin was the transgression of the law of God. But Dr. Wayland held that a thing might be permitted to exist by the divine will and still be a sin. In other words, the Bible permitted sin to exist for a period on the ground of expediency.[35] To the Southern group of theologians, there was implicit in this argument an absolute denial of the authority of the Bible.

Ultimately this question led the slaveholder to speculate as to the relation of the Deity to absolute right and wrong. They did not all reach the same conclusion. Dr. Smith, professor of moral and intellectual philosophy at Randolph-Macon College, for instance, thought that the will of God was the rule of right in the sense that it always conforms to that which in itself is right, but not in the sense that it is absolutely in itself the only rule of right. He would not assign to the Deity "the power to make the wrong the right, and the right the wrong." According to his view, the slavery that God provided for the Jews being right in principle, therefore, was right for all time.[36] A similar idea was expressed

[34] See Sawyer, *op. cit.*, p. 36.

[35] *Domestic Slavery Considered as a Scriptural Institution* (New York and Boston, 1845). See also a review, "Slavery in the Southern States," in *Southern Quarterly Review*, VIII (1845), 317-360.

[36] *Op. cit.*, pp. 145-146.

by R. H. Rivers, professor of moral philosophy at Wesleyan College, Florence, Alabama. In answering Mahan's contention that slavery was established by human law, he insisted that it was divine legislation, which, if it did not make it right, did prove that it was right: "We maintain that God's law is always right, and that whatever God established is right, not because he established it, but we maintain that God established it *because he saw that it is right*."[37] Dr. Ross of Alabama took a different view. He thought that right and wrong were made to exist solely by the will of God, that rectitude and turpitude were conformity or non-conformity to His law. He explained that "sin is the transgression of the law and where there is no law there is no sin." Thus polygamy was not sin until God made it so; slavery was never sin because God early commanded it and had never prohibited it.[38]

Besides attempting to explain away the Old Testament sanction, it was equally important that the anti-slavery group account for the fact that Christ had nowhere condemned slavery and that the Apostles had preserved His silence. The same reason of expediency and policy was offered in this case. God might make known his will in many ways, either directly or indirectly. As it happened Christ and the Apostles determined that the best way to rebuke the sin was to say nothing about it, to regulate the manner in which it should be indulged, and to leave it to the general spirit of Christianity eventually to abolish the evil. Dr. Paley, the eminent Scotch moral philosopher of the late eighteenth century, had suggested that the reason for the silence of the scriptures was twofold, that Christianity seeking admission into all nations abstained from an interference with civil institutions, and secondly that to have preached immediate freedom would

[37] *Elements of Moral Philosophy* (Nashville, 1860), p. 330.
[38] *Op. cit.*, pp. 39-45.

have resulted in a great servile war.[39] Paley had a great influence upon the development of the expediency argument by the anti-slavery moralists.[40]

The ultimate task of the school of moralists who attacked the pro-slavery case built on the scriptures was to state the general tendencies of Christianity that were subversive of slavery. What were the principles of the Gospel which were intended as a substitute for a direct condemnation of wrong and sin, and under the operation of which slavery would gradually disappear? The precept most often cited and the one upon which the chain of reason depended was the Golden Rule. It is interesting to know that this principle pervaded the moral discussion from the very earliest conflict of opinion on slavery. It might well be called the first principle of the moral question, determining the ultimate justice of either position. It will be seen that the pro-slavery theorist harmonized the principle of the Golden Rule with the scriptural defense, while the opposition used it to destroy the entire defense. In fact, all schools of anti-slavery opinion, when arguing on moral grounds, were forced to this rule as their citadel of strength. Dr. Wayland outlined the significance of it as follows:

The moral precepts of the Bible are diametrically opposed to slavery. They are, Thou shalt love thy *neighbor* as *thyself*, and *all things whatsoever* ye would that men should do unto you, do ye even so unto them.

1. The application of these precepts is universal. Our neighbor is *every one whom we may benefit*. The obligation respects *all*

[39] *Works*, I, 147.
[40] See for examples of the acceptance of Paley's reasoning, Francis Wayland, *The Elements of Moral Science* (Boston, 1848), p. 202; Channing, *op. cit.*, p. 122; and Barnes, *op. cit.*, p. 228 *ff.* The reasons of Paley were quoted with approval in Congress as early as 1790 in the abolition petition debate. See speech of Boudinot, of New Jersey, March 22nd, *Annals of Congress*, 1st Cong., 1st Sess., p. 1468.

things whatsoever. The precept, then, manifestly, extends to *men, as men,* or *men* in *every condition;* and if to all things what soever, certainly to a thing so important as the right to personal liberty.

2. Again. By this precept, it is made our duty to cherish as tender and delicate a respect for the right which the meanest individual possesses over the means of happiness bestowed upon him by God, as we cherish for our own right over our own means of happiness, or as we desire any other individual to cherish for it. Now were this precept obeyed, it is manifest that slavery could not in fact exist for a single instant. The principle of the precept is absolutely subversive of the principle of slavery. That of the one is the entire equality of right; that of the other, the entire absorption of the rights of one in the rights of the other.[41]

Likewise, Dr. Channing contended that slaveholding was an infraction of the Golden Rule because every man feels "that nothing, could induce him to become a slave . . . if reduced to this abject lot, his whole nature, reason, conscience, affections would cry out against it." Applying the rule of scriptural criticism, that particular texts should be interpreted according to the general tenor and spirit of Christianity, the Golden Rule, the great perpetual teaching of Christianity in regard to social duty, would override the few texts designed for temporary and local use.[42]

To the mind of the slaveholder such reasoning did not carry great weight as an ethical argument. Having given up the notion of any direct and explicit condemnation in the scriptures, he charged that the attempt of the anti-slavery moralist to show that the genius and spirit of Christianity were opposed to slavery resulted from a distortion and a misapplication of the great commandment. The monstrous perversion of the Golden Rule that generated the abolition

[41] *Elements of Moral Science,* p. 209.
[42] *Op. cit.,* pp. 124-125.

philosophy came from the idea that it required one "to change places with your neighbor, and make your imaginary wishes if in his place, the law for you in yours." Doing good according to such a rule became "the natural problem of a sinful humanity, for it is doing good upon one's own principles; his own wisdom, his own passions, his own will, determine what is benevolent and philanthropic; every man is left to eat at the tree of his own knowledge of what is good and evil."[43] The slaveholder felt that the abolitionist made the capital mistake of assuming without evidence to support it that the Golden Rule opposed the slave relation. To him the Golden Rule of Christ embodied the same soul as the moral injunction of Moses: "Thou shalt love thy neighbor as thyself." (Leviticus XIX:18). The two must have the same import because Jesus said that there were but two principles in God's moral government, one including all that is due to God, the other all that is due to man. Consequently, Christ added no new moral principle that would prohibit slavery, and under the law of Moses the principle and slavery were reconciled.[44]

Again it was often pointed out that even conceding that in logic the Golden Rule was a condemnation of slavery; yet, if slavery was afterward expressly mentioned and treated as lawful, it would obviously follow that slavery was excepted by necessary implication. Therefore those who extracted the prohibition from the rule begged the question in dispute.[45] In other words, according to the construction of the slaveholder, the rule did not reveal at all what man's relations should be, but informed him what to do under those relations. In regard to slavery, instead of requiring the master to withdraw his care and protection, the rule required the main-

[43] J. C. Coit, *A Discourse upon Government, Divine and Human* (Columbia, 1853), p. 45.

[44] Thornton Stringfellow, "The Bible Argument: or, Slavery in the Light of Divine Revelation," *Cotton Is King*, p. 479.

[45] Thornwell, "Address," *Southern Presbyterian Review*, XIV (1862), 541.

tenance of the relation as a duty, and operated on the master only by requiring him to do what was just and benevolent under the relation, to use the slave well and to treat him with humanity. Following out the theory of the church, it was a command to perfect and improve the character of both parties.

It was with such an idea that Beverley Tucker took a realistic approach to the ethics of slavery. He observed that the relation subsisting between master and slave was favorable to the growth of religion in the hearts of both and to the fruition of the Christian rule of love. Not only did he believe that slavery had proved "a nurse to virtue through the agency of religion" but that it came "in aid of religion to carry on the work of reformation in the heart and life of the slave." The appropriate manifestation of those affections which it was the office of religion to cultivate in man, incident to the slave relation, had a mute language "in the cheerful humility, the liberal obedience, the devoted loyalty of the slave, and in the gentleness, the kindness, the courtesy of the master."[46]

Looking at the other side of the relation, the slaveholder said that it was not what the individual desired that became his right under the Rule, but what he ought to desire. As Bledsoe concluded, "the whole question of right turns upon what he ought to wish or desire in such a condition."[47] Thus the command extended only to cases where the slave's condition ought to be changed and it completely lost its force in reference to the slaveholder who was striving to make the condition of the slave better. The same idea was clearly expressed by Dr. Dabney of Virginia as follows:

[46] "An Essay on the Moral and Political Effects of the Relation Between the Caucasian Master and the African Slave," *Lectures on the Science of Government*, pp. 307-317. Also published in *Southern Literary Messenger*, X (1844), 329-339 and 470-480.

[47] *Op. cit.*, p. 68.

The meaning . . . , is, not that we must do to our fellow all that our caprice might desire, if our positions were inverted; but what we should believe ourselves morally entitled to require of him, in that case. Here, then, is the true basis of human equality. Men are all children of a common Father, brethren of the same race, each one entitled by the same right to his own appropriate share of well-being. Hence, by a single and conclusive step, as the foundation of civil government is moral, its proper object is the good of all, governors and governed.[48]

His conclusion was that the rule of love was simply "the inculcation of universal equity," which regulated the ranks and gradations of society but did not abolish them.

To interpret the rule in any other way, the slaveholder contended, was tantamount to a repudiation of all authority, for the authority of the master was based upon the same principle as that of the father, the husband, and even of the state.[49] Dr. Thornwell inquired: "Who is authorized to limit the application of this sweeping principle to the sole relation of slavery? It is as much the weapon of the socialist and the leveler as of the abolitionist." In the last analysis, the Golden Rule became, according to the interpretation of the two schools, on the one side, the principle of essential equality between individuals, and on the other, the principle of authority and subordination. There was a counterpart to this moral principle in the political realm, where pro-slavery and anti-slavery theory definitely divided betwen individualism and societarianism.

Apart from the field of moral arguments based on scripture, there was a field of ethical discussion dealing with human rights. Essentially moral science dealt with relation-

[48] *Op. cit.*, p. 254.

[49] The following passage from Dabney is in point: "If then the necessities of order justify the subjection of a whole nation . . . to one man, will not the same reasons justify the far milder and more benevolent authority of masters over their servants?" *Ibid.*, p. 258.

ships of man to man, and it became important to determine whether slavery was such a relation. It might be proved contrary to moral science on the ground that it reduced the nature of the slave below that of a person or that it divested him of certain rights essential to his humanity. The anti-slavery school of moral philosophers argued against the morality of slavery upon these grounds. Probably the most extreme concept of the unmoral nature of slavery was expressed by Professor Whewell as follows:

Slavery is contrary to the Fundamental Principles of Morality. It neglects the great primary distinction of Persons and Things; converting a Person into a Thing, an object merely passive, without any recognized attributes of Human Nature. A slave is, in the eye of the State which stamps him with that character, not acknowledged as a man. . . . He is reduced to the level of the brutes.[50]

Wayland took a somewhat milder view, as follows:

It supposes at best, that the relation between master and slave, is not that which exists between man and man, but is a modification, at least, of that which exists between man and the brutes.[51]

Thus the first accusation was that slavery turned the nature of a moral being into that of a thing. The second accusation under moral science held that slavery was the infraction of human rights. To begin with, it destroyed the essential equality of men. Dr. Wayland said that it violated the "personal liberty of man as a physical, intellectual, and moral being." It thus subjected "the duty of man to God, entirely to the will of man." In this light then the moral agency of the slave was destroyed, as the master had control

---

[50] William Whewell, *The Elements of Morality Including Polity* (New York, 1852), I, 372.

[51] *Op. cit.*, p. 206. Channing, *op. cit.*, p. 13, speaks of a slave: "to be another's instrument," and p. 15, "an article of property."

of the soul of the slave.[52]   With the same idea, Dr. Channing brought out his seven famous arguments against the right of property in man, for property was an exclusive right and shut out all claims but that of the possessor.[53]   Summing up the arguments of these moral scientists, Dr. Smith of Virginia commented:

Following these we should adopt the belief that the principle of slavery in question is, as they express it, "an absorption of the humanity of one man into the will of another"; or, in other words, that "slavery contemplates him, not as a responsible, but as a mere sentient being—not as a man, but a brute."[54]

These views were flatly denied by the slaveholder.   Dr. Thornwell said that "the constitution of the human mind is in flagrant contradiction to the absorption of the conscience, will, and understanding of one man into the personality of another—it is a thing which cannot be conceived,"[55] and Dr. Smith said that "this is a state of things which the human mind cannot even conceive to be possible, but does intuitively perceive to be utterly impossible."[56]   It was ridiculous to say that human legislation could convert mind into matter or matter into mind.   The Southern school distinctly recognized the personality of the slave.   They said that the soul could be lost but not sold, and denied that the master's right of property destroyed the rights of the slave as man.   In fact the Southern school of moral philosophers based their argument on the human nature of the slave, and accepted the same principle of moral science, namely—that in all relations of man to man, every right involved a corresponding duty.   They claimed that correlative rights and duties pervaded the whole system of Southern slavery.   Here again they pointed

[52] Thornwell said that their logic reduced the question to such a point, *Rights and Duties of Masters*, p. 22.

[53] *Op. cit.*, pp. 13-30.   [54] *Op. cit.*, p. 147.

[55] *Rights and Duties of Masters*, p. 22.

[56] *Op. cit.*, p. 148.

to the Bible as establishing the rights and duties. In the last analysis, it was claimed that the slave possessed certain rights which the master could not justly disregard.

It was at this point that the moral philosopher of slavery ran into conflict with the school of ethnological defenders, because the latter seemed to the former to deny the essential humanity of the slave. The former charged that because the latter based the justification of bondage on the inferior intellect and faculties of the Negro, he also denied his Christian responsibilities and his claims to be treated as a human being under the care of man and the concern of God. Thornwell deplored the fact that in the South "science, falsely so called may attempt to exclude him from the brotherhood of humanity" and deny to him "the same humanity in which we glory as the image of God."[57]

Thus the slave moralist definitely claimed that the relation of slavery recognized the human rights of the slave and insisted that their protection was fundamental to the entire moral defense. Further dispute arose as to the nature and content of those rights. As both schools acknowledged basic human rights, this discussion was reduced to the question of what was included under those rights. But the pro-slavery theorist denied that rights arose from an essential equality of individuals. The rights of individuals differed according to their different characters and relations. The pro-slavery theory of rights in moral science was probably best expressed by Dr. Thornwell thus:

As to the endless declamation about human rights, we have only to say that human rights are not a fixed but a fluctuating quantity. Their sum is not the same in any two nations on the globe. . . . There is a minimum without which a man cannot be responsible; there is a maximum which expresses the highest degree of civiliza-

---

[57] *Rights and Duties of Masters*, p. 11. Whewell made a similar attack on the ethnologist from the anti-slavery viewpoint, *op. cit.*, I, 375-376.

tion and of Christian culture. The education of the species con-
sists in its ascent along this line. As you go up, the number of
rights increases, but the number of individuals who possess them
diminishes. As you come down the line, rights are diminished,
but the individuals are multiplied. It is just the opposite of the
predicamental scale of the logicians, there comprehension diminishes as you ascend, and extension increases, and comprehension
increases as you descend and extension decreases. Now when it
is said that slavery is inconsistent with human rights, we crave to
understand what point in this line the slave is conceived to occupy.
There are, no doubt, many rights which belong to other men
which are denied him. But is he fit to possess them? Has God
qualified him to meet the responsibilities which their possession
necessarily implies? His place in the scale is determined by his
competency to fulfill his duties. There are other rights which he
certainly possesses, without which he could be neither human nor
accountable. Before slavery can be charged with doing him injustice it must be proved that the minimum which falls to his lot, at
the bottom of the line, is out of proportion to his capacity and
culture. The truth is, the education of the human race for liberty
and virtue, is a vast Providential scheme, and God assigns to every
man . . . the precise place he is to occupy in the great moral
school of humanity.[58]

Dabney expressed the theory in somewhat different form:

Now it is clear, that the several rights of different individuals in
the same society must differ exceedingly, because the persons differ
indefinitely in powers, knowledge, virtue, and natural relations to
each other. From that very law of love and equity, whence the
moral equality of men was inferred, it must also follow, that one
man is not entitled to pursue his natural well-being at the expense
of that of other men, or of society. Each one's right must be so
pursued, as not to infringe other's rights. The well being of all
is interconnected. Hence equity, yea, a true equality itself, demands a varied distribution of social privilege among the members,
according to their different characters and relations. . . . To at-

[58] "Address," *Southern Presbyterian Review*, XIV (1862), 541.

tempt an identical and mechanical equality . . . would be essential inequality; for it would clothe the incompetent and undeserving with power to injure the deserving and capable, without real benefit to themselves.[59]

It was with like reasoning that Professor Rivers answered Wayland's alphabetical argument of the unmoral quality of the slave relation. Wayland had argued in this fashion:

Suppose that A has a right to use the body of B according to his, that is, A's will. Now, if this be true, it is true universally; hence A has the control over the body of B, and B has control over the body of C, C of that of D, etc., and Z again over the body of A; that is, every separate will has the right of control over some other body or intellect besides its own, and has no right of control over its own body or intellect.[60]

Rivers pointed out that the fallacy in the argument was the assumption that all men are equally capable of self-government. If there were no more difference between men than there is between the letters of the alphabet then the alphabetical argument would have some force. But so long as there is not only difference in men but in races of men which varies their capacity for self-government, it had no force.[61]

Furthermore, the Southern school contended that human rights in moral science were not synonymous with the so-called natural rights. The rights of a father were natural rights, but they belonged only to fathers; the rights of property were natural, but belonged only to property holders.[62] In many other cases of this sort, natural rights did not arise because of one's humanity, but because of his position in society.

Finally, the last phase of the moral question, the clash resulting from the logic of the two schools, will be examined.

[59] *Op. cit.*, pp. 255-256.
[60] *Op. cit.*, p. 202.   [61] *Op. cit.*, p. 367.
[62] For a clear explanation of the whole theory of the difference between human rights and natural rights, see Adger, *The Christian Doctrine of Human Rights and Slavery* (Columbia, 1849).

In passing a judgment upon the essential right and wrong of slaveholding, it became necessary to determine the source of all moral rectitude. The slaveholder said that the law which determined good and evil must come from a source above man, for man had contradictory and confused views. Man must submit to the revealed work of God, as the universal and infallible rule of action. Since the scriptures contained the only standard of morals that the Almighty had revealed; therefore, the Bible forever settled abstract questions of morality. Dr. Thornwell said: "We must not repeat that a sound philosophy must ever coincide with revelation, but what we insist upon is that in cases of conflict the scriptures must be supreme. Man may err, but God can never lie."[63]

On the other side, the anti-slavery school in their argument adopted certain principles that seemed to deny that a plenary revelation was made in the Bible and seemed to attack the authority of the Bible. They contended that there was a multitude of truths in the depths of ethics which the scriptures did not specifically mention, and that the Bible presupposed in man a knowledge of principles of natural justice taught by reason, observation, and experience. In this view, the authority of the Bible as a complete revelation was denied; and reason was established as equally authoritative in determining right and wrong.[64] As the slaveholder viewed

[63] *Report on Slavery*, p. 12.

[64] It is difficult to say how far the pro-slavery moralist would have gone in denying the authority of reason. Probably the most philosophical statement of the relative place of reason and scripture in making a determination of truth was stated by Dr. Thornwell in his *Discourses on Truth* (New York, 1855), Ch. I. "So far as the simple knowledge of duty is concerned, we may err, on the one hand by exaggerating the necessity of revelation, and, on the other, by exaggerating the sufficiency of reason. . . . The elemental principles of right, therefore, which are involved in the very conception of a moral nature, must be conceded to man as man. They are the birth rights of his being, and not the legacy of a subsequent revelation. . . . But it is equally an error to maintain that, because the Scriptures presuppose the moral constitution of man, they are of little or no importance, considered as a *rule* of life. It is one thing to say that

it, this was an attack that robbed the scriptures of their supremacy and made them defective as a system of morality.

Certain of the New England thinkers went farther and proclaimed the doctrine that man possessed a distinct moral faculty, by which he was enabled to discover right and wrong without the aid of observation or revelation. This intuitive sense, by which man perceived the morality of his actions, was the voice of God itself. Dr. Wayland gave expression to the doctrine in this way:

It seems, then, . . . that we are all endowed with conscience, or a faculty for discerning a moral quality in human actions, impelling us towards right, and dissuading us from wrong, and that the dictates of this faculty are felt and known to be of supreme authority.[65]

And Dr. Channing said: "We believe that all virtue has its foundation in the moral nature of man, that is, in conscience; or his sense of duty and in the power of forming his temper and life according to conscience."[66] Adopting the concept of a distinct moral faculty, the conclusion was that it taught infallible truth and was above all other law that conflicted with its dictates. Here was the moral basis of the higher law doc-

---

reason is law, and another to say that it is a perfect law." It was because of our fallen condition that our passions and prejudices prevent the original principles of right. "It is only of the law of the Lord, as contained in the Scriptures, that we can justly say that it is perfect." At another time, he said: "We admit that there are primitive principles in morals which be at the root of human consciousness. But the question is how are we to distinguish them? The subjective feeling of certainty is no adequate criterion, as that is equally felt in reference to crotchets and hereditary prejudice. The very point is, to know when this certainty indicates a primitive cognition, and when it does not. There must therefore be some external test." "Address," *Southern Presbyterian Review*, XIV (1862), 543.   [65] *Op. cit.*, p. 83.

[66] *Works* (Tenth Complete Edition, 1849), III, 93. The idea of a separate moral faculty was traced by Fletcher, *op. cit.*, p. 19, back to Lord Shaftesbury, Dr. Hutchinson, and Dr. Reid. Paley discussed the theory in *op. cit.*, Ch. V, but dismissed it as a question of pure curiosity.

trine in the political field and here again was the moral basis
of political individualism.

This doctrine was energetically opposed by the pro-slavery
school. Dr. Fletcher attempted a refutation of it. He
adopted the reasoning of Locke that "moral good and evil
are the conformity or disagreement of our voluntary actions
to some law, whereby good or evil is drawn upon us from
the will or power of the maker."[67] As men disagreed about
the moral quality of different acts, there could not be an infallible faculty of determination in the individual. He explained the mental process of determining truth in this way:

The truth is, we have no such infallible guide. The idea of right
and wrong . . . is always fixed through an exertion of the
powers of the understanding. We have no instinctive power
reaching the case. Our judgment, our feelings are often unstable,
irregular, and sometimes antagonistic. . . . On every decision on
a question of right or wrong, a train of mental action is called into
operation, comparing the ideas already in the mind with the facts of
the case under review, and noting the similarity of these facts to
our idea of right, or whether the facts conform to our idea of
wrong. This decision we call judgment: but when the decision
reaches to the question of right or wrong, touching our own
conduct only, logicians have agreed to call it conscience; not a
distinct action from judgment much less a distinct faculty; and by
no means carrying with it more proof of accuracy and correctness
than is our judgment about any other matter.[68]

Rivers also argued against the supremacy of conscience as
a faculty for discerning good and evil. In any conflict with
any other principle of our nature conscience was the higher
principle and should be obeyed; but "no one should place
conscience above God, or above his law," for there is not a
"higher law in his moral nature which is above God's re-

[67] *Op. cit.*, p. 196.　　　　　　[68] *Ibid.*, p. 20.

vealed law."[69]   P. R. Leatherman in his work on moral
science devoted a section to a refutation of the conscience doctrine of the abolitionists.   To him man had no gift or faculty
which was an unerring guide to truth.   Instead of man being
able to depend upon his conscience as a moral sense by which
he was enabled to decide immediately concerning the moral
quality of an action, he thought that "the nearer an individual's standard of right approaches to the great standard of
moral law, the Bible, the more correctly he will be able to
decide concerning the moral quality of actions."[70]   In fact,
had God bestowed such an instinctive and intuitive faculty
upon man then His revelation would have been unnecessary
and mere surplusage.   Nevertheless, a somewhat different
answer was given to this question by W. S. Grayson, who admitted: "I am perfectly aware that slavery is repugnant to
the *natural* emotions of men. . . . But I take the stand on
the position that our natural feelings are unsafe guides for
us to follow in the social relations."   He explained that they
had become a fallible guide because of the fall of man.[71]

Regardless of the doctrine of conscience, the slaveholder contended that opposition to slavery had never been
the offspring of the Bible, but had sprung from the misguided
reason of man in applying natural not revealed law.   It was
the product of the rationalism of the age, which proceeded on
the ground that the human mind was itself capable of deciding what revelation ought to be, and of elaborating its own
system of divine truth.   Thus the conflict between the anti-
slavery school and the Southern school of moral philosophers,
to the mind of the slaveholder, reduced itself into a clash between rationalism and what some called scripturalism.   A

[69] *Op. cit.*, p. 68.

[70] *Elements of Moral Science* (Philadelphia, 1860), pp. 58-73.

[71] "Is Slavery Right, or, Natural and Moral Philosophy Contradistinguished,"
Southern Literary Messenger, XXXI (1860), 248.

brilliant explanation of the differences in these systems of logic was given by a Southern divine:

Scripturalism is the inductive philosophy of religion. By an induction of facts we prove that the Bible comes from God. This determined, we ask what does the Bible teach. To find out this we examine its contents, and by plain and ordinary laws of language we decide. . . . To the Scripturalist these doctrines are true, because he finds them in the Bible.

This was the logic technique of the pro-slavery school, while the anti-slavery school practiced a fundamentally different one.

Rationalism, however, proceeds upon a different principle. Exalting the human reason above the Scriptures, many go to the word of God determined to make its teachings bend to their preconceived notions of what a revelation ought to be. . . . Being independent of the Scriptures, they are tolerated rather than received, and as often as their teachings come into conflict with the more reliable deductions of the inner man, they must be set aside.[72]

Thus the Southern moralist went so far as to attribute infidelity to the abolitionist, who in order to establish the evil of slavery, was compelled to abandon the Bible wherever it did not sustain his principles.[73] It was just as dangerous to deviate to the one side as to the other in interpreting scrip-

[72]S. W. Stanford, "Scripturalism versus Rationalism," *Southern Presbyterian Review*, V (1851), 271. The charge of rationalism upon abolition is also made by Thornwell, *Report on Slavery*, p. 12: "The very same spirit of rationalism which has made the prophets and apostles succumb to philosophy and impulse in relation to the doctrine of salvation, lies at the foundation of modern speculation in relation to the rights of man."

[73] See for example in Wayland and Fuller, *op. cit.*, pp. 83-84 the statement of Dr. Wayland: "If the religion of Christ allows such a license (to hold slaves) from such percepts as these, the New Testament would be the greatest curse that ever was inflicted on our race." See also Barnes, *op. cit.*, p. 381. "If the Bible could be shown to defend and countenance slavery as a good institution, it would make thousands of infidels." On these grounds the anti-slavery moralists were often charged with infidelity.

ture, and those who declared things sinful that it instituted did more to destroy its authority than the avowed atheist. They claimed that the divines of New England had established a transcendental religion as a counterpart of their transcendental philosophy. Their argument was strengthened by the fact that a number of New England scholars had, about this period, accepted the higher criticism of the Bible from the German rationalists.[74] Thus the clash between the two schools of slavery moralists was characterized by orthodoxy versus liberalism, which has become fundamentalism versus modernism of the present day.

In order to combat the general tendency toward rationalism, the orthodox thinkers of the South found it necessary to publish new texts in the field of moral science for use in instructing the youth. The traditional texts were entirely unsuitable for use in building a militant defense of slavery, so that during the 1850s a number of new ones were published written from the "Southside" view of morals. These texts in presenting a systematic moral science were distinctive in that they contained sections presenting the scriptural argument, sections outlining the duties of both parties to the slave relation, and in that they attempted to refute the conscience doctrine of ultimate truth.[75]

To the slaveholder, furthermore, the rationalistic method in moral science had a far reaching significance; it involved a principle that struck at every fibre of society. Rationalism in morals was closely related to radicalism in politics. The transcendentalist taught political concepts that were out of harmony with the scriptural grounds of government; and the attack upon the authority of the Bible grew into an attack upon the principle of authority embedded in all institutions,

---

[74] Among others, the names of Channing, Norton, Parker, and Palfrey stand out.

[75] The two best examples are Rivers, *op. cit.*, and Leatherman, *op. cit.*

the family, the church, and the state. The doctrine of the conscience in moral science had its counterpart in the political theory of the sovereignty of the individual.[76]

It was at this point, moreover, that the orthodoxy of the moral philosopher conflicted with the ethnological school of pro-slavery thought. To the moralist it was another evidence of the radical and rationalistic method that enabled the ethnologist to harmonize the doctrine of universal emancipation and the defense of slavery. The ethnologist had attempted to prove by deductions from science that the Bible doctrine of the unity of the races was not true, that Negroes belonged to a different species, were not human and, therefore, might be enslaved with perfect consistency with the theory of absolute social equality. While rationalism on the part of the abolitionists rejected the scriptures "because they do not denounce slavery as a sin"; radicalism on the part of the ethnologist attacked the authority of the scriptures "because they teach us that the negroes are human beings, fellow creatures of God, and that though in God's providence they are slaves, God requires that we care for them as brethren."[77]

The justification for Southern secession drew much from the school of moralists. They held that secession was as much a moral as a political necessity, for no people could work out their destiny in a nation pervaded with rationalistic and atheistic principles, such as the old government was founded upon. Bishop Elliott accounted for the moral obloquy of the nation which had made secession necessary in one of his eloquent sermons early in the war. He believed that there had been

no necessity to cast to the winds all conservatism, and to lay down principles, as the foundation of our government, which were con-

<hr />

[76] George Frederick Holmes correlated these two theories as a part of the anti-slavery thought in an article, "The Theory of Political Individualism," *DeBow*, XXII (1857), pp. 133-149.   [77] Stanford, *loc. cit.*, p. 281.

trary to Revelation, and therefore, to Truth. Carried away by our opposition to monarchy and an established Church, we declared war against all authority and against all form. The reason of man was exalted to an impious degree and in the face not only of experience, but of the revealed word of God, all men were declared equal, and man was pronounced capable of self-government. . . . Two greater falsehoods could not have been announced, because the one struck at the whole constitution of civil society as it had ever existed, and because the other denied the fall and corruption of man.[78]

He felt that the remedy lay not in a change of the form of government, but in the modification of the principles upon which it was founded. These principles of the old government having the force of authority, had influenced the spirit of the people toward insubordination. Carefully differentiating between subordination and inferiority, he declared that "subordination rules supreme in heaven and must rule supreme on earth." Dr. Palmer in a great sermon on the eve of the war also declared that subordination was the theistic principle upon which governments are founded:

Last of all, in this struggle, we defend the cause of God and religion. The abolition spirit is undeniably atheistic. The demon which erected its throne upon the guillotine in the days of Robespierre and Marat, which abolished the Sabbath and worshipped *reason* in the person of a harlot, yet survives to work other horrors, of which those of the French Revolution are but the type. . . . From a thousand Jacobin clubs here, as in France, the decree has gone forth which strikes at God by striking at all subordination and law.[79]

The idea that the spirit of rationalism exemplified by abolition would inevitably lead to a repetition of the French Revolution was one of the most common manifestations of pro-

[78] *A Sermon, Christ Church, Savannah, Feb. 28, 1862* (Savannah, 1862), p. 8.
[79] *A Discourse. The South: Her Peril and Her Duty* (New Orleans, 1860), p. 10.

slavery theory.   As a result, the school of moralists, led by the brilliant James Henley Thornwell, launched a movement to give explicit recognition to the moral concepts in the new constitution to be framed.   It was considered a glaring error that no recognition of God was made by the old Constitution and the proposal was made to include a clause in the Confederate Constitution recognizing God.   The moral rationale of slavery culminated in an endeavor to create a theistic state in the slaveholding South.

CHAPTER VI

THE ETHNOLOGICAL JUSTIFICATION OF SLAVERY

THE ethnological justification of slavery carries us into the field of positive philosophy. In one sense of the word, it was an appeal to nature as the proper moral foundation upon which the institution could be placed. It was an extension of the moral defense in that whatever harmonizes with nature may be said to accord with the will of the Creator and thereby to be His revelation. The chief significance of the ethnological argument, however, was apart from ethics. It was rather an attempt to find a scientific foundation for slavery. By means of the inductive method, through the application of new information derived from the natural sciences, the speculation made long before by Aristotle that slavery grew out of an inequality in nature was given verification. Making use of the exact sciences, with the knife of the anatomist and the spade of the anthropologist as tools, the naturalist laboriously collected and carefully analyzed a large array of facts upon which was built the positive philosophy of slavery. In this chapter of experimental philosophy, induction confirmed what had long been but a preconceived hypothesis. The conclusion reached was that slavery did not spring from any disorder in nature nor from a struggle for race supremacy, but that it grew out of nature's well ordered plans.

In the American slavery system the ethnic factor was of basic significance because of the presence of distinct races upon which it was founded, the Negro and the Caucasian. The real problem of the positivist was to study the relation of natural laws to these races living in juxtaposition. Jefferson, the great theoretical equalitarian, had early insisted that the ultimate decision of the abolition question would depend upon the results of research in the field of ethnology, the science that investigates the mental and physical differences of mankind. Jefferson believed that the Negro lacked native ability for the higher pursuits of civilization. From the Colonial period on, the inferiority of the Negro was an assumption made by the slaveholder for which he required little or no demonstration. Accepting this premise without question, to the mind of the Southerner there could be no alternative to a system of slavery, except a condition of race conflict which would, after horrible experiences, eventuate in the extermination of the inferior race. The entire pro-slavery thought was imbued with the belief of Negro inferiority. An English traveler of the fifties was so impressed with its prevalence that he wrote:

There seems, in short, to be a fixed notion throughout the whole of the States, whether slave or free, *that the colored is by nature a subordinate race;* and that, in no circumstances, can it be considered equal to the white. Apart from commercial views, this opinion lies at the root of American slavery; and the question would need be argued less on political and philanthropic than on physiological grounds.[1]

The problem in constructing the ethnological defense, therefore, was a problem of verification and substantiation of the inferiority belief. It was necessary to demonstrate that the faculties of the Negro, as compared with those of the Saxon, qualified him for a state of servitude and made him unfit for the enjoyment of freedom. The ethnologist argued that slavery needed no other justification, excuse or apology than the proof that the Negro race was weak and imperfectly developed in mind and body and, therefore, belonged to a

[1] William Chambers quoted in *DeBow*, XVIII (1855), 449.

lower order of man. One of them freely admitted that "if this be not true, American slavery is a monstrous wickedness."[2]

THE ARGUMENT OF DIVERSITY OF RACES

Let us then review the arguments brought forth by Southern ethnologists to establish the physical and mental difference between the races to the slave relationship. These may be divided into two types, historical and physiological. From a comparative study of the races throughout the course of history certain conclusions were drawn significant to a proper understanding of race relationship. In the records of the earliest civilization discovered at that time, the monuments of the Egyptians, the Negro was pictured as occupying a servile position in human society;[3] and, as the history of the race was traced through succeeding civilizations, the Negro was found to have remained the subject of continued enslavement. Moreover, when left alone in his native land, he had never of his own initiative advanced from a state of barbarism to develop a civilization of his own. This fact was considered as strong proof of his lack of capacity to advance. Moreover, the large continent of Africa stood in plain view as an ever present reminder, a rank wilderness, where the various tribes engaged in incessant attempts to subject each other to slavery. This phase of the historical argument was stated very clearly and succinctly by Sawyer in the following paragraph:

The social, moral, and political, as well as the physical history of the negro race bears strong testimony against them; it furnishes

[2] [Sidney George Fisher], *The Laws of Race as Connected with Slavery* (Philadelphia, 1860), p. 32.

[3] John Campbell, *Negro Mania. Being an examination of the falsely assumed equality of the races of men* (Philadelphia, 1851), p. 421, quoting from Morton, *Crania Ægyptiaca*, pp. 22-29. "We have the most unequivocal evidence, historical and monumental, that slavery was among the earliest of the social institutions of Egypt, and that it was imposed on all conquered nations, white as well as black. . . . Of negro slavery in particular, the paintings and sculptures give abundant illustration."

the most undeniable proof of their mental inferiority. In no age or condition has the real negro shown a capacity to throw off the chains of barbarism and brutality that have long bound down the nations of that race; or to rise above the common cloud of darkness that still broods over them.[4]

Herodotus, it is true, had said that the Egyptians were "of a black complexion and woolly haired," indicating that their traits were negroid. The abolitionist invoked his statement as authority to prove that the Egyptian had been a Negro culture. The slaveholder, however, questioned the accuracy of Herodotus and countered with the finding of modern Egyptologists as more cogent proof to establish the claim that the Egyptian was a race *sui generis*.[5] From the vain search for an indigenous civilization, the conclusion was drawn that the history of the Negro race could not represent a chapter of mere accidents but that it was the fulfillment of manifest destiny.

As a further link in the chain of the historical argument, the slaveholder pointed out that on every occasion on which the servile race had gained freedom, after once having been held in bondage, that it had inevitably within a time lapsed into barbarism. A most vivid illustration of this tendency was found in the history of Santo Domingo and Haiti. The results of emancipation in this island were a powerful object lesson, a timely and salutary warning to the Southerner. Closely scrutinizing the situation, an official representative of the United States in Haiti wrote it was a conviction forced upon him by his observations that "negroes only cease to be children when they degenerate into savages." He was convinced that a short residence there would cause "the most determined philanthropist to entertain serious doubts of the

---

[4] *Op. cit.*, p. 192.

[5] See Cobb, *op. cit.*, pp. 41-42 where the matter is discussed.

possibility of their ever attaining the full stature of intellectual and civilized manhood."[6]

Another lesson in the retrograding tendency of the race just as conclusive and even nearer home was the record of the free Negro element in the States. Its condition led Professor Dew to a typical remark: "Taken as a whole class the latter [the free blacks] must be considered the most worthless and indolent of the citizens of the United States. It is well known that throughout the whole extent of our Union they are looked upon as the very *drones* and *pests* of society."[7] Judge Conrad expressed the same opinion in even stronger terms: "The free blacks are, in the mass, the most ignorant, voluptuous, idle, vicious, impoverished, and degraded population of this country. . . . They have sunk lower than the Southern slaves, and constitute but a melancholy proof of the advantages of abolition."[8] The Southerner pointed out that even the free States recognized the inferiority of the race for they refused to grant to the free blacks the political rights granted to the white man. To complete the case, statistics were used. The census figures showed that the Negro was in a better condition under slavery than in freedom. Crime, poverty, and disease all attained a much higher percentage among the free black element of the population than among either the whites or the slaves. This type of argument had its principal cogency when directed against the abolitionist who claimed that the Negro race was not inferior but merely degraded by the whites through slavery.[9]

[6] Taken from a report of Robert M. Walsh to Daniel Webster, Secretary of State, published in *DeBow*, XIV (1853), p. 276. The researches of Charles Hamilton Smith in the West Indies leading to the same conclusion were often cited. See *The Natural History of the Human Species* (Boston, 1851). See also "Slavery in the United States," *Southern Quarterly Review*, XII (1846), 91-134.

[7] *Loc. cit.*, p. 422.

[8] Cobb, *op. cit.*, p. 40 quoting from *A Plea for the South*, (1836), p. 230.

[9] Among many others, this definite claim of the abolitionist may be found in John Rankin, *Letters on American Slavery* (Newburyport, 1836), p. 118.

The other type of argument used to prove the inferiority of the Negro may be characterized as physiological. In order to prove that the Negro was physically an inferior being, comparative anatomy was utilized. The peculiarities of the physical structure of the Negro were pointed out in studies of minute detail, and many differences from the white race were found in the organization of the brain, the nerves, and the vital organs.[10] Here we shall notice only a few of the more essential of these.

Of much importance was the explanation of the color of the Negro. To prove that color was an evidence of an elemental difference, it became necessary to refute the hypothesis that the blackness of the Negro was due to the effects of climate. In order to discredit the climate theory, it was shown that the blackest parts of the body were not those that were exposed to the sun.[11] At that time, Blumenbach and Samuel Stanhope Smith, well known scientists, had advanced the theory that the Negro's blackness was caused by the secretion of a greater quantity of carbon, or bilious fluid, and its fixation by uniting with oxygen in the *rete mucosum,* one of the middle layers of the skin.[12] This hypothesis was subject to attack, however, on the ground that the secretion of the two races was identical; and secondly, that the same operation went on in the lungs, where the carbon of the blood readily combined with the oxygen of the air so that the blood returned to the heart purified and the carbon became atmospherized.[13] As further evidence that color was elemental,

[10] In this work the pro-slavery writers drew very largely from the researches of scientists who had investigated the field; such as Lawrence, Prichard, and Morton. However, Dr. Nott of Alabama, Dr. Van Evrie of Washington, and Dr. Cartwright of Louisiana made studies with the slavery question primarily in view.

[11] W. G. Ramsay of Charleston was one of the earliest Southerners to write upon this phase of slavery.

[12] Blumenbach was one of the first scientists to advance the idea. He was followed by Smith, see Richard Colfax, *Evidences against the Views of the Abolitionists* (New York, 1833), p. 8.   [13] *Ibid.*

it was said that not only the skin, but the membranes, the tendons, and the fluids of the Negro were black, and that even his brain and nerves were tinctured with a shade of darkness.[14]

Another theory concerning racial diversity that was somewhat generally held throughout the South related to the Negro's ability to endure heat better than the white man, an idea confidently believed to be a fact by slaveholders. Governor Hammond, of South Carolina, for instance, gave expression to it in a letter to a friend:

Have your Science and Philosophy of man furnished you with any *certain knowledge* of the causes which enable the negro to stand heat better than the Caucasian, and live longer in a warm climate and not so long in a cold one? . . . I have formed a theory. . . . You know that in summer as well as in winter a negro habitually, of choice, sleeps with his head closely wrapped in a thick blanket. Caucasians would instantly suffocate on the quantity of air a negro appropriates as ample for his use. Now the chief [—] in supporting life is [—] to provide oxygen which provides combustion of the food in our stomachs and supplies the vital heat. A negro then requires less oxygen, less combustion, less vital heat, is as we would say *colder natured*. Now in cold latitudes the air has more oxygen in it, in warmer less. Hence he [dies] out in colder climates and flourishes in hot ones. Now there is another view the *rationale* of which is nearly the reverse of this, but the results the same. A little oxygen may produce a great deal of combustion in the negroes' stomach and enable them to digest their food. . . . Hence they can digest better and live longer in hot climates. . . . And this great ability to combustion may furnish them with excessive internal heat which radiates through their thick black skins and repels external heat. . . . May not the truth be sought with one or the other of these?[15]

[14] S. A. Cartwright, "Diseases and Peculiarities of the Negro Race," *DeBow,* XI (1851), 64-69.

[15] Letter to Nott, Aug. 3, 1845, MS. MSS. in this Chapter, unless otherwise indicated are in the Library of Congress. Nott replied: "Your views about combustion are not very orthodox." Letter of Nott to Hammond, Aug. 12, 1845, MS.

Dr. Cartwright gave voice to a similar observation as to the peculiar habits of the Negro.

This is proved by the fact of the universal practice among them of covering their heads and faces during sleep, with a blanket or any kind of covering. . . . The natural effect of this kind of respiration is imperfect atmospherization of the blood in the lungs, and a hebetude of intellect from the defective vitalization of the blood distributed to the brain.[16]

Cartwright claimed that the Negro was enabled to withstand the heat of the sun when at work because of a peculiarity in the structure of his eye. He had an "additional anatomical contrivance, consisting of a membranous wing expanded underneath a portion of the upper eyelid, and that when the eye is exposed to a bright light, the membranous wing covers a considerable portion of the globe of the eye."[17] Matthew Estes called this the "nictitating membrane" which protected the eye and directed the course of tears.[18]

From a study of craniology evidence was also found of the mental inferiority of the Negro. In the first place, it was claimed that his brain was smaller in size and lighter in weight than that of the Caucasian. As the highest available authority, the results of the researches of Samuel George Morton, the most eminent craniologist of the day, were cited. He had concluded from various tests and measurements that the mean internal capacity of the Negro cranium was less by twelve cubic inches than that of the Anglo-Saxon.[19]

[16] "Disease and Peculiarities," *The Industrial Resources, Statistics, etc., of the Southern States* (New York, 1854), III, 316.

[17] *Essays*, p. 14.   [18] *Op. cit.*, p. 63.

[19] See Sawyer, *op. cit.*, pp. 194-195 noting the result of Morton's research. Morton published his researches in *Crania Ægyptiaca* (Philadelphia, 1844) and *Crania Americana* (Philadelphia, 1839). Dr. Nott in his analysis of Morton's contribution to science said that his books created an era in anthropology, *Types of Mankind: Or ethnological researches, based upon the ancient monuments, paintings, sculptures, and crania of races, and upon their natural, geographical, philological and Biblical history* (Philadelphia, 1854). Chapter on the comparative anatomy of Races, p. 417.

A statement of the eminent naturalist, Louis Agassiz, was often quoted to show the difference in the mental capacity of the two races:

A peculiar conformation characterizes the brain of an adult negro. Its development never gets beyond that observable in the Caucasian in boyhood. And, besides other singularities, it bears a striking resemblance, in several particulars to the brain of an ourang-outang.[20]

The Negro's brain also was supposed to have a peculiar form due to the shape of his head. The slanting forehead and depressed summit contracted the size of the cerebrum, the seat of the intellectual faculties, and increased the size of the cerebellum, the seat of the animal propensities. It was claimed that the facial angle of the Caucasian was eighty degrees, that of the Negro seventy degrees, while that of the ourang-outang was only fifty-eight degrees. Hence it appeared that low vertices and slanting heads were indicative of inferior mentality.[21] The corollary drawn from the fact of the peculiar development of the Negro's brain was that his nerves were larger than those of the white man and that his animal attributes had grown proportionately to the size of his nerves, or his "sensate organism." Cartwright offered an explanation of this anatomical peculiarity:

The nerves of the spinal marrow and the abdominal viscera, being more voluminous than in other races, and the brain being ten per cent less in volume and in weight, he is, from necessity, more under the influence of his instincts and *animality*, than other races of men and less under the influence of his reflective faculties. . . . The former predominating rules the intellect and chains the mind to slavery—slavery to himself, slavery to his appetites, and a radical savage in his habits, whenever he is left to himself. His

[20] Sawyer, *op. cit.*, p. 195 quoting Agassiz.
[21] Colfax, *op. cit.*, p. 25. See also an article on phrenology by Thomas Cooper, *Southern Literary Journal*, I (1835), 188.

mind being thus *depressed* by the excessive development of the nerves of organic life, nothing but arbitrary power, prescribing and enforcing *temperance* in all things, can restrain the excesses of his animal nature and restore reason to her throne.[22]

Another proof that the Negro was structurally different from the white was drawn from the belief that he was immune to certain diseases and susceptible to others to which the white man was not. For example, the Southern physicians gave it as their testimony from experience that the Negro race was almost totally immune to yellow fever.[23]

In close connection with the arguments of inferiority drawn from a difference in organic structure of the two races was the group of arguments that these specific differences were designed to fit the black for a status of slavery. It was the general testimony of slaveholders that the Negro was imitative, but never inventive or suggestive; and by consequence, he could never create a civilization of his own. Moreover, he was habitually indolent and opposed to exertion, which condition necessitated a master to force him to work. An idea, probably entertained by others, was expressed by Dr. Cartwright, who claimed that the Negro was endowed by nature with a principle of self-protection against "wanton abuses and tyrannical oppression of masters," a principle that had been denied to all other races of men. He believed that the master could not force the slave beyond a reasonable amount of service. It was due to this characteristic that the Negro race, beyond all others, was so perfectly fitted for a state of slavery.[24] Estes likewise attributed to the character of the Negro

[22] *Essays*, p. 12.

[23] Ramsay, *op. cit.*, thought that Negroes were not altogether immune but that cases were always very mild. Nott in his "Statistics of Southern Slave Population," *DeBow*, IV (1847), 284, contended that not only were Negroes exempt but even the quadroon, to a greater degree than the white. See also Cartwright, "Diseases," *loc. cit.*

[24] *Essays*, p. 18.

"a kind of stubbornness which induces him to resist every attempt to force him to the performance of more than a reasonable amount of labor."[25]   The white man, on the other hand, as proved by free society, could easily be forced to perform a degree of labor far beyond his strength and capacity.

The inferiority of the Negro was almost universally accepted in the South by all groups of pro-slavery theorists as a great primary truth.   It led to the belief that slavery was the condition prepared for him by nature, and that it was the only condition that he could occupy for the time being.   This law of race relationship, derived from the study of ethnology, became the true "higher law" of the defense, and placed the black forever in subordination to the white.   Negro slavery, so called, was found to be no slavery at all, but the natural relation of the races—the mere external adaptation of natural law.

Many Southerners were willing to rest the positive defense of slavery here; having established diversity of races, they were not concerned with finding its cause or inquiring into its origin.   Dr. Thomas Cooper reflected this attitude in a letter to Senator Mahlon Dickerson in 1826 when he wrote "I do not say that blacks are a distinct race: but I have not the slightest doubt of their being an inferior variety of the human species and not capable of the same improvement as the whites."[26]   The scientific method, however, led to an inquiry into the cause of diversity.   To a large group of thinkers it seemed sufficient to attribute racial differences to a direct act of God.   Reinforced by Biblical authority, many asserted the occasion to have been the curse on Canaan.   Dr. Cartwright thought that such a miraculous explanation was essential for even the scientist to understand diversity.

[25] *Op. cit.*, p. 79.
[26] Letter published in *The American Historical Review*, VI, 729.   See also Dumas Malone, *op. cit.*, p. 289.

The recent anatomical and physiological discoveries were mysteries, or locked up treasures to the medical world—the key to them is found by searching the Scriptures in the original language. The physiological peculiarities of the Ethiopian race, corresponding to the peculiar anatomical structure discovered by modern anatomists, and the history of the race for thousands of years marking the essential difference in mind between that and all other races of men, are beautifully, succinctly and definitely expressed in the language in which Moses wrote.[27]

Not only the theologians generally but a number of the adherents to the scientific school explained the phenomenon in such a way. The two outstanding scientific treatises produced in the South upholding the unity of the races explained diversity on supernatural grounds and traced the origin of the races to the three sons of Noah.[28] Matthew Estes, who also maintained that all races of men sprang from the same original stock, could not explain diversity as a result of ordinary circumstances and accepted the trinitarian account in the Bible.[29] The most ambitious attempt to reconcile the findings of the ethnologist with the prophecy of the Bible and trace the origin of the races to the Noachian family was the book written by Samuel Davies Baldwin, entitled *Dominion: or, the Unity and Trinity of the Human Race; with the Divine Political Constitution of the World, and the Divine Rights of Shem, Ham and Japheth* (Nashville, 1858). A variant of the Noachian theory held that the races had actually been transformed by God at the Tower of Babel by the same instantaneous fiat by which He had confounded the languages and dispersed mankind throughout the world. God had ef-

---

[27] *Essays*, pp. 12-13.

[28] John Bachman, *The Doctrine of the Unity of the Human Race: Examined on the principles of science* (Charleston, 1850), pp. 290-292. Thomas Smyth, *The Unity of the Human Races: Proved to be the doctrine of scripture, reason and science* (New York, 1850) republished in *Works* (J. W. Flinn, ed.) VIII, 12-389; see pp. 110-115.

[29] *Op. cit.*, p. 69.

fected diversity of complexion and structure at that time so that the races would be adapted respectively to the regions of their future abodes.[30]   One of the most fanciful ideas about the Negro's origin was that advanced by Dr. Cartwright. His desire to find God's revelation in it finally led him to accept a theory of Dr. Adam Clark and identify the Negro with the serpent which had tempted Eve in the Garden of Eden. He wrote as follows:

Fifty years ago, Dr. Adam Clark, the learned commentator of the Bible, from deep reading in the Hebrew, Arabic, and Coptic languages, was forced to the conclusion that the creature which beguiled Eve was an animal formed like man, walked erect, and had the gift of speech and reason. He believed it was an ourang-outang and not a serpent. If he had lived in Louisiana, instead of England, he would have recognized the *negro gardener*.[31]

Cartwright insisted that the word *Nachash* in Genesis should have been translated Negro and not snake.

THE THEORY OF PLURAL ORIGINS OF THE RACES

It is difficult to determine how early the theory of a separate origin of the white and black races became current in the South. It is likely that the suggestion came to the minds of many from the earliest experience of the two races living together on the continent. Voltaire, Hume, and Lord Kames had advanced theories of the separate origin of the Negro and even Jefferson speculated about it. Until about 1830, however, the large majority of naturalists of repute in both America and Europe held to the unity of origins theory, and the plurality theory had not influenced the development of

[30] This theory was expounded by Wm. T. Hamilton in *The "Friend of Moses,"* or, *a defense of the Pentateuch as the production of Moses and an inspired document, against the objections of modern skepticism* (Mobile and New York, 1852), p. 500.

[31] "The Unity of the Human Race Disproved by the Hebrew Bible," *DeBow,* XXIX (1860), 130.

pro-slavery thought to any degree. After that date a scientific hypothesis was worked out and advanced as a definite part of the Southern defense of slavery. In that year Dr. Charles Caldwell of Philadelphia published *Thoughts on the Original Unity of the Human Race* in which he presented a strong case against the unity theory. The earliest evidence that the author has found of the use of the plurality theory as a part of the pro-slavery argument was a pamphlet published by Richard H. Colfax in 1833 in answer to arguments of the abolitionists. His specific purpose was to refute their contention that the Negro instead of being an innately inferior race had been degraded under the slave system.[32] J. J. Flournoy, the expounder of the expulsion philosophy, in his pamphlets during the 1830s emphasized the importance of the plurality theory in understanding the Negro problem.[33]

Morton was probably the first of the natural scientists to bring out significant facts in support of the plural origins hypothesis. By 1838 his researches with Egyptian and American craniums showed that the same diversity of race had existed for over four thousand years. Such an indication of permanency of type forced him to doubt the climatic explanation of diversity. Nevertheless, he was slow to place himself openly as a sponsor of the idea of the creation of a number of original types. At first he attempted to explain the fact of permanency on the theory that God had stamped the marks of race upon the immediate family of Adam. He soon gave up such a notion. In a letter to Estes in 1845 he wrote he had become convinced from extensive observation and much reflection that the physical differences among men were coeval with the primitive dispersion of the race; and that external agents; such as, climate, locality, food and moral

---

[32] *Op. cit.*, at p. 8 he cites Boyle, Gibbon, Lord Kames, Voltaire, Jefferson, and Sir William Lawrence as believing in two distinct varieties of the *genus homo*. He also refers to the work of Caldwell.   [33] See *supra*, pp.

causes had never "converted a white man into a Negro, or a Negro into a white man." Moreover, he ridiculed the idea that the Negro was descended from Ham. In answer then to the inquiry, from whence the Negro came, he merely suggested that ethnology was still a new science and he was but a learner.[34]

Dr. Josiah Clark Nott, a physician of Mobile, Alabama, who had been a student under Morton, first advanced his ideas on plurality in an article in the *Philadelphia Medical Journal* about 1842.[35] This article brought the praise of Morton, and by 1845 Nott claimed that they were in agreement on the matter.[36] The two were in regular correspondence and Morton had probably assured Nott of his support long before he publicly clarified his position. But not until 1847 did he openly avow a belief in diverse origins and not until 1850 did he make his position in the matter clear to Dr. Bachman and the unitary school.[37]

Meanwhile, interest in the subject had run far in advance in the South due to the stimulating researches of Dr. Nott, who had been practicing medicine for a number of years among the Negroes of the lower South. Through his professional experiences with that race he had early come to the conclusion that the Negro was a separate species from the white man. In 1845 he wrote to Governor Hammond of South Carolina: "Science has done nothing (and probably never will) towards explaining the effects of climate on whites and blacks. . . . Though I have been much in want of materials to work with, I have caught glimpses here and there which satisfy me that the Unity of Race must be given up."[38]

---

[34] Letter of Oct. 22, 1845, published in Estes, *op. cit.*, p. 70.

[35] I have been unable to check on this article. Nott mentions it in a letter to Ephriam G. Squier, Sept. 30, 1848. MS.

[36] See Nott's article, *Southern Quarterly Review*, VIII (1845) 160.

[37] See Morton's letter to Bachman, March 30, 1850, published in *Types of Mankind*, p. xlix.   [38] Letter of August 12, 1845. MS.

Dr. Nott's first attempt to expound publicly his idea of a plural creation was made in two lectures on the natural history of the races in 1844.[39] He stated his general thesis briefly in this fashion:

I set out then with the proposition, that there is a genus, man, comprising two or more species—that physical causes cannot change a white man into a Negro, and that to say this change has been effected by a direct act of Providence, is an assumption which cannot be proven, and is contrary to the great chain of nature's laws.[40]

In writing Governor Hammond, moreover, he was frank to admit that "the negro question was the one that I wished to bring out and embalmed it in Egyptian ethnography, etc., to excite a little more interest."[41] He wrote shortly afterward that "the nigger business has brought me into a large and heterogeneous correspondence" and if he could get the materials he "should like to follow out the Negro, moral and physical in all his ramifications."[42]

The lectures were reviewed in the *Southern Quarterly Review* by Moses Ashley Curtis, a botanist of fine reputation and an Episcopal clergyman from North Carolina.[43] He based his attack on science and religion. He advanced the view that the opposite of Nott's conclusion was proved by analogies in the animal and vegetable kingdoms, where mutation of types was clearly discernible. Moreover, he resented as an attack on revealed religion Nott's questioning the validity of the orthodox Biblical chronology.

[39] *Two Lectures on the Natural History of the Caucasian and Negro Races* (Mobile, 1844).

[40] *Ibid.*, p. 7, quoted in the *Southern Quarterly Review*, VII (1845), 392.

[41] Letter of August 12, 1845. MS.

[42] Letter to Hammond, September 4, 1845. MS.

[43] "The Unity of Races," *Southern Quarterly Review*, VII (1845), 372-448. Nott replied *ibid.*, XIII (1845), 148-190. Curtis rejoined, *ibid.*, IX (1846), 372-391.

Dr. Nott observed, nevertheless, that the ideas expounded in his lectures, while new to the masses, were much talked of and read and that public opinion, in the South, was coming over to him. Even those who held out against him admitted that "it is debatable ground and ought to be investigated." He expressed confidence that if "I have not traveled the exact road, I have indicated the direction which this discussion should take." For after all he realized the abolition question could never be settled by reason or religion and a study of ethnology offered its only sure solution.[44]

He continued his investigations, some of which were published in the Southern reviews. He next delivered a series of lectures at the University of Louisiana on the connection between the Biblical and physical history of man.[45] In accepting the invitation tendered by Professor J. D. B. DeBow he felt that it would give him "a fine opportunity of sowing seed broadcast." He would be able to tell about the significant findings of men of science; such as, "Luke Burke, Bunsen, DeWette, Norton, Stroup, Morton, etc., and above all that infamous sinner Squier who has hardihood to assert that the Indians were making potato hills in the *Valley* before Eve was convicted and punished for stealing apples." He realized that he would "be abused by somebody, but that does good to the cause."[46] On the occasion of the lectures he asserted that viewed simply as a question of science the theory of the unity of the races had been fairly settled in the negative. Years of study of the Negro's diseases and anatomy, together with a careful perusal of foreign works on the history of man, and an examination of the earliest human records had led him to "a firm conviction that the Almighty in

[44] Letter to Hammond, July 25, 1845. MS.
[45] *Two Lectures on the Connection between the Biblical and Physical History of Man* (New York, 1849).
[46] Letter to Squier, September 30, 1848. MS.

his wisdom has peopled our vast planet from many distinct centers, instead of one, and with races or species originally and radically distinct."[47] Moreover, he pointed out that during the past twenty years the great number of systematic writers in Europe in the field of natural history, and Morton, Pickering, Bartlett, Caldwell, Gliddon, Squier, and Davis in America had abandoned the unity hypothesis. He believed that the inspired writers of the Bible were uninformed on questions of science, that their knowledge of ethnology was circumscribed and limited. His main object in the lectures, therefore, was "to cut loose the natural history of mankind from the Bible, and to place each upon its own foundation, where it might remain without collision or molestation."[48]

He was not successful in his purpose, however, and drew an attack from the "natural theologians," who would make all science conform to the Bible. Dr. George Howe reviewed these lectures in the *Southern Presbyterian Review*, describing Nott as "an assailant of religion" and as "uttering opinions dangerous to religious morality and law."[49] Especially was he denounced for appealing to the German critics of the Bible in order to support his views. His defense was that he had only turned to Biblical criticism in an attempt to reconcile embarrassing difficulties, as recent archaeological discoveries had destroyed the accuracy of orthodox chronology.[50] He wrote Squier in regard to the attack upon his orthodoxy, "I have no intention which would induce me to war against the Christian religion, though I was against all dogmas which conflict with the demonstrated facts of science."[51] While pre-

---

[47] *Two Lectures*, p. 6.   [48] *Ibid.*, p. 7.

[49] "A Review," *Southern Presbyterian Review*, III (1849) 124.

[50] For Nott's rejoinder see "Ancient and Scriptural Chronology," *Southern Quarterly Review*, XVIII (1850) 385-426. He wrote to Squier after having read Bunsen's *Egypt:* "He is a good authority and does give Moses some awful digs under the short ribs. . . . The game is nearly played out and the parsons must look out for a new humbug." Letter of September 30, 1848, MS.

[51] Letter of February 14, 1849. MS.

paring his lectures in book form, he was confident they would sell because "the subject attracts and all the title articles I have written on *niggerology* have been eagerly sought for at the South, and in the present excited state of the political world I think the thing will go well, though I have never [written] to please the crowd, but for the advancement of truth. . . . Science will gain by discussion and I can't be injured at home."[52]

For a few years Dr. Nott had to fight his battle alone, but as his ideas began to receive more publicity others came to his rescue. By 1850 he could write optimistically: "My great object for several years has been to get the world quarreling about niggerology and I have at last succeeded, and I think I shall sit on the fence now and enjoy the fight." It seemed that the line was rapidly forming to support him. Agassiz had come out with an article in the *Christian Examiner* which "is a clincher" and "backs me fully"; and "Morton is coming out dead against Moses and the prophets, and I think we have the game started now and will give them hell before we stop." Squier's book on the antiquity of the Indians was a strong spoke in the wheel. Lepsius had practically settled the question of Egyptian Chronology. In the final analysis it appeared to him that "with Agassiz, Morton, Pickering and the Egyptologists with me on diversity, I think the world will come to its senses on so plain a point."[53]

In 1850 Dr. Bachman of Charleston, an eminent naturalist and a Lutheran minister, published *The Doctrine of the Unity of the Human Race* in which he strongly supported the unity theory. In the course of his argument he took occasion to attack Nott, Morton, and Agassiz for their recent publications advancing the plurality doctrine. His main evidence presented in favor of unity rested upon analogies from the animal kingdom. Nott severely criticised the work because

[52] *Ibid.*   [53] Letter to Squier, May 4, 1850. MS.

it "omits the strong examples against him, dodges the chronology, historical evidence of permanence of type in man, the monumental evidence of early diversity—and perverts facts from beginning to end."[54] There ensued between Morton and Bachman a hot controversy on the question of hybridity as a test of the specific difference of species. Bachman's work, nevertheless, became recognized as the most authoritative statement of the case of the unity school.

Dr. Nott's interest and researches in the field of ethnology led him into a wide correspondence and a resultant interchange of ideas with naturalists abroad. Aside from an association with the leading men of science of his day in America, he corresponded with the Humboldts, Lepsius, and Bunsen.[55] He contributed articles to the leading scientific journals of America and to the *London Ethnological Journal*, the editor of which, Luke Burke, considered him one of the outstanding of the new American school of ethnologists. In addition to membership in the American Ethnological Society, he became an honorary member of the Anthropological Societies of London and Paris, and of the Tyro-Egyptian Society of London.[56] He was generally looked upon by naturalists abroad as the leader of the plurality school in America. Hugh Miller, a leader of the English unity school, singled him out as the pluralist to be refuted.[57]

A full and exhaustive statement of the plurality theory was finally worked out in the monumental treatise of Dr. Nott in collaboration with George R. Gliddon, an archaeologist of many years' experience in Egypt, which they entitled *Types of Mankind*. This volume became a virtual source

---

[54] Letter to Hammond, June 3, 1850. MS.

[55] Letter from S. D. Nott, wife of J. C. Nott, to Squier, May 5, 1873, telling of his foreign associations. MS.

[56] *Ibid.*

[57] See his article, "The Unity of the Human Race," *Essays, Historical and Biographical, Political, Social, Literary, and Scientific* (Boston, 1866), pp. 394-403.

book for pro-slavery theorists as it explained every phase of the ethnic question. In thanking Squier for his highly complimentary review in the *New York Herald*, Nott wrote that he did not "care a curse . . . what the crowd say or think about the book," but confessed he felt "gratified to think that *men of science* should think that the book with all its imperfections may assist in developing the truths involved in the discussion."[58] As a consequence of the circulation of the book many writers accepted the plurality theory, and by the middle of the fifties, the followers of Nott had grown to a very sizable group throughout the South. *The Southern Quarterly Review* and *DeBow's Review* became avowed exponents and many of their articles reflect the same trend of opinion among their contributors. The influence of the ethnological argument was very definitely mirrored in books of the type of Sawyer's *Southern Institutes* and Cobb's *Law of Negro Slavery*. In 1857, Nott and Gliddon published a second work of ethnological researches which they called *Indigenous Races of the Earth*.[59] Dr. John H. Van Evrie also became a disciple of the plurality theory and published books to substantiate it.[60]

The growth of the pluralist school, of course, caused an increased energy on the part of those who believed in the unity of the race. Dr. Bachman again came out for the unity

[58] Letter of April 30, 1854, MS. Squier's review appeared in *The Herald*, April 23, 1854.

[59] The complete title was *Indigenous Races of the Earth; or new chapters of ethnological inquiry; including monographs on special departments of philology, iconography, cranioscopy, palaeontology, pathology, archaeology, comparative geography, and natural history* (Philadelphia, 1857). Nott summarized the scientific facts bearing upon the question of the unity and plurality of species and published it as an appendix to Hotz's translation of Count de Gobineau's *The Moral and Intellectual Diversity of Races* (Philadelphia, 1856).

[60] *Negroes and Negro "Slavery": The first an inferior race: The latter its normal condition* (New York, 1861), and *White Supremacy and Negro Subordination; or, Negroes a subordinate race and (so called) slavery its normal condition* (New York, 1868).

group and reviewed *Types of Mankind*.[61]   James L. Cabell, Professor of Comparative Anatomy and Physiology in the University of Virginia, brought his knowledge of racial characteristics and the testimony of modern science to support the theory of the specific unity and common origin of all mankind.[62]   Those believing in unity, moreover, were strongly supported by the religious periodicals, especially the *Southern Presbyterian Review* (Columbia).   The book published by Thomas Smyth in 1850, presenting arguments for unity from Scripture, reason, and science, also remained in current use.[63]

THE CONTROVERSY BETWEEN "UNITARISTS" AND "PLURALISTS"

It is now pertinent to examine briefly the scientific controversy that ensued between the two schools, those accepting the theory of the unity of all races and those declaring for a plural origin.   These schools may be distinguished by applying the terms "unitarist" and "pluralist."   The technique of both led to a search for the physical likenesses and peculiarities of the separate races, and the drawing of a conclusion from a preponderance of fact on the one side or the other.   Neither school could claim complete success, however, as it was difficult to ascertain which was the more striking, the similarity or the dissimilarity between the races.

One of the arguments in favor of unity was drawn from the study of philology, through the attempt to trace all the existing groups of languages to one root language.   The plu-

[61] *A Notice of the "Types of Mankind," with an Examination of the Charges Contained in the Biography of Dr. Morton* (Charleston, 1854), and *A Continuation of the Review of "Nott and Gliddon's Types of Mankind"* (Charleston, 1855).   These were originally published in the *Charleston Medical Journal*.

[62] *The Testimony of Modern Science to the Unity of Mankind; being a summary of the conclusions announced by the highest authorities in the several departments of physiology, zoölogy, and comparative philology in favor of the specific unity and common origin of all the varieties of man* (New York, 1859).   This work was originally published in two parts as reviews of *Types of Mankind* and *Indigenous Races* in the *Protestant Episcopal Review and Church Register.*

[63] *Op. cit.*

ralist denied first that there was such a connection; and secondly, granting its existence, claimed that it could be explained by an intermingling of races in prehistoric times. Furthermore, he pointed out that because the organs of speech of all races were similar a great diversity of sound was precluded.

Another factor that played an essential part in the dispute was hybridity. Dr. Bachman and Dr. Nott reached different conclusions from their study of the question of the relation of the mulatto to the laws of hybridity. The former was well qualified to speak on this subject, for his researches among the lower animals were recognized as authority among naturalists. In fact, his line of argument was drawn from analogies between man and the animal kingdom. He contended that man was a single species in the animal kingdom, and that the laws of hybridity applied equally to all species. His conclusions were briefly stated:

Since no two species of animals have ever been known to produce a prolific hybrid race, therefore hybridity is a test of specific character.

Consequently, the fact that all the races of mankind produce with each other a fertile progeny, by which means new varieties have been produced in every country, constitutes one of the most powerful and undeniable arguments in favor of the unity of the races.[64]

In other words, the mule is a hybrid, incapable of reproducing, which proves that the horse and the ass are different species; but the mulatto reproduces; therefore, the parent races are of the same species. Thus his definition of species was based on the capacity for successive reproduction.

Dr. Nott, on the other hand, defined species to mean "a type, or organic form, that is permanent; or which has re-

[64] *Unity of the Human Race*, p. 119. See also Smyth, *op. cit.*, Chapter XII.

mained unchanged under opposite climatic influences for ages."[65]   His definition was based on permanency of type. Species in relation to each other might be "remote," "allied," or "proximate" according to their "disparity" or "affinity." Consequently, hybridity could not be treated as a unit under which an analogy could be drawn between man and the lower animals.   Rather the laws of hybridity must be classified in their application to different species.   He established at least four degrees of hybridity.

That in which hybrids never reproduce; in other words, where the mixed progeny begins and ends with the first cross.

That in which the hybrids are incapable of reproducing *inter se*, but multiply by union with the parent stock.

That in which animals of unquestionably distinct species produce a progeny which is prolific *inter se*.

That which takes place between closely proximate species— among mankind for example, and among those domestic animals most essential to human wants and happiness: here the prolificacy is unlimited.[66]

In regard to the mulatto, he concluded from his observations that they were the shortest lived of any race of human beings, that they were intermediate in intelligence between the parent races, that they were less capable of undergoing fatigue than either of the parent races, that the women were unhealthy and bad breeders, that intermarriages were less prolific than when crossed with a parent stock, that the offspring partook more largely of the Negro type than of the Caucasian, and that they had an inherent tendency to run out.[67]   Another fact of lesser importance was that they were

---

[65] *Types of Mankind*, p. 375.   [66] *Ibid.*, p. 376.

[67] Nott first stated his views on hybridity in 1842. This was before Morton became interested in that question, and Morton complimented him upon his work, *ibid.*, p. 373. For another statement of Nott's early views see *DeBow* IV (1847)

more exempt from yellow fever than the white race. Consequently, Nott argued, on the one hand, that no definition or final law of hybridity could be laid down; and, on the other, that mulattoes partook to some extent of the nature of the hybrid. Furthermore, he claimed that certain "affinities" and "repulsions" existed among the various races which caused the blood of the Negro to mingle more or less perfectly. On this ground, he explained the comparative "longevity" and "prolificacy" of the mulattoes of the Gulf region as to those of the upper South. There was a disparity of type among the Caucasian races of the two sections, the former being of closer affinity to the Negro than the latter. Squier, in his review of *Types of Mankind*, summarized Nott's theory of hybridity and explained the consequences to be drawn from it:

Dr. Nott claims that the mixture of races can never be perfect or permanent, and that it is more or less imperfect as the various races themselves approximate to or diverge from each other. . . . He contends further, not only that no intermixture can be permanent, but that no intermixture has come to constitute a permanent variation in type, or a permanent race, with powers of perpetuation, that is to say, the offspring of whites and negroes are either speedily merged in one or the other of the original types, or be-

p. 284. Morton later entered the field in his dispute with Bachman. He argued in direct contradiction to Bachman that fertility of hybrids existed in some cases among the lower animals. See *Additional Observations on Hybridity in Animals, and on Some Collateral Subjects; being a reply to the objections of the Rev. John Bachman, D.D.* (Charleston, 1850) and *Letter to the Rev. John Bachman, on the Question of Hybridity in Animals, Considered in Reference to the Unity of the Human Species* (Charleston, 1850). Both were originally published in the *Charleston Medical Journal*. Another scientist that Nott quoted on this subject was M. Honoré Jacquinot of France. See *Considérations Générales sur l'Anthropologie* (Paris, 1846) (J. S. C. Dumont d'Urville, *Voyage au pôl sud, Zoologie*, v. II.). For authority that the mulatto tended to run out he cited Caldwell, *op. cit.*, Jacquinot, *op. cit.*, and Professors Dickson and Holdbrook of Charleston, who held that the mulattoes became extinct when held apart from parent stocks, *Types of Mankind*, p. 398. Of course, Bachman contended that the mulatto had no such tendency.

come extinct from defective organization, the necessary consequence of an unnatural intermixture. He affirms, as a result of
his own observations and study, that the seeds of decay and extinction are visible in the very first departure from this primitive
type.[68]

Dr. Van Evrie gave expression to a very similar belief. He
thought that

had the orator of the Colonization Society said that amalgamation
with separate *races* of men, as ourselves and the Negro, is followed
by a mongrel brood, however superior mentally to the Negro, yet
vastly inferior to the white, and as certain to perish as the mule, or
any other hybrid generation; but that amalgamation with the
Irishman or German, or any other variety of our own *species* or
race, would be followed by a more vigorous stock than either of
the originals, he would have declared an *eternal truth*.[69]

The importance of this branch of the theory can readily
be seen. It was the case against amalgamation. Not that the
races would not mix, but that they were not intended to mix
and a violation of the law would reduce the white race to inferiority. The Caucasian races had always been the rulers
and would always remain so if left unmixed. Nott said that
"the superior races ought to be kept free from all adultera-
tions, otherwise the world will retrograde, instead of advancing, in civilization."[70] Amalgamation thus became re-

[68] *Loc. cit.* Here it should be pointed out Nott thought that the Negro race
alone may have come from a hundred original pairs. Originally all the pairs had
been distinct, but proximate, and a mixture had been going on for ten thousand
years or longer. Letter to Hammond, July 10, 1850, MS. He wrote Squier one
of the points he would make in *Types of Mankind* was that "each grand division
ias Caucasian, Negro, Indian, etc., contains many primitive races, which though
resembling, are of different grades." Letter of September 26, 1852, MS. Many
pluralists, however, held that the Negro had been a permanent type from the creation down.

[69] *Op. cit.*, p. 8.

[70] *Types of Mankind*, p. 405. Nott's final conclusion was that some day
man might wholly disappear from the earth: "When the inferior types of mankind
shall have fulfilled their destiny and passed away, and the superior, becoming

pulsive to anyone who understood the proper destiny of the white race.

A third subject of dispute between the two schools related to the origin of the races. If the unity of mankind be established, then the diversity of race must be explained. On this point, the pluralist remained on the defense while it became necessary for the unitarist to make out a case. Nott said that one could explain the existence of race, if he accepted the unity theory, in only three ways.

A *miracle*, or direct act of the Almighty, in changing one type into another.

The gradual action of physical causes, such as climate, food, mode of life, etc.

Congenital or accidental varieties.[71]

There was absolutely no reliable evidence that the first had ever taken place; therefore, the pluralist discounted it as unscientific. The unitarist, however, contended that if one admitted the creative power of an Almighty in the first instance, then the same omnipotence might have caused diversity at some subsequent time.[72] The exact time and manner was not essential. At most such reasoning provided only a possible origin of the races which could not be substantiated scientifically.

In regard to the second possible cause, the effects of nat-

---

intermingled in blood, have wandered from their primitive zoölogical provinces, and overspread the world, what will be the ultimate result? May not that law of nature, which so often forbids the commingling of species, complete its work of destruction, and at some future day leave the fossil remains alone of man to tell the tale of his past existence." This is a clear example of the influence of the science of geology as it had developed at that date, the idea that the world had passed through a number of periods, each requiring a new creation. See also Estes, *op. cit.*, for the same idea, except that he adds the cataclysmic destruction of each period.

[71] *Types of Mankind*, p. 57.

[72] This argument was stated by Curtis, *loc. cit.*, p. 393; and by Smyth, *op. cit.*, p. 313. See also Bachman, *Unit of the Human Race*, pp. 291-292.

ural forces, the unitarist had the support of the noted authority, James Cowles Prichard, who had maintained this conclusion through years of research.[73]   Dr. Bachman suggested that in early ages, before the earliest evidence of existence of types, "causes operated under a special providence, with rapidity far beyond that which is ordinary now."[74] Although many cases of minor change could be found of the effects of these forces upon man, yet it was necessary to resort again to analogy with the animal and plant kingdoms to find cases of actual mutation of type.   Here definite cases were pointed out.[75]

The third possibility—accidental varieties—was regarded as rather fanciful by both schools.   The unitarist merely pointed to such peculiar occurrences as club feet and six fingers to show that nature often worked in queer ways.   The pluralist laughed at the idea of a race originating in such a way, declaring that crossed eyes were never transmitted to children.

The pluralist directed the full force of his argument against the possibility of change under the forces of nature. It was irreconcilable with the Egyptian discoveries, which proved permanency of type for at least five thousand years. This was the basic support of the theory of the types of man, for if permanency could be traced back so near the creation, then physical forces could not have had sufficient time

[73] *Natural History of Man and Physical Researches into the Natural History of Mankind* (1813, 1826, 1847).   In order to maintain the theory of natural forces as a cause of races he was forced to conclude that chiliads of years were necessary to effect this change, an admission which destroyed the whole force of his thesis for the natural theologian.

[74] Quoted in "Ancient and Scriptural Chronology," *Southern Quarterly Review,* XVIII (1850), 403.   This led to an interesting question concerning the primitive color of the race.   Bachman held that it was intermediate between black and white and that the present races are equally removed, from the original colors, *Unity of the Human Race,* pp. 155-156.

[75] See, Curtis, *loc. cit.,* pp. 427-440; Bachman, *Unity of the Human Race, passim.*

to effect the diversity.   In fact, the reasoning of the pluralist was conclusive, premised upon the idea of a recent creation. Only with the idea of a very great antiquity of man, which would give the evolutionary hypothesis an incalculably long period of time to work, was the case of the pluralist subject to attack.   Neither school in the South accepted such an idea at the time the pro-slavery argument was being formulated.

To secure a supplementary proof of permanency of type, the history of the Hebrew race, which remained in its original type, was traced.   Dr. Nott said in this relation:

That, although the Jewish race has been subjected, during this immense extent of time, to every possible variety of moral and physical influences, in the four quarters of the earth, yet, in *no instance*, has it lost its own type or approximated to that of other races.

From this he believed that it followed as "a corollary that no physical causes exist which can transform one race into another, as the negro into the white man."[76]

Refuting in this manner the possibilities by which the unitarists claimed diversity of race might have originated, the way lay open for the pluralist to prove that there had been a plural creation.   Aside from the arguments from history and archaeology, and the arguments from anatomy, there was the theory of the "centers of creation."   This was the theory that God had created the races to correspond to the conditions of the different centers of the earth.   The great scientist Louis Agassiz developed this hypothesis.[77]   He con-

[76] "Physical History of the Jewish Race," *Southern Quarterly Review*, XVII (1850), 429.

[77] See his chapter in *Types of Mankind*, p. lviii, "Sketch of the Natural Provinces of the Animal World in Relation to the Different Types of Man;" see also his article in the *Christian Examiner*, March, 1850.   He was answered by Smyth, *op. cit.*, Ch. XI, and by Bachman, *An Examination of Professor Agassiz's Sketch of the Natural Provinces of the Animal World and Their Relation to the Different Types of Man* (Charleston, 1855).

tended that there was a natural relation between the types of man and the animals and plants inhabiting a region. Furthermore, he found that the different regions of the earth had their different fauna and flora, circumscribed within certain limits. Some were peculiar to the tropical regions, others to the temperate regions; and they did not intermingle with each other but were confined within a definite range as if originally intended for it. To support these contentions, the pluralist also drew upon the science of geology to prove that the fossil beds conformed to the theory of "zoölogical provinces" or "centers of creation."

Finally, we come to the last subject of dispute between the two schools, the conflict over the Bible. The unitary school held that the entire spirit of the Bible taught the unity of the races from a single pair. Certain passages were quoted as authority:

And Adam called his wife's name Eve; because she was the mother of all living. (Genesis III:20)

These are the three sons of Noah; and of them was the whole earth replenished. (Genesis IX: 19)

And [God] hath made of one blood all nations of men, for to dwell on all the face of the earth; . . . (Acts XVII:26)[78]

The theory, furthermore, held that all the races must be of Adamite origin because the command of Christ was to preach the gospel to all nations; and, therefore, that they must be of the same original family. Smyth said that "the unity of the human race is absolutely necessary, therefore, to account for the present condition of human nature in consistency with the wisdom and justice of God, and also to render salvation possible to any human being."[79] The unitarists accepted the Mosaic account as the history of all races.

---

[78] These are the texts used by Bachman in his reply to Morton, *Charleston Medical Journal*, V, 508.   [79] Smyth, *op. cit.*, p. 105.

The pluralists did not openly repudiate the scriptures; rather they attempted to reconcile pluralism and the Bible. Bowing before the strength of scientific discovery, they contended that either the scriptures must be interpreted in harmony with the idea of diverse origins or it must be recognized that the writers were not qualified to speak on scientific problems. Nott said that he found nothing in the Pentateuch which induced him to believe that its author knew or cared anything about the unity or diversity of races.[80] In order to reconcile pluralism and the Bible, the school brought forth the theory of pre-Adamite people, that the Mosaic account related only to the history of one race, and that Adam and Eve were only one among a number of pairs created. Thus they said that the word "Adam" meant a "blusher" or "red blooded," which was a term for the white races, instead of its being the "generic name of the entire human species."[81] They believed that the Negro race was not even known to the writer of Genesis.[82]

The acceptance of the archaeological discoveries as trustworthy authority, however, led the pluralist school to cast doubt upon the accuracy of Biblical chronology. By 1850, the Egyptologists had proved the existence of a civilization too remote to be reconciled with any of the several tables of chronology.[83] Nott pointed out that the orthodox position was confused because there had been three distinct Pentateuchs, the Greek, the Hebrew, and the Samaritan, which

[80] "Ancient and Scriptural Chronology," *loc. cit.*, p. 392. He and Agassiz held that the Bible supposed other races because the marriage of Cain could not be explained on any other ground. Cited by Smyth, *op. cit.*, p. 107.

[81] *Types of Mankind*, p. 573, and Smyth, *op. cit.*, p. 117.

[82] *Types of Mankind* chapter on Biblical Chronology. Nott ridiculed Cartwright's attempt to identify Canaan with Ethiopia.

[83] Nott cited the findings of Bunsen, Birch, Barruchi, and Gliddon, "Ancient and Scriptural Chronology," *loc. cit.*, p. 403. He wrote Hammond that the recent book of Lepsius had definitely settled the chronology question. Letter, June 3, 1850. MS.

had come down from antiquity and all of which differed as to dates and length of periods. Both the chronology of the English Bible, worked out by Archbishop Ussher, and the more ancient chronology of the Septuagint, nevertheless, fell far short of the actual antiquity of the races. Furthermore, it was a known fact that the Chinese and the Hindu chronologies went back full 3000 years B.C., a date too close to the flood to provide time for the origin of those races from natural causes.[84]

Not being willing to accept the orthodox interpretation of the Mosaic narrative, the pluralists turned to the higher criticism of the German commentators. They felt that the Bible had come down in a mutilated form, but that it need not stand or fall as a whole. In other words, the pluralists of the South rejected a literal interpretation; and by so doing identified themselves with the critical theologians of New England who were attacking the authority of the scriptures in order to break down the Bible defense of slavery.[85] Thus in the last analysis the dispute over the unity and diversity of the races definitely divided pro-slavery thought between scripturalism and rationalism.

Viewed in the light of scientific progress of their day, the pluralists of the South cannot be considered as pseudo-ethnologists. They brought to bear upon the problem of diverse

[84] Letter to Hammond, August 12, 1845. MS.

[85] Nott quoted Channing, Norton, Palfrey, and Parker to show that the historical accuracy of the Pentateuch was doubted in this country. *Two Lectures on the Biblical and Physical History of Man.* See also D. J. McCord, "How the South is affected by her Slave Institution," *DeBow,* XI (1851), 349, which is a reconciliation of the theory of types of man with the Bible. He cites Arnold, *Miscellanies,* pp. 147, 160, 161, who held that revelation to the Patriarchs was only partial, or limited to certain points. On the other side Bachman said: "In a political point of view, we regard the effort made by Nott and Gliddon, to establish their theory by a denial of the veracity of the historical Scriptures, as more dangerous to our institutions than all the ravings of the abolitionists." Quoted by Bacon, *loc. cit.*

races all the facts that had been made available in the field of the natural sciences at that time. Nott was thoroughly convinced that his conclusions were supported by the strongest scientific information and the best authorities of his day. Aside from applying a thoroughly scientific technique to the problem within his own fields of anatomy and medicine, he utilized the findings of the great men in all the allied fields of natural science in order to construct a comprehensive and conclusive case in support of pluralism. It must be recalled that Darwin did not publish his researches until 1859 in *The Origin of Species*. This book, which offered the first really scientific evidence to support a progression theory, came too late to influence the pro-slavery ethnologists.[86] It was with high praise, therefore, that Squier reviewed *Types of Mankind* as a great contribution to the science of ethnology. He referred to its authors as students, who

have achieved results in this department which must forever constitute landmarks and fixed points of departure, for future researches in the same field of inquiry. Founded upon a large array of facts laboriously collected and carefully analysed and digested, they have come to form parts of the permanent results of the great system of positive philosophy, which holds, in respect to general science, the same relation, which, in physics, is sustained by experimental philosophy.[87]

[86] Nott's first reaction after reading *The Origin of Species* was expressed in a letter to Squier August 22, 1860, MS.: "I have been well enough to skim Darwin's book—the man is clearly crazy, but it is a capital dig into the parsons—it stirs up Creation and much good comes out of such thorough discussions." In 1866, Nott still holding to permanency of type, had this to say in regard to the evolutionary hypothesis: "It is true that Lamarck, Geffroy, Saint Hillaire, Darwin, and other naturalists have contended for the gradual change or development of organic forms from the physical causes, yet even this school require *millions* of years for their theory, and would not contravene the facts and deductions I have laid down." "The Problem of the Black Races," *DeBow*, I (after the War Series, 1860), 272, note.   [87] *Loc. cit.*

Looking back today to the stage of scientific development of the 1850s it would seem that pluralism was the most plausible positive philosophy of slavery that could have been constructed.

THE CONTRIBUTION OF THE ETHNOLOGICAL ARGUMENT TO PRO-SLAVERY THOUGHT

We now pass to an analysis of the theory which may be designated as that of "types of man," and its bearing upon the pro-slavery argument.   First, there were certain conclusions drawn in regard to the Negro.   He was not considered a brute, or a lower species of animal than man, but a totally distinct and inferior sort of man from the Caucasian.   He was not a "lamp-blacked white man" that might slowly change his color; but, just as he was of a different original nature, so he must remain.   "The Ethiopian could not change his skin," nor could he add one cubic inch to his brain.   It was the idea of permanence of condition, both physical and intellectual.   As a consequence, not only was the barrier between the races insurmountable, but nature had set limits beyond which the Negro was totally incapable of improvement.   The pluralist went so far as to deny the possibility of the schemes of the philanthropist and even of the moralist benefiting the race.   Sawyer, who became one of the chief advocates of the theory, remarked on this point: "We would not decry or discourage missionary labors among them, if they can by any means ameliorate their condition. . . . But we fear that they are 'casting their pearls before swine.' "[88]   They even viewed the colonization scheme as futile and believed that Liberia could not be maintained except under the guiding hand of the white man.   Here is found the true basis of the perpetualism theory of slavery, for, as the authors of *Types of*

[88] *Op. cit.*, p. 193, note 3.

Mankind contended "no philanthropy, no legislation, no missionary labors can change this law: it is written in man's nature by the hand of his Creator."[89]

Thus Nott, with grave concern as to the consequences to Southern society from the attempt of the Freedmen's Bureau to educate the Negro, wrote to General Howard in 1866 that the Bureau was "the most mischievous institution ever established in this country. . . . Your great object . . . is to elevate the negro above the condition from which you have removed him, and to place him in every respect upon a full equality with the whites." He went on to show that the whole action of the Bureau was based upon an unsound assumption, directly opposite to facts established by naturalists, for the permanency of the Negro's intellectual faculties was not less certain than that of his physical.[90] When the Bureau took over his pet, the Medical College of Mobile, he wrote to Squier in utter disgust: "God Almighty made the Nigger, and no dam'd Yankee on top of the earth can bleach him."[91] It being impossible to reconcile himself to the reconstruction program, which ran counter to the conclusion of a lifetime of research, he finally felt that he was driven out of the South and went to New York City to pass the declining years of his life.

Beyond the idea of the intellectual permanency of the Negro, the theory of types of man had an important political significance. The advocates of pluralism identified unity of origin with equality among races. Nott declared that upon the question of unity or plurality depended "the more practical question of the equality and perfectibility of races."[92] To the statesman, consequently, this point became a practical

[89] *Types of Mankind,* p. 79. For a much earlier view of Nott to the same effect, see *DeBow,* IV (1847), 275.

[90] "The Problem of the Black Races," *Debow,* I (1866), 266-270.

[91] Letter of December 5, 1865, MS.

[92] *Types of Mankind,* p. 50.

problem in the development of his political theories.   The editor of *DeBow's Review* pointed out this fact:

> If the whole race have but a common original, then common systems may be applied to all; and the greatest license is given to the "latter day" theorists, who would organize the world upon certain uniform bases and fit the same institutions and laws to every stage and condition of civilization.   If, on the contrary, this assumption be false and groundless, these mad dreamers will at once be refuted, and the world discover that parliament and congress are unsuited to the Hottentot and the African, and the ballot-box and trial by jury not altogether the sort of things to flourish in all their vigor among the snows of Russia or the shores of the Bosphorus.   Our faith in political theories has never exceeded a mustard seed.[93]

Thus in one sense the theory of types of man was directed against the many radical movements of the day that proposed to abolish all distinctions and organize society on the basis of universal equality.

> The Proudhons and Fouriers, French Socialists, Continental Republicans, Northern Abolitionists, who, setting out with the perfect *equality* in every respect of all the nations and families of men, proclaim the doctrines of universal republicanism, *universal agrarianism,* and in addition, the fulness of liberty and freedom from all restraint, stand ready to fit, as in the bed of Procrustes, Hottentot and Bushman, semi-civilized Negro and Caucasian, to institutions of a common shape and character![94]

In another sense, the whole defense of slavery turned on the theory of types of man.   If Negroes were of the same species, they were capable of the same enlightenment; consequently, they should not be held in bondage, which was opposed to improvement.   The pluralist maintained that upon this basis alone could slavery be justified.   He frankly

[93] "Editorial," *DeBow*, IX (1850), 243.
[94] J. D. B. DeBow, "The Earth and Man," *De Bow*, X (1851), 287.

admitted that "every race capable of self-government, has a right to liberty, and that no one has a right to withhold it." Nott confessed that he was ready to avow emancipation whenever proof was sufficient that "the present condition of our slaves can be changed for the better."[95]

Thus the often quoted dogma that "all men are born *free* and *equal*," usually attributed to Mr. Jefferson by the slaveholder, was denied as unsound when applied to all races universally. DeBow could see no ground for presuming the equality of mankind "as we are created with different intelligences little less than angels and idiots; with different constitutions, Hercules and imbeciles; in frozen climates of the poles, where bread must be earned by struggles with terrible nature—or about the equator, where spontaneous fruits make earth a garden of paradise." He saw no argument *a priori* in favor of equality. If there were an argument it had to come from facts, and the facts were opposed to the theory of equality.[96]

Dr. Van Evrie explained the meaning of true equality as follows: "All men are created equal, or all the forms of existence that are organized alike, *are equal:* thus "equality" is a fact, while those created unlike, are *unequal;* and to seek to contradict this, to force the Negro to an 'equality' with the white man . . . is equally a violation of the fact of 'equality,' as it is an outrage on nature."[97] On the other hand, the pluralist accepted the Jeffersonian dogma as being possible of fulfillment only under a system of slavery. Thus they con-

[95] "Physical History of the Jewish Race," *Southern Quarterly Review*, XVII (1850), 951.

[96] "Emancipation in the West Indies," *DeBow*, V (1848), 487.

[97] *Op. cit.*, p. 9. In the Declaration it is stated that "all men are created equal," and Jefferson probably never asserted the dogma that "all men are born free and equal." Nevertheless, the slaveholder identified the two. As a matter of fact, it was the idea of equality that the slaveholder could not accept, and conceived of the principles of abolition, of the Declaration, of the Jeffersonian school, and of the entire natural rights school as based upon the equality of all men.

tended that they occupied the high ground of defense because under the theory of diversity of races there could exist actual republican equality. As they would say, they drew a distinction between the true and the false interpretation of the theory of freedom.

This reasoning, however, drew an attack from another school of pro-slavery thinkers, who held that the sole question in dispute was whether equals by nature could be placed upon a footing of inequality. Their argument was that slavery must be defended on principle, not on race, that slavery existed in free society as well as in slave society, and that to concede the dogma of equality was to recognize the creed of socialism, which held it to be unjust to subject equals by nature to the inequalities of society. George Fitzhugh was the chief exponent of the theory, which has been referred to earlier under the slavery principle. He contended that "Southern thought must be a distinct thought—not a half thought, but a whole thought. Domestic slavery must be vindicated in the abstract, and in the general, as a normal, natural, and *in general*, necessitous element of civilized society, without regard to race or color."[98]

The interesting question arises as to the actual influence of the school of pluralists on the political thought of the Southern people. Pluralism was late in being developed and only in the decade of the fifties was an attempt made to propagate the doctrine. It was faced with the tremendous disadvantage of running counter to the principles of the well established Bible defense. Furthermore, an understanding of the theory necessitated a scientific knowledge beyond the reach of the average man. For these and other reasons pluralism never became the popular accepted defense, and the school was looked upon as a small group of radical thinkers. To the educated man, however, who attempted to form

[98] "Southern Thought," *DeBow*, XXIII (1857), 347.

a systematic and logical defense of slavery, pluralism offered a more rational and a less fanciful argument than any system developed by pro-slavery thought. It would seem that the logical thinker unaffected by religious dogma would have been driven to this position. It remains a problem that well deserves study to determine whether the profound political thinkers of the South accepted the theory of the types of man as the ultimate basis upon which they built their masterly arguments on political rights. Of primary significance is a determination of the influence of the pluralist school upon the thinking of Calhoun. There is no doubt that he believed in the inferiority of the Negro race; his whole political theory was based on that premise. But how did he arrive at the premise, by deduction from history or by the induction of science? Upon the answer to this question, must depend our final estimate of whether his thinking was merely *a priori* or truly *a posteriori*.[99]

It now remains by way of conclusion to show the results of the conflict that arose in the South between the pro-slavery school that drew its arguments from moral philosophy and the school that appealed to nature to find a valid defense for the system of slavery. One cause of this cleavage between the two schools that stands out clearly was the fact that the

[99] Calhoun was familiar with Nott and made him several visits. He was also familiar with the scientific work of Morton and Gliddon. The pluralists considered him to be an adherent of their school and claimed that he made use of ethnology in formulating his policy toward England while he was Secretary of State—in his letters to Wm. R. King. See *Types of Mankind,* pp. 50-52. See also *DeBow,* X (1851), 282, where the claim is made that ethnology was the motivating influence in his last speech in Congress. See also, letter of Dr. Cartwright in Van Evrie, *op. cit.,* p. 33. The only claim that a definite influence existed that I have found among later writers is the statement of Woodbridge Riley, *American Thought,* p. 182. "Morton's views were spread in the South by his pupil Knott of Mobile. They came to a curious use at the hands of the politician, J. C. Calhoun, who argues that if all men had a common origin, whites and blacks would be equal; but there has been a plurality of origins, and one of these primordial varieties was the negro, who was originally created the inferior of the Caucasian, therefore, between whites and blacks there is no real equality."

principles of pluralism ran counter to the teachings of the church. Not only upon the question of Scriptural interpretation, on which the schools divided on lines of orthodoxy and liberalism, but in two other respects was this fact evident. First, the church viewed the theory of types of man as a denial of the humanity of the slave, an essential of the moral defense. On the basis of humanity alone, the divines insisted, could slavery be reconciled with Christianity and the New England moralist be answered.[100]   Secondly, the theory of the two schools conflicted on the problem of improvement of the Negro. The moralist claimed that the definite results of religious instruction had been to elevate him. They claimed that the work of the missionaries had incidentally thrown much light on the ethnological question, because "they have demonstrated, that whatever causes may have led to the deteriorations of the African race in the scale of civilized nations, and whatever inferiority of mind and position may belong to it, when compared with other varieties of the human family, it nevertheless belongs to that family, in the highest human capabilities—those of religion."[101]   They contended that the adaptation of Christianity to the understanding and moral sentiments of the Negro had been fully tested and justified.   Bachman asserted that "our experience has produced—a conviction that the African race is capable of considerable advance."[102]   The pluralist conceived of this as being a physical impossibility.

[100] Whewell, op. cit., I, Secs. 525-530 deals with morality and the plural defense. See also Bacon, loc. cit., pp. 640-642, "Our readers are aware that certain sciolists at the South have undertaken to vindicate the institution of slavery, in the form which it exists there, and to reconcile it with the moral sense, by denying that the enslaved are of the same species with the enslavers. The principle of those philosophers is, that though all men ought to be free, Africans . . . are not of the same species with the European race and therefore are not men in the sense of the proposition that affirms that liberty is an inalienable human right. . . ."

[101] "Report of the South Carolina Methodist Episcopal Church Missionary Society" quoted in Smyth, op. cit., p. 150.   [102] Quoted ibid., p. 253.

For these reasons the divines of the South almost invariably wrote and preached in opposition to the new school.[103] Their plea was that the church was in danger; her duties taught by the Bible were spurned. Consequently, they called for a renewed stand on the Bible defense. On this ground they had been able to give an unanswerable reply to all "fanatical impugners" of the rights of slaveholding, and on the same ground could they hope to gain the approval of the "Christian mind" throughout the world. One writer said:

> We cannot deem it right or wise or becoming, and we cannot consent, that the defences of our position be transformed from this foundation of rock, to the shifting quicksands of less than doubtful theories. It is not in our view just, and we will not even tacitly allow our enemies the moral advantage of representing, that we hold our slaves only as a higher race of Ourangs, not really contemplated in the authoritative precepts on which the morality of Christendom is founded.[104]

The real importance of the clash of opinion went beyond the conflict over these principles. It was once again the age old fight between religion and science. The very fact that Voltaire had advanced a theory of the separate origin of the Negro was sufficient reason for placing the stigma of infidelity upon the later school of pluralists. In all things they became identified with the school of the eighteenth century. Beyond this, moreover, pluralism was viewed as a part of the worldwide scientific movement of the age, which was atheistic in tendency and directed against the church. The theory of the types of man was identified with the progression theories of Lamarck and Comte.[105] It is rather

[103] For this attitude see such important works as, Wm. Smith, *op. cit.*; R. L. Dabney, *op. cit.*; J. H. Thornwell, *The Rights and Duties of Masters*; J. B. Adger, *op. cit.*

[104] "The Human Family," *Southern Quarterly Review*, XXVII (1855), 119.

[105] *The Origin of Species* was not written until 1859; consequently it did not influence slavery thought. However this may be, Maillet and Lamarck had de-

strange that the pluralist should have been identified with the scientists who were the founders of the evolutionary hypothesis; for the theory of types of man, instead of destroying the line between species and even genera, denied all mutation whatsoever. The pluralists believed in the very antithesis of that with which the moralists connected them. In fact, it was only through the theory of evolution that a sound scientific basis could be laid for the doctrine of the unity of the races, which the moralists accepted. Sawyer showed the inconsistency in the charge that pluralism was evolutionary and, therefore, tended toward infidelity:

The doctrine of the plurality of original types or races of men has been denounced as anti-scriptural, and tending to infidelity; but in truth, the danger lies upon the other side of the question. For if the physical organization of the animal kingdom is progressive, and one type of man or beast may, from external causes, gradually approximate, and finally lose itself in another, higher than itself, the skeptic has but to seize upon the retrograde course and there is no stopping till he reaches the mineral kingdom. It puts a magic wand into his hand, that enables him to smite the whole framework of natural theology. . . . He may thus run the race out into a Monad.[106]

The only ground on which one might consider the theory of types of man evolutionary was the fact that the pluralists often declared the Negro to be midway between the Caucasian and the ourang in intelligence and physical structure. They held, nevertheless, that his condition was absolutely static.

---

vised scientific theories of development and Comte represented the theory of progression in the philosophical school. In 1844 [Robert Chambers] published in England *Vestiges of the Natural History of the Creation*, a development hypothesis proved by geology. He was answered by Hugh Miller, *The Footprints of the Creator*, based also on geological research and advancing the cataclysmic theory. These two works were transferred to America and became identified, the one with pluralism, the other as the defender of the orthodox school.

[106] *Op. cit.*, 195.

However that may be, the whole scientific attempt of the ethnologists was denounced as advocating a theory of natural causation and denying God a place in the universe.[107]

In regard to the slavery defense, the real importance of the conflict between science and religion was an attempt to establish the source of morality. Should the standard of right upon which slavery was to be justified be natural law or revealed law? The moralist looked upon nature as a fallible standard, while the scientist saw a harmony between the natural and the moral.

[107] See "The Human Family," *Southern Quarterly Review*, XXVII (1855), 116-174, where the charge is made on the grounds that Nott accepted Comte's positivism, for which see *Types of Mankind*, p. 576. On this question the pluralist felt that his case was the stronger. This was pointed out by Hammond to Nott, Aug. 3, 1845, MS. "If there was no other creation all these things must have been affected by secondary causes. . . . But if these natural and secondary causes —without any special intervention of God—acting merely as conformity with the *instinct of the universe* according to the *Law of Development*, could effect such wonders what becomes of *mind*, of God? What then have we for him if nature without his aid can change the Caucasian into the Malay and the Negro, and develop plants unknown to Noah? If we can conceive of any power to do all this without God, then is it not superfluous to have a God at all?"

CHAPTER VII

THEORIES OF SLAVE SOCIETY

SO FAR in this study, slavery has been treated as an institution, as a moral relationship, and as a government for races of diverse character. Now another set of theories respecting slave society will be considered. These theories deal with the position and relation of the different classes that made up slave society. There were theories defining the order and rank of the classes, and theories concerning slavery as a system of capital and labor. A third body of theory dealt with a comparison of slave society and free society, with the idea of finding the most perfect form. Taken as a whole, social theory pronounced a vindication of slavery and offered to the world slave society as the panacea for the many radical and revolutionary movements running current in free society.

The slaveholder believed that he lived in a perfectly ordered society, where each class filled a natural position for the advancement of civilization. Governor McDuffie gave expression to the theory when he said: "In the very nature of things there must be classes of persons to discharge all the different offices of society. Some of those offices are regarded as degrading, though they must and will be performed."[1] Southerners contended that they had made a contribution to the science of society in that they had perfected a division of labor between classes naturally constituted for their particular functions. As Calhoun so vividly pictured it, the unequal races occupied "the front and rear ranks in the march of progress."

[1] "Message on the Slavery Question," *American History Leaflets*, No. X, p. 2.

The menial and laborious tasks, which were always distasteful to man, had to be performed by some class.   Here
was the office of the slave class.   Beverley Tucker, of Virginia, thought that "it is here on this point, of the necessity
of forcing those to labor who are unable to live honestly
without labor, that we base the defense of our system."[2]
Likewise, Governor Hammond expressed the view that "this
idea that slavery is so necessary to the performance of the
drudgery so essential to the subsistence of man, and the advance of civilization, is undoubtedly the ground on which
the reason of the institution rests."[3]   From this idea, he developed his famous mud-sill theory of the structural basis of
all society:

In all social systems there must be a class to do the menial duties,
to perform the drudgery of life.   That is, a class requiring but a
low order of intellect and but little skill.   Its requisites are vigor,
docility, fidelity.   Such a class you must have or you would not
have that other class which leads progress, civilization, and refinement.   It constitutes the very mud-sill of society and of political
government; and you might as well attempt to build a house in
the air, as to build either the one or the other, except on this mud-
sill.   Fortunately for the South, she found a race adapted to that
purpose to her hand. . . .   We use them for our purpose and call
them slaves.[4]

[2] "Note to Blackstone's Commentaries," *Southern Literary Messenger*, I
(1835), 230.
[3] Letter to Matthew Estes, quoted in Estes, *op. cit.*, p. viii.
[4] Speech in the Senate, March 4, 1858, *Congressional Globe*, 35th Congress, 1st
Session, Appendix, p. 71.   This expression of Hammond's made late in the slavery
controversy probably caused more sensation than any single defense of slavery
ever attempted in Congress.   He wrote shortly afterward: "While the papers come
down on me column after column, not a speech here since has not been over
half in answer to me, and I get ten to twenty letters daily from the North. . . .
To make capital of 'white slaves' will be choruses of every campaign speech
and song next summer."   Letter to William Gilmore Simms, March 22, 1858, MS.
in the Library of Congress.   The thought that the white laborer of the North
was merely a white slave, a mud-siller of society, became very distasteful.   Yet
Hammond did receive many letters from the laboring class expressing thanks

Hammond's mud-sill theory was not new in the South but never had it been so well expressed before. So effective was his description that Lincoln in criticising the Southern theory of the structure of society singled out Hammond and replied to his mud-sill theory. Years earlier Calhoun had declared in the Senate that there had never been "a wealthy and civilized society in which one portion of the community did not, in point of fact, live on the labor of the other."[5] It was simply the age-old saying that there must be, at all times and in all countries, "hewers of wood and drawers of water" to form the basis of human society. It was a universal phenomenon and slave society differed from other types only in the fact that an inferior race had been found to do the inferior duties. Hence, at the South, the slave class formed the substratum of the entire structure of society.

Since slave labor filled the low and degrading stations, doing all the tasks of mere brute strength, the freeman did the services that required trust, confidence, and skill. These gave him a sense of respectability, made him more honorable, chivalrous and self-governed, and fitted him to be the director. Slave society was often pictured as a great organism where the mind of the master directed the physical faculties of the slave. Moreover, the system made pos-

---

for his exposure of their servile condition. The opinion of Southerners was well expressed by W. J. Grayson in "The Dual Form of Labor," *DeBow*, XXVIII (1860), 49: "The phrase 'mud-sill' is not elegant, perhaps, but it is very expressive. It indicates forcibly the two forms or classes of labor. In this country, these two forms are composed of different races and different colors—one of African, and the other of European descent. Negroes only, with us, are slaves. Hired men are whites. The negro is an inferior race. The black mud-sill is not made from as good stuff as the white. This is admitted, and this is the ground of offense. But the inferiority of race admitted, why may we not . . . compare the darker with the lighter color?" Lincoln attempted to refute the mud-sill theory of society on several occasions. See *Works* (Nicolay and Hay, ed.), I, 580; II, 105.

[5] *Works*, II, 631. The speech was delivered in 1837. For a similar view expressed in 1820 see *supra*, p. 66.

sible a large leisure class which devoted its attention to the
cultural and political spheres of life. The Southerner was
proud of naming the great political leaders produced under
slavery and of boasting of the culture attained on the Southern plantation.

It is erroneous, of course, to think of the whites as a
single class in society. They were sub-divided among themselves into a number of classes. But the argument of the
slaveholder was that domestic slavery caused an identity of
interests among all the whites to the extent that they approached singleness of class. Color really became the badge
of distinction and all classes of whites were interested in
maintaining that distinction. Color, so noticeable to the eye,
inspired the most humble white man to a sense of his comparative dignity and importance. As one writer remarked,
"however poor, or ignorant, or miserable he may be, he has
yet the consoling consciousness that there is a still lower condition to which he can never be reduced." But beyond the
color line which was the basis of class unity, in slave society
the interests of the different orders were the most identical,
their habits the most uniform, and their pursuits the most
permanent. And this resulted from two principal reasons
—the upper order were all owners of slaves and cultivators
of the soil. Whatever of diversity was maintained in their
occupations, the largest interest of all was in their slaves.
This reasoning led Judge Upshur to declare: "We have
among us, but one great class, and all who belong to it have
a necessary sympathy with one another; we have but one
great interest, and all who possess it are equally ready to
maintain and protect it."[6]

The charge was often made that this caste system of
Southern society was aristocratic in its nature, and, conse-

---

[6] "Domestic Slavery," *Southern Literary Messenger*, V (1839), 685.

quently, denied the genius of free institutions. The slave-holder admitted that it was indeed aristocratic. For example, Governor Hammond remarked that "slavery does indeed create an aristocracy—an aristocracy of talents, of virtue, of generosity and courage. . . . It is a government of the best, combining all the advantages and possessing but few of the disadvantages of the aristocracy of the old world." Instead of fostering "the pride, the exclusiveness, the selfishness, the thirst for sway, the contempt for the right of others" which characterized European nobility, it provided "their education, their polish, their munificence, their high honor, their undaunted spirit."[7]   In fact, every freeman in slave society was an aristocrat. In the same strain of thought Chancellor Harper explained that "ours is indeed an aristocracy, founded on the distinction of races, and conformable, as we believe, to the order of nature." To him it had the advantage "that the privileged class is larger in proportion to the whole society." He thought that the advantage of rank was conferred on a larger number than the world had known in any other society.[8]

If one looks at the classes in terms of averages instead of in terms of individual differences within the classes, one gets the slaveholder's conception. The slaveholder felt that he had found the true basis of aristocracy in diverse races that must inherit an equal social rank as a whole. It was the old argument of Aristotle that nature provided a scale for social rank. On the other hand, in his claim of the aristocratic nature of his society, he did not look at the other angle, the differences within the races. Consequently, the ultimate validity of his argument for aristocracy was reduced to the

[7] Speech in the House of Representatives, Feb. 1st, 1836, *Debates in Congress*, 24th Congress, 1st Session, p. 2460; *Letters and Speeches*, p. 44.
[8] *Anniversary Oration* (Columbia, 1836), p. 11.

necessity of establishing the inferiority of the subordinated race.[9]

Holding to the aristocratic nature of society was far from admitting the second contention—that slavery destroyed free institutions. The slaveholder argued that free institutions had their only natural basis in slave society. It was because of the aristocracy in the first place that there was "less of any other invidiously aristocratic distinction, and that every free-man may claim to be the peer of any other freeman."[10] Here arose one of the most important elements in the slavery defense, the reconciliation of slavery with the principles of republican liberty. In order to do so, the opinion of Edmund Burke was cited as authority. The influence of Burke upon Southern minds was probably as great as that of either Carlyle or Aristotle. He was considered "the most profound of political philosophers." More quotations probably can be found from his speech on conciliation with America than from any single work of any other writer. At the time of the Revolution he had declared: "These people of the Southern (American) colonies are much more strongly, and with a higher and more stubborn spirit, attached to liberty than those of the northward." . . . "It is because freedom is to them not only an enjoyment, but a kind of rank and privilege."[11]

Again, they often pointed to the fact that it was in the ancient republics of Greece and Rome, where slavery flourished,

[9] Calhoun developed the theory of aristocracy in *A Disquisition on Government*, see *Works*, vol. I. The whole theory goes back to Aristotle, who probably had more influence on other thinkers than Calhoun had. In the *Politics*, Aristotle lays down the maxim that a complete household or community is one composed of freemen and slaves. For the influence of Aristotle on Calhoun see W. J. Grayson, *loc. cit.*, p. 60.

[10] Harper, *op. cit.*, p. 44.

[11] Quoted in Dew, *loc. cit.*, p. 461. The influence of this passage on the pro-slavery writers is inestimable; thousands of references were made to it. See, *The Works of Edmund Burke* (Boston, 1865), II, 123-125.

that the spirit of freedom was born. This fact led Senator Toombs to remark that "public liberty and domestic slavery were cradled together."[12] Another line of argument pointed to the fact that the old whig principle of liberty, which restricted the powers of government to the limits of the Constitution, had always maintained its stronghold in the slave-holding States of the South. They had ever been the chief barrier to centralization which they viewed as the greatest destroyer of local freedom.[13]

Beverley Tucker thought that the influence of slavery as a preservative of the spirit of freedom grew out of the peculiar organization of Southern society. He held that there was an element in every community that must be restricted by coercion to its proper place, the performance of labor; but, "if there is strength enough in the frame of government to make this coercion effectual, that strength may be dangerous to the freedom of all." In the slave régimes of the past it was necessary for the government to possess too much power in order to maintain them. However, where society was so organized, as in the South, "that the element in question can be restrained and directed by other energies than those of government, we escape the difficulty."[14] Tucker was continually emphasizing the fact that the peculiar organization of slave society narrowed the scope of powers that it was necessary to vest in government.

The same fact led others to view slave society as having a "quasi military constitution." Since the power of restrain-

[12] *An Oration, Slavery in the United States; Its Consistency with Republican Institutions, and Its Effect upon the Slave and Society* (Augusta, 1853), p. 22.

[13] This argument was expressed by McDuffie, *op. cit.*

[14] *Lectures,* pp. 340-341. Also published as "An Essay on the Moral and Political Effects of Slavery," *Southern Literary Messenger,* X (1844), 477. Again in "Note to Blackstone," *ibid.,* I (1835), 230, he said: "But to a people jealous of freedom, it is a delicate question whether such a power over the citizen can be safely trusted to the municipal authority. To make it effectual it must be a power dangerous to liberty."

ing the slaves in their proper position was in the hands of the masters, it became necessary for them to be clothed with military authority over their servants. While peace would be the ultimate aim, yet in order to secure it on a permanent basis, a military spirit had to be cultivated.[15] This view, rarely expressed, may be contrasted with the more commonly expressed concept of the patriarchal form of slave society. Public opinion and domestic discipline exerted all the power necessary for subjection of the slave. Moreover, the color of the slave was cause sufficient to maintain the system over and beyond any governmental interference or restraint.

Returning to the question of republican liberty, it was contended that its true basis, actual equality, was attained only in slave society. Professor Dew declared that in the South had been accomplished equality among the whites "as nearly as can be expected or desired in the world."[16] Their very sympathy, which arose from their identity of interests was favorable to equality. Judge Upshur explained the effect of slavery as an equalizer of wealth. He recognized that no government could preserve an equality of wealth, even for a day. But he thought that domestic slavery "approaches that result much more nearly than any other civil institution, and it prevents, in a very great degree, if not entirely, that gross inequality among the different *classes* of society, from which alone liberty has anything to fear."[17] In free society there was no such influence and there, the Southerner pointed out, the basis of class was wealth. The only force acting to maintain the equality in the Northern States was the westward movement of the population, which

[15] This view was developed in an article, "The Black Race in America," *DeBow*, XX (1856), 190.

[16] *Loc. cit.*, p. 461.

[17] Upshur, *loc. cit.*, p. 685. For an early statement of influence of wealth in free society see the message of Governor Miller of S. C. in 1829, *supra*, p. 76.

acted as a safety valve to those who were falling behind in the race of life.

But there was another reason why this aristocracy of race and color really maintained the true republican principles. This was because it offered the only sure protection of property. The poorest man in slave society felt an interest in the laws which protected the rights of property, "for, though he has none as yet, he has the purpose and the hope to be rich before he dies, and to leave property to his children." Consequently, Tucker thought that suffrage might be given to all the whites in slave society, because the temptation of the lower class to abuse power was diminished.[18] Where all have property, the right of property is held sacred by all; and there will be no misgovernment, for what is best for one is best for all. There could be no ground for jealousy between rich and poor. In other words, the argument of the Southerner was that all classes felt a security of rights in slave society, and therefore were in the true sense of the word freemen. There was no oppressive force of government, for this constitution of society made the tasks of government easy, since there were no classes to be reconciled. The result was domestic peace, order, and security. In the last analysis, slavery was the ideal force and security for perfect social control.

On the other hand, the slaveholder thought that if the man who had no property be allowed to vote, there could be no security to the rights of people who owned property. Property would be voted robbery. This was the cause for the weakness of universal suffrage in free society, where the large propertyless class was enfranchised. There, in place of a force acting to identify the classes, wealth was rapidly distributing men into classes of diverse interests. The prog-

[18] Tucker, *Lectures,* p. 336.

ress of society would increase these diversities until the classes would begin to war upon each other. The powerful class would always sacrifice the interests of the weaker. Hence, the power of government must be increased to maintain social order and to secure the rights of individuals.[19] But in order to do so the power of government must necessarily become burdensome upon some element.

Going a step further, the slaveholder doubted if the government based upon equal political rights in every member of the community, from the highest to the lowest, could maintain itself when society had reached the stage where wealth was centered in the hands of the few and the great number were reduced to poverty. To such a condition all free society was rapidly progressing. The agrarian spirit was already apparent in the Northern States, and here again, it was shown, only the influence of the westward movement held it in check. The final result, however, could not long be delayed and free society in the North must find some other solution for the class conflict that was imminent.

The result of the reasoning led the slaveholder to picture slavery as the strongest conservative force in society and a bulwark against agrarianism. As Judge Upshur expressed it: "There is then in this institution something which courts and solicits good order; there is a principle in it which avoids confusion and repels faction; its necessary tendency is to distract the purposes and to bind the arm of the agrarian

[19] De Tocqueville criticised American society on the ground that "while the poorer classes are secure in the enjoyment of their rights, except so far as they are endangered by their own caprices, the wealthier have not the same immunity. The right to fill that place in society to which the merit of the individual entitles him and the right to discharge those public functions for which he is better qualified than other men . . ." were not recognized. Tucker said that had De Tocqueville come South he would have found society organized according to his plan. See *ibid.*, pp. 342-343.

and the leveler."[20] This resulted from the facts that "equal in our rank, the spirit of levelling sees nothing to envy; equal in our fortune, the spirit of agrarianism sees nothing to attack."[21] Truly the agrarian spirit was divided against itself in slave society and there were no revolutionary movements to overthrow the harmony of social order or the security of vested rights. Hence, Governor McDuffie declared that slavery was the "cornerstone of our republican edifice," and with the same confidence the Southern leaders declared that the last stronghold of republicanism would be in the slaveholding States. Consequently, South Carolina, when she came to secede from the Union, declared "we are vindicating the great cause of free government, more important, perhaps, to the world, than the existence of all the United States."[22]

SLAVERY AS A SYSTEM OF CAPITAL AND LABOR

The second phase of social theory dealt with slavery as a system of capital and labor. The slaveholder believed that a perfect organization of these two elements of society flourished in the South. Here again an identity of interests, between employee and employer, was the first principle of the system. By making the labor itself capital, the conflict of interests, so evident in other labor systems, lost its foundation. This unity was effected because slave labor was the property of slave capital. Consequently, the interest of capital and labor became identical. T. R. R. Cobb was of the opinion that "there is perhaps no solution of the great problem of reconciling the interests of labor and capital, so as to protect each from the encroachments and oppressions of the other, so simple and effective as negro slavery."[23] Another writer drew a picture of the whole system.

[20] Upshur, *loc. cit.*, p. 686.
[21] *Ibid.*, p. 685.
[22] *Address to the People* (1860), p. 15.
[23] *Op. cit.*, p. ccxiv.

Slavery, in the South, is the days-man between capital and labour. It beautifully blends, harmonizes, and makes them as one. It mingles and unites the wealth, the labour, and industry of the country, in all their varied and diversified interests and conditions; because the labour of the South—the slaves—constitute a great part of the wealth and capital of the South. This union of labor and capital in the same hands, counteracts . . . all those social, moral, material, and political evils which afflict the North and Western Europe.[24]

Here lay the second reason for the conservatism of slave society.

From this idea, there developed the practice of comparing the two systems of labor, free and slave. In the South, the free laborer of the North was called a hireling and his condition in society was compared with that of the slave.[25] It was the contention of the pro-slavery theorist that the status of the two was essentially the same in whatever form of society they toiled. In the last analysis, both were compelled to labor and both received the reward of subsistence. Consequently, they were both slaves under a different name. In order to establish this contention, the servile condition of free labor was pictured. They said that "the poor man has only changed his name. He was once called a serf, then a villein, and now a laborer; but in reality he is now, more than ever, a slave."[26] In fact, the poor of free society were pauper slaves depending upon meager wages for subsistence. Many went so far as to claim that all service was slavery and that the form of labor differed only in name.

But there was one important distinction in the status of the two types of laborers. The slave was assured work and the

---

[24] "American Slavery in 1857," *Southern Literary Messenger*, XXV (1857), 85.

[25] See W. J. Grayson, *The Hireling and the Slave* (Charleston, 1855). Review in *DeBow*, XVIII (1855), 459-462. This was a lengthy poetic defense of slavery as a system of labor.

[26] [R. E. Colston], *The Problem of Free Society* (n. p., n. d.), p. 17.

subsequent reward which was necessary for his comfort, while the hireling was not always able to obtain the labor he sought, and consequently, often suffered. The pro-slavery theorist proceeded on the idea that in all conditions labor remained dependent on capital.[27] Fletcher explained it in this way:

Capital and labor can exist in but two relations; congenerous or antagonistic. They are never congenerous only when it is true that labour constitutes capital, which can only happen through slavery. The deduction is then clear, that capital forever governs labour; and the deduction is also as clear, that, out of slavery, capital and labour must be forever antagonistic. But, again, capital governs labour, because, while capital *now exists*, labour can possess it only by its own consumption. But when the two are congenerous, labour, as a tool, is not urged to its injury, because the tool itself is capital; but when antagonistic, the tool is urged to its utmost power, because its injury, its ruin touches not the capital.[28]

In fact the condition of the slave was preferable to that of the hireling because of the protecting care of the system

---

[27] Those arguing for the free labor system denied the truth of the theory that labor was always dependent on capital. See L. Bacon, *loc. cit.*, p. 647: "Under a just government, recognizing the laborer as having in every respect the same personal rights with the capitalist, labor . . . and capital are mutually dependent and mutually subservient. . . . It is as necessary for capital to seek investment as it is for labor to seek employment . . . it is never employed as capital without giving employment to labor. . . . Out of this blunder comes the assumption that the free laborer like a slave, gets no just compensation for his labor—nothing but what the employer wishes to give him." Likewise, Lincoln argued against the Southern theory of the relation of labor and capital: "Now there is no such relation between capital and labor as assumed, nor is there any such thing as a free man being fixed for life in the condition of a hired laborer. . . . Labor is prior to and independent of capital. Capital is only the fruit of labor, and could never have existed if labor had not first existed. Labor is the superior of capital, and deserves much the higher consideration. . . . The error is in assuming that the whole labor of community exists within that relation. . . . A large majority belong to neither class—neither work for others nor have others working for them." "Annual Message to Congress," 1861, *Works* (Lapsley, ed.), V, 406-407.   [28] *Op. cit.*, p. 219.

for the individual. Not only was the slave assured of work while he was able-bodied, but when he became aged or infirm, he was cared for and given the comforts of life. The slave had no anxieties from want, misfortune, or disability. He was cared for in infancy, in sickness, and in old age. Hence one of the strongest arguments for the system was that it provided a preventive for pauperism. As Cobb said, "Slavery is a protection from pauperism, the bane for which the wisdom of civilized man has not yet prepared an antidote."[29] The profits of capital were reduced to the extent that the welfare of labor was first provided for. George Fitzhugh remarked that "every Southern slave has an estate in tail, indefeasible by fine and recovery, in the lands of the South. If his present master cannot support him, he must sell him to one who can."[30]

Another characteristic of the free labor system was the keen competition that resulted between the individual laborers. Its influence was so intense in free society because of the surplus labor population. This pressure of population upon the means of subsistence, which necessitated the laborers to bid against each other for available work and provided the reason why capital was able to exploit labor, was the real cause of the evils of free society. Although wages were often reduced to the minimum, the hireling was forced to accept because of the pressure of hunger. He was a slave of hunger. Again, it was pointed out that a great loss of time and labor resulted from the competitive economic system of free society.

On the other hand, slavery was said to provide a perfect association of economic factors. First, the slaveholder showed that under slavery the population increased more slowly and

[29] *Op. cit.*, p. ccxiv.
[30] *Sociology for the South, or the Failure of Free Society* (Richmond, 1854), pp. 67-68.

thus did not overtake subsistence at the same pace as in free society. This self-protecting power of slavery against over-population applied to the slave class as well as to the employing class. Furthermore, the slave system provided the means of perfect distribution of labor, it being transferred from place to place with the ease and facility of capital itself. Again the system made the indolent do their share of the work along with the industrious. And it provided a diversion from unproductive to productive consumption. Instead of the wealthy spending their profits upon superfluities, they were taxed with the comfortable support of the laboring class. Finally, the result of directing the products of the soil into their proper channels was that the means of existence kept pace with the increase of population. Hence the strain of population upon subsistence did not result as in free society. So the slaveholder concluded that slavery was the best answer to the gloomy speculation advanced under the Malthusian law.

SLAVE VERSUS FREE SOCIETY

Passing into the last division of social theory, we shall consider the relation of the social movements of the time to the social theories of slavery. It was the contention of the slaveholder that society in the South was more perfect than any other form because it was well ordered and gave no occasion for the rise of radical movements. Here was his strongest defense before the tribunal of civilization. Slave society was free from the many "isms" that ran rampant throughout free society. He often asked the question why he should fly to the evils that he knew not of rather than to cherish the blessings that slavery provided?

Consequently, the first tendency of the social theorists seems to have been a repudiation of all the social movements that grew up during the nineteenth century. In this respect they made no distinction between them, but opposed them all simply because they had in common the revolutionary purpose of changing, in some manner, the existing status of society. Moreover, to the slaveholder, all alike were mere expressions of the problem faced by free society, the discontent of the under class. The Southern writer was fond of calling these movements the social reform theories. He classed anarchism, communism and socialism, Proudhonism and Fourierism, in the same category with abolitionism, free rentism, free love, and perfectionism, as illustrations of the revolutionary temper of the time. It was, however, not strange that he should have conceived of the natural opposites, anarchism and socialism, as kindred theories. At the time neither had been clearly and systematically formulated and differentiated. Besides, in two fundamentals they were alike. To the slaveholder, these were of paramount importance. They alike attacked the sanctity of property and they alike attempted to organize society on the basis of individual equality of rights.

With the idea of property in mind, the pro-slavery theorists drew a definite parallel between abolitionism and socialism. Jefferson Davis once pointed out this fact in an address before the Senate of the United States.

And the current suggestion, that slave property exists but by the local law, is no more true of this than it is of all other property. In fact, the European Socialists, who, in wild radicalism, [. . .] are the correspondents of the American abolitionists, maintain the same doctrine as to all property, that the abolitionists do as to slave property. He who has property, they argue, is the robber of him who has not. *"La propriété c'est le vol,"* is the famous theme of the Socialist, Proudhon. And the same precise theories of attack at the North on the slave property of the South would, if carried out to their legitimate and necessary logical consequences, and will, if successful in this, their first stage of action, superinduce at-tacks on all property, North and South.[31]

The one said that all property in man was sin while the other declared that all property in land was wrong. In principle they were the same, and, as the slaveholder pointed out, to admit the principle in the case of one form of property was to recognize it in regard to all forms, which meant a social revolution. Such would be the outcome of the abolition doc-trine, if once accepted.

Viewed from another angle the social reform theories offered proof of the failure of free society. Socialism and many other movements would not have arisen had free so-ciety been able to cope with the problems of the day. It was because the social structure was not well ordered that these movements arose as attempted cures for the exploited classes. As examples of the failure of free society, the many schemes of social philosophers were reviewed. The plan of Fourier and the schemes of Saint-Simon of France were examples. In England the work of John Stuart Mill and Herbert Spencer illustrated the failure and dangers which attended the free competitive labor system, and indicated the necessity of par-tial reform.[32] Another example of the necessity of some re-form were the poor laws of England. One writer expressed it in this way:

The hirelings of the old world are consequently discontented. They clamour for change. They demand communism, socialism,

[31] Quoting from a letter of Caleb Cushing, "Speech, Jan. 26, 1860, *Works*, IV, 183; for a similar view see W. J. Grayson, *A Reply to Dr. Dewey's Address* (Charleston, 1856), *passim*. Proudhon was not a socialist, as the Southern writers often indicated, but an anarchist, a follower of the Englishman, Godwin. Godwin himself was also referred to on many occasions, but he did not influence Southern thinking to the degree that Proudhon did, probably because Proudhon's first book *What Is Property?* was published in 1840. For Proudhon's theories, see Dunning, *op. cit.*, III, 344, 365-370; for Godwin, *ibid.*, pp. 208, 362-364. Smylie, *op. cit.*, connected the writings of Godwin with the abolitionists.

[32] For a review of the significance of Mill see, "Slavery and Freedom," *Southern Quarterly Review*, XXIX (1856), 62.

the organization of labor—something different from the present
system—anything rather than pauperism, misery, and starvation
to which they are exposed. Society in England and France is con-
vulsed with [discontent] for this very reason and it is hard to say
where the remedy will come from.[33]

The slaveholder also pointed to the reform movements
of the Northern States which were manifestations of the
failure of society there. Horace Greely, the editor of
the *New York Tribune*, probably influenced the Southern
mind to the greatest extent. He had for many years advocated, as a follower of Fourier, a theory of general proprietorship and association of laboring families in which there
would be no hired labor.[34] As another radical manifestation
of discontent, the Southern writer pointed to Stephen Pearl
Andrews, who expounded a complete theory of anarchism.[35]
The view of the slaveholder in regard to the theories of these
men was expressed as follows:

Here, then, are two witnesses, both natives of the enlightened
North, both hostile to slavery, both favorable to the widest dis-
semination of liberty, both cognizant or professing to be cognizant
of the condition of the labouring class in the Northern and North-
western States of the Union, both resident in the free States, both
occupied with the study of the social condition of the free population there, both engaged in devising and popularizing patent meth-

[33] W. J. Grayson, *Letters of Curtius* (Charleston, 1851).

[34] For the influence of Greely see: Fitzhugh, *Cannibals All! or Slaves without
Masters* (Richmond, 1857); "The War upon Slavery—Socialism," *DeBow*, XXII
(1857), 633; "The Declaration of Independence," *ibid.*, XXIX (1859), 178;
D. Lee, "The Laborer—His Rights and Duties," *ibid.*, p. 487.   For Greely's
views see *Hints Toward Reforms* (New York, 1850).

[35] See, *The True Constitution of Government in the Sovereignty of the Indi-
vidual as the Final Development of Protestantism, Democracy and Socialism* (New
York, 1853), and *Cost the Limit of Price: A scientific measure of honesty in
trade, as one of the fundamental principles in the solution of the social problem*
(New York, 1853).   The influence of Andrews on Fitzhugh was very pronounced.
For other examples, see, "Slavery and Freedom," *Southern Quarterly Review*,
XXIX, (1856), 65; G. F. Holmes, "Theory of Political Individualism," *DeBow*,
XXII (1857), 133.

ods of reform, who both attest so far as their observation extends, the pernicious accompaniments of the existing free society.[36]

There were many other illustrations used at various times to bring out this point. Fitzhugh concluded that "the great socialist and communist movement of the day, which is co-extensive with free society, whilst it has not yet invoked reëstablishment of domestic slavery, asserts, in a thousand forms, the utter failure of existing social institutions, which have arisen from the ruins of feudal servitude."[37]

Returning to the other side of the question, the slave-holder argued that slavery, although it acted as a protection against all social reform theories, yet in reality it attained for the masses that which those movements were striving for. This idea led many Southern thinkers to declare that slave society was in fact the only practicable form of socialism. Edmund Ruffin of Virginia declared that "in the institution of domestic slavery, and in that only, are most completely realized the dreams and sanguine hopes of the socialist school of philanthropists."[38] Grayson, one of the ablest of the social theorists, pictured slavery in this light:

Slave labor is the only organized labor ever known. It is the only condition of society in which labor and capital are associated on a large scale in which their interests are combined and not in conflict. Every plantation is an organized community, a pha-lanstery, as Fourier would call it—where all work, where each member gets subsistence and a home and the more industrious larger pay and profits to their own superior industry.[39]

Association of labor, in order to destroy competition among the laborers, certainly was one of the ends all socialists desired. Fitzhugh said that slavery did away with free com-

[36] "Slavery and Freedom," *Southern Quarterly Review*, XXIX (1856), 67.
[37] "The Counter Current," *DeBow*, XXI (1856), 91.
[38] *Op. cit.*, p. 10.   [39] *Letters of Curtius*, p. 8.

petition, afforded support at all times to laborers, brought about a qualified community of property, and associated labor. In all these respects, it carried out the principles of socialism. In fact he thought "a well-conducted farm in the South is a model of associated labor that Fourier might envy."[40] Again he pictured the socialistic nature of the Southern plantation:

A Southern farm is a sort of joint stock concern or social phalanstery, in which the master furnishes the capital and skill, and the slaves the labor, and divide the profits, not according to each one's in-put, but according to each one's wants and necessities.[41]

In one respect, however, slavery and socialism differed. Slavery provided the one directing mind and controlling will of the master as the head and governing power of the association. Socialism had offered no substitute for this authority of the master as a controlling force. This fact led Fitzhugh to declare: "Socialism is already slavery in all save the master. It had as well adopt that feature at once, as come to that it must to make its schemes at once humane and efficient."[42] Socialism differing from slavery in this one respect, would be totally ineffective without it. Hence Fitzhugh advocated slavery as the best social system in all forms of society. It was his contention that slavery was not only suited for diverse races, but was the proper relation between unequal individuals within the races. In fact, he declared that the true and best slave race was the white race.[43] On this point, he was thinking of the large class of unfortunate hirelings to whom the protective principle of slavery would ensure a life of comfort and contentment.

Although the pro-slavery philosophy rejected the many innovating movements of the nineteenth century, yet there was one social philosopher whose writings were in harmony

---

[40] *Sociology for the South*, p. 45.
[41] *Ibid.*, p. 48.   [42] *Ibid.*, p. 70.
[43] "Origin of Civilization," *DeBow*, XXV (1858), 653.

with the principles of slavery. The influence of Carlyle became pronounced upon the thought of Southern people from the time of his earliest edition of *Sartor Resartus* (1833). Later his *Past and Present* (1843) and his *Latter Day Pamphlets* (1850) had a widespread influence upon the slaveholder.[44] His essay on the West India emancipation, *Occasional Discourse on the Nigger Question,* published in *Frazer's Magazine* (December, 1849) did most to establish him in the Southern mind as an advocate of their form of society. Beverley Tucker was so impressed with the likeness between Carlyle's ideas and his own that he sent him a copy of his *Lectures,* which led to a brief correspondence and a consequent interchange of political ideas between them.[45] Fitzhugh thought that Aristotle's *Politics* and "the *Latter Day Pamphlets* of Mr. Carlyle, furnish the best refutations of socialism and abolition. They should both be text books in all our colleges."[46] The following passage was quoted with high approval and satisfaction to demonstrate the kindred nature of Carlyle's philosophy to that of the slaveholder:

Liberty, I am told, is a divine thing. Liberty, when it becomes the liberty to die by starvation, is not so divine! The true liberty of a man, you would say, consisted in his finding out, or being forced to find out, the right path, and to walk therein. To learn, or to be taught what work he actually was able for, and then, by permission, persuasion, and even compulsion, to set about doing of the same! That is his true blessedness, honour, liberty, and maximum of well-being: if liberty be not that, I, for one, have small care about liberty. . . . If thou do know better than I what is good and right, I conjure thee, in the name of God, force me to

[44] For reviews of Carlyle's works, see, *DeBow,* VIII (1850), 527; *Southern Quarterly Review,* XVIII (1850), 313-356; *ibid.,* XXIV (1853), 369.

[45] Letter of Tucker to Hammond, May 29, 1849, MS. in the Library of Congress.

[46] "Black Republicanism in Athens," *DeBow,* XXIII (1857), 22.

do it; were it by never such brass collars, whips and handcuffs, leave me not to walk over precipices![47]

The slaveholder felt that the principles of slave philosophy were inculcated throughout the writings of Carlyle. Fitzhugh declared that "Mr. Carlyle boldly proclaims slavery as the only cure for existing social evils."[48] How accurately the slaveholder interpreted the philosophy of Carlyle as he translated it into the pro-slavery argument may best be determined by Carlyle's own words as he commented upon the Southern problem in answer to a specific inquiry from Beverley Tucker.

For you and other men of sense and manfulness of spirit, who stand in the very coil of Negro complications, and feel practically that you must retain command of your servants, or else quit your place and task in the world I find it altogether natural that you should in silence resolve to front all extremities rather than yield to an extrinsic clamour of that nature, however big-voiced and sententious it become: in which quarrel too, what can I say, except "God stand by the right," which I clearly perceive you in part are!

But, alas, the question is deep as the foundations of society; and will not be settled this long while! For this cry about emancipation, so well pleased with itself on Humanity Platforms, is but the keynote of that huge anarchic roar, now rising from all nations, for good reasons too,—which tends to abolish all mastership and obedience whatsoever in this world, and to render society impossible among the Sons of Adam! And I doubt we have hardly got to the crisis of that yet,—at least among speakers in England I find myself in a painful minority of one in regard to it;—and *after* the crisis, when the minority shall have become considerable, I feel too well what a task will be ahead of them! It is truly time

[47] See "British and American Slavery," *Southern Quarterly Review*, XXIV (1853), 410, quoting from *Past and Present* (1843), p. 148. The passage varies slightly from the text in *Works* (Centenary ed.), pp. 212-213.

[48] "Centralization and Socialism," *DeBow*, XX (1856), 692.

that each brave man consulted solemnly his own most religious oracles on the subject; and stand piously prepared to do whatever God's mandate he felt to be laid on him in regard to it.

Give me leave, in my dim light, but in my real sympathy with your affairs, to hint another thought I have. It is, that this clamour from your "Exeter Hall" and ours, which few persons can regard with less reverence than I, was nevertheless a thing *necessary*. My notion is, that the relation of the white man to the black is *not* at present a just one, according to the Law of the Eternal; and though "abolition" is by no means the way to remedy it, and would be a "remedy" equivalent to killing it (as I believe); yet, beyond all question, remedied it must be; and peace upon it is not possible till a remedy be found, and begin to be visibly applied. "A servant hired *for life*, instead of by the day or month": I have often wondered that wise and just men in your region (of whom I believe there are many) had not come upon a great many methods, or at least some methods better than those yet in use, of justly enunciating this relation, and relieving such asperities of it as become intolerable. . . . I shall say only the Negro question will be left in peace, when God Almighty's Law about it *is* (with tolerable approximation) actually found out, and practiced; and never till then. Might this also be a word to the wise!— . . ."[49]

This commentary on Southern institutions seen through foreign eyes was passed on by Tucker to Hammond "as a sort of cordial to grave heartedness."[50]

In conclusion, let us point out the culmination of social theory. Not only did the slaveholder reject the "isms" of free society, but he denied the soundness of the principle upon which that society was founded, the philosophy of *laissez faire*, which required each individual to shift for himself and the devil take the hindmost.[51] Rather he showed that slave so-

[49] Letter of Carlyle to Tucker, Oct. 31st, 1850. MS. in a private collection. Italics and capitalization as in the original.

[50] Letter of Jan. 2nd, 1851. MS. in the Library of Congress.

[51] This reasoning led Fitzhugh to reject the science of political economy as a whole. See *Sociology for the South, passim.* In fact, he associated in his mind

ciety was based upon the opposite principle, the protective philosophy, where the weak were taken care of. In the last analysis, he contended that the *laissez faire* doctrine destroyed the social spirit itself, while the protective doctrine carried out the true societarian principle.

---

the *laissez faire* doctrine of Adam Smith and his school of political economists with the entire science of political economy. This fallacy was pointed out by an article "Slavery and Political Economy," *DeBow*, XXI (1856), 331-349, 442-467, which showed that the science of political economy merely took utility as the test of right. In this respect, it was of great value in justifying slavery.

BIBLIOGRAPHY

PRIMARY MATERIALS

MANUSCRIPTS

(A) Manuscripts in the Library of Congress:

James Henry Hammond Papers, including correspondence with the following: J. C. Calhoun, Thomas Cooper, Robbert Y. Hayne, George McDuffie, J. C. Nott, W. G. Simms, Louis Tappan, N. Beverley Tucker and others.

George Frederick Holmes Papers: miscellaneous correspondence; observations on a passage in Aristotle's *Politics*.

Ephriam G. Squier Papers, including letters from the following: Luke Burke, George R. Gliddon, J. H. Hammond, Samuel George Morton, J. C. Nott.

(B) Manuscripts in the Collection of Mr. George P. Coleman, Williamsburg, Virginia:

St. George Tucker Papers.

Nathaniel Beverley Tucker Papers, including letters from the following: Thomas Carlyle, J. H. Hammond, Francis Lieber, Edmund Ruffin, W. G. Simms, Abel P. Upshur, and others; an essay written by J. H. Hammond: Laws of Nature, Natural Rights, Slavery.

H. A. Washington, Class Notebook.

(C) Manuscripts in the McClung Collection, Lawson McGhee Library, Knoxville, Tennessee:

Letters of J. G. M. Ramsey to L. W. Spratt.

(D) Manuscripts in the Department of Archives, Montgomery, Alabama:

Letter of John W. Walker to Charles Tait, February 11, 1820.

PRINTED SOURCES

Collections

The Athenian Oracle: An entire collection of all the valuable questions and answers in the old Athenian mercuries. 6 v., London, 1728.

Candler, A. D., ed. The Colonial Records of Georgia. 25 v., Atlanta, 1908.

Catterall, Mrs. Helen Honor (Tunnicliff), ed. Judicial Cases Concerning American Slavery and the Negro. 3 v., Washington, 1926-1932.

Cooper, Thomas and McCord, D. J. Statutes at Large of South Carolina. 10 v., Columbia, 1836-1841.

DeBow, J. D. B., ed. The Industrial Resources, Statistics, etc., of the United States and More Particularly of the Southern and Western States. 3 v., New York, 1854.

Force, Peter. American Archives: Fourth series containing a documentary history of the English Colonies in North America, from the King's message to Parliament, of March 7, 1774, to the Declaration of Independence. 6 v., Washington, 1837-1846.

Georgia Historical Society Collections. 9 v., 1840-1916.

Hening, W. W., ed. The Statutes at Large, being a collection of the laws of Virginia. 13 v., New York, 1823.

Massachusetts Historical Society Collections. 70 v., Boston, 1792+

Thorpe, F. N., ed. Federal and State Constitutions, Colonial Charters, and Other Organic Laws. 7 v., Washington, 1909.

Official Reports, Debates, and Proceedings

The Address of the People of South Carolina Assembled in Convention to the People of the Slaveholding States of the United States. Charleston, 1860.

Annals of the Congress of the United States (1st Congress 1st session, 1789 to 18th Congress 1st session, 1824). Washington.

The Congressional Globe, containing sketches of the debates and proceedings of the Congress (23rd Congress 1st session, 1834 to 36th Congress 2nd session, 1861). Washington.

"The Debates in the Virginia House of Delegates on Emancipation" published in the *Richmond Enquirer*, January to May, 1832.

The Debates of the General Conference, of the Methodist Episcopal Church, May, 1844. To which is added a review of the proceedings of said conference. By Rev. Luther Lee and Rev. E. Smith. New York, 1845.

Declaration of the Immediate Causes Which Induce and Justify the Secession of South Carolina from the Federal Union and the Ordinance of Secession. Charleston, 1860.

Elliot, Jonathan, ed. The Debates in the General State Conventions, on the Adoption of the Federal Constitution, as Recommended by the General Convention at Philadelphia, in 1787. Together with the journal of the Federal Convention, Luther Martin's Letter, Yates's Minutes, etc. 4 v., Washington, 1836.

English Reports. 176 v., London, 1900-1932.

Ford, W. C., Hunt, Gaillard, Fitzpatrick, J. C., eds. Journals of the Continental Congress. 31 v., Washington, 1904-1934.

Hayne, Robert Y., ed. Proceedings of the Citizens of Charleston, on the Incendiary Machinations Now in Progress against the Peace and Welfare of the Southern States. Charleston, 1835.

Journal of the Convention of the State of Tennessee, convened for the purpose of revising and amending the Constitution thereof. Held in Nashville. Nashville, 1834.

Journal of the State Convention, held in Milledgeville, in December, 1850. Milledgeville, 1850.

Official Reports of the Debates and Proceedings of the Southern Commercial Convention Assembled at Knoxville, Tennessee, August 10, 1857. Appendix, proceedings of Southern Convention at Savannah. December 8, 1856. Knoxville, 1857.

Proceedings and Debates of the Virginia State Convention of 1829-30, to which are subjoined the new Constitution of Virginia, and the votes of the people. Richmond, 1830.

Proceedings of the Meeting in Charleston, South Carolina, May 13-15, 1845, on the Religious Instruction of the Negroes. Charleston, 1845.

Proceedings of a Meeting of Citizens of Central Mississippi, in Relation to the Slavery Question: Also the proceedings of the State convention, on the same subject, held at the city of Jackson, October, 1849. Published by order of the Legislature. Jackson, 1850.

Register of Debates in Congress, comprising the leading debates and incidents of the Congress (18th Congress 2nd session 1824 to 25th Congress 1st Session 1837). Washington.

A Report and Treatise on Slavery and the Slave Agitation (Printed by order of the House of Representatives of Texas). Austin, 1857.

United States Supreme Court Reports. 4 v., Dallas, ed., 1789-1800; 9 v., Cranch, ed., 1801-1815; 12 v., Wheaton, ed., 1816-1827; 16 v., Peters, ed., 1828-1842; 24 v., Howard, ed., 1843-1860. Washington.

Legal Commentaries

Burge, William. Commentaries on Colonial and Foreign Laws Generally, and in their conflict with each other, and with the law of England. 4 v., London, 1838.

Cobb, Thomas R. R. An Inquiry into the Law of Negro Slavery in the United States of America. To which is prefixed an historical study of slavery. Philadelphia and Savannah, 1858.

Cooper, Thomas. The Institutes of Justinian with Notes. Philadelphia, 1812.

Dane, Nathan. A General Abridgment and Digest of American Law, with occasional notes and comments. 9 v., Boston, 1823.

Goodell, William. The American Slave Code in Theory and Practice: Its distinctive features shown by its statutes, judicial decisions, and illustrative facts. New York, 1853.

Hurd, John C. The Law of Freedom and Bondage in the United States. 2 v., Boston, 1857-1862.

O'Neall, John Belton. The Negro Law of South Carolina. Columbia, 1848.

Stroud, George M. A Sketch of the Laws Relating to Slavery in the Several States of the United States of America. Philadelphia, 1827.

Tucker, St. George. Blackstone's Commentaries: With notes of reference, to the Constitution and laws of the United States; and of the Commonwealth of Virginia. 5 v., Philadelphia, 1803.

Wheeler, Jacob D. A Practical Treatise on the Law of Slavery. Being a compilation of all the decisions made on that subject in the general courts of the United States, and State courts. With copious notes and references to the statutes and other authorities, systematically arranged. New York and New Orleans, 1837.

Special Treatises

Aristoteles. The Politics of Aristotle, translated with an analysis and critical notes, by J. E. C. Welldon. London, 1883.

Grotius, Hugo. De Jure Belli et Pacis, accompanied by an abridged translation by William Whewell, with the notes of the author, Barbarac, and others. 3 v., Cambridge, n. d.

Horn, Andrew. The Mirrour of Justices, written originally in the old French, long before the conquest; and many things added. . . . (W. C. Robinson, ed.). Washington, 1903.

Montesquieu, Charles Louis de Secondat. The Spirit of Laws. With D'Alembert's analysis of the work. . . . With additional notes . . . by J. V. Prichard. 2 v., London, 1900-1902.

Published Works—Correspondence, Speeches, Memoirs, and Journals

Adams, Charles Francis, ed. Memoirs of John Quincy Adams, comprising portions of his diary from 1795 to 1848. 12 v., Philadelphia, 1874-1877.

———— The Works of John Adams. 10 v., Boston, 1856.

Bergh, A. E., ed. The Writings of Thomas Jefferson. 20 v., Washington, 1917.

Berkeley, George. Works, to which is added an account of his
    life and several of his letters. 3 v., London, 1820.

Boucher, Chauncey Samuel, ed. Correspondence Addressed to
    John C. Calhoun, 1837-1849. (American Historical Asso-
    ciation Annual Report for 1929), Washington, 1930.

The Works of the Right Honorable Edmund Burke. 12 v. (re-
    vised ed.), Boston, 1865-1867.

The Works of Thomas Carlyle. 30 v. (Centenary ed.), New
    York, 1896-1901.

Channing, William Ellery. Works. 6 v., Boston, 1849.

Conway, M. D., ed. The Writings of Thomas Paine. 4 v., New
    York, 1894.

Crallé, Richard K., ed. The Works of John C. Calhoun. 6 v.,
    New York, 1853.

Flinn, J. W., ed. Complete Works of Rev. Thomas Smyth.
    10 v., Columbia, 1910.

Hammond, James Henry. Selections from the Letters and Speeches
    of the Hon. James Henry Hammond of South Carolina. New
    York, 1866.

Hunt, Gaillard, ed. The Writings of James Madison. 9 v., New
    York, 1910.

Jameson, J. F., ed. Correspondence of John C. Calhoun.
    (American Historical Association Annual Report for 1899,
    II). Washington, 1900.

King, C. R., ed. The Life and Correspondence of Rufus King;
    comprising his letters, private and official, his public documents,
    and his speeches. 6 v., New York, 1894-1900.

Lapsley, A. B., ed. The Writings of Abraham Lincoln. 8 v.,
    New York, 1906.

The Life, Travels and Opinions of Benjamin Lundy, including his
    journeys to Texas and Mexico; with a sketch of contemporary
    events, and a notice of the revolution in Haiti, compiled under
    the direction and on behalf of his children. Philadephia, 1847.

Nicolay, John G. and Hay, John, eds. Abraham Lincoln; Com-
    plete Works, comprising his speeches, letters, state papers, and
    miscellaneous writings. 2 v., New York, 1922.

Orme, Rev. William, ed. The Practical Works of the Rev. Richard Baxter: With a life of the author and a critical examination of his writings. 21 v., London, 1830.

Reynolds, I. A., ed. The Works of the Rt. Rev. John England. 5 v., Baltimore, 1849.

Rowland, Dunbar, ed. Jefferson Davis, Constitutionalist, his letters, papers and speeches. 10 v., Jackson, Mississippi, 1840.

Sparks, Jared, ed. The Works of Benjamin Franklin. 10 v., Boston, 1840.

Tipple, E. S., ed. The Heart of Asbury's Journal. New York, 1904.

Tyerman, L. The Life and Times of John Wesley, Founder of the Methodists. 3 v., New York, 1872.

Wayland, D. S., ed. The Works of William Paley, D.D. 5 v. London, 1837.

Wheaton, Henry. Some Account of the Life, Writings and Speeches of William Pinkney. New York, 1826.

Woolman, John. A Journal of the Life, Gospel Labours, and Christian Experiences of the Faithful Minister of Christ, John Woolman, late of Mt. Holly, New Jersey, to which is added his works. Dublin, 1776.

Contemporary Newspapers and Periodicals

Charleston Courier. Charleston, 1829-1833.

Charleston Medical Journal and Review. 15 v., Charleston, 1846-1860.

Charleston Mercury. Charleston, 1829-1833.

De Bow's Commercial Review of the Southern and Western States. 34 v., New Orleans, Charleston, Columbia, 1846-1864. After the War Series, 8 v., New Orleans, 1866-1870.

Farmer's Register. 10 v., Shellbanks and Petersburg, Va., 1833-1842.

Gospel Messenger and Southern Episcopal Review. 29 v., Charleston, 1824-1853.

Richmond Enquirer. Richmond, 1830-1833.

Russell's Magazine. 6 v., Charleston, 1857-1860.

Southern Agriculturalist, Horticulturalist, and Register of Rural Affairs. 12 v., Charleston, 1828-1839.

Southern Literary Journal and Magazine of Arts. 6 v., Charleston, 1835-1838.

Southern Literary Messenger. 38 v., Richmond, 1834-1864.

Southern Presbyterian Review. Columbia, 14 v., 1847-1862.

Southern Quarterly Review. 30 v., New Orleans, Charleston, Columbia, 1842-1857.

Contemporary Books

Adams, Nehemiah, D.D. A South-Side View of Slavery; or three months at the South, in 1854. Boston, 1854.

———— The Sable Cloud: A Southern tale, with Northern comments by the Author of "A South-Side View of Slavery." Boston, 1861.

Andrews, E. A. Slavery and the Domestic Slave-Trade in the United States. In a series of letters addressed to the executive committee of the American Union for the Relief and Improvement of the Colored Race. Boston, 1836.

Andrews, Stephen Pearl. The True Constitution of Government in the Sovereignty of the Individual as the Final Development of Protestantism, Democracy, and Socialism. New York, 1853.

———— Cost the Limit of Price: A scientific measure of honesty in trade, as one of the fundamental principles in the solution of the social problem. New York, 1853.

———— Love, Marriage and Divorce, and the Sovereignty of the Individual: A discussion by Henry James, Horace Greely, and Stephen Pearl Andrews, including the final replies of Mr. Andrews, rejected by the *Tribune*. New York, 1853.

Armstrong, George D. The Christian Doctrine of Slavery. New York, 1857.

Bachman, John. The Doctrine of the Unity of the Human Race —Examined on the principles of science. Charleston, 1850.

Bacon, Thomas. Two Sermons Preached to a Congregation of Black Slaves, at the parish church of St. Peter in the Province of Maryland. By an American Pastor. London, 1749.

————— Four Sermons upon the Great Indispensable Duty of All Christian Masters and Mistresses to Bring up Their Negro Slaves in the Knowledge and Fear of God. Preached at the parish church of St. Peter in Talbot Co., in the Province of Maryland. London, 1750.

Bailey, William Rufus. The Issue, presented in a series of letters on slavery. New York, 1837.

Baldwin, Samuel Davies. Dominion; or, the Unity and Trinity of the Human Race; with the divine political constitution of the world, and the divine rights of Shem, Ham, and Japheth. Nashville, 1858.

Barnes, Albert. An Inquiry into the Scriptural Views of Slavery. Philadelphia, 1846.

————— The Church and Slavery. Philadelphia, 1857.

[Bellon de Saint Quentin, J.]. Dissertation sur la Traite et le Commerce des Nègres. Paris, 1764.

Blake, W. O. The History of Slavery and the Slave Trade, Ancient and Modern. The forms of slavery that prevailed in ancient nations, particularly in Greece and Rome. Columbus, 1860.

Bledsoe, Albert Taylor. An Essay on Liberty and Slavery. Philadelphia, 1856.

Boucher, Jonathan. Causes and Consequences of the American Revolution. London, 1797.

Bowditch, William Ingersoll. Slavery and the Constitution. Boston, 1849.

Brown, David. The Planter: Or Thirteen Years in the South. By a Northern Man. Philadelphia, 1853.

Brownlow, W. G. and Pryne, Rev. A. Ought American Slavery To Be Perpetuated? Philadelphia, 1858.

Buckingham, J. S. The Slave States of America. 2 v., London and Paris, n.d.

Cabell, J. L., M.D. The Testimony of Modern Science to the Unity of Mankind; being a summary of the conclusions announced by the highest authorities in the several departments of physiology, zoölogy, and comparative philology in favor of the specific unity and common origin of man. With an introductory notice by James W. Alexander, D.D. New York, 1859.

Cairnes, J. E. The Slave Power, Its Character, Career and Probable Designs: Being an attempt to explain the real issues in the American contest. New York, 1862.

Caldwell, Charles. Thoughts on the Original Unity of the Human Race. New York, 1830.

Campbell, John. Negro-Mania: Being an examination of the falsely assumed equality of the various races of men; demonstrated by the investigations of Champollion, Wilkinson, Rosellini, Van-Amringe, Gliddon, Young, Morton, Knox, Lawrence, Gen. J. H. Hammond, Murray, Smith, W. Gilmore Simms, English, Conrad, Elder, Prichard, Bluemenbach, Cuvier, Brown, Le Vaillant, Carlyle, Cardinal Wiseman, Burckhardt, and Jefferson. Together with a concluding chapter, presenting a comparative statement of the condition of the Negroes in the West Indies before and since emancipation. Philadelphia, 1851.

Carey, H. C. The Slave Trade, Domestic and Foreign: Why it exists, and how it may be extinguished. Philadelphia, 1853.

[Chambers, Robert]. Vestiges of the Natural History of Creation. (Introduction by Rev. George B. Cheever). New York, 1845.

Chambers, William. American Slavery and Colour. London and New York, 1857.

Channing, William E. Essays on Slavery. Boston, 1835.

———— Slavery. Boston, 1836.

Chase, Henry and Sanborn, C. H. The North and the South: Being a statistical view of the condition of the free and slave States. Boston and Cleveland, 1857.

Cheever, George Barrell. God Against Slavery: And the freedom and duty of the pulpit to rebuke it, as a sin against God. New York, 1857.

———— The Guilt of Slavery and Crime of Slaveholding. Boston, 1860.

Christy, David. Cotton Is King: Or the culture of cotton, and its relation to agriculture, manufacture and commerce; to the free colored people; and to those who hold that slavery is in itself sinful. . . . By an American. Cincinnati, 1855.

———— Pulpit Politics: Or ecclesiastical legislation on slavery, in its disturbing influences on the American Union. Cincinnati, 1862.

Clarkson, Thomas. An Essay on the Slavery and Commerce of the Human Species, Particularly the African, translated from a Latin dissertation, which was honored with the first prize in the University of Cambridge, for the year 1785, with additions. London and Philadelphia, 1786.

———— The History of the Rise, Progress, and Accomplishment of the Abolition of the African Slave Trade by the British Parliament. 2 v. London, 1808.

Cobb, Howell. A Scriptural Examination of the Institution of Slavery in the United States. [Perry?], Georgia, 1856.

Coffin, Joshua. A Sketch of the History of Newbury, Newburyport, and West Newbury, from 1635 to 1845. Boston, 1845.

Copley, Esther. A History of Slavery. London, 1839.

Dabney, Robert L. A Defense of Virginia [and through her of the South,] in the recent and pending contests against the sectional party. New York, 1867.

Delaney, Martin Robison. The Condition, Elevation, Emigration, and Destiny of the Colored People of the United States. Philadelphia, 1852.

Dew, Thomas R. Review of the Debate [on the Abolition of Slavery] in the Virginia Legislature of 1831 and 1832. Richmond, 1832.

———— An Essay on Slavery. Richmond, 1849.

Drayton, John. A View of South Carolina, as Respects Her Natural and Civil Concerns. Charleston, 1802.

[Drayton, William]. The South Vindicated from the Treason and Fanaticism of the Northern Abolitionists. Philadelphia, 1836.

Elliott, Rev. Charles. Sinfulness of American Slavery. 2 v., Cincinnati, 1851.

Elliott, E. N., ed. Cotton Is King, and Pro-Slavery Arguments: Comprising the writings of Hammond, Harper, Christy, Stringfellow, Hodge, Bledsoe, and Cartwright, on this important subject. Augusta, 1860.

Ellison, Thomas. Slavery and Secession in America, Historical and Economical. London, 1861.

England, Bishop John. Letters of the Late Bishop [John] England to the Hon. John Forsyth, on the Subject of Domestic Slavery: To which are prefixed copies, in Latin and English, of the Pope's Apostolic letter, concerning the African slave trade, with some introductory remarks, etc. Baltimore, 1844.

Estes, Matthew. A Defense of Negro Slavery, as It Exists in the United States. Montgomery, 1846.

Farrar, C. C. S. The War, Its Causes and Consequences. Cairo, Ill.; Memphis, Tenn.; Paducah, Ky., 1864.

Featherstonhaugh, G. W. Excursion Through the Slave States, from Washington on the Potomac to the Frontier of Mexico; with sketches of popular manners and geological notices. 2 v., London, 1844.

Felt, Joseph B. Annals of Salem. 2 v., Salem, 1845-1849.

Fitzhugh, George. Sociology for the South: Or the failure of free society. Richmond, 1854.

———— Cannibals All! Or slaves without masters. Richmond, 1857.

Fletcher, John. Studies on Slavery, in Easy Lessons. Compiled into eight studies, and subdivided into short lessons for the convenience of readers. Natchez, 1852.

Freeman, Rev. F. Africa's Redemption the Salvation of Our Country. New York, 1852.

Freeman, O. S. *Pseud.*-Rogers, Edward Coit. Letters on Slavery Addressed to the Pro-Slavery Men of America; showing its illegality in all ages and nations: its destructive war upon society and government, morals and religion. Boston, 1855.

French, Mrs. A. M. Slavery in South Carolina and the Ex-Slaves; or, the Port Royal mission. New York, 1862.

Fuller, Rev. Richard and Wayland, Rev. Francis. Domestic Slavery Considered as a Scriptural Institution: In a correspondence between the . . . New York and Boston, 1845.

Gobineau, Joseph Arthur, Comte de. The Moral and Intellectual Diversity of Races, with particular reference to their respective influence in the civil and political history of mankind. From the French by . . . with historical notes by H. Hotz. To which is added an appendix containing a summary of the latest scientific facts bearing upon the question of unity or plurality of species by J. C. Nott. Philadelphia, 1856.

Godwyn, Morgan. The Negroes' and Indians' Advocate, sueing for their admission into the Church. London, 1680.

Goodell, William. Slavery and Anti-Slavery; a history of the great struggle in both hemispheres; with a view of the slave question in the United States. New York, 1843.

———— Views of American Constitutional Law, in Its Bearing upon American Slavery. Utica, New York, 1845.

Grahame, James. Who Is to Blame? Or Cursory Review of "American Apology for American Accession to Negro Slavery." London, 1842.

Grayson, William J. The Hireling and the Slave. Charleston, 1855.

Gurowski, Adam. Slavery in History. New York, 1860.

Hamilton, William T. The "Friend of Moses"; or, a defense of the Pentateuch as the production of Moses and an inspired document, against the objections of modern skepticism. Mobile and New York, 1852.

Handlin, W. W. American Politics, a moral and political work, treating of the causes of the Civil War, the nature of government, and the necessity for reform. New Orleans, 1864.

Harper, William, Hammond, J. H., Simms, W. G. and Dew, T. R. The Pro-Slavery Argument; as maintained by the most distinguished writers of the Southern States: Containing the several essays, on the subject, of Chancellor Harper, Governor Hammond, Dr. Simms, and Professor Dew. Charleston, 1852.

Helper, Hinton Rowan. The Impending Crisis of the South. New York, 1857.

———— Compendium of the Impending Crisis of the South. New York, 1859.

———— Nojoque; a Question for a Continent. New York and London, 1867.

Hildreth, Richard. Despotism in America: An inquiry into the nature, results, and legal basis of the slave-holding system in the United States. Boston, 1854.

Hopkins, John Henry. A Scriptural, Ecclesiastical, and Historical View of Slavery, from the days of the Patriarch Abraham to the nineteenth century, addressed to the Right Rev. Alonzo Porter, D.D., Bishop of Pennsylvania. New York, 1864.

Hosmer, William. The Higher Law in Its Relations to Civil Government: With particular reference to slavery, and the fugitive slave law. Auburn, 1852.

Hughes, Henry. Treatise on Sociology, Theoretical and Practical. Philadelphia, 1854.

Humphrey, David. An Historical Account of the Incorporated Society for the Propagation of the Gospel in Foreign Parts, containing their foundation, proceedings, and the success of their missionaries in the British Colonies to the year 1728. London, 1730.

Hundley, D. R. Social Relations in Our Southern States. New York, 1860.

Jay, William. Inquiry into the Character and Tendency of American Colonization. New York, 1835.

———— Miscellaneous Writings on Slavery. Boston, 1853.

Jones, Charles Colcock. The Religious Instruction of the Negroes in the United States. Savannah, 1842.

Kettell, T. P. Southern Wealth and Northern Profits as Exhibited in Statistical Facts and Official Figures: Showing the necessity of union to the future prosperity and welfare of the republic. New York, 1860.

Lay, Benjamin. All Slave-Keepers that keep the Innocent in Bondage, Apostates pretending to lay Claim to the Pure and

Holy Christian Religion; of what Congregation so ever; but especially in their Ministers, by whose example the fillthy Leprosy and Apostacy is spread far and near; it is a notorious Sin, which many of the true Friends of Christ, and his pure Truth, called Quakers, has been for many Years and still are concern'd to write and bear Testimony against; as a Practice so gross and hurtful to Religion, and Destructive to Government, beyond what Words set forth, or can be declared of by Men or Angels, and yet lived in by Ministers and Magistrates in America . . . Written for a General Service, by him that truly and sincerely desires the present and eternal Welfare and Happiness of all Mankind, all the World over, of all Colours, and Nations, as his own Soul. Philadelphia, 1737.

Leatherman, P. R. Elements of Moral Science. Philadelphia, 1860.

McHenry, George. The Cotton Trade: Its bearing upon the prosperity of Great Britain and commerce of the American Republics considered in connection with the system of Negro slavery in the Confederate States. London, 1863.

MacMahon, T. W. Cause and Contrast: An essay on the American crisis. Richmond, 1862.

McTyeire, Holland Nimmons. Duties of Masters to Servants. Charleston, 1851.

Mather, Cotton. Essays To Do Good, addressed to all Christians, whether in public or private capacities. Boston (Massachusetts Sabbath School Society ed.), 1845.

Mellen, G. W. F. An Argument on the Unconstitutionality of Slavery, embracing an abstract of the proceedings of the national and State conventions on the subject. Boston, 1841.

Moore, George H. Notes on the History of Slavery in Massachusetts. New York, 1866.

Nott, Josiah Clark. Two Lectures on the Connection between the Biblical and Physical History of Man. Delivered by invitation, from the chair of political economy, etc., of the Louisiana University, in December, 1848. New York, 1849.

———— and Gliddon, George R. Types of Mankind: Or, ethnological researches, based upon the ancient monuments, paintings, sculptures, and crania of races, and upon their natural geographical, philological, and Biblical history: Illustrated by selections from the inedited papers of Samuel George Morton, M.D., and by additional contributions from Prof. L. Agassiz, LL.D.; W. Usher, M.D.; and Prof. H. S. Patterson, M.D. Philadelphia, 1854.

———— Indigenous Races of the Earth; or, new chapters of ethnological inquiry; including monographs on special departments of philology, iconography, cranioscopy, palaeontology, pathology, archaeology, comparative geography, and natural history: Contributed by Alfred Maury, Francis Pulszky, and J. Aitken Meigs, M.D. (With communications from Prof. James Leidy, M.D., and Prof. L. Agassiz, LL.D.) presenting fresh investigations, documents, and materials. Philadelphia and London, 1857.

O'Kelly, James. Essay on Negro Slavery. Baltimore, 1789.

Olmsted, Frederick Law. A Journey in the Seaboard Slave States, with remarks on their economy. New York and London, 1856.

———— The Cotton Kingdom: A traveller's observations on cotton and slavery in the American slave States. Based upon three former volumes of journeys and investigations by the same author. 2 v., Boston and London, 1861.

Palmer, B. M., Thornwell, J. H., etc. Fast Day Sermons, or the pulpit on the state of the country. New York, 1861.

Parsons, C. G., M.D. Inside View of Slavery: Or a tour among the planters. (Introduction by Mrs. H. B. Stowe). Boston and Cleveland, 1855.

Paulding, James Kirke. Slavery in the United States. Philadelphia, 1836.

Paxton, J. D. Letters on Slavery. Lexington, Kentucky, 1833.

Peissner, Elias. The American Question in Its National Aspect. Being also an incidental reply to Mr. H. R. Helper's "Compendium of the Impending Crisis of the South." New York, 1861.

Phelps, Amos A. Lectures on Slavery and Its Remedy. Boston, 1834.

Pollard, Edward A. Black Diamonds Gathered in the Darkey Homes of the South. New York, 1859.

Priest, Rev. Josiah. Bible Defence of Slavery; and origin, fortunes, and history of the Negro race. Glasgow, Kentucky, 1852.

———— Slavery, as It Relates to the Negro, or African Race, Examined in the Light of Circumstances, History and the Holy Scriptures; with an account of the origin of the black man's color, causes of his state of servitude and traces of his character as well in ancient as in modern times: With strictures on abolitionism. Albany, 1845.

Rankin, John. Letters on American Slavery Addressed to Mr. Thomas Rankin, Merchant at Middlebrook, Augusta Co., Virginia. Newburyport, 1836.

Rivers, R. H. A Defence of Negro Slavery as It Exists in the United States. Nashville, 1860.

———— Elements of Moral Philosophy. Nashville, 1860.

Romans, Bernard. A Concise Natural History of East and West Florida. New York, 1775.

Ross, Frederick A. Slavery Ordained of God (Several speeches before general assembly at Buffalo and New York—and a series of letters to Albert Barnes). Philadelphia, 1857.

Sawyer, George S. Southern Institutes; or, an inquiry into the origin and early prevalence of slavery and the slave trade: With an analysis of the laws, history, and government of the institution in the principal nations, ancient and modern, from the earliest ages down to the present time. With notes and comments in defence of the Southern institutions. Philadelphia, 1858.

[Scott, John]. The Lost Principle; Or the Sectional Equilibrium: How it was created—how destroyed—how it may be restored. By "Barbarossa." Richmond, 1860.

Seabury, Samuel. American Slavery Distinguished from the Slavery of English Theorists and Justified by the Law of Nature. New York, 1861.

Smith, Charles Hamilton. The Natural History of the Human Species. Boston, 1851.

Smith, Samuel Stanhope. An Essay on the Causes of the Variety of Complexion and Figure in the Human Species. To which is added strictures on Lord Kaims' discourse on the original diversity of mankind. Philadelphia, 1787.

Smith, William A., D.D. Lectures on the Philosophy and Practice of Slavery, as exhibited in the institution of domestic slavery in the United States: With the duties of masters to slaves. Nashville, 1856.

Smyth, Thomas. The Unity of the Human Races: Proved to be the doctrine of scripture, reason, and science. With a review of the present position and theory of Professor Agassiz. New York, 1850.

Spooner, Lysander. The Unconstitutionality of Slavery: Including parts first and second. Boston, 1847.

Stiles, Joseph C. Modern Reform Examined; or, the union of North and South on the subject of slavery. Philadelphia, 1857.

Stirling, James. Letters from the Slave States. London, 1857.

Stringfellow, Thornton, D.D. Scriptural and Statistical Views in Favor of Slavery. Richmond, 1856.

Taylor, John. Arator; being a series of agricultural essays, practical and political. Baltimore, 1817.

Thornton, T. C. An Inquiry into the History of Slavery; its introduction into the United States; causes of its continuance, and remarks upon the abolition tracts of William E. Channing, D.D. Washington, 1841.

Thornwell, James Henley. Discourses on Truth. New York, 1855.

Tucker, N. Beverley. A Series of Lectures on the Science of Government, intended to prepare the student for the study of the Constitution of the United States. Philadelphia, 1845.

Tucker, St. George. A Dissertation on Slavery with a Proposal for the Gradual Abolition of It in the State of Virginia. Philadelphia, 1796.

Van Evrie, J. H. Negroes and Negro "Slavery"; The first an inferior race: The latter its normal condition. New York, 1861.

——— White Supremacy and Negro Subordination; or, Negroes a subordinate race, and (so-called) slavery its normal condition. With an appendix showing the past and present condition of the countries south of us. New York, 1868.

Vaux, Robert. Memoirs of the Lives of Benjamin Lay and Ralph Sandiford; two of the earliest of the public advocates for the emancipation of the enslaved Africans. Philadelphia, 1815.

Walsh, Robert. An Appeal from the Judgments of Great Britain Respecting the United States of America. Philadelphia, 1819.

Warren, E. W. Nellie Norton; or Southern Slavery and the Bible; a Scriptural refutation of the principal arguments upon which the abolitionists rely. Macon, 1864.

Wayland, Francis, D.D. The Elements of Moral Science. Boston, 1848.

Wheat, M[arvin] T. The Progress and Intelligence of Americans; collateral proof of slavery, from the first to the eleventh chapter of Genesis, as founded on organic law; and from the fact of Christ being a Caucasian, owing to his peculiar parentage; progress of slavery south and southwest, with free labor advancing, through the acquisition of territory; advantages enumerated and explained. Louisville, Kentucky, 1862.

Whewell, William, D.D. The Elements of Morality, Including Polity. 2 v., New York, 1852.

Wise, Henry A. Territorial Government and the Admission of New States into the Union: A historical and constitutional treatise. N. p., n. d.

Wolfe, Samuel M. Helper's Impending Crisis Dissected. Philadelphia, 1860.

Contemporary Pamphlets: Speeches, Sermons, Addresses

Adams, James H. Message No. 1 of His Excellency James H. Adams to the Senate and House of Representatives at the Session of 1856. Columbia, 1856.

Adger, J. B.   The Christian Doctrine of Human Rights and of Slavery.   In two articles from the *Southern Presbyterian Review* for March, 1849.   Columbia, 1849.

Agassiz, Louis.   The Diversity of Origin of the Human Races. (From the *Christian Examiner* for July, 1850).   N.p., n.d.

———— On the Principles of Classification in the Animal Kingdom; on the Structure of the Halcyonoid Polypi; on the Morphology of the Medusae.   Charleston, 1850.

Alexander, Ann.   An Address to the Inhabitants of Charleston, South Carolina.   Philadelphia, 1805.

Armstrong, Geo. D.   A Discussion on Slaveholding.   Philadelphia, 1858.

Atkinson, Rev. Thomas.   On the Causes of National Troubles. Wilmington, 1861.

Austin, James T.   Remarks on Dr. Channing's Slavery.   Boston, 1835.

Bachman, John, D.D.   A Continuation of the Review of "Nott and Gliddon's Types of Mankind."   Charleston, 1855.   ,

———— An Examination of the Characteristics of Genera and Species as Applicable to the Doctrine of the Unity of the Human Race.   Charleston, 1855.

———— An Examination of Professor Agassiz's Sketch of the Natural Provinces of the Animal World and Their Relation to the Different Types of Man, with a tableau accompanying the sketch.   Charleston, 1855.

———— A Notice of the "Types of Mankind," with an Examination of the charges contained in the biography of Dr. Morton, published by Nott and Gliddon.   (From *Charleston Medical Journal and Review* for September).   Charleston, 1854.

———— A refutation of the theory of Dr. Morton, Professor Agassiz, and Dr. Nott, on the characteristics of genera and species.   Nashville, 1855.

Baker, J. L.   Slavery.   Philadelphia, 1860.

Barnwell, W. H.   Views upon the Present Crisis.   Charleston, 1850.

———— "The Divine Trust"—a Sermon, November 21, 1851.   Charleston, 1851.

Bascom, H. B., D.D. Methodism and Slavery: With other matters controversial between the North and the South; being a review of the manifesto of the majority, in reply to the protest of the minority, of the late general conference of the Methodist Episcopal Church, in the case of Bishop Andrew. Frankfort, 1845.

Batchelder, Samuel. The Responsibility of the North in Relation to Slavery. Cambridge, 1856.

Bell, Marcus A. Message of Love. Southside view of cotton is king and the philosophy of African slavery. Atlanta, 1860.

Bellinger, Edmund, Jr. A Speech on the Subject of Slavery; delivered 7th of September, 1835, at a public meeting of the citizens of Barnwell district, South Carolina. Charleston, 1835.

Benezet, Anthony. A Caution to Great Britain and Her Colonies, in a short representation of the calamitous state of the enslaved Negroes in the British Dominions. Philadelphia and London, 1784.

————— A Serious Address to the Rulers of America, on the Inconsistency of Their Conduct Respecting Slavery, forming a contrast between the encroachments of England on American liberty and American injustice in tolerating slavery. Trenton, 1783.

————— Notes on the Slave Trade. Philadelphia, 178-.

————— Observations on the Enslaving, Importing, and Purchasing of Negroes, with some advice thereon, extracted from the epistle of the yearly meeting of the people called Quakers, held at London in the year 1748. Germantown, 1759.

————— A Short Account of That Part of Africa Inhabited by the Negroes. With respect to the fertility of the country; the good disposition of many of the natives, and manner by which the slave trade is carried on. Philadelphia, 1762.

Berry, Rev. Philip. A Review of the Bishop of Oxford's Council to the American Churches with Reference to the Institution of Slavery—Supplementary remarks with reference to the relation of the Wilmot Proviso to the interests of the colored class. Washington, 1848.

Blair, Frank P.   The Destiny of the Races of this Continent. An address delivered before the Mercantile Library Association of Boston, Massachusetts, on the 26th of January, 1859. Washington, 1859.

[Blunt, Joseph].   An Examination of the Expediency and Constitutionality of Prohibiting Slavery in the State of Missouri. By Marcus. New York, 1819.

[Bourne, George].   A Condensed Antislavery Bible Argument. By a Citizen of Virginia. New York. 1845.

Bowen, Nathaniel, D.D.   A Pastoral Letter on the Religious Instruction of the Slaves of Members of the Protestant Episcopal Church in the State of South Carolina, at request of the convention of churches of the diocese. Charleston, 1835.

Boyden, E.   The Epidemic of the Nineteenth Century. Richmond, 1860.

Branard, Thomas.   Who is Responsible for the Present Slavery Agitation. Philadelphia, 1860.

Brisbane, William H.   The Constitution of the United States versus Slavery. Philadelphia, 1846.

[Brookes, Rev. Iveson L.]   A Defence of the South against the Reproaches and Incroachments of the North: In which slavery is shown to be an institution of God intended to form the basis of the best social state and the only safeguard to the permanence of a republican government. Hamburg, South Carolina, 1849.

[————] A Defence of Southern Slavery. Against the attacks of Henry Clay and Alexander Campbell. Hamburg, 1851.

Brown, Edward.   Notes on the Origin and Necessity of Slavery. Charleston, 1826.

Browne, Willliam H.   Speech of Mr. William H. Browne of King George and Stafford in the House of Delegates of Virginia, on the removal from the Commonwealth of the free colored population, delivered February 23, 1853. Richmond, 1853.

Brownlow, W. G.   A Sermon on Slavery, a Vindication of the Methodist Episcopal Church, South. Knoxville, 1857.

Bryan, Edward B. Letters to the Southern People: The rightful remedy, addressed to the slaveholders of the South. Charleston, 1858.

———— Report of the Special Committee of the House of Representatives, of South Carolina, on So Much of the Message of His Excellency Governor James H. Adams, as Relates to Slavery and the Slave Trade. Columbia and Charleston, 1857.

Buchanan, George. An Oration upon the Moral and Political Evil of Slavery, delivered at a public meeting of the Maryland Society for Promoting the Abolition of Slavery, July 4, 1791. Baltimore, 1793.

Burling, William. An Address to the Elders of the Church. N. p., 1718.

Caldwell, John H. Slavery and Southern Methodism. Two sermons preached in the Methodist Church in Newman, Georgia. N.p., 1865.

Camden, Peter G. Common Sense, Matter of Fact Examination and Discussion of Negro Slavery in the United States. St. Louis, 1855.

Carey, John L. Slavery in Maryland Briefly Considered. Baltimore, 1845.

———— Some Thoughts Concerning Domestic Slavery, in a Letter to ———— ———— Esq. of Baltimore. Baltimore, 1839.

Carey, Matthew. Considerations on the Impropriety and Inexpediency of Reviving the Missouri Question. Philadelphia, 1820.

———— Letters on The Colonization Society and on Its Probable Results. . . . Addressed to the Hon. C. F. Mercer. Philadelphia, 1832.

Carpenter, Russell Lant. Observations on American Slavery after a Year's Tour in the United States. London, 1852.

Cartwright, Samuel A., M.D. Essays, being inductions drawn from the Baconian philosophy proving the truth of the Bible and the justice and benevolence of the decree dooming Canaan to be a servant of servants: And answering the question of

Voltaire: "On demande quel droit des étrangers tels que les Juifs avaient sur le pays de Canaan?" In a series of letters to the Rev. William Winans. Natchez, 1843.

Cheves, Langdon. Speech of Hon. Langdon Cheves, in the Southern Convention at Nashville, Tennessee, November 14, 1850. [Nashville] 1850.

Child, Lydia Maria. An Appeal in Favor of That Class of Americans Called Africans. Boston, 1833.

Clapp, Theodore. Slavery, a Sermon—First Congregational Church in New Orleans, April 15, 1838. New Orleans, 1838.

Clay, Thomas S. Detail of a Plan for the Moral Improvement of Negroes on Plantations. Read before the Georgia Presbytery. N. p., 1833.

Coit, J. C. A Discourse upon Government, Divine and Human. Columbia, 1853.

Coleman, Elihu. A Testimony against the Antichristian Practice of Making Slaves of Men, wherein it is shewed to be Contrary to the Dispensation of the Law and Time of the Gospel, and very Opposite both to Grace and Nature. New Bedford, 1733.

Colfax, Richard H. Evidence against the Views of the Abolitionists, consisting of physical and moral proofs of the natural inferiority of the Negroes. New York, 1833.

Collins, Robert. Essay on the Treatment and Management of Slaves. Written for the seventh annual fair of the Southern Central Agricultural Society. Boston, 1853.

[Colston, R. E.] The Problem of Free Society. By R. E. C. N. p., n. d.

[Colwell, Stephen.] The Five Cotton States and New York; or, remarks upon the social and economic aspects of the Southern political crisis. Philadelphia, 1861.

[———] The South: A Letter from a Friend in the North. With special reference to the effects of disunion upon slavery. Philadelphia, 1856.

Cooper, Thomas. Two Essays: (1) On the Foundation of Civil Government. (2) On the Constitution of the United States. Columbia, 1826.

Crawford, Charles. Observations upon Negro-Slavery. Philadelphia, 1784.

[Dalcho, Frederick.] Practical Considerations Founded on the Scriptures Relative to the Slave Population of South Carolina. Charleston, 1823.

Darling, Henry. Slavery and the War. A historical essay. Philadelphia, 1863.

Day, Thomas. A Letter from . . . in London to His Friend in America on the Subject of the Slave Trade, together with some approved extracts. New York, 1784.

De Bow, J. D. B., and others. Interest in Slavery of the Southern Non-Slaveholder. Charleston, 1860.

Dewey, Chester. Examination of Some Reasonings against the Unity of Mankind. (From the *Princeton Review*, July, 1862). N. p., n. d.

Dickson, S. Henry, M.D. Remarks on Certain Topics Connected with the General Subject of Slavery. Charleston, 1845.

Drisler, Henry. Bible View of Slavery, by John H. Hopkins, D.D., Bishop of Vermont, Examined. New York, 1863.

Dupré, Lewis. An Admonitory Picture, and a Solemn Warning: Principally addressed to professing Christians in the Southern States of North America. Being an introduction and pressing invitation to the establishment of a system of progressive emancipation. N. p, 1810.

———— A Political View of the Evils of Slavery; by way of appendix to a system of progressive emancipation. [Raleigh?], 1810.

———— A Rational and Benevolent Plan for Averting Some of the Calamitous Consequences of Slavery, being a practicable, seasonable, and profitable institution for the progressive emancipation of Virginia and Carolina slaves. [Charleston?], 1810.

Edwards, Jonathan. The Injustice and Impolicy of the Slave Trade and of the Slavery of the Africans. Illustrated in a sermon. Providence, 1792.

Elliott, James H.   Are These Thy Doings—St. Michael's, Charleston, November 21, 1860.   Charleston, 1860.

Elliott, Stephen.   A High Civilization, the Moral Duty of Georgians—Georgia Historical Society, February 12, 1844.   Savannah, 1844.

———— Sermon—Christ Church, Savannah, Georgia.   Savannah, 1861.

———— Address to the 39th Annual Convention of the Diocese of Georgia.   Savannah, 1861.

———— Sermon, Christ Church, Savannah, February 28, 1862.   Savannah, 1862.

Elliott, William.   Annual Address to the State Agricultural Society of South Carolina, November 30, 1848.   Charleston, 1849.

Ewart, David.   A Scriptural View of the Moral Relations of African Slavery, 1849.   Charleston, 1849.

Ewbank, Thomas.   Inorganic Forces Ordained to Supercede Human Slavery.   New York, 1860.

Ferguson, J. B.   Address on the History, Authority and Influence of Slavery Delivered in the First Presbyterian Church, Nashville.   November 21, 1850.   Nashville, 1850.

Fisher, Elwood.   Lecture on the North and the South.   Richmond, 1849.

[Fisher, Sidney George.]   The Law of the Territories.   Philadelphia, 1859.

———— The Trial of the Constitution.   Philadelphia, 1862.

[————]   The Laws of Race as Connected with Slavery—by the Author of "The Law of the Territories," "Rustic Rhymes," etc.   Philadelphia, 1860.

Fitzhugh, George.   Slavery Justified, by a Southerner.   Fredericksburg, 1850.

Flournoy, John Jacobus.   An Essay on the Origin, Habits, etc., of the African Race, incidental to the propriety of having nothing to do with Negroes: Addressed to the good people of the United States.   New York, 1835.

———— Expulsion the Best Earthly Conservative of Peace in Our Country.   Athens, 1837.

———————— Much Prefatory Declarations, tending to throw farther light upon the annexed second edition of scriptural examination into the question of whom and what are the evil genii,
of the objects portrayed by the Apostle St. John. Athens,
1838.

———————— A Reply, to a Pamphlet Entitled "Bondage, a Moral
Institution, Sanctioned by the Scriptures and the Savior, etc.,
etc.," so far as it attacks the principles of expulsion. With no
defence, however, of abolitionism. Athens, 1838.

———————— A Series of Separate Pamphlets, Elucidatory and De-
fenditory of the New Doctrine of Expulsion. By its originator.
Athens, 1838.

Ford, Timothy. The Constitutionalist, or an inquiry how far it
is expedient and proper to alter the Constitution of South Carolina—published in *City Gazette* and *Daily Advertiser* in 1792.
By Americanus. Charleston, 1794.

Forsyth, John. Address to the People of Georgia. Including—
Letter of Pope Gregory XVI on Slavery and Resolutions of
the General Anti-Slavery Convention held in London, June
12-23, 1840. Fredericksburg, Virginia, 1840.

Freeman, G. W. Rights and Duties of Slaveholders; two discourses delivered on Sunday, November 27, 1836—in Christ
Church, Raleigh. Raleigh, 1836.

Fuller, Richard. Our Duty to the African Race. An address
delivered at Washington, D. C., January 21, 1851. Baltimore, 1851.

Furman, Dr. Richard. Exposition of the Views of the Baptists
Relative to the Colored Population of the United States in a
Communication to the Governor of South Carolina. Charles-
ton, 1823.

———————— Sermon on the Anniversary of American Independence,
July 4, 1802. Charleston, 1802.

Godwyn, Morgan. Trade Preferred Before Religion, and Christ
Made To Give Place to Mammon: Represented in a sermon
relating to the plantations. First preached at Westminster
Abbey, and afterwards in divers churches in London. London, 1685.

———— A Supplement to the Negro's and Indian's Advocate: Or, some further considerations and proposals for the effectual and speedy carrying on of the Negro's Christianity in our plantations. London, 1685.

[Goodloe, Daniel R.] Inquiry into the Causes Which Have Retarded the Accumulation of Wealth and Increase of Population in the Southern States: In which the question of slavery is considered in a politico-economical point of view. By a Carolinian. Washington, 1846.

[————] The South and the North: Being a reply to a lecture on the North and the South, by Ellwood Fisher, delivered before the Young Men's Mercantile Library Association of Cincinnati, January 16, 1849. By a Carolinian. Washington, 1849.

———— The Southern Platform: Or, manual of Southern sentiment on the subject of slavery. Boston, 1858.

Grattan, Peachy R. Speech in General Assembly, Cleveland, June 2, 1857. Richmond, 1857.

Grayson, William John. Reply to Dr. Dewey's Address Delivered at the Elm Tree, Sheffield, Mass., with extracts from the same. Charleston, 1856.

[————] Letters of Curtius. Published originally in the *Charleston Currier*. Charleston, 1851.

Gregg, William. Essays on Domestic Industry, or an inquiry into the expediency of establishing cotton manufacturing in South Carolina. Charleston, 1845.

[Gridley, Rev. Wayne.] Slavery in the South: A review of Hammond's and Fuller's letters, and Chancellor Harper's memoir on that subject. (From October number 1845 of *Southern Quarterly*, signed W. G.). N. p., n. d.

Gurley, R. A. Remarks on the South Carolina Opinions of the American Colonization Society from the *African Repository* of 1830. N. p., 1830.

[Habich, Edward.] The American Churches the Bulwarks of American Slavery. By an American. Newburyport, 1842.

Hague, William. Christianity and Slavery: A review of the Correspondence between Richard Fuller, D.D., of Beaufort, S. C., and Francis Wayland, D.D., of Providence, R. I., on domestic slavery, considered as a Scriptural institution. Boston, 1847.

Hales, Stephen. A Sermon Preached before the Trustees for Establishing the Colony of Georgia in America; and before the Associates of the late Rev. Dr. Thomas Bray, for converting the Negroes in the British Plantations, and for other good purposes; at their anniversary meeting in the Parish Church of St. Brides, Fleet Street, on Thursday, March 21, 1734. London, 1734.

[Hamilton, James.] An Account of the Late Intended Insurrection among the Blacks of the City. Charleston, 1822.

Hamilton, Rev. W. T. The Duties of Masters and Slaves Respectively: Or domestic servitude as sanctioned by the Bible: A discourse, delivered in the Government Street Church, Mobile, Alabama, on Sunday night, December 15, 1844. Mobile, 1845.

Hammond, James Henry. An Address Delivered before the South Carolina Institute, at Its First Annual Fair, on the 20th November, 1849. Charleston, 1849.

———— Two Letters on Slavery in the United States, Addressed to Thomas Clarkson, Esq. Columbia, 1845.

———— Speech, Delivered at Barnwell Courthouse, October 29th, 1858. Charleston, 1858.

Hampton, Wade. Speech on the Constitutionality of the Slave Trade Laws—Delivered in the Senate of South Carolina, December 10, 1859. Columbia, 1860.

Harper, Robert G. An Argument against the Policy of Reopening the African Slave Trade. Atlanta, 1858.

Harper, William. Anniversary Oration. South Carolina Society for Advancement of Learning. Columbia, 1836.

———— Memoir on Slavery, read before the Society for the Advancement of Learning of South Carolina at its annual meeting at Columbia, 1837. Charleston, 1838.

Harris, Rev. Raymond. Scriptural Researches on the Slave Trade, shewing its conformity with the principles of natural and revealed religion, delineated in the sacred writings of the word of God. London, 1788.

[Harrison, Jesse Burton]. Review of the Slave Question, extracted from the *American Quarterly Review*, December, 1832; based upon the speech of Thomas Marshall of Fauquier: Showing that slavery is the essential hindrance to the prosperity of the slaveholding States; with particular reference to Virginia, though applicable to other States where slavery exists. By a Virginian. Richmond, 1833.

Hepburn, John. The American Defence of the Christian Golden Rule. London, 1713.

Hobby, W. J. Remarks upon Slavery; occasioned by attempts made to circulate improper publication in the Southern States. Augusta, 1835.

Hodge, Rev. Charles. The State of the Country. Philadelphia, 1861.

Hoit, T. W. The Right of American Slavery. St. Louis, 1860.

Holcombe, James Phileman. Is Slavery Consistent with Natural Law? An address delivered before the seventh annual meeting of the Virginia State Agricultural Society, November 4, 1858. Richmond, 1858.

————— The Election of a Black Republican President an Overt Act of Aggression on the Right of Property in Slaves: The South urged to adopt concerted action for future safety. A speech before the people of Albemarle on the second day of January, 1860. Richmond, 1860.

Holcombe, William H. The Alternative: A Separate Nationality or the Africanization of the South. New Orleans, 1860.

————— Suggestions as to the Spiritual Philosophy of African Slavery. New York, 1861.

[Holland, Edwin C.] A Refutation of the Calumnies Circulated against the Southern and Western States, Respecting the Institution and Existence of Slavery among Them. To which is added a minute and particular account of the actual state and condition of their Negro population. Together with historical notices of all the insurrections that have taken place since the settlement of the country. By a South-Carolinian. Charleston, 1822.

Hornsby, T. N. The Anatomy of Slavery. Louisville, 1846.

How, Samuel B., D.D. Slaveholding Not Sinful. Slavery, the punishment of man's sin, its remedy, the gospel of Christ. An argument before the General Synod of the Reformed Protestant Dutch Church, October, 1855. New Brunswick, N. J., 1856.

Hughes, Henry. A Report on the African Apprentice System, read at the Southern Commercial Convention held at Vicksburg, May 10, 1859. Vicksburg, 1859.

———— State Liberties or the Right to African Contract Labor. Port Gibson, 1858.

Ingersoll, C[harles] J[ared]. African Slavery in America. Philadelphia, 1856.

———— Letter to a Friend in a Slave State. Philadelphia, 1826.

Jacobs, Curtis M. Speech of Colonel Curtis M. Jacobs, on the Free Colored Population of Maryland, Delivered in the House of Delegates, on the Seventeenth of February, 1860. Annapolis, 1860.

[Johnson, Reverdy]. Slavery, Its Institution and Origin. Its status under the law and under the gospel. Its agricultural, commercial and financial aspects. N. p., n. d.

Johnson, S. M. The Dual Revolutions. Anti-Slavery and Pro-Slavery. Baltimore, 1863.

Jones, Charles Colcock, D.D. Religious Instruction of the Negroes. An address delivered before the Presbyterian Church, at Augusta, Georgia, December 10, 1861. Augusta, 1861.

Junkin, Rev. George, D.D. The Integrity of Our National Union vs. Abolitionism: an Argument from the Bible. Cincinnati, 1834.

Kenrick, John. Horrors of Slavery. In two parts: Part I. Containing observations, facts and arguments extracted from speeches of Wilberforce, Grenville, Pitt, Burke, Fox, Martin, Whitehead. . . . Part II. Containing extracts, chiefly American, compiled from authentic sources; demonstrating that slavery is impolitic, antirepublican, unchristian, and highly criminal: And proposing measures for its complete abolition through the United States. Cambridge, 1817.

Ker, Rev. Leander. Slavery Consistent with Christianity, with an introduction, embracing a notice of the "Uncle Tom's Cabin" movement in England. Weston, Missouri, 1853.

[Kingsley, Z.] A Treatise on the Patriarchal System of Society, as it exists in some governments and colonies in America and in the United States, under the name of slavery, with its necessity and advantages. N. p., 1833.

Laurens, Edward R. A Letter to the Hon. Whitemarsh B. Seabrook of St. John's Colleton; in explanation and defence of an act to amend the law in relation to slaves and free persons of color. Charleston, 1835.

Learned, Joseph D. A View of the Policy of Permitting Slaves in the States West of the Mississippi: Being a letter to a member of Congress. Baltimore, 1820.

[Lee, Arthur.] An Essay in Vindication of the Continental Colonies of America from the Censure of Mr. Adam Smith, in His Theory of Moral Sentiments. With some reflections on slavery in general. By an American. London, 1764.

[Leigh, Benjamin Watkins]. The Letter of Appomatox to the People of Virginia: Exhibiting a connected view of the recent proceedings in the House of Delegates, on the subject of the abolition of slavery; and a succinct account of the doctrines broached by the friends of abolition, in debate, and the mischievous tendency of those proceedings and doctrines. Richmond, 1832.

Leigh, E., M.D. Birds-Eye View of Slavery in Missouri. St. Louis, 1862.

Letcher, John. Speeches and Extracts from Speeches of the Honorable John Letcher, Democratic Candidate for Governor of Virginia, touching the subject of slavery during his several terms as representative in Congress from the State of Virginia. Washington, 1859.

Lewis, Seth. A Review of Abolitionism, or the Question of Slavery as it Exists in the United States Considered. Presented to the Conservative Society of Citizens of Louisiana. N. p., n. d.

Lipscomb, A. A. North and South. Impressions of Northern Society upon a Southerner. Mobile, 1853.

Littell, John S. Letter from Governor R[ichard] K. Call, of Florida, to John S. Littell, of Germantown, Pennsylvania. Philadelphia, 1861.

Longstreet, A. B. A Voice from the South, Comprising Letters from Georgia to Massachusetts and to the Southern States. Baltimore, 1847.

———— Letters on the Epistle of Paul to Philemon. Charleston, 1845.

Lumpkin, James H. Address Delivered before the South Carolina Institute at Its Second Annual Fair, 19 November, 1850. Charleston, 1851.

Lundy, Benjamin. The War in Texas: A review of facts and circumstances, showing that this contest is a crusade against Mexico, set on foot and supported by slaveholders, land speculators, etc., in order to reëstablish, extend, and perpetuate the system of slavery and the slave trade. By a citizen of the United States. Philadelphia, 1837.

McCaine, Alexander. Slavery Defended from Scripture against the Attacks of the Abolitionists, in a speech delivered before the general conference of the Methodist Protestant Church, in Baltimore, 1842. Baltimore, 1842.

McDonogh, John. Letter of John McDonogh on African Colonization: Addressed to the editors of the *New Orleans Commercial Bulletin*. New Orleans, 1842.

McDuffie, George. National and State Rights, considered by the Honorable George McDuffie, under the signature of one of the people, in reply to the "Trio," with the advertisement prefixed to it, generally attributed to Major James Hamilton, Jr., when published in 1821. Charleston, 1830.

Meade, Rt. Rev. William. Pastoral Letter—Religious Instruction of Slaves. Richmond, 1854.

Memminger, C. G. Lecture before the Young Men's Library Association of Augusta, Georgia, showing American slavery to be consistent with moral and physical progress of a nation. Augusta, 1851.

[Middleton, Henry]. Economical Causes of Slavery in the United States, and Obstacles to Abolition. By a South Carolinian. London, 1857.

[Mifflin, Warner]. A Serious Expostulation with the Members of the House of Representatives of the United States. Philadelphia, 1793.

———— The Defence of Warner Mifflin against Aspersions Cast on Him on Account of His Endeavors to Promote Righteousness. . . . Philadelphia, 1796.

Miles, William Porcher. Republican Government, an Address. Charleston, 1852.

———— An Oration, July 4, 1849. Charleston, 1849.

———— The Ground of Morals, a discourse delivered before the graduating class of the College of Charleston, March 28, 1852. Charleston, 1852.

Mills, Rev. J. W. The Relation of the Races at the South. Charleston, 1861.

[Mitchell, James]. Letter on the Relation of the White and African Races in the United States, showing the necessity of the colonization of the latter. Washington, 1862.

Mitchell, J. C. A Bible Defence of Slavery, and the Unity of Mankind. Mobile, 1861.

Morton, Samuel George, M.D. Hybridity in Animals and Plants, Considered in Reference to the Question of the Unity of the Human Species. Read before the Academy of Natural Sciences of Philadelphia, November 4 and 11, 1846. New Haven, 1847.

———— Additional Observations on Hybridity in Animals, and on Some Collateral Subjects; being a reply to the objections of the Rev. John Bachman, D.D. (From *Charleston Medical Journal and Review*). Charleston, 1850.

———— Letter to the Rev. John Bachman, D.D., on the Question of Hybridity in Animals, Considered in Reference to the Unity of the Human Species. Charleston, 1850.

Mussey, Osgood. Review of Ellwood Fisher's Lecture on the North and the South. Cincinnati, 1849.

[Nisbet, Richard]. Slavery Not Forbidden by Scripture. Or a defence of the West-India planters, from the aspersions thrown out against them by the author of a pamphlet entitled, "An Address to the Inhabitants of the British Settlements in America, upon Slave Keeping." By a West-Indian. Philadelphia, 1773.

Nott, Josiah Clark, M.D. The Physical History of the Jewish Race. Charleston, 1850.

———— Two Lectures on the Natural History of the Caucasian and Negro Races. Mobile, 1844.

———— The Negro Race. Its Ethnology and History. By the author of "Types of Mankind." To Major-General O. O. Howard, Superintendent of Freedman's Bureau, etc. Mobile, 1866.

Nott, Samuel. Slavery and the Remedy; or principles and suggestions for a remedial code. New York, 1856.

———— The Present Crisis: With a reply and appeal to European advisers, from the sixth edition of "Slavery and the Remedy." Boston, 1860.

———— The Necessities and Wisdom of 1861. A Supplement to the sixth edition of "Slavery and the Remedy." Boston, 1861.

O'Connor, Charles. Negro Slavery not Unjust. Union Meeting, New York, December 19, 1859. New York, 1859.

Otis, James. The Rights of the British Colonies Asserted and Proved. Boston, 1764.

———— A Vindication of the House of Representatives of the Province of Massachusetts Bay. Boston, 1762.

Palfrey, J. G. Papers on the Slave Power First Published in the Boston Whig. Boston, 1846.

Palmer, B. M. The South: Her Peril and Her Duty. New Orleans, 1860.

———— Slavery a Divine Trust. New Orleans, 1860.

———— National Responsibility Before God. New Orleans, 1861.

———— A Discourse before the General Assembly of South Carolina, December 10, 1863. Columbia, 1864.

Parker, Theodore.   The Relation of Slavery to a Republican Form of Government.   A speech delivered at the New England Anti-Slavery Convention, Wednesday Morning, May 26, 1858.   Boston, 1858.

Parrish, John.   Remarks on the Slavery of Black People: Addressed to the citizens of the United States, particularly to those who are in legislative or executive stations in the general or State governments; and also to such individuals as hold them in bondage.   Philadelphia, 1806.

[Parsons, Theodore and Pearson, Eliphalet].   A Forensic Dispute on the Legality of Enslaving the Africans.   Held at public commencement in Cambridge, N. E., July 21, 1773.   By two candidates for the Bachelors Degree.   Boston, 1773.

Perry, B. F.   Address before the South Carolina Institute at Their Annual Fair, November, 1856.   Charleston, 1857.

Pettigrew, J. Johnston.   Report of the Minority of the Special Committee of Seven, to Whom Was Referred So Much of His Late Excellency's Message No. 1, as Relates to Slavery and the Slave Trade.   Columbia, 1857, and Charleston, 1858.

Phillips, Wendell.   Review of Lysander Spooner's Essay on the Unconstitutionality of Slavery.   Reprinted from the *Anti-Slave Standard*.   Boston, 1847.

Pickens, F. W.   Speech Delivered at a Public Meeting of the People of the District, Held at Edgefield Court House, South Carolina, July 7, 1851.   Edgefield, South Carolina, 1851.

[Pinckney, Charles?]   Answer to "A Dialogue between a Federalist and a Republican."   Charleston, 1800.

Pinckney, C. C.   An Address Delivered in Charleston before the Agricultural Society of South Carolina, at Its Anniversary Meeting, on Tuesday, the 18th of August, 1829.   Charleston, 1829.

Pinckney, Henry Laurens.   Address to the Electors of Charleston District, South Carolina, on the Subject of the Abolition of Slavery.   Washington and Charleston, 1836.

————— Report of The Select Committee upon the Subject of Slavery in the District of Columbia, Made by Honorable H. L. Pinckney, to the House of Representatives, May 18, 1836, to which is appended the votes in the House of Representatives upon the general resolutions with which the Report concludes. Washington, 1836.

———— "The Spirit of the Age," an address delivered before the two literary societies of the University of North Carolina. Raleigh, 1836.

Pinckney, Thomas. Reflections Occasioned by the Disturbances in Charleston. Charleston, 1822.

Pinkney, William. Speech of William Pinkney, Esq. in the House of Delegates of Maryland, at Their Session in November, 1789. Philadelphia, 1790.

[Pollard, E. A.] The Southern Spy: Or, curiosities of Negro slavery in the South. Letters from a Southerner to a Northern friend. Washington, 1859.

[Postlewayt, Malachy]. The African Trade, the Great Pillar and Support of the Plantation Trade in America. London, 1745.

Powell, Samuel. Notes on "Southern Wealth and Northern Profits." Philadelphia, 1861.

Power, John H. Review of the Lectures of William A. Smith on "The Philosophy and Practice of Slavery." Cincinnati, 1859.

Prentiss, W. O. Sermon, St. Peter's Church, Charleston, November 21, 1860. Charleston, 1860.

Pridgen, H. McBride. Address to the People of Texas on the Protection of Slave Property. Austin, 1859.

Pringle, Edward J. Slavery in the Southern States. By a Carolinian. Cambridge, 1852.

Quarterman, Rev. Robert. Ninth Annual Report of the Association for the Religious Instruction of the Negroes in Liberty County, Georgia; together with the address to the association by the president. Savannah, 1844.

Quincy, Josiah. Address Illustrative of the Nature and Power of the Slave States and the Duties of Free States, June 5, 1856. Boston, 1856.

Ramsay, James, A.M. Objections to the Abolition of the Slave Trade, with answers to which are prefixed, stricture on a late publication entitled "Considerations on the Emancipation of

Negroes and the Abolition of the Slave Trade, by a West India Planter." London, 1788.

———— Examination of The Rev. Mr. [Raymond] Harris' Scriptural Researches on the Licitness of the Slave Trade. London, 1788.

———— Essay on the Treatment and Conversion of African Slaves in the British Sugar Colonies. London, 1784.

Randolph, Peter. Sketches of Slave Life: Or, illustrations of the peculiar institution. Boston, 1855.

Raymond, James. Prize Essay on the Comparative Economy of Free and Slave Labor in Agriculture. Frederick, Maryland, 1827.

Reed, Henry. Southern Slavery and Its Relations to Northern Industry: A lecture delivered at the Catholic Institute, in Cincinnati, January 24, 1862. Cincinnati, 1862.

Rhett, Robert Barnwell. Address to the people of Beaufort and Colleton Districts upon the Subject of Abolition. Charleston, 1838.

Rice, David. Slavery Inconsistent with Justice and Good Policy; proved by a speech delivered in the convention held at Danville, Kentucky. Philadelphia, 1792.

Rice, N. L., D.D. Lectures on Slavery, Delivered in First Presbyterian Church on July 1 and 3, 1845. Cincinnati, 1845.

———— Ten Letters on the Subject of Slavery Addressed to the Delegates from the Georgetown Association to the Last General Assembly of the Presbyterian Church. St. Louis, 1855.

———— and Blanchard, Rev. J. A Debate on Slavery: Held in the city of Cincinnati, on the first, second, third, and sixth days of October, 1845, upon the question: Is slave-holding in itself sinful, and the relation between master and slave, a sinful relation? Cincinnati, 1846.

Rice, W. Vindex: On the Liability of the Abolitionists to Criminal Punishment, and on the Duty of Non Slave-Holding States to Suppress Their Efforts. Charleston, 1835.

Robinson, Conway. An Essay upon the Constitutional Rights as to Slave Property. Republished from the *Southern Literary Messenger,* for February, 1840. Richmond, 1840.

Ross, F. A.   Position of the Southern Church in Relation to Slavery, as illustrated in a letter of Dr. F. A. Ross to Rev. Albert Barnes with an introduction by a constitutional Presbyterian.   New York, 1857.

Ruffin, Edmund.   Address to the Virginia State Agricultural Society, on the effects of domestic slavery on the manners, habits and welfare of the agricultural population of the Southern States; and the slavery of class to class in the Northern States. Read at the first annual meeting, in the hall of the House of Delegates, December 16, 1852.   Richmond, 1853.

———— African Colonization Unveiled.   N. p., n. d.

———— Slavery and Free Labor Described and Compared. N. p., n. d.

———— The Political Economy of Slavery.   Richmond, 1857.

Ruffner, Henry, D.D.   Address to the People of West Virginia; shewing that slavery is injurious to the public welfare; and that it may be gradually abolished, without detriment to the rights and interests of slaveholders.   Louisville, 1847.

Rush, Benjamin.   An Address to the Inhabitants of the British Settlements in America, upon Slave-Keeping.   Philadelphia, 1773.

———— A Vindication of the Address to the Inhabitants of the British Settlements, on the Slavery of the Negroes in America, in Answer to a Pamphlet Entitled, "Slavery not Forbidden by Scripture; or, a Defense of the West India Planters. . . ." Philadelphia, 1773.

Rushton, Edward.   Expostulatory Letter to George Washington, of Mount Vernon, in Virginia, on His Continuing To Be a Proprietor of Slaves.   Liverpool, 1797.

Saffin, John.   A Brief and Candid Answer to a late printed sheet, entituled The Selling of Joseph whereunto is annexed, a True and Particular narrative by way of Vindication of the Author's Dealing with and Prosecution of his Negro Man Servant for his vile and exhorbitant Behavior towards his Master and his Tenant, Thomas Shepard; which hath been wrongfully represented to their Prejudice and Defamation.   Boston, 1701.

Sandiford, Ralph. A Brief Examination of the Practice of the Times, By the Foregoing and the Present Dispensation: Whereby is manifested, how the Devil works in the Mystery, which none can understand and get the Victory over but those that are armed with the Light that discovers the Temptation and the Author thereof, and gives Victory over him and his Instruments, who are now gone forth, as in the Beginning, from the true Friends of Jesus, having the Form of Godliness in Words, but in Deeds deny the Power thereof; from such we are commanded to turn away. Philadelphia, 1729.

Schade, Louis. A Book for the "Impending Crisis!" Appeal to the common sense and patriotism of the people of the United States. "Helperism" annihilated! The "Irrepressible Conflict" and its consequences! Washington, 1860.

Seabrook, Whitemarsh B[enjamin]. A Concise View of the Critical Situation and Future Prospects of the Slave-Holding States, in Relation to Their Colored Population. Charleston, 1825.

———— An Essay on the Management of Slaves and Especially on Their Religious Instruction Read before the Agricultural Society of St. John's Colleton. Charleston, 1834.

[————] An Appeal to the People of the Northern and Eastern States on the Subject of Negro Slavery in South Carolina. New York, 1834.

[————] Emancipation. By a South Carolinian. New York, 1843.

Sewell, Samuel. The Selling of Joseph, A Memorial. Boston, 1700.

Shannon, James. The Philosophy of Slavery, as Identified with the Philosophy of Human Happiness; An Essay. Frankfort, Kentucky, 1849.

[————] An Address Delivered before the Pro-Slavery Convention of the State of Missouri; held in Lexington, July 13, 1855, on domestic slavery, as examined in the light of Scripture, of natural rights, of civil government, and the constitutional power of Congress. St. Louis, 1855.

Simms, William Gilmore. The Morals of Slavery. Charleston, 1837.

[————] Slavery in America, being a brief review of Miss Martineau on that subject. By a South Carolinian. Richmond, 1838.

Sims, A. D. A View of Slavery, Moral and Political. Charleston, 1834.

Smith, Whitefoord. God the Refuge of the People. A sermon, General Assembly of South Carolina, December 6, 1850. Columbia, 1850.

Smith, William. An Oration Delivered July Fourth at Charleston. Charleston, 1796.

Smylie, Rev. James, A.M. A Review of a Letter from the Presbytery of Chillicothe, to the Presbytery of Mississippi, on the Subject of Slavery. Woodville, Mississippi, 1836.

Spratt, L. W. The Foreign Slave Trade. The source of political power—of material progress, of social integrity, and of social emancipation to the South. Charleston, 1858.

———— Speech upon the Foreign Slave Trade, before the Legislature of South Carolina. Columbia, 1858.

———— Virtue of Slavery: A series of articles on the value of the Union to the South, lately published in the *Charleston South Carolina Standard*. Charleston, 1855.

[Stephens, Thomas] Brief Account of Causes That Have Retarded the Progress of the Colony of Georgia, in America, etc., etc. London, 1743.

Stringfellow, B. F., Chairman. Negro-Slavery No Evil, or the North and the South. The effects of Negro slavery as exhibited in the census, by a comparison of the condition of the slaveholding and non-slaveholding States. Considered in a report to the Platte County Self-Defense Association. By a Committee. St. Louis, 1854.

Stringfellow, Thornton. A Brief Examination of Scripture Testimony on the Institution of Slavery. In an essay first published in the *Religious Herald*, and republished by request: With remarks on a letter of Elder Galusha of New York to Dr. Richard Fuller of S. C. Washington, 1850.

———— Slavery and Government. Washington, 1841.

———— Slavery: Its Origin, Nature and History, considered in the light of Bible teachings, moral justice, and political wisdom. New York, 1861.

Swain, William, ed. Address to the People of North Carolina on the Evils of Slavery by the Friends of Liberty and Equality. Greensboro, 1830.

T[hornton], W. Political Economy: Founded in justice and humanity. In a letter to a friend. Washington, 1804.

Thornwell, James Henley, D.D. Hear the South! The State of the Country: An article republished from the *Southern Presbyterian Review*. Columbia, 1861.

———— Our Danger and Our Duty. Columbia, 1862.

———— Report on the Subject of Slavery. Presented to the Synod of South Carolina, at their sessions in Winnsborough, November 6, 1851. Adopted by them and published by their order. Columbia, 1852.

———— A Review of J. B. Adger's Sermon on The Religious Instruction of the Colored Population. Charleston, 1847.

———— The Rights and Duties of Masters. A sermon preached at the dedication of a church, erected in Charleston, South Carolina, for the benefit and instruction of the coloured population. Charleston, 1850.

Thrasher, J. B. Slavery a Divine Institution. A speech before the Breckenridge and Lane club, November 5, 1860. Port Gibson, Mississippi, 1861.

Toombs, Robert. A Lecture Delivered in the Tremont Temple, Boston, Massachusetts, on the 24th January, 1856. Slavery —its constitutional status—its influence on the African race and society. Washington, 1858.

———— An Oration, Delivered before the Few and Phi Gamma Societies of Emory, at Oxford, Georgia, July, 1853. Slavery in the United States; its consistency with republican institutions, and its effects upon the slave and society. Augusta, 1853.

Torrey, Jesse. A Portraiture of Domestic Slavery in the United States: Proposing measures for the education and gradual emancipation of the slaves, without impairing the legal privileges of the possessor: And a project of a colonial asylum for free Negroes of color: Including memoirs of facts on the interior traffic in slaves, and in kidnapping. Philadelphia, 1818.

Townsend, John. The Doom of Slavery in the Union: Its Safety Out of It. Charleston, 1860.

———— The Southern States, Their Present Peril, and Their Certain Remedy. Why do they not right themselves? And so fulfill their glorious destiny. Charleston, 1850.

Trescott, William H. The Position and Course of the South. Charleston, 1850.

Trimble, Robert. The Negro, North and South: The status of the coloured population in the Northern and Southern States of America compared. London, 1863.

Tucker, John Randolph. Republicanism and Slavery: An address delivered before the Phoenix and Philomathean Societies of William and Mary College, July 3, 1854. Richmond, 1854.

Tucker, Nathaniel Beverley. A Discourse on the Dangers that Threaten the Free Institutions of the United States, being an address to the literary societies of Hampden Sidney College, Virginia. Richmond, 1841.

———— Prescience. Speech delivered in the Southern Convention, held at Nashville, Tennessee, April 13, 1850. Richmond, 1862.

Tyson, Bryan. The Institution of Slavery in the Southern States, religiously and morally considered in connection with our sectional troubles. Washington, 1863.

Upshur, Abel P. Speech of Judge Abel P. Upshur, as Delivered in the Convention of Virginia, on Tuesday, October 27, 1829, upon the Subject of the Basis of Representation. Richmond, 1829.

Van Evrie, J. H., M.D. Negroes and Negro "Slavery"; the first an inferior race—the latter its normal condition. Introductory number: Causes of popular delusion on the subject. New York, 1853.

[————] Subgenation: The Theory of the Normal Relation of the Races; An Answer to "Miscegenation." New York, 1864.

Webster, Noah, Jun. Effects of Slavery, on Morals and Industry. Hartford, 1793.

Wesley, John. Thoughts upon Slavery. London, 1774.

Weston, George M. The Progress of Slavery in the United States. Washington, 1858.

———— The Poor Whites of the South. Washington, 1856.

Wheaton, N. S., D.D. A Discourse on St. Paul's Epistle to Philemon—exhibiting the duty of citizens of the Northern States in regard to the institution of slavery, December 22, 1850. Hartford, 1851.

Whitaker, Daniel K. Reflections on Domestic Slavery, elicited by Judge Harper's Anniversary Oration, delivered before the South Carolina Society for the Advancement of Learning, 7th December, 1835. Charleston, 1836.

[————] Sidney's Letters to William E. Channing, occasioned by his letter to Hon. Henry Clay on the annexation of Texas to the United States. Charleston, 1837.

Wiley, C. H. Sober View of the Slavery Question. By a Citizen of the South. N. p., 1849.

Wilson, Rev. J. Leighton, D.D. The Foreign Slave Trade—can it be revived without violating the most sacred principles of honor, humanity, and religion. N. p., 1859.

Winchester, Elhanan. The Reigning Abominations, Especially the Slave Trade, Considered as Causes of Lamentation; being the substance of a discourse delivered in Fairfax County, Virginia, December 30, 1774, and now published with several additions. London, 1788.

Woolman, John. Some Considerations on the Keeping of Negroes. Recommended to the professors of Christianity of every denomination. Philadelphia, 1754.

[Worcester, Samuel Melanthon, D.D.] Essays on Slavery, republished from the *Boston Recorder and Telegraph* for 1825. By Vigornius and others. Amherst, 1826.

Yeadon, Richard, Jr. The Amenability of Northern Incendiaries as Well to Southern as to Northern Laws. Without prejudice to the right of free discourse; to which is added an inquiry into the lawfulness of slavery under the Jewish and Christian dispensations; together with other views of the same subject. Being a series of essays recently published in the *Charleston Courier*. Charleston, 1835.

Anonymous

Address to the Citizens of South Carolina on the Approaching Election of President and Vice President of United States. By a Federalist. Charleston, 1800.

Authentic and Impartial Narrative of the Tragical Scene Which Was Witnessed in Southampton County (Virginia) on Monday the 22d. of August Last. . . . Communicated by those who were eye witnesses of the bloody scene. N. p., 1831.

Bondage a Moral Institution Sanctioned by the Scriptures of the Old and New Testaments, and the Preaching and Practice of the Savior and His Apostles. By a Southern Farmer. Macon, 1837.

A Brief Statement of the Rise and Progress of the Testimony of the Religious Society of Friends, against Slavery and the Slave Trade. [Yearly Meeting, Philadelphia, April, 1843.] Philadelphia, 1843.

The Constitutional Duty of the Federal Government to Abolish American Slavery, an Exposé of the Abolition Society of New York. New York, 1855.

A Controversy between Caius Gracchus and Opimius, in reference to the American Society for the Colonization of Free People of Colour of the United States. (Originally published in the *Richmond Enquirer*, October, 1825, to August 8, 1826.) Georgetown, D. C., 1827.

An Essay in Defence of Slaveholding, as existing in the Southern States of Our Union. By a Citizen of New York. New York, 1837.

Examination by a South Carolinian. New York, 1843.

An Exposition of the African Slave Trade, from the Year 1840 to 1850 Inclusive, prepared from official documents, and published by direction of the religious society of Friends, in Pennsylvania, New Jersey, and Delaware. Philadelphia, 1851.

Free Negroism; or, Results of Emancipation in the North, and the West India Islands; with statistics of the decay of commerce, idleness of the Negro, his return to savagism, and the effect of emancipation upon the farming, mechanical and laboring classes. New York, 1862.

Free Remarks on the Spirit of the Federal Constitution, the Practice of the Federal Government, and the Obligations of the Union Respecting the Exclusion of Slavery from the Territories and New States. By a Philadelphian. Philadelphia, 1819.

Letter Addressed to the Hon. John C. Calhoun, on the Law Relating to Slaves, Free Negroes, and Mulattoes. By a Virginian. Washington, 1845.

Letters from the South, or Northern and Southern views respecting slavery and the American Tract Society. (First published in the *Boston Courier*.) By O. C. 'S. Boston and New York, 1857.

Letters of Nathaniel Macon to Charles O'Connor: The destruction of the Union is emancipation. Philadelphia, 1862, and Montgomery, 1860.

Letters on the Condition of the African Race in the United States. By a Southern Lady. Philadelphia, 1852.

The North and the South, or the question stated and considered by one of the people. (From the *Daily Telegraph*). Columbia, 1850.

Personal Slavery Established by the Suffrages of Custom and Right Reason, being a full answer to the gloomy and visionary reveries of all the fanatical and enthusiastical writers on that subject. By Machiavelus Americanus. Philadelphia, 1773.

A Plea for the South [Anti-Slavery]. By Massachusetts Junior. Boston, 1847.

The Question Examined; or a brief reply to a pamphlet on the "Jurisdiction of Our State Courts over the Violators of Our Slave Laws." By a Citizen of the South. Charleston, 1835.

Remarks on the Decision of the Appeal Court of South Carolina, in the Case of Wells: And on the abolition movement at the North, being a series of numbers originally published in the *Charleston Mercury* under the signature of "A States' Rights man" and "a South Carolinian," during the month of August, 1835. Charleston, 1835.

A Review of the Decision of the Supreme Court of the United States in the Dred Scott Case. By a Kentucky Lawyer. Louisville, 1857.

A Series of Letters Addressed to the Public on the Subject of Slaves as Free People of Color in *South Carolina Gazette*, September and October, 1822. By a Columbian. Columbia, 1822.

Slaveholding, Proved To Be Just and Right to a Demonstration, from the Word of God. Dedicated to Elder Richard Fuller of Beaufort, S. C. By Doulophilus. N. p., 1846.

Slavery: A Treatise, Showing That Slavery Is Neither a Moral, Political, nor Social Evil. Penfield, Georgia, 1844.

Slavery: Indispensable to the Civilization of Africa. Baltimore, 1855.

Southern Slavery Considered on General Principles; or, a Grapple with Abstractionists. By a North Carolinian. New York, 1861.

Views of American Slavery Taken a Century Ago. Philadelphia, 1858.

Magazine Articles

Allison, Samuel. "Notes on Early Books on Slavery," *The Non Slaveholder*. Philadelphia, II, 1847.

[Bacon, L.] "The Southern Apostasy," *The New Englander*. New Haven, XII, 1854.

Keith, George. "An Exhortation and Caution to Friends Concerning Buying or Keeping of Negroes," *The Pennsylvania Magazine of History and Biography*. Philadelphia, XIII, 1889.

Moore, George H. "Additional Notes on the History of Slavery in Massachusetts," *The Historical Magazine*, Boston, X, 1866.

SECONDARY MATERIALS

A SELECTIVE LIST OF MONOGRAPHS AND SPECIAL STUDIES

Adams, Alice Dana. The Neglected Period of Anti-Slavery in America, 1808-1831. Boston and London, 1908.

Barnes, Gilbert Hobbs. The Antislavery Impulse, 1830-1844. New York, 1933.

Carlyle, R. W. and Carlyle, A. J. A History of Mediaeval Political Theory in the West. 5 v, Edinburgh and London, 1909-1928.

Chase, Ezra B. Teachings of Patriots and Statesmen; or, the Founders of the Republic on Slavery. Philadelphia, 1860.

Collins, Winfield H. The Domestic Slave Trade of the Southern States. New York, 1904.

Dodd, William E. The Cotton Kingdom, a Chronicle of the Old South. New Haven, 1921.

Drewry, William Sidney. The Southampton Insurrection. Washington, 1900.

DuBois, W. E. B. The Suppression of the African Slave-Trade to the United States of America, 1638-1870. New York and London, 1896.

Dunning, W. A. A History of Political Theories. 3 v., New York, 1922-1923.

Fox, E. L. The American Colonization Society, 1817-1840. Baltimore, 1919.

Henry, H. M. The Police Control of Slavery in South Carolina. Emory, Virginia, 1914.

Holdsworth, William Searle. A History of English Law. 9 v., Boston, 1922-1926.

Livermore, George. An Historical Research Respecting the Opinions of the Founders of the Republic on Negroes as Slaves, as Citizens, and as Soldiers. Boston, 1862.

Locke, Mary Stoughton. Anti-Slavery in America, from the introduction of African slaves to the prohibition of the slave trade (1619-1808). Boston, 1901.

McDougall, Marion Gleason. Fugitive Slaves (1619-1865). Boston, 1891.

McDougle, Ivan Eugene. Slavery in Kentucky, 1792-1865. Lancaster, Pennsylvania, 1918.

McIlwain, Charles Howard. The Growth of Political Thought in the West. New York, 1932.

Martin, Asa Earl. The Anti-Slavery Movement in Kentucky Prior to 1850. N. p., 1918.

Matlock, L. C. The Anti-Slavery Struggle and Triumph in the Methodist Episcopal Church. New York and Cincinnati, 1881.

Merriam, Charles E. A History of American Political Theories. New York, 1924.

Munford, B. B. Virginia's Attitude toward Slavery and Secession. New York, 1909.

Norwood, John Nelson. The Schism in the Methodist Episcopal Church, 1844. A study of slavery and ecclesiastical politics. New York, 1923.

Parrington, V. L. Main Currents in American Thought; an interpretation of American literature from the beginning until 1920. 3 v., New York, 1927-1930.

Pennypacker, Samuel W. "The Settlement of Germantown and the Causes which Led to It," *The Pennsylvania Magazine of History and Biography*, Philadelphia, IV, 1880.

Phillips, Ulrich B. American Negro Slavery. New York, 1918.

Poole, Frederick William. Anti-Slavery Opinions before the Year 1800. Cincinnati, 1873.

Putnam, Mary Burnham. The Baptists and Slavery, 1840-1845. Ann Arbor, Michigan, 1913.

Smith, Thomas Vernon. The American Philosophy of Equality. Chicago, 1927.

Smith, William Henry. A Political History of Slavery. 2 v., New York, 1903.

Swaney, C. B. Episcopal Methodism and Slavery with Sidelights on Ecclesiastical Politics. Boston, 1926.

Whitfield, Theodore M. Slavery Agitation in Virginia 1829-1832. Baltimore, 1930.

Wright, Benjamin Fletcher. American Interpretations of Natural Law: A study in the history of political thought. Cambridge, 1931.

Wylly, Charles Spalding. The Seed That Was Sown in the Colony of Georgia, the Harvest and the Aftermath, 1740-1870. New York and Washington, 1910.

INDEX

ABOLITION, in Massachusetts. 26 and n., petition for to Congress, 50, 53, 79; by formal amendment, 168. *See also* Emancipation.

Abstract theory, reaction to in pro-slavery thought, 61-65.

Acts, cited, 271.

Adams, James H., on reopening the slave trade, 95; quoted on labor need argument, 99; on the vacillation of Hammond, 102 n.

Adams, John, on Otis, 24 n.; on natural rights, 25 n.; on Declaration of Rights, 25 n.

Adams, John Quincy, Conversation of with Calhoun, 66, 190; on Rufus King's speech in Missouri debates, 69 n.; as introducer of petition for exercise of the guaranty clause, 183-184.

Adger, J. B., opposed reopening slave trade, 98; on human rights of slave, 232 n.; cited, 213 n., 282 n.

Agassiz, Louis, on Negro capacity, 250; on plural origins theory, 260; on centers of creation theory, 270; on pre-Adamite races, 272 n.

Agrarianism, relation of to types of man theory, 277; slavery as a check to 294-295.

Aldrich, O. P., cited, 160 n.

Allison, Samuel, cited, 8 n.

The American Defense of the Christian Golden Rule, 8. *See also* Hepburn.

Anarchy. *See* Reform movements, Authority, principle of.

Anatomy, relation of to Aristotelian theory, 137. *See also* Physiological argument.

Andrews, Stephen Pearl, theory of as evidence of failure of free society, 302 and n.

The Antelope, 144 and n.

Apology, as a form of defense, 48-49, 55, 70, 79, 87, 88 n., 89, 104-105.

Apprentice system, proposal of to circumvent slave trade acts, 101. *See also* Slave trade.

Aquinas, Thomas. *See* St. Thomas.

Aristocracy, theories of in slave society, 289-295.

Aristotle, 1; early influence of, 41; influence on G. F. Holmes, 110; on natural origin theory, 120; refutation of by Bodin, 121; ideas of on naturalness of slavery, 137; influence of on Calhoun, 137 n., 290 n.; verification of by natural scientist, 242; influence of on theory of aristocracy, 289-290 and n.; Fitzhugh on influence of, 305.

Asbury, Bishop Francis, views of as to difficulty of instructing slaves, 15 n.; on pro-slavery opinion in Virginia, 54; cited, 12 n.

Atheism, relation of to abolition, 239-241; and pluralism, 282.

Athenian Oracle, on baptism and slavery, 17, 18 n.

Augustine, St. *See* Saint Augustine.

Authority, principle of, in early pro-slavery thought, 45-46; in all social relations, 116; as origin of slavery, 120; and Golden Rule, 227; and revelation, 233-239; and rationalism, 237-239.

Authority of scriptures. *See* Authority, principle of.

BACHMAN, John, on value of Bible argument, 207; on miraculous theory of origin of races, 253, 268; on the unity of mankind theory, 260, 262-263 and n.; on hybridity, 264, 265 n.; on the climatic theory of the origin of races, 269; on the Bible